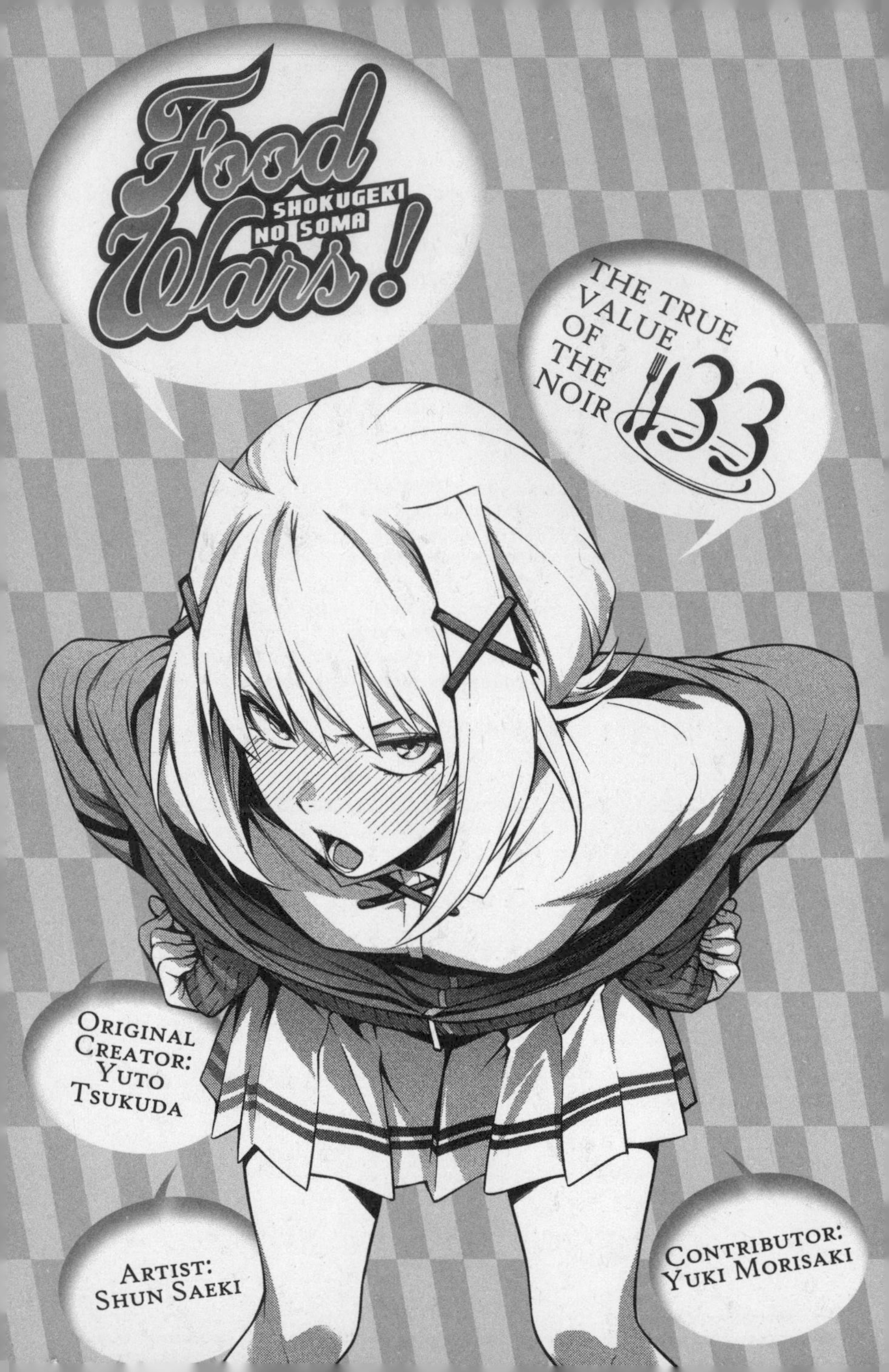
Food Wars!
SHOKUGEKI NO SOMA
THE TRUE VALUE OF THE NOIR
133
Original Creator: Yuto Tsukuda
Artist: Shun Saeki
Contributor: Yuki Morisaki

CHARACTERS

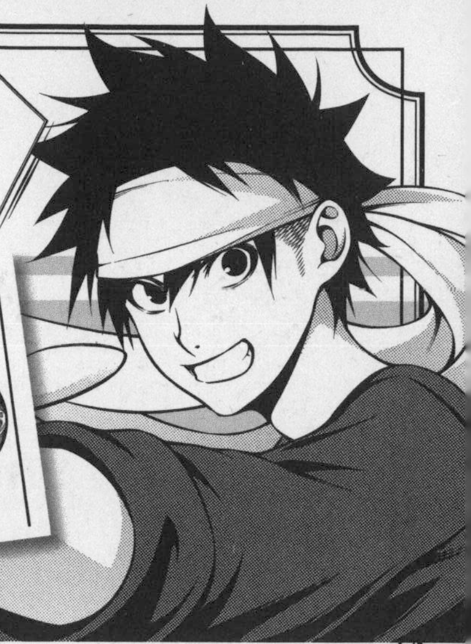

SOMA YUKIHIRA Second Year High School

The current first seat on Totsuki's Council of Ten. Unbound by traditional notions and with a natural inquisitiveness and passion for cooking, his fresh take on cuisine leads him to create dishes no one has ever thought of before. Resides in Polaris Dormitory.

Shokugeki no SOMA

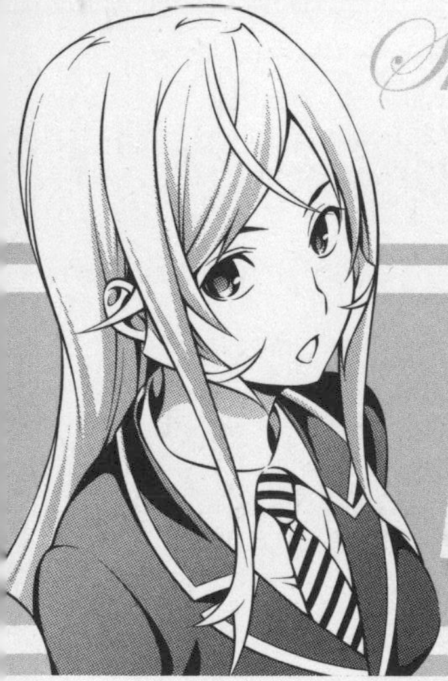

ERINA NAKIRI Second Year High School

The current dean of Totsuki Institute and granddaughter of former dean Senzaemon Nakiri. Her sense of taste is so refined it's known as "the Divine Tongue." Though normally strict and proper, she has a girly side that loves shojo manga.

STORY

Soma grew up helping to cook at his family's restaurant, Yukihira. But one day his father enrolls him in Japan's premier culinary school, Totsuki Institute. Having met other students as skilled as he is and with similar goals, Soma has grown a little as a chef.

Soma, Erina and the others try to trace the whereabouts of the mysterious Asahi Saiba to no avail. Then one day, Soma visits new Totsuki instructor Suzuki and is challenged to a cooking battle. In an unexpected turn of events, it's Soma who's blown out of the water. Instructor Suzuki's skill is leagues beyond anything Soma has ever seen…perhaps because he's actually Asahi Saiba! Blissfully unaware of instructor Suzuki's true identity, Soma vows to get a rematch. But then a certain someone pays Soma a visit.

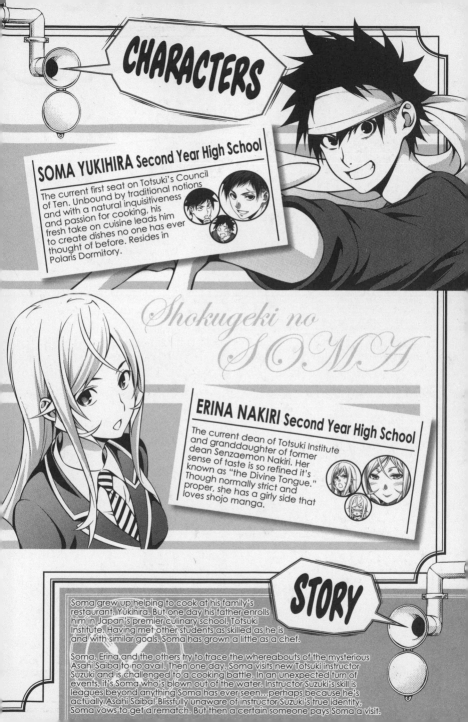

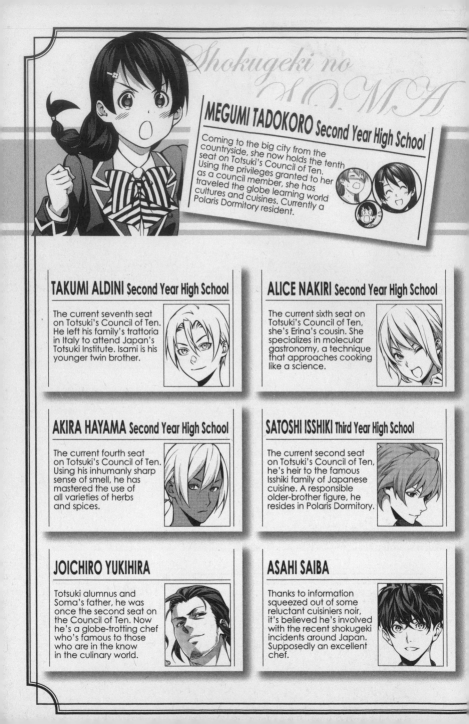

Shokugeki no SOMA

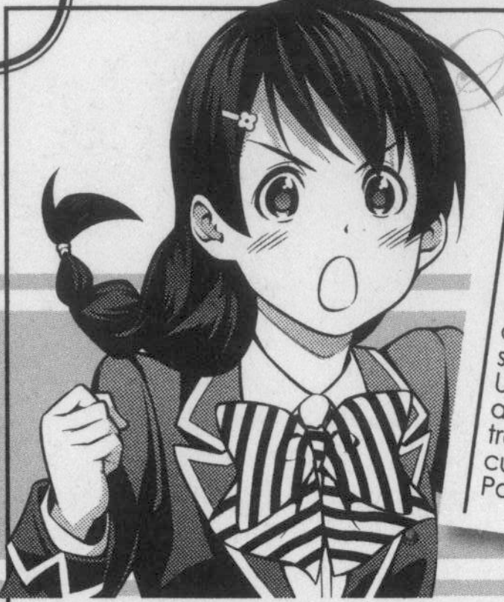

MEGUMI TADOKORO Second Year High School

Coming to the big city from the countryside, she now holds the tenth seat on Totsuki's Council of Ten. Using the privileges granted to her as a council member, she has traveled the globe learning world cultures and cuisines. Currently a Polaris Dormitory resident.

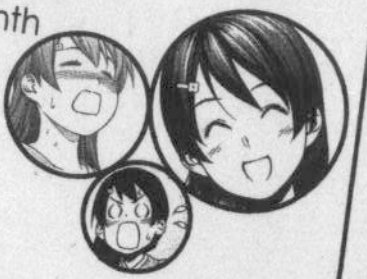

TAKUMI ALDINI Second Year High School

The current seventh seat on Totsuki's Council of Ten. He left his family's trattoria in Italy to attend Japan's Totsuki Institute. Isami is his younger twin brother.

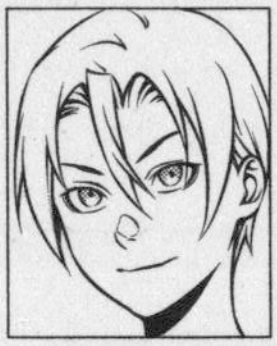

ALICE NAKIRI Second Year High School

The current sixth seat on Totsuki's Council of Ten, she's Erina's cousin. She specializes in molecular gastronomy, a technique that approaches cooking like a science.

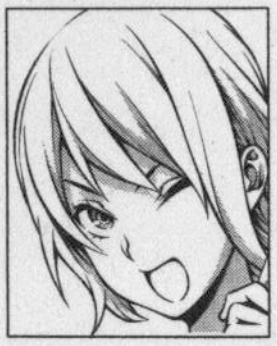

AKIRA HAYAMA Second Year High School

The current fourth seat on Totsuki's Council of Ten. Using his inhumanly sharp sense of smell, he has mastered the use of all varieties of herbs and spices.

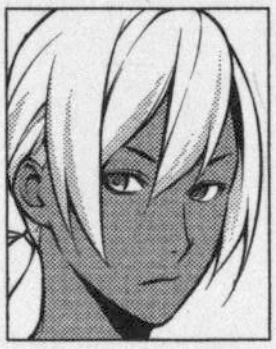

SATOSHI ISSHIKI Third Year High School

The current second seat on Totsuki's Council of Ten, he's heir to the famous Isshiki family of Japanese cuisine. A responsible older-brother figure, he resides in Polaris Dormitory.

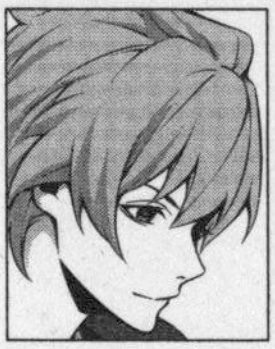

JOICHIRO YUKIHIRA

Totsuki alumnus and Soma's father, he was once the second seat on the Council of Ten. Now he's a globe-trotting chef who's famous to those who are in the know in the culinary world.

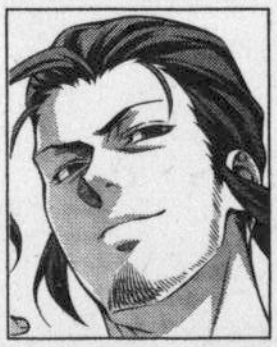

ASAHI SAIBA

Thanks to information squeezed out of some reluctant cuisiniers noir, it's believed he's involved with the recent shokugeki incidents around Japan. Supposedly an excellent chef.

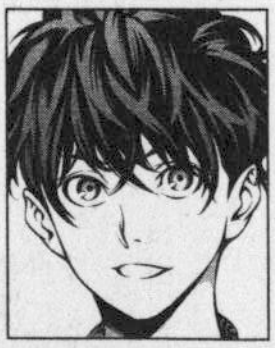

Food Wars!

SHOKUGEKI NO SOMA

33

Table of Contents

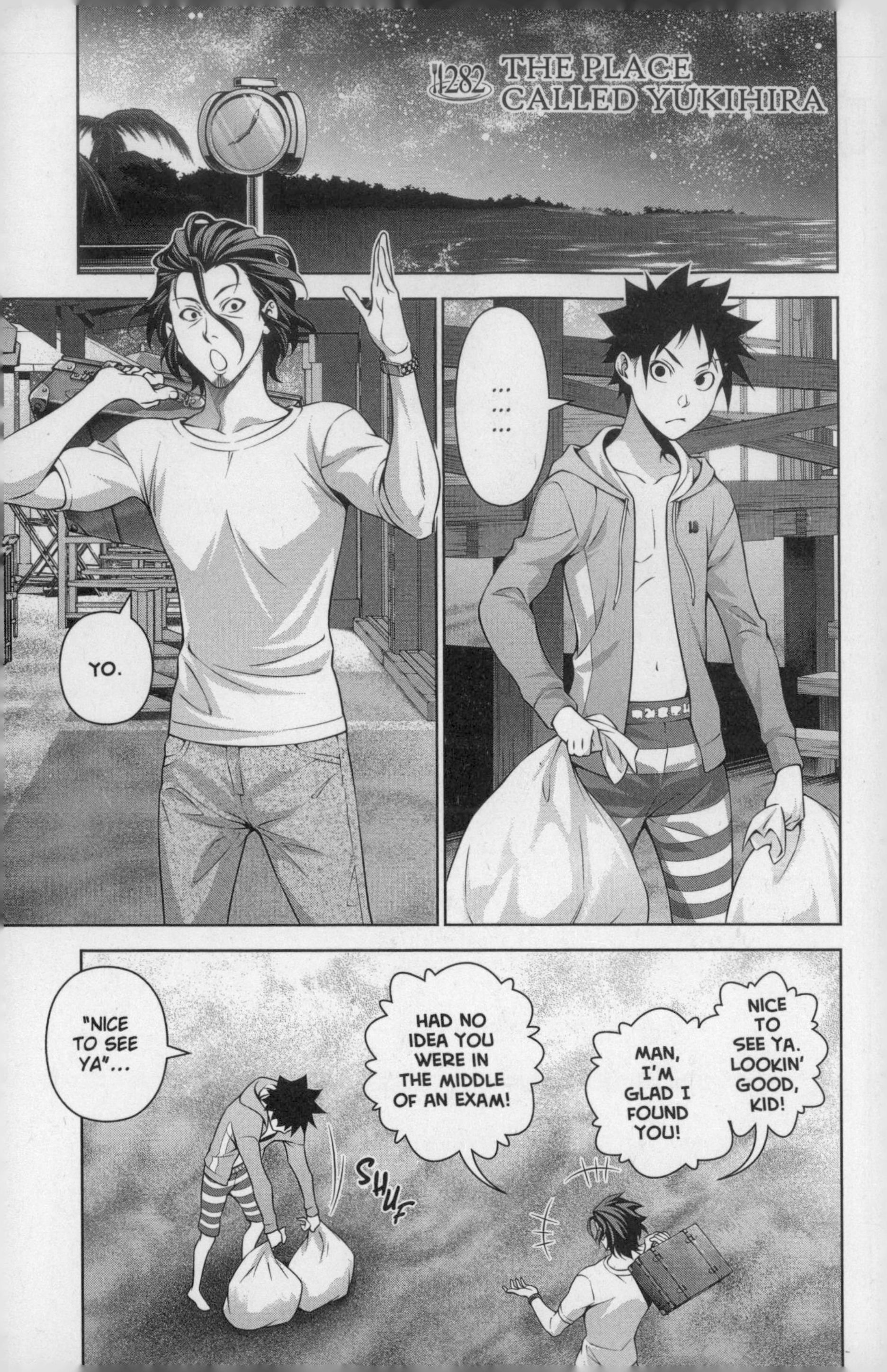
282 THE PLACE CALLED YUKIHIRA
......
YO.
NICE TO SEE YA. LOOKIN' GOOD, KID!
MAN, I'M GLAD I FOUND YOU!
HAD NO IDEA YOU WERE IN THE MIDDLE OF AN EXAM!
SHUF
"NICE TO SEE YA"...

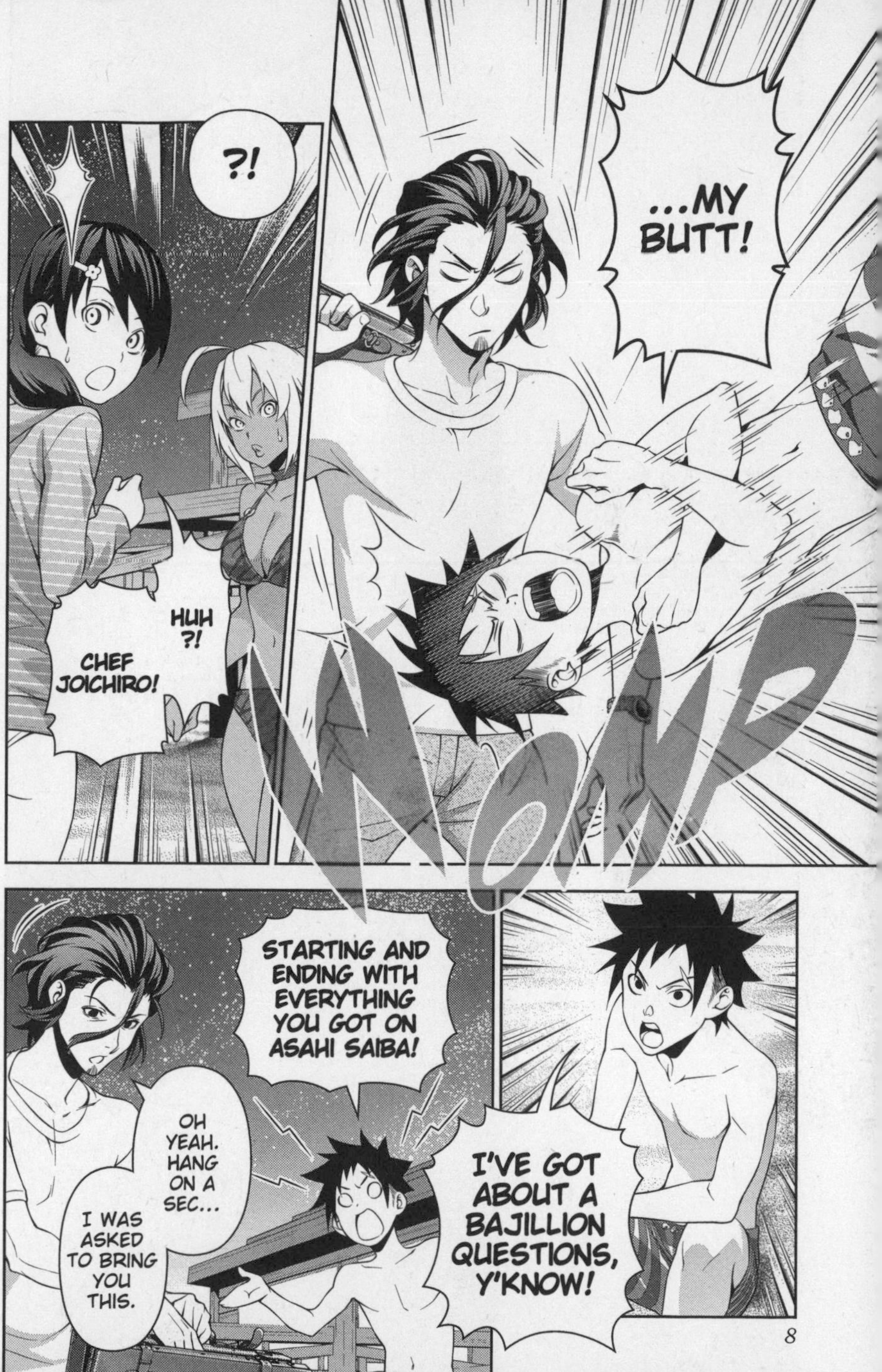
...MY BUTT!
WOMP
?!
HUH ?!
CHEF JOICHIRO!
I'VE GOT ABOUT A BAJILLION QUESTIONS, Y'KNOW!
STARTING AND ENDING WITH EVERYTHING YOU GOT ON ASAHI SAIBA!
OH YEAH. HANG ON A SEC...
I WAS ASKED TO BRING YOU THIS.

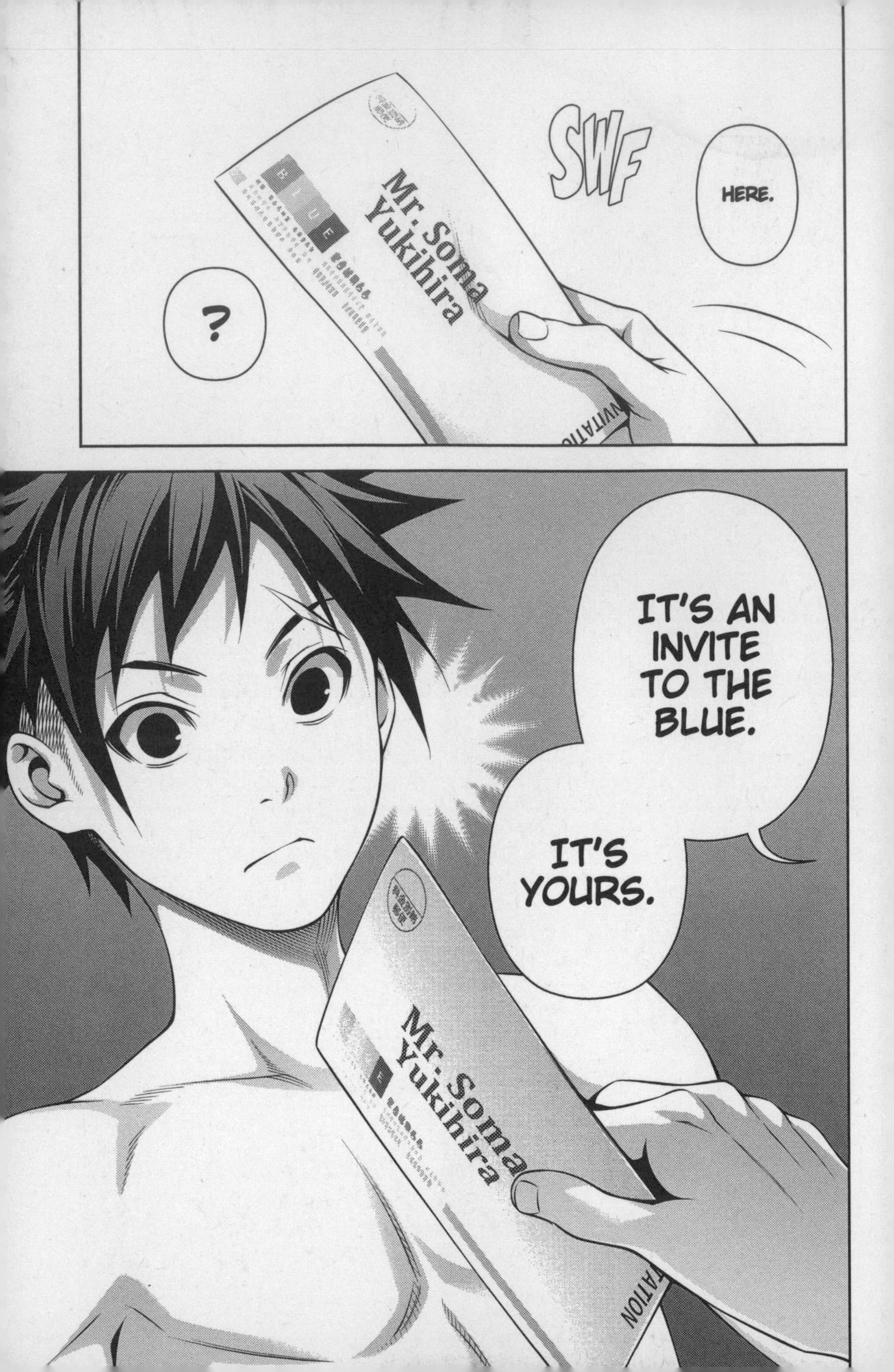
HERE.
SWF
Mr. Soma Yukihira
INVITATION
?
IT'S AN INVITE TO THE BLUE.
IT'S YOURS.
Mr. Soma Yukihira
INVITATION

282 THE PLACE CALLED YUKIHARA

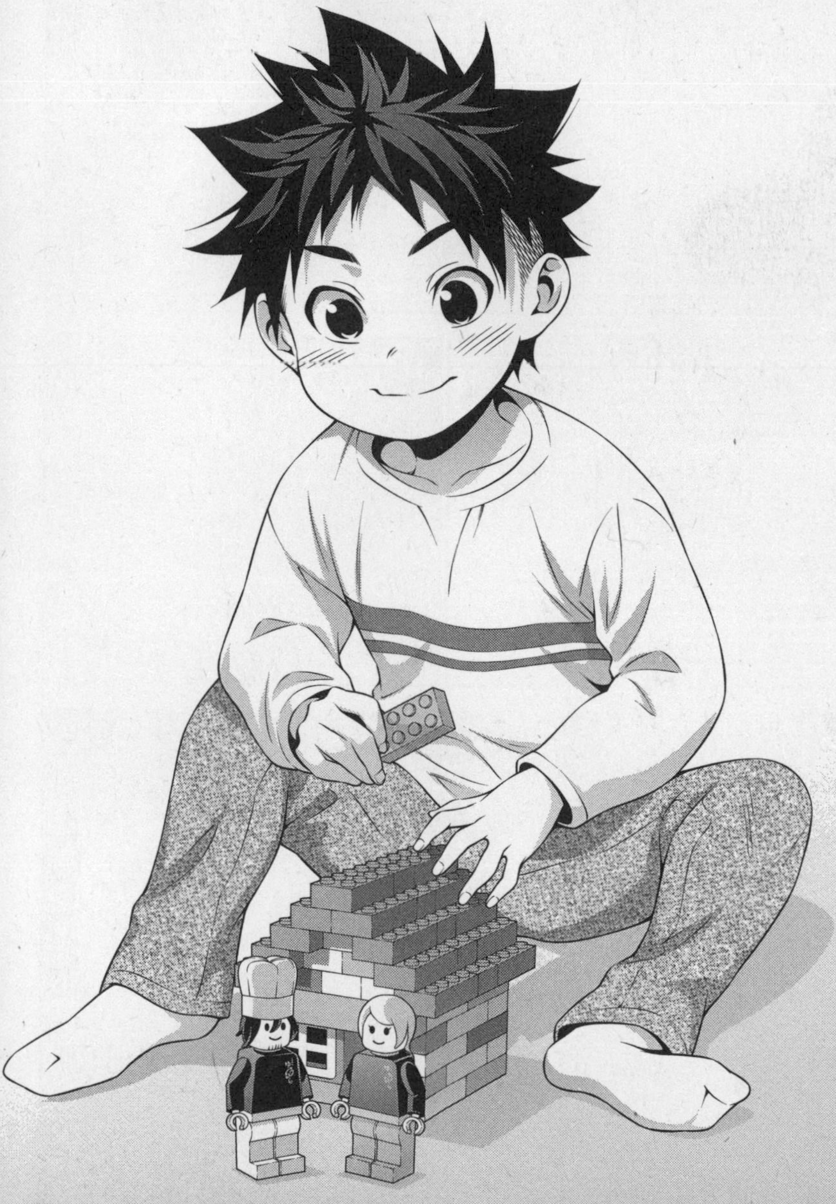

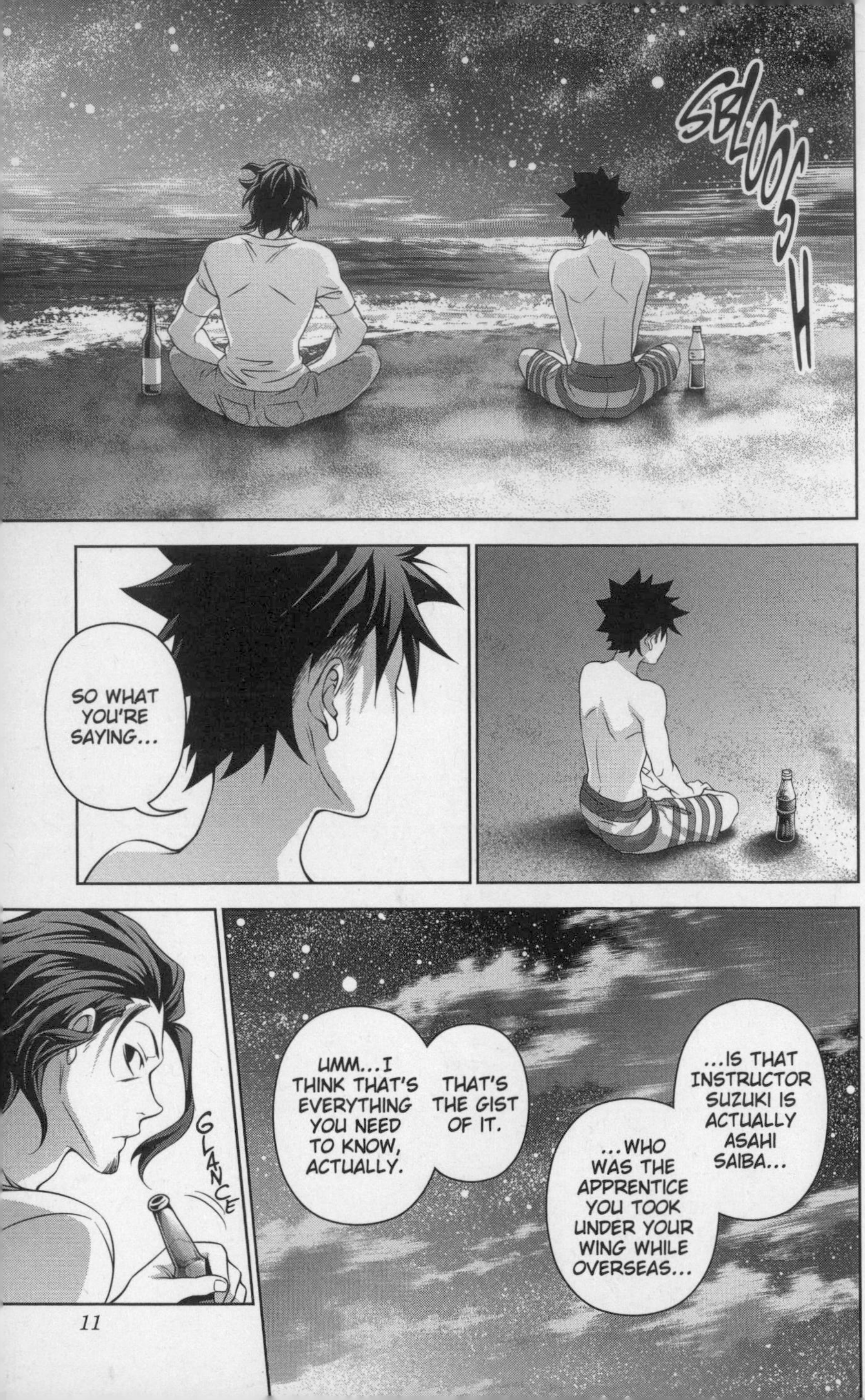
SBLOOSHH
SO WHAT YOU'RE SAYING...
...IS THAT INSTRUCTOR SUZUKI IS ACTUALLY ASAHI SAIBA...
...WHO WAS THE APPRENTICE YOU TOOK UNDER YOUR WING WHILE OVERSEAS...
THAT'S THE GIST OF IT.
UMM...I THINK THAT'S EVERYTHING YOU NEED TO KNOW, ACTUALLY.
GLANCE

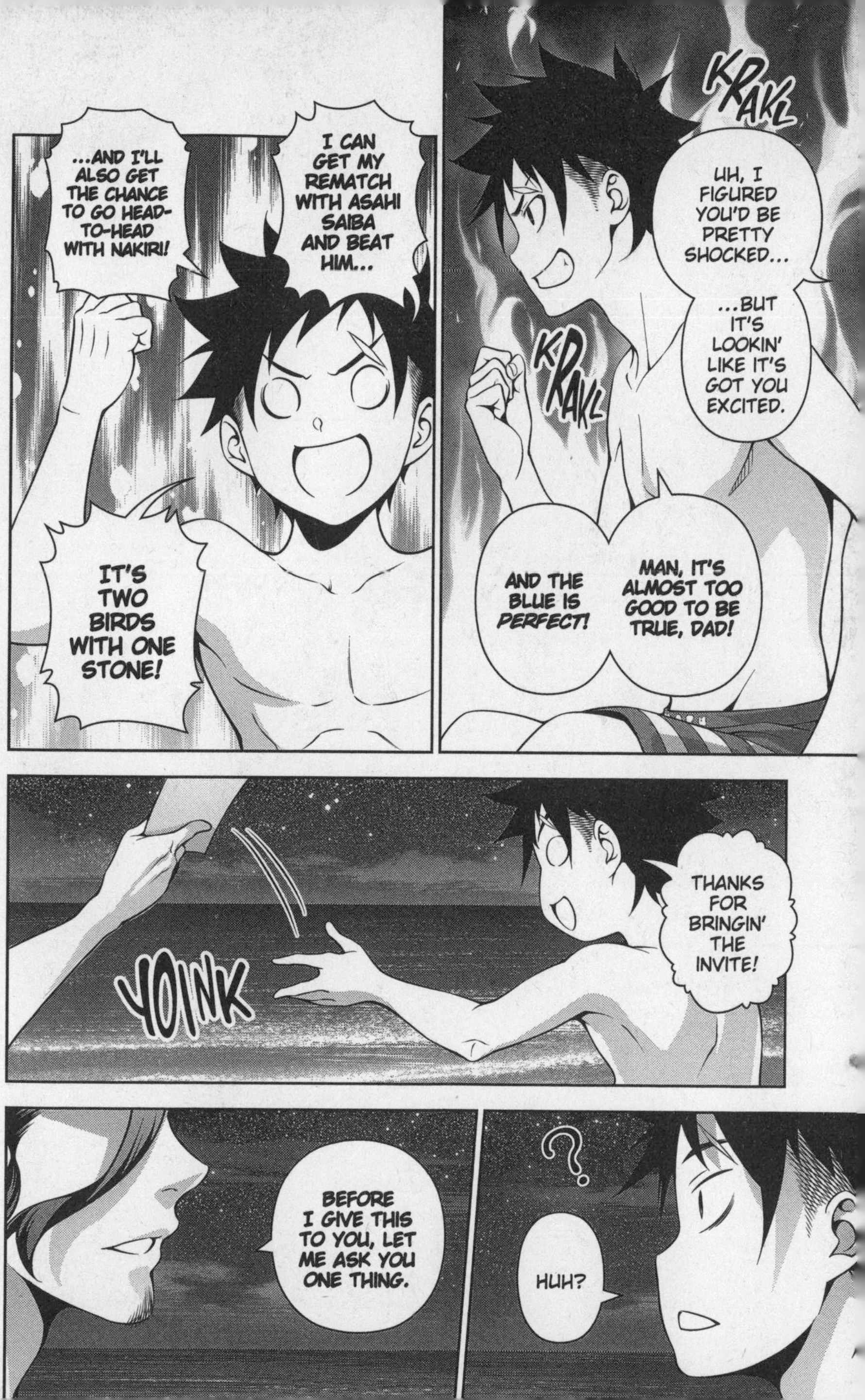
KRAKL
UH, I FIGURED YOU'D BE PRETTY SHOCKED...
...BUT IT'S LOOKIN' LIKE IT'S GOT YOU EXCITED.
KRAKL
MAN, IT'S ALMOST TOO GOOD TO BE TRUE, DAD!
AND THE BLUE IS *PERFECT!*
I CAN GET MY REMATCH WITH ASAHI SAIBA AND BEAT HIM...
...AND I'LL ALSO GET THE CHANCE TO GO HEAD-TO-HEAD WITH NAKIRI!
IT'S TWO BIRDS WITH ONE STONE!
THANKS FOR BRINGIN' THE INVITE!
YOINK
?
HUH?
BEFORE I GIVE THIS TO YOU, LET ME ASK YOU ONE THING.

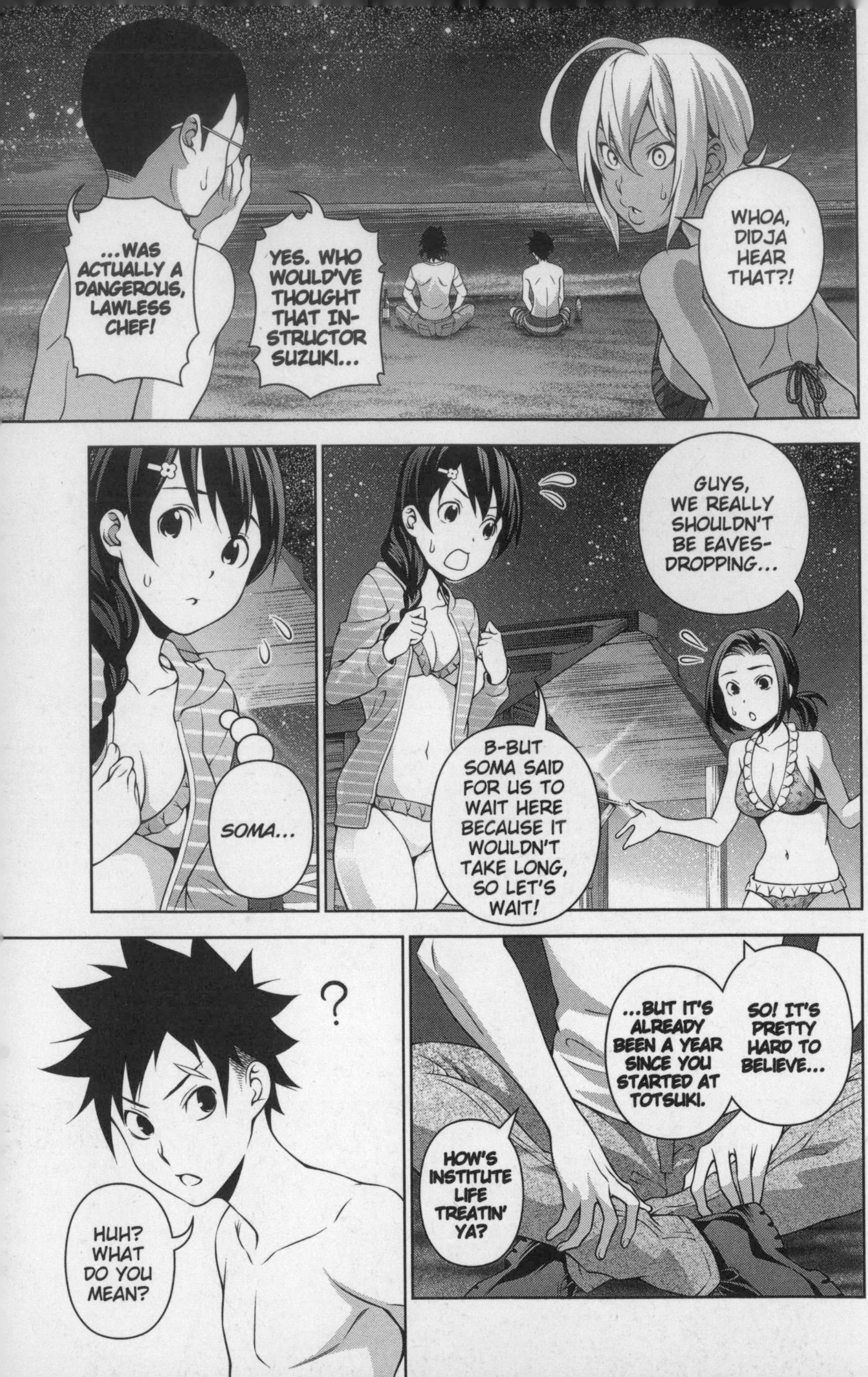
WHOA, DIDJA HEAR THAT?!
YES. WHO WOULD'VE THOUGHT THAT INSTRUCTOR SUZUKI...
...WAS ACTUALLY A DANGEROUS, LAWLESS CHEF!
GUYS, WE REALLY SHOULDN'T BE EAVES-DROPPING...
B-BUT SOMA SAID FOR US TO WAIT HERE BECAUSE IT WOULDN'T TAKE LONG, SO LET'S WAIT!
SOMA...
SO! IT'S PRETTY HARD TO BELIEVE...
...BUT IT'S ALREADY BEEN A YEAR SINCE YOU STARTED AT TOTSUKI.
HOW'S INSTITUTE LIFE TREATIN' YA?
?
HUH? WHAT DO YOU MEAN?

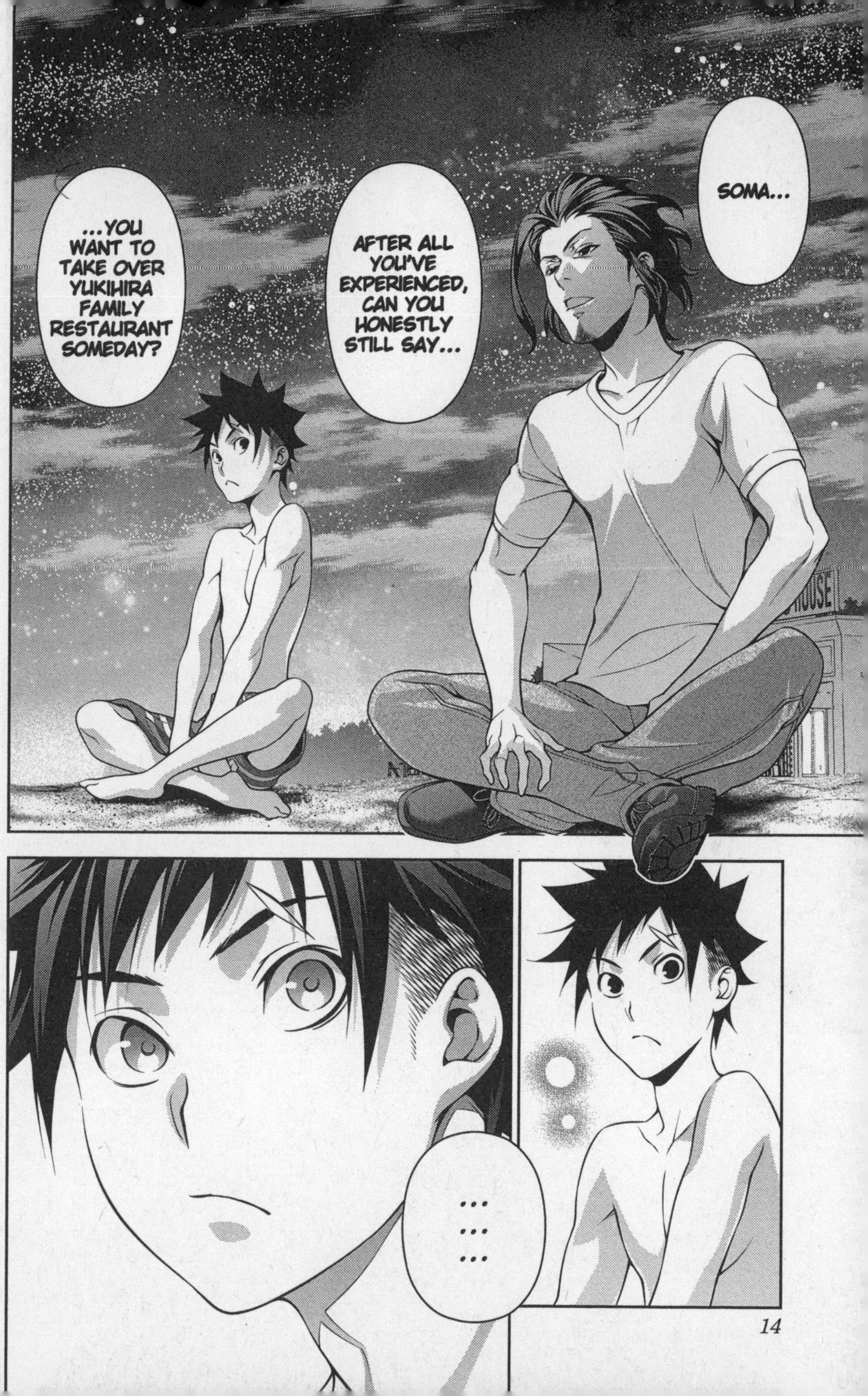
SOMA...
AFTER ALL YOU'VE EXPERIENCED, CAN YOU HONESTLY STILL SAY...
...YOU WANT TO TAKE OVER YUKIHIRA FAMILY RESTAURANT SOMEDAY?
...
...
...

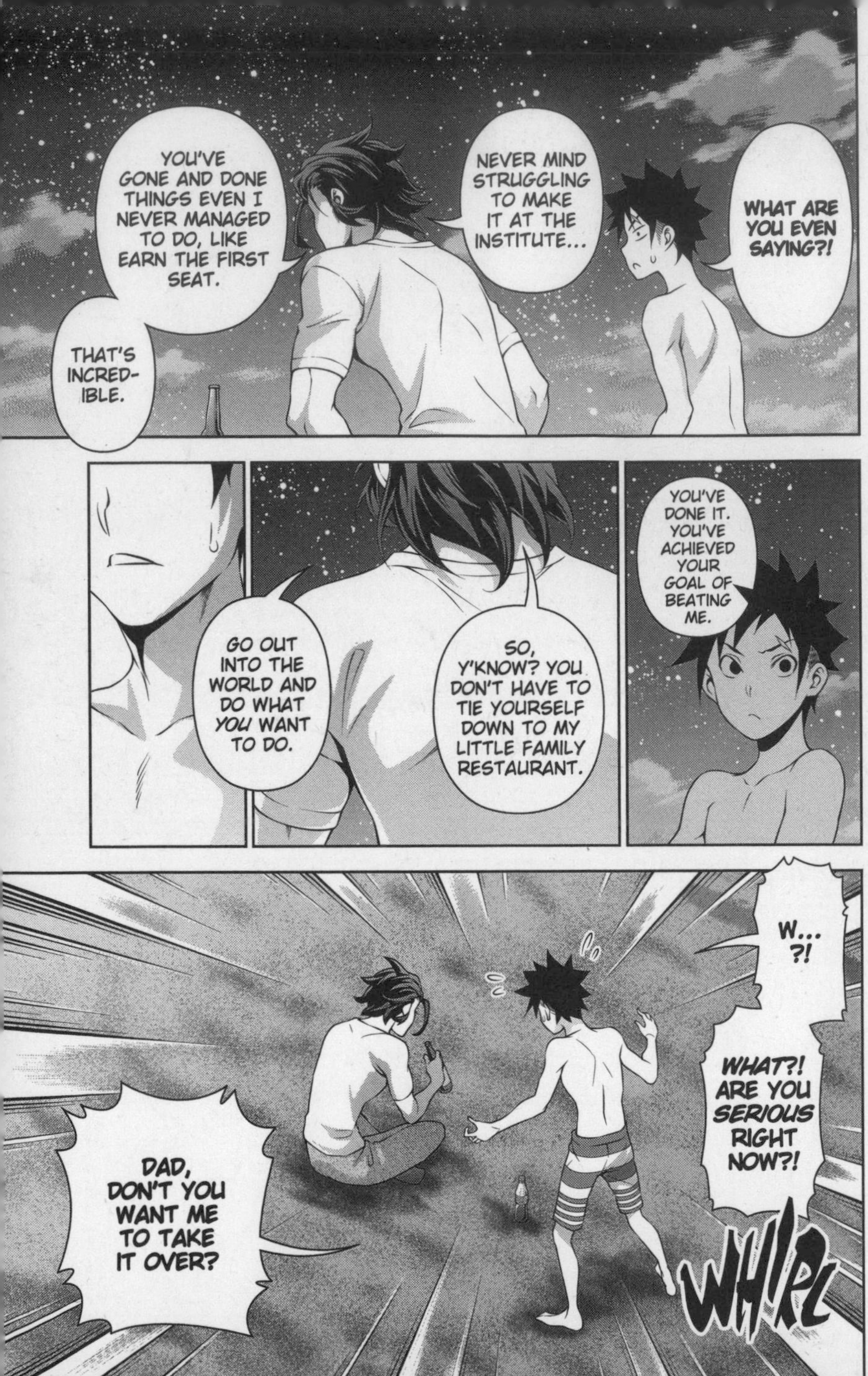
WHAT ARE YOU EVEN SAYING?!
NEVER MIND STRUGGLING TO MAKE IT AT THE INSTITUTE...
YOU'VE GONE AND DONE THINGS EVEN I NEVER MANAGED TO DO, LIKE EARN THE FIRST SEAT.
THAT'S INCRED-IBLE.
YOU'VE DONE IT. YOU'VE ACHIEVED YOUR GOAL OF BEATING ME.
SO, Y'KNOW? YOU DON'T HAVE TO TIE YOURSELF DOWN TO MY LITTLE FAMILY RESTAURANT.
GO OUT INTO THE WORLD AND DO WHAT *YOU* WANT TO DO.
W... ?!
WHAT?! ARE YOU *SERIOUS* RIGHT NOW?!
WHIRL
DAD, DON'T YOU WANT ME TO TAKE IT OVER?

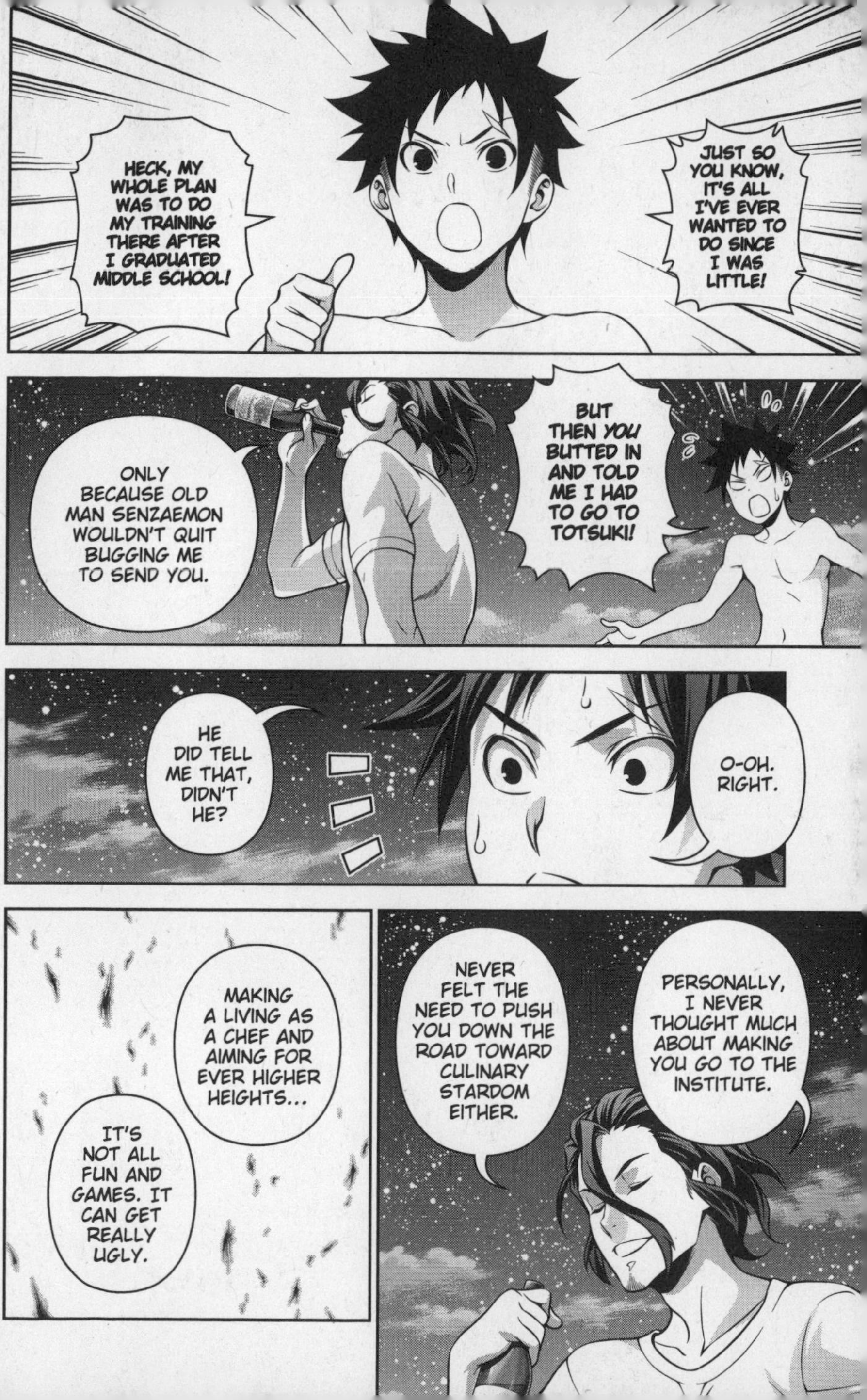
JUST SO YOU KNOW, IT'S ALL I'VE EVER WANTED TO DO SINCE I WAS LITTLE!
HECK, MY WHOLE PLAN WAS TO DO MY TRAINING THERE AFTER I GRADUATED MIDDLE SCHOOL!
BUT THEN *YOU* BUTTED IN AND TOLD ME I HAD TO GO TO TOTSUKI!
ONLY BECAUSE OLD MAN SENZAEMON WOULDN'T QUIT BUGGING ME TO SEND YOU.
O-OH. RIGHT.
HE DID TELL ME THAT, DIDN'T HE?
PERSONALLY, I NEVER THOUGHT MUCH ABOUT MAKING YOU GO TO THE INSTITUTE.
NEVER FELT THE NEED TO PUSH YOU DOWN THE ROAD TOWARD CULINARY STARDOM EITHER.
MAKING A LIVING AS A CHEF AND AIMING FOR EVER HIGHER HEIGHTS...
IT'S NOT ALL FUN AND GAMES. IT CAN GET REALLY UGLY.

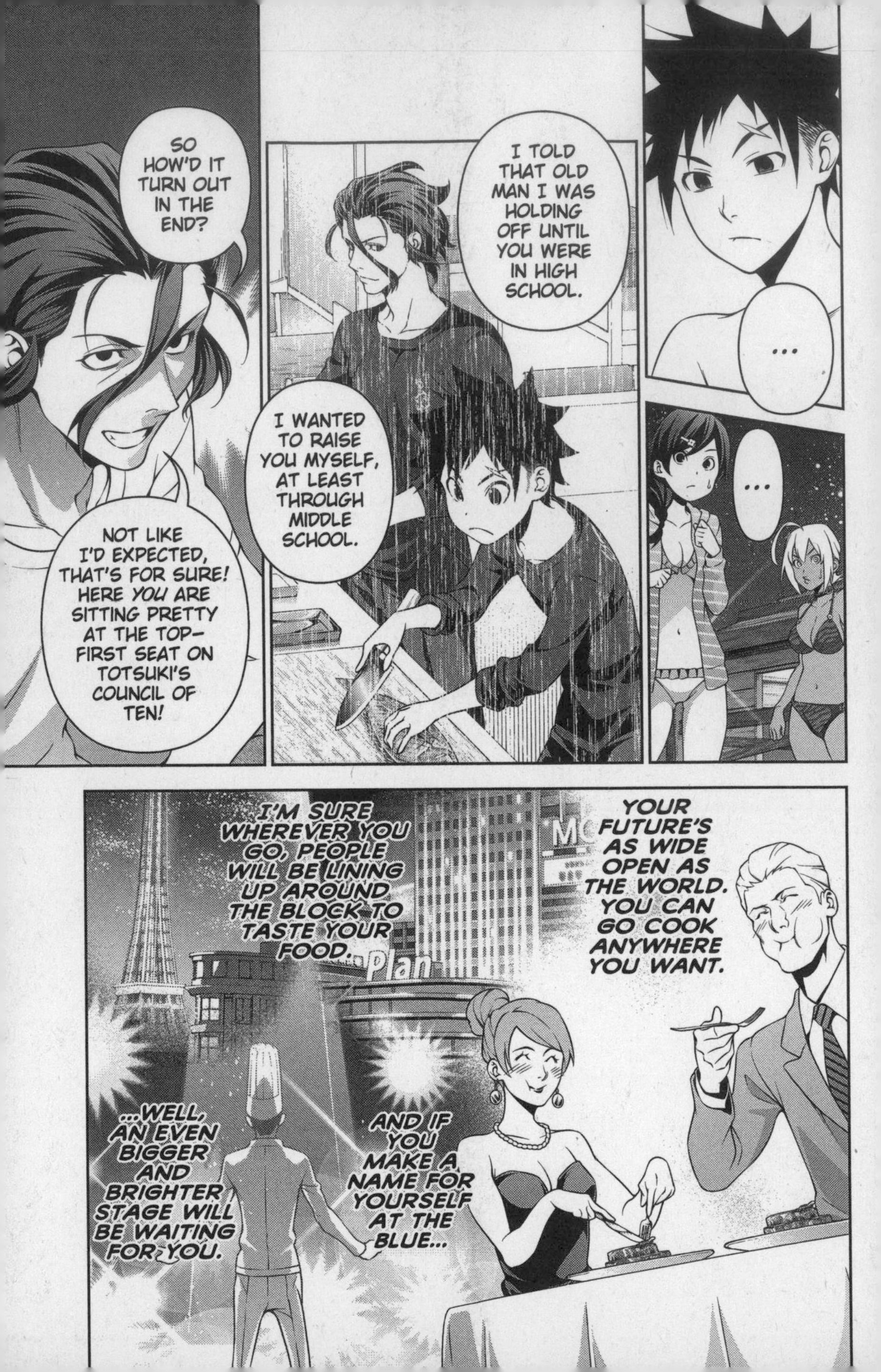
...
...
I TOLD THAT OLD MAN I WAS HOLDING OFF UNTIL YOU WERE IN HIGH SCHOOL.
I WANTED TO RAISE YOU MYSELF, AT LEAST THROUGH MIDDLE SCHOOL.
SO HOW'D IT TURN OUT IN THE END?
NOT LIKE I'D EXPECTED, THAT'S FOR SURE! HERE *YOU* ARE SITTING PRETTY AT THE TOP—FIRST SEAT ON TOTSUKI'S COUNCIL OF TEN!
YOUR FUTURE'S AS WIDE OPEN AS THE WORLD. YOU CAN GO COOK ANYWHERE YOU WANT.
I'M SURE WHEREVER YOU GO, PEOPLE WILL BE LINING UP AROUND THE BLOCK TO TASTE YOUR FOOD.
AND IF YOU MAKE A NAME FOR YOURSELF AT THE BLUE...
...WELL, AN EVEN BIGGER AND BRIGHTER STAGE WILL BE WAITING FOR YOU.

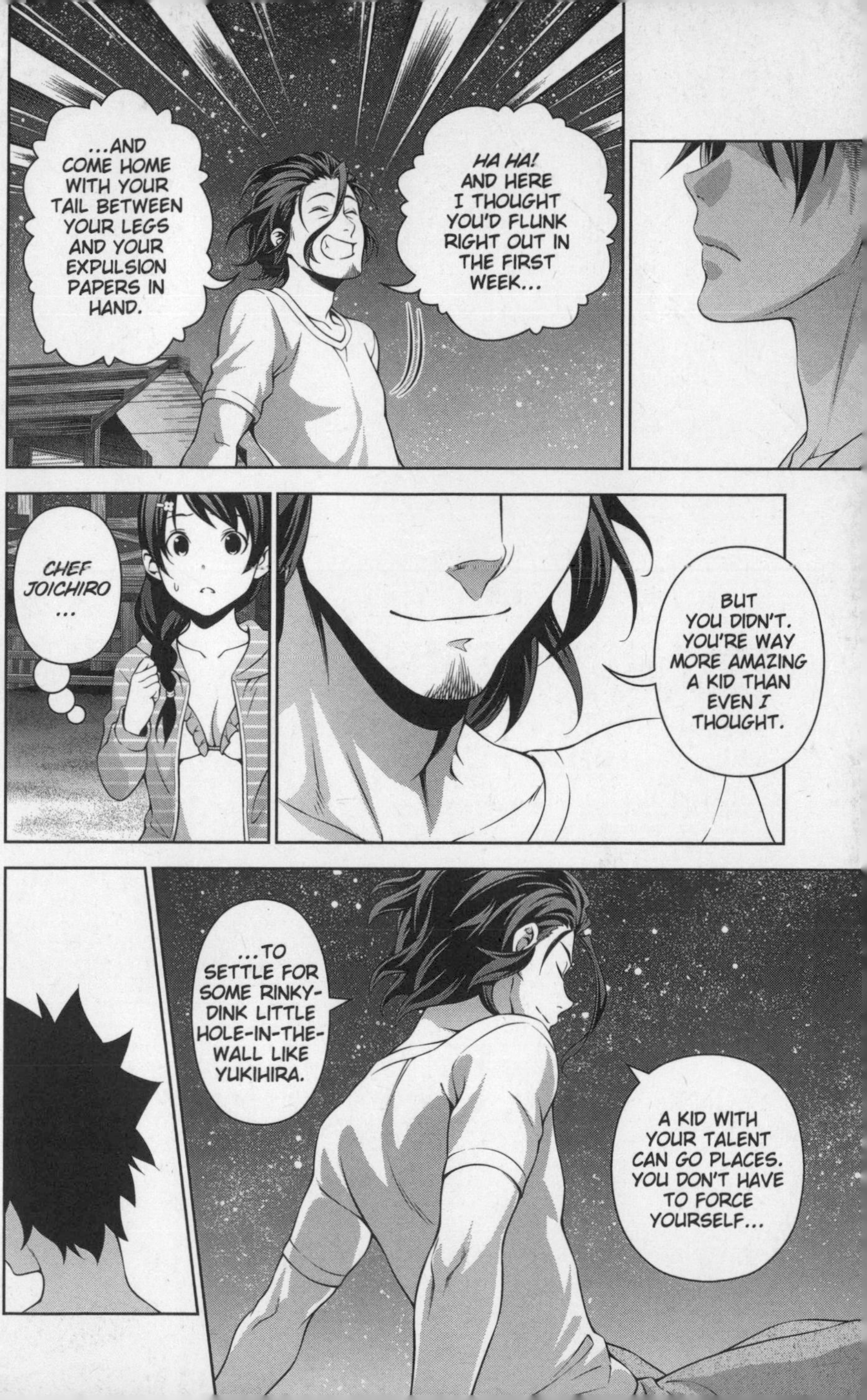
HA HA! AND HERE I THOUGHT YOU'D FLUNK RIGHT OUT IN THE FIRST WEEK...
...AND COME HOME WITH YOUR TAIL BETWEEN YOUR LEGS AND YOUR EXPULSION PAPERS IN HAND.
BUT YOU DIDN'T. YOU'RE WAY MORE AMAZING A KID THAN EVEN I THOUGHT.
CHEF JOICHIRO ...
A KID WITH YOUR TALENT CAN GO PLACES. YOU DON'T HAVE TO FORCE YOURSELF...
...TO SETTLE FOR SOME RINKY-DINK LITTLE HOLE-IN-THE-WALL LIKE YUKIHIRA.

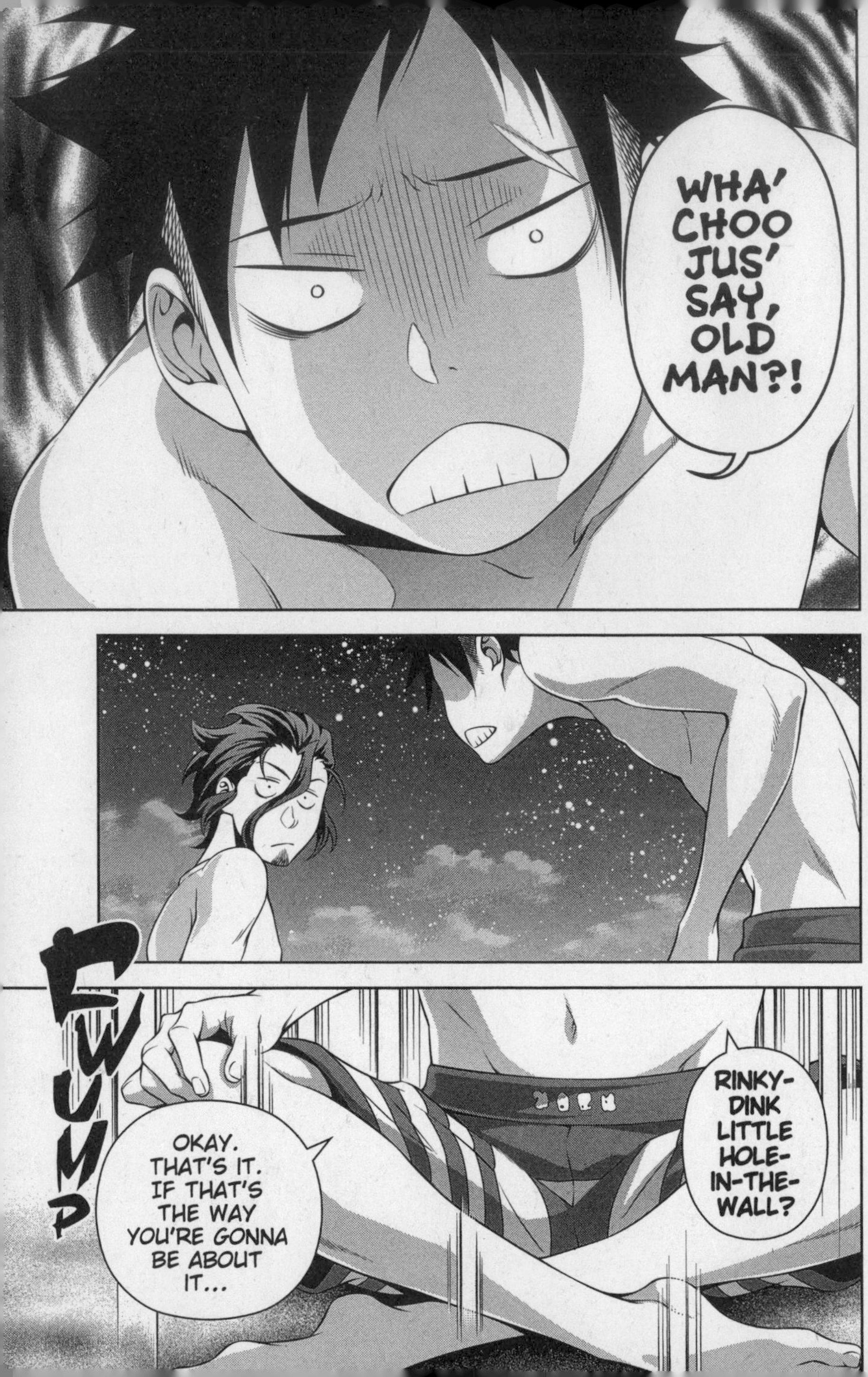
WHA' CHOO JUS' SAY, OLD MAN?!
FWUMP
RINKY-DINK LITTLE HOLE-IN-THE-WALL?
OKAY. THAT'S IT. IF THAT'S THE WAY YOU'RE GONNA BE ABOUT IT...

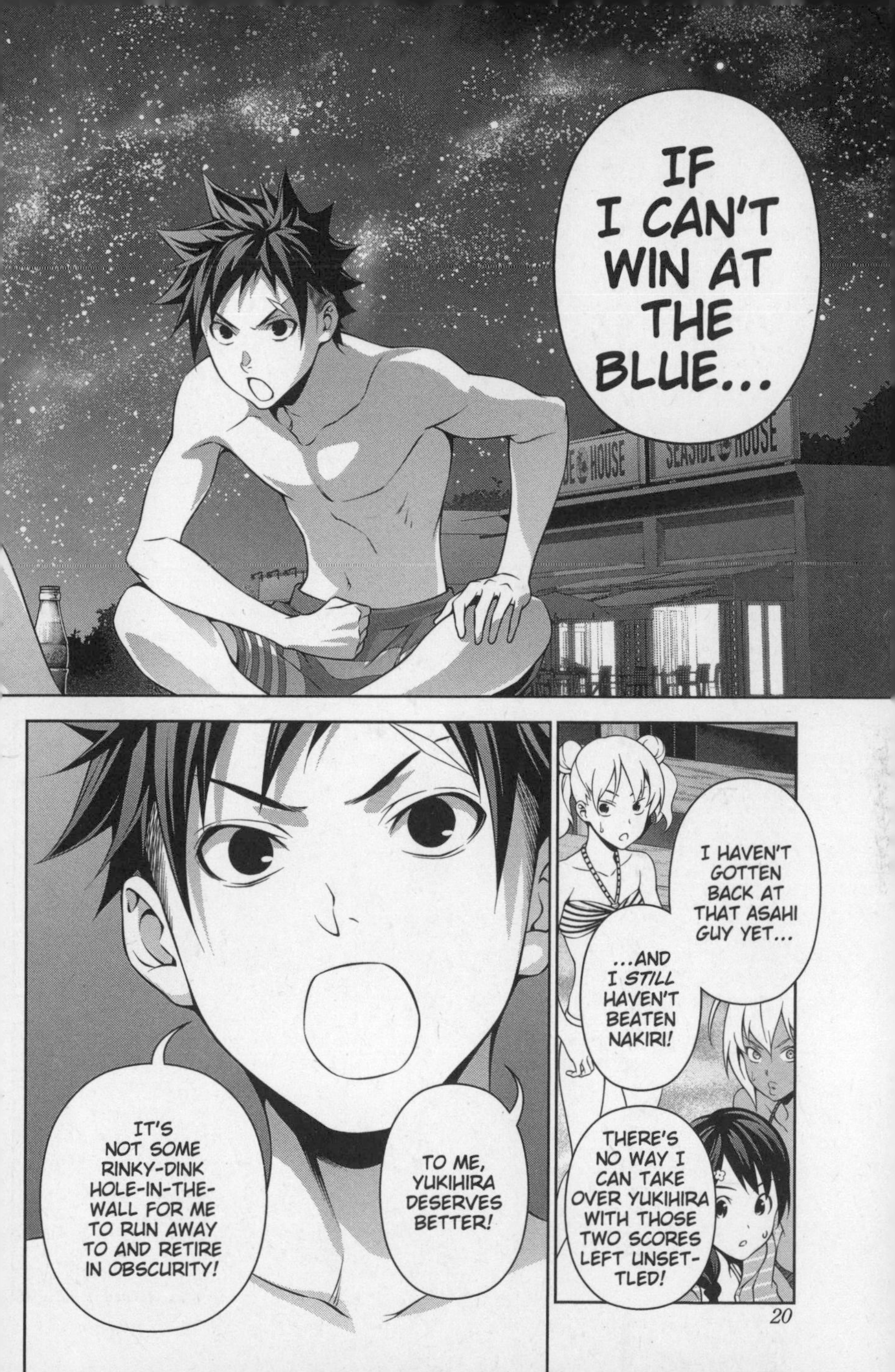
IF I CAN'T WIN AT THE BLUE...
SEASIDE HOUSE
I HAVEN'T GOTTEN BACK AT THAT ASAHI GUY YET...
...AND I *STILL* HAVEN'T BEATEN NAKIRI!
THERE'S NO WAY I CAN TAKE OVER YUKIHIRA WITH THOSE TWO SCORES LEFT UNSET-TLED!
TO ME, YUKIHIRA DESERVES BETTER!
IT'S NOT SOME RINKY-DINK HOLE-IN-THE-WALL FOR ME TO RUN AWAY TO AND RETIRE IN OBSCURITY!

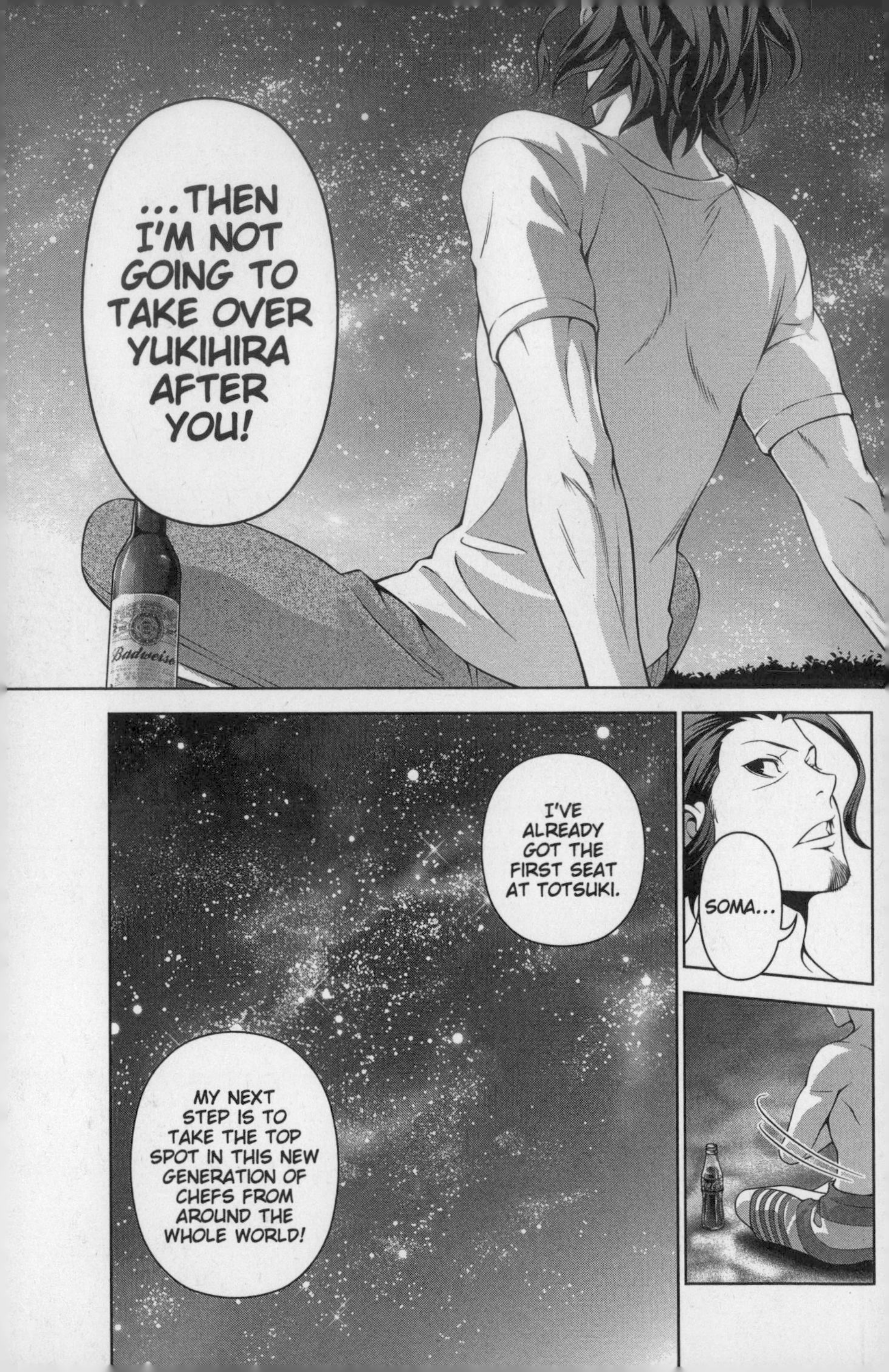
...THEN I'M NOT GOING TO TAKE OVER YUKIHIRA AFTER YOU!
SOMA...
I'VE ALREADY GOT THE FIRST SEAT AT TOTSUKI.
MY NEXT STEP IS TO TAKE THE TOP SPOT IN THIS NEW GENERATION OF CHEFS FROM AROUND THE WHOLE WORLD!

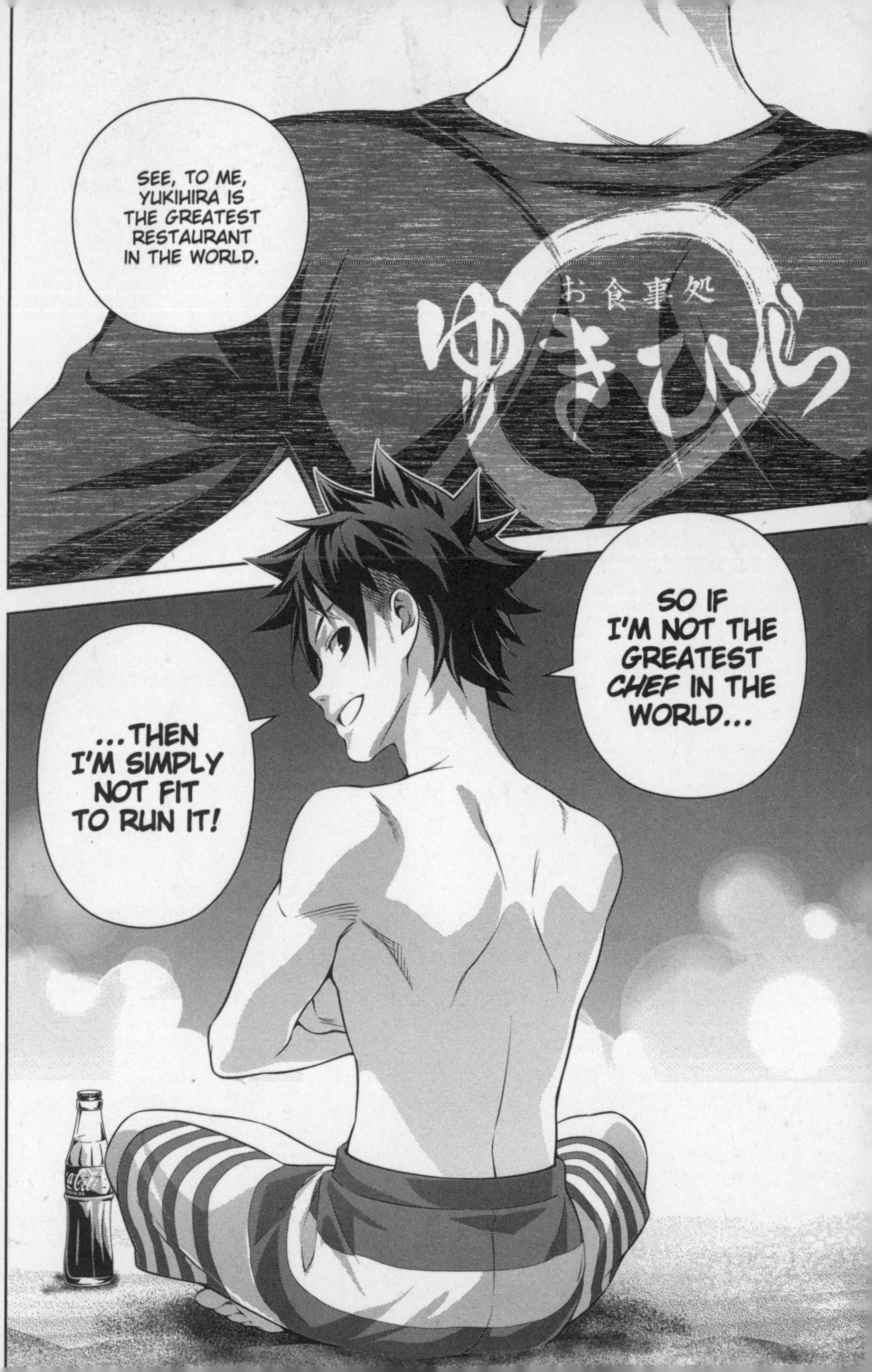
お食事処
ゆきひら
SEE, TO ME, YUKIHIRA IS THE GREATEST RESTAURANT IN THE WORLD.
SO IF I'M NOT THE GREATEST *CHEF* IN THE WORLD...
...THEN I'M SIMPLY NOT FIT TO RUN IT!

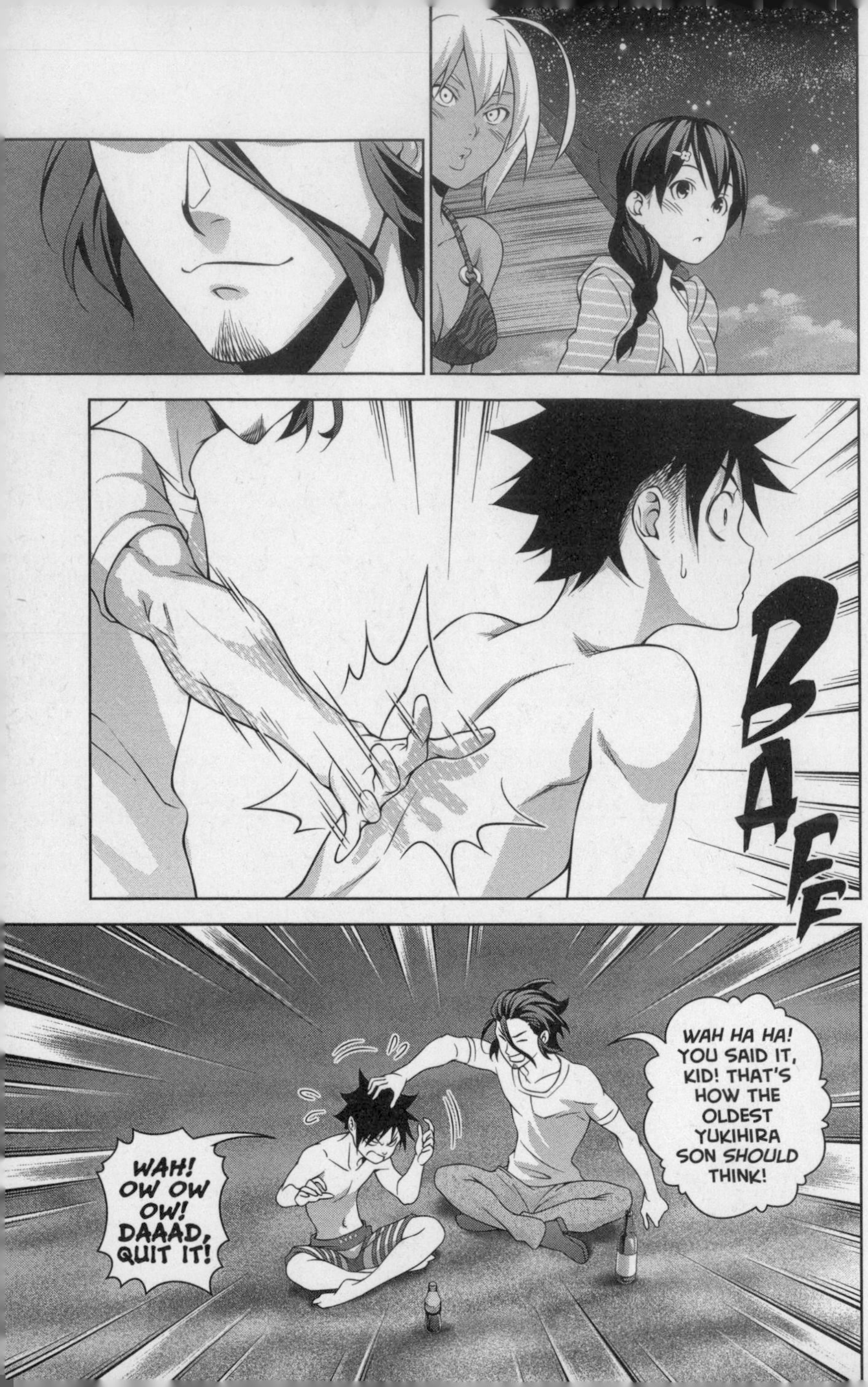
BAFF
WAH HA HA! YOU SAID IT, KID! THAT'S HOW THE OLDEST YUKIHIRA SON SHOULD THINK!
WAH! OW OW OW! DAAAD, QUIT IT!

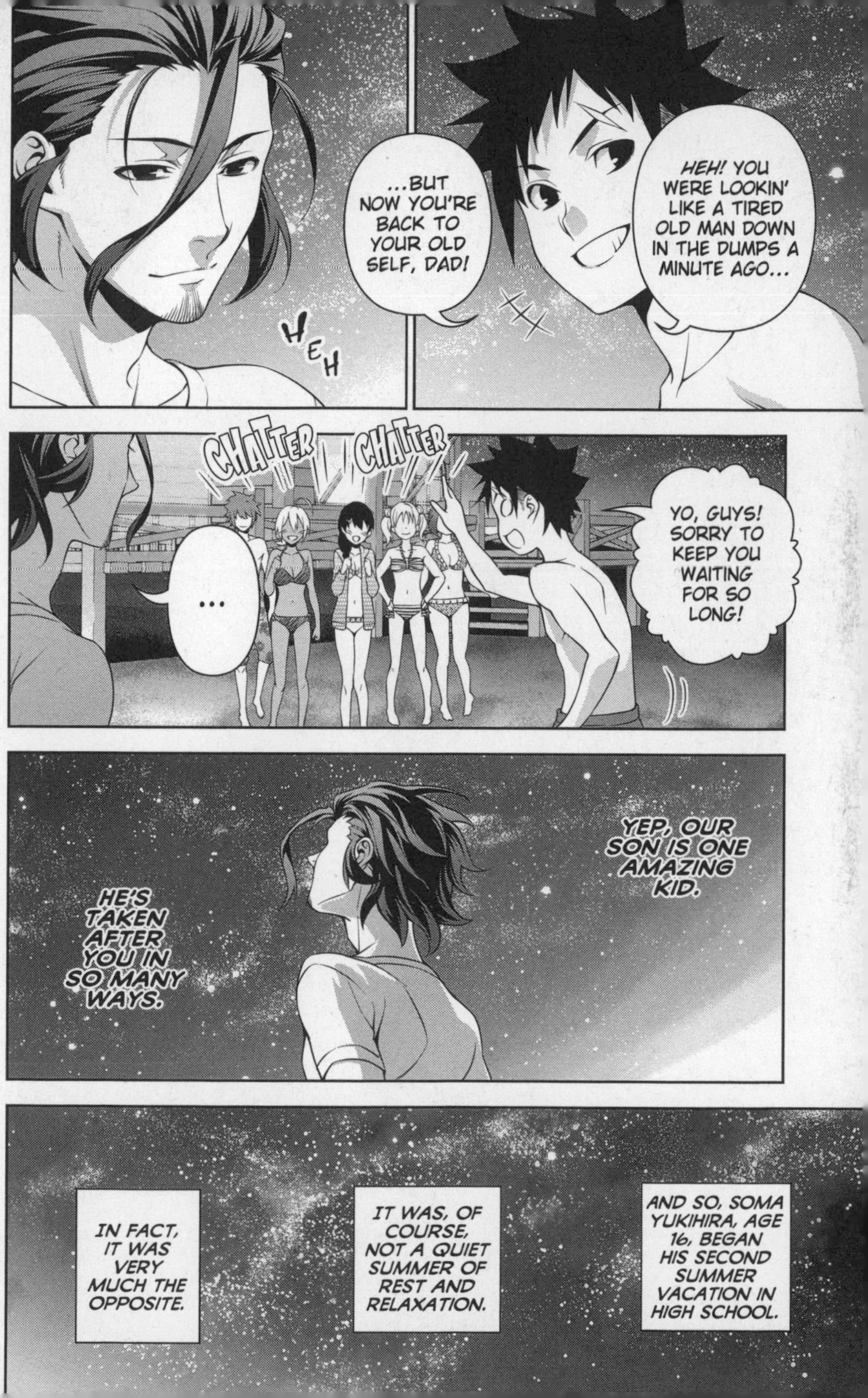
HEH! YOU WERE LOOKIN' LIKE A TIRED OLD MAN DOWN IN THE DUMPS A MINUTE AGO...
...BUT NOW YOU'RE BACK TO YOUR OLD SELF, DAD!
HEH
YO, GUYS! SORRY TO KEEP YOU WAITING FOR SO LONG!
CHATTER
CHATTER
...
YEP, OUR SON IS ONE AMAZING KID.
HE'S TAKEN AFTER YOU IN SO MANY WAYS.
AND SO, SOMA YUKIHIRA, AGE 16, BEGAN HIS SECOND SUMMER VACATION IN HIGH SCHOOL.
IT WAS, OF COURSE, NOT A QUIET SUMMER OF REST AND RELAXATION.
IN FACT, IT WAS VERY MUCH THE OPPOSITE.

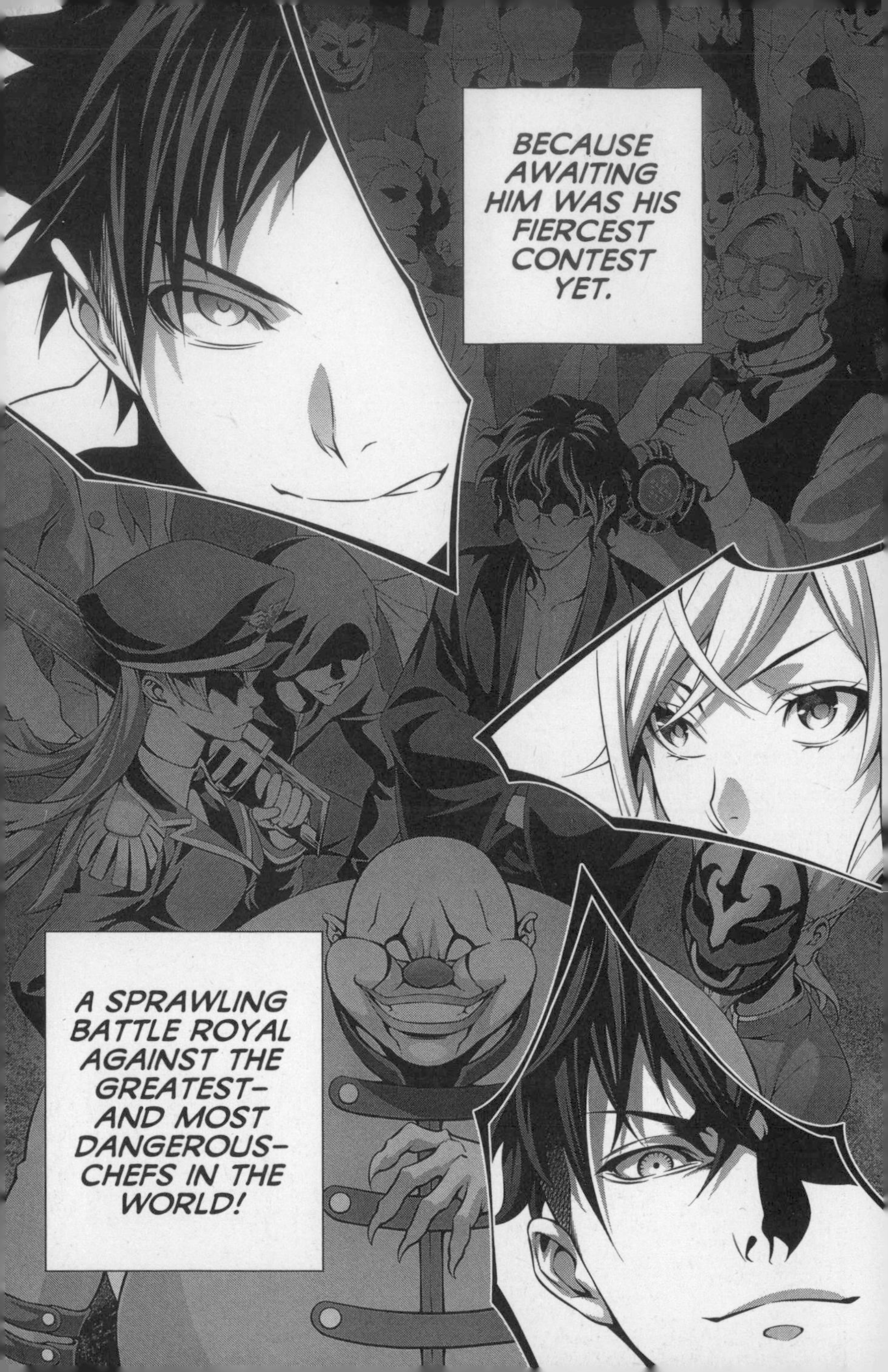
BECAUSE AWAITING HIM WAS HIS FIERCEST CONTEST YET.
A SPRAWLING BATTLE ROYAL AGAINST THE GREATEST—AND MOST DANGEROUS—CHEFS IN THE WORLD!

BLUE

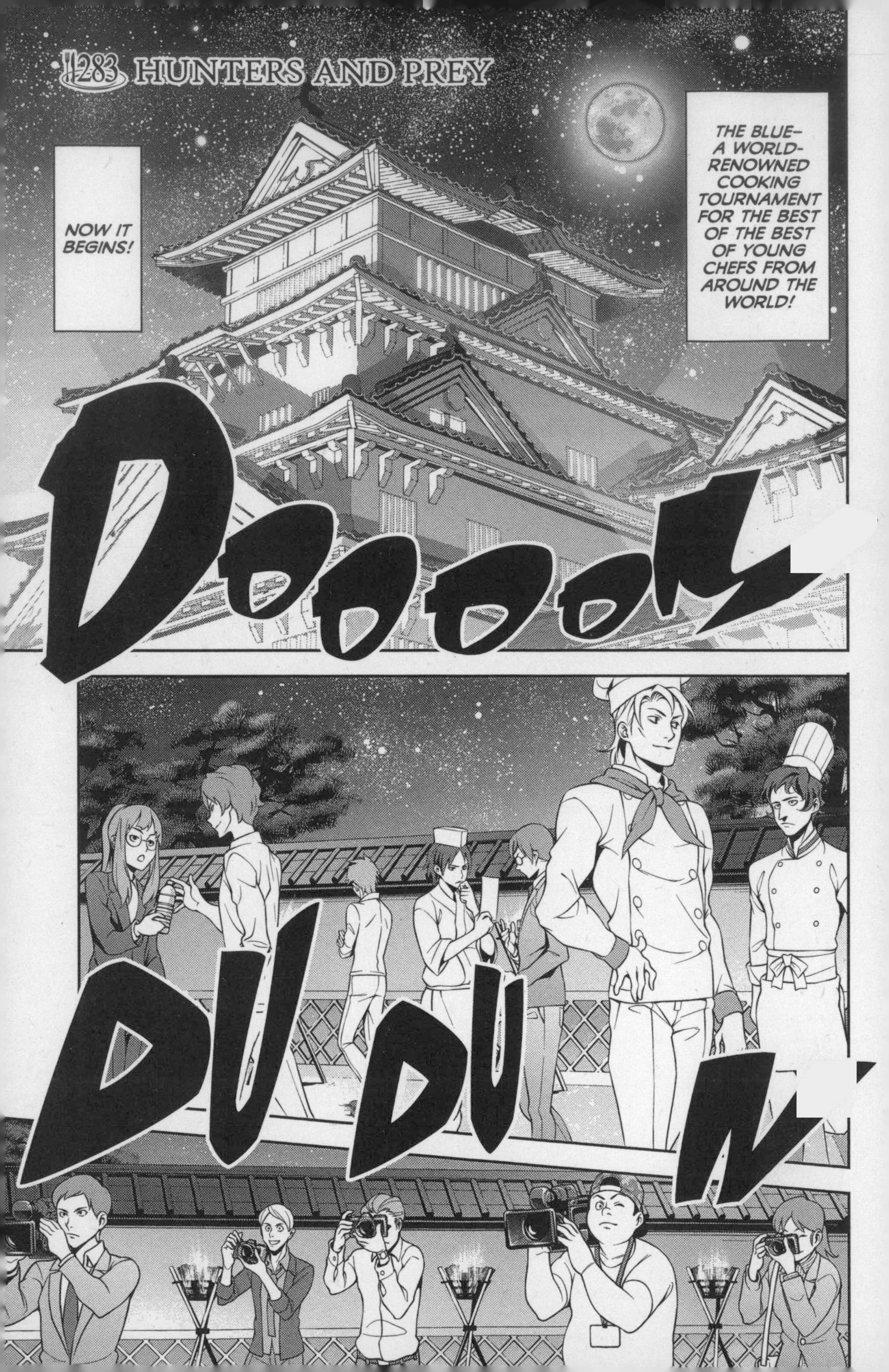
#283 HUNTERS AND PREY
THE BLUE– A WORLD-RENOWNED COOKING TOURNAMENT FOR THE BEST OF THE BEST OF YOUNG CHEFS FROM AROUND THE WORLD!
NOW IT BEGINS!
DOOOOOM
DUDUN

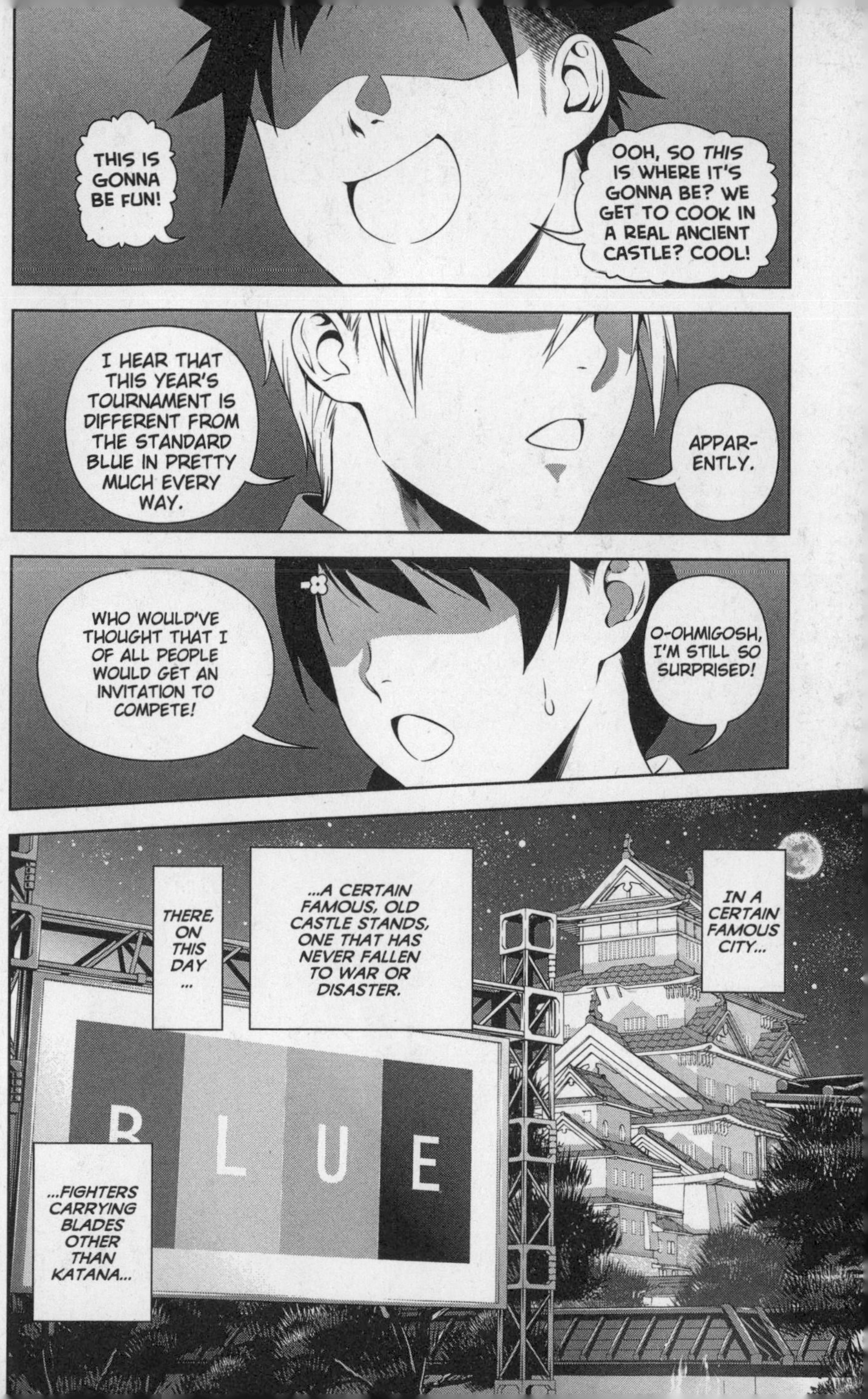
OOH, SO THIS IS WHERE IT'S GONNA BE? WE GET TO COOK IN A REAL ANCIENT CASTLE? COOL!
THIS IS GONNA BE FUN!
APPARENTLY.
I HEAR THAT THIS YEAR'S TOURNAMENT IS DIFFERENT FROM THE STANDARD BLUE IN PRETTY MUCH EVERY WAY.
O-OHMIGOSH, I'M STILL SO SURPRISED!
WHO WOULD'VE THOUGHT THAT I OF ALL PEOPLE WOULD GET AN INVITATION TO COMPETE!
IN A CERTAIN FAMOUS CITY...
...A CERTAIN FAMOUS, OLD CASTLE STANDS, ONE THAT HAS NEVER FALLEN TO WAR OR DISASTER.
THERE, ON THIS DAY...
BLUE
...FIGHTERS CARRYING BLADES OTHER THAN KATANA...

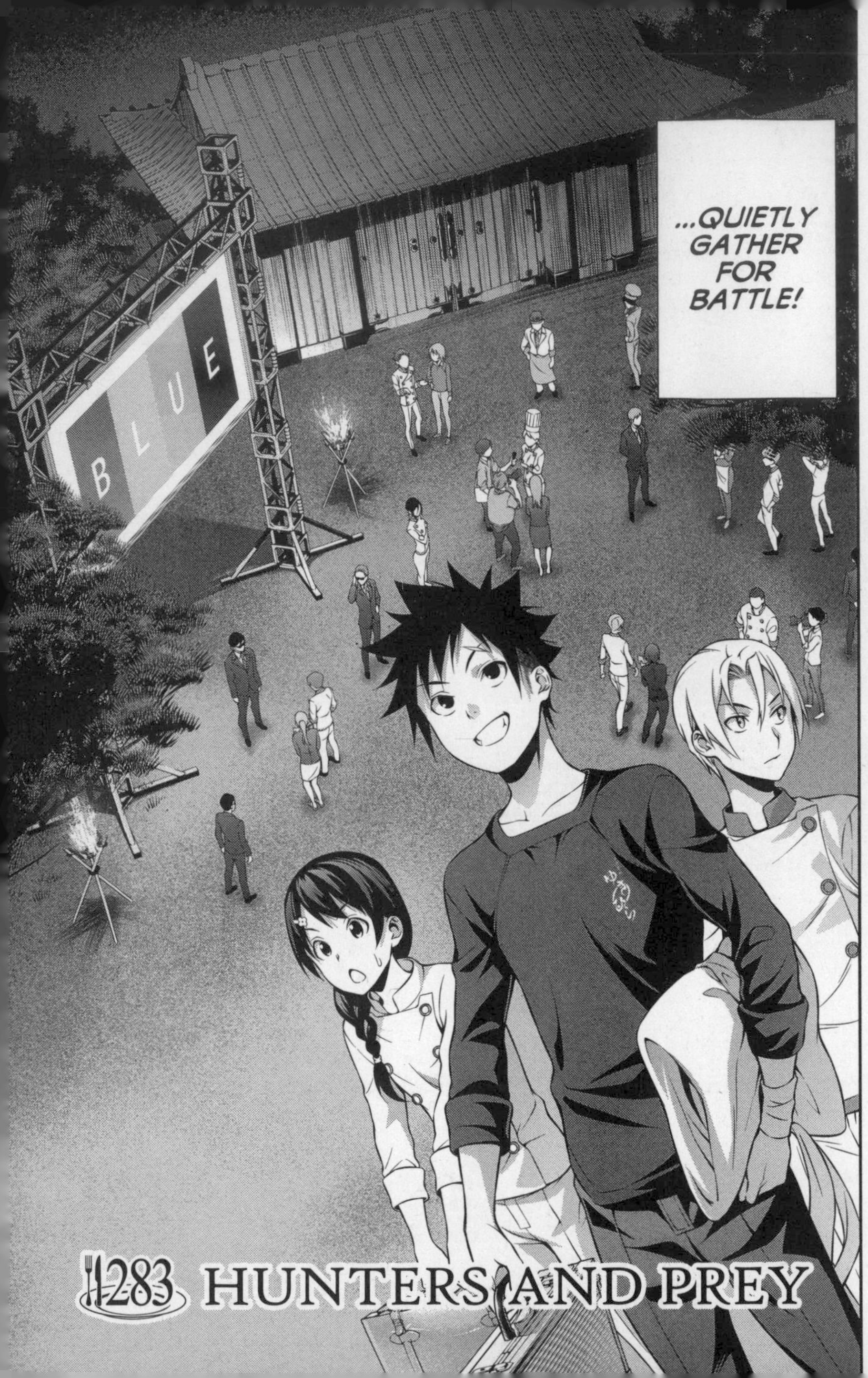
...QUIETLY GATHER FOR BATTLE!
BLUE
283 HUNTERS AND PREY

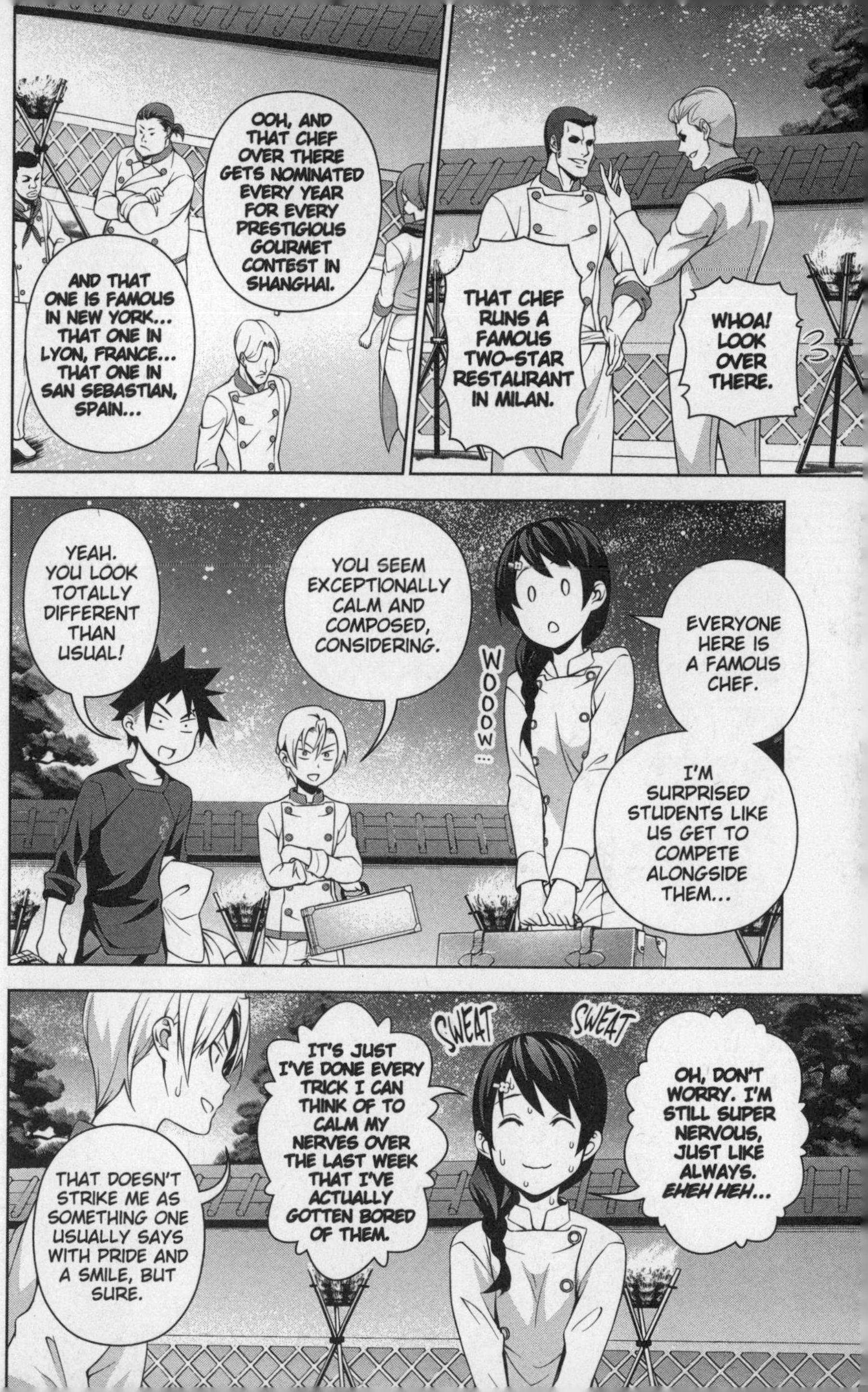
WHOA! LOOK OVER THERE.
THAT CHEF RUNS A FAMOUS TWO-STAR RESTAURANT IN MILAN.
OOH, AND THAT CHEF OVER THERE GETS NOMINATED EVERY YEAR FOR EVERY PRESTIGIOUS GOURMET CONTEST IN SHANGHAI.
AND THAT ONE IS FAMOUS IN NEW YORK... THAT ONE IN LYON, FRANCE... THAT ONE IN SAN SEBASTIAN, SPAIN...
EVERYONE HERE IS A FAMOUS CHEF.
I'M SURPRISED STUDENTS LIKE US GET TO COMPETE ALONGSIDE THEM...
WOOOOW...
YOU SEEM EXCEPTIONALLY CALM AND COMPOSED, CONSIDERING.
YEAH. YOU LOOK TOTALLY DIFFERENT THAN USUAL!
OH, DON'T WORRY. I'M STILL SUPER NERVOUS, JUST LIKE ALWAYS. *EHEH HEH...*
SWEAT
SWEAT
IT'S JUST I'VE DONE EVERY TRICK I CAN THINK OF TO CALM MY NERVES OVER THE LAST WEEK THAT I'VE ACTUALLY GOTTEN BORED OF THEM.
THAT DOESN'T STRIKE ME AS SOMETHING ONE USUALLY SAYS WITH PRIDE AND A SMILE, BUT SURE.

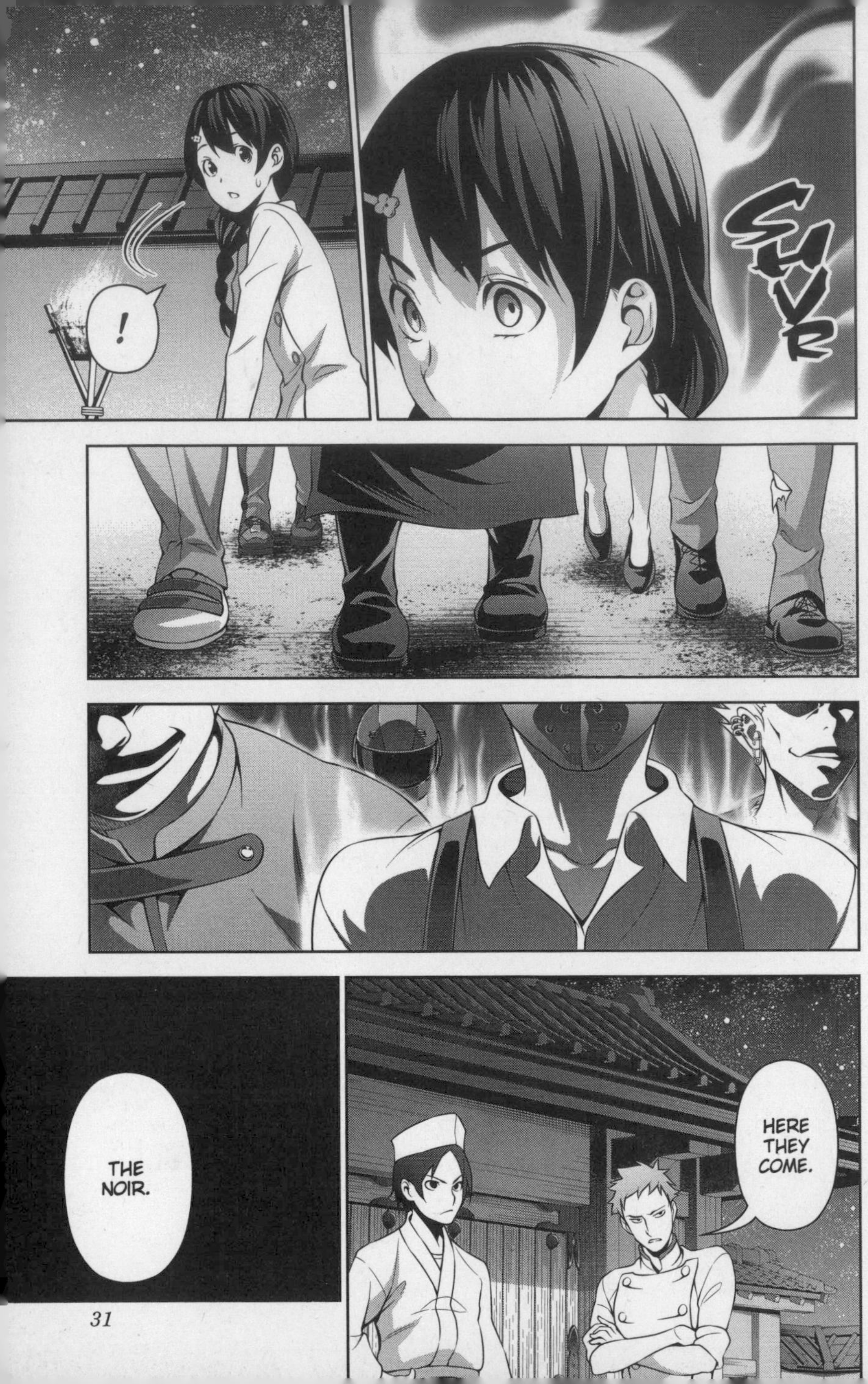
SHVR
!
HERE THEY COME.
THE NOIR.

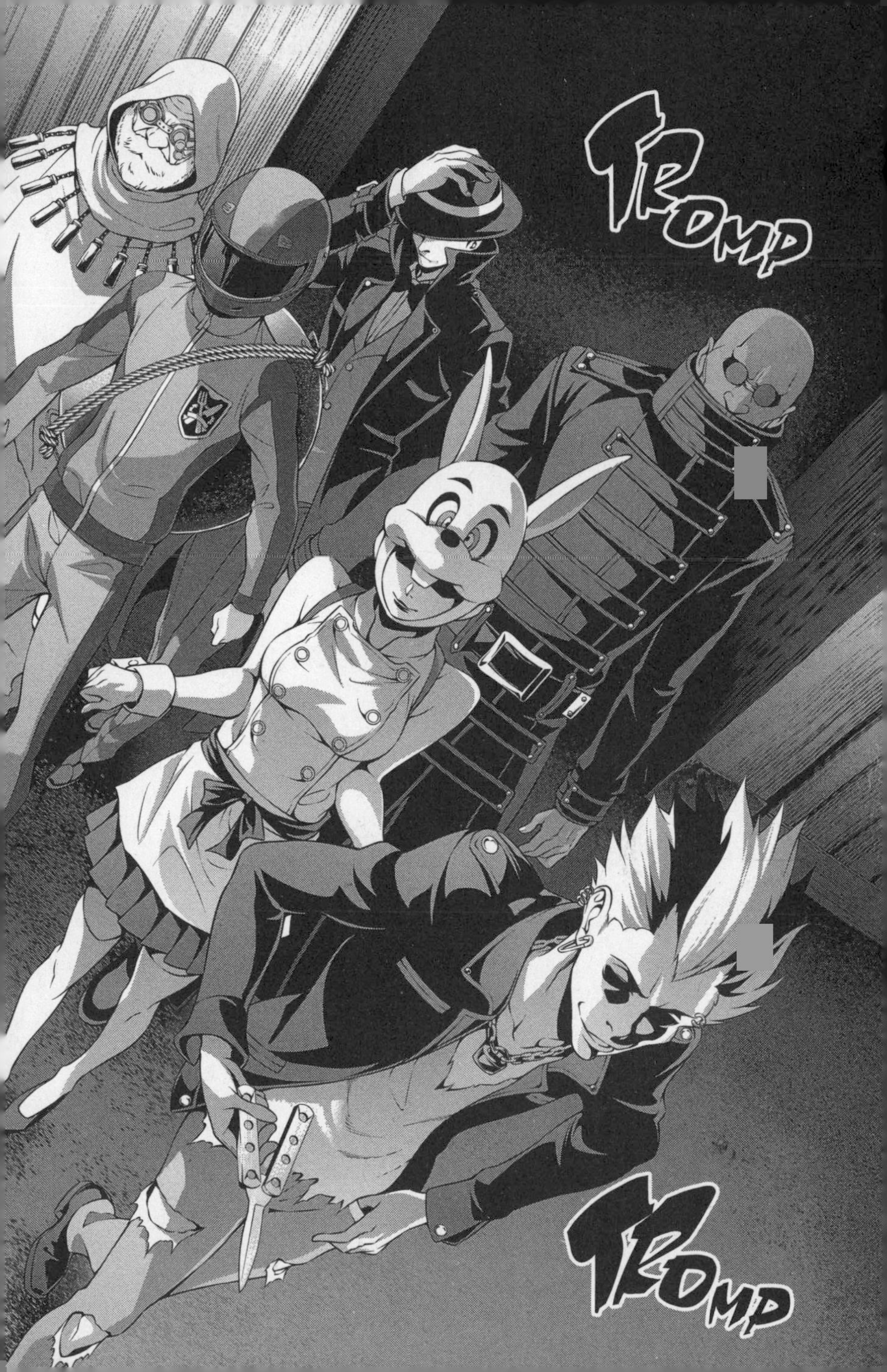
TROMP
TROMP

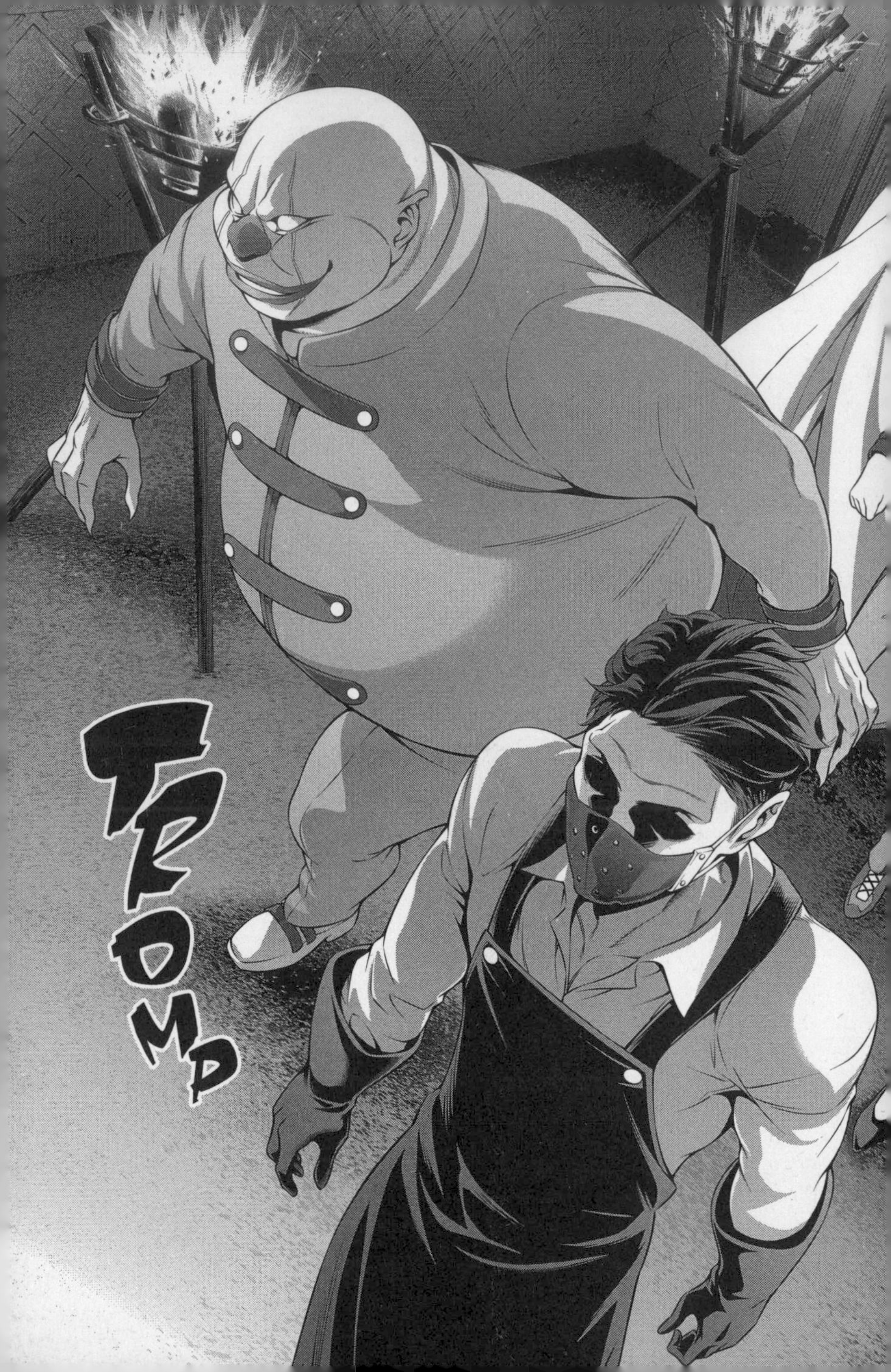
TROMP

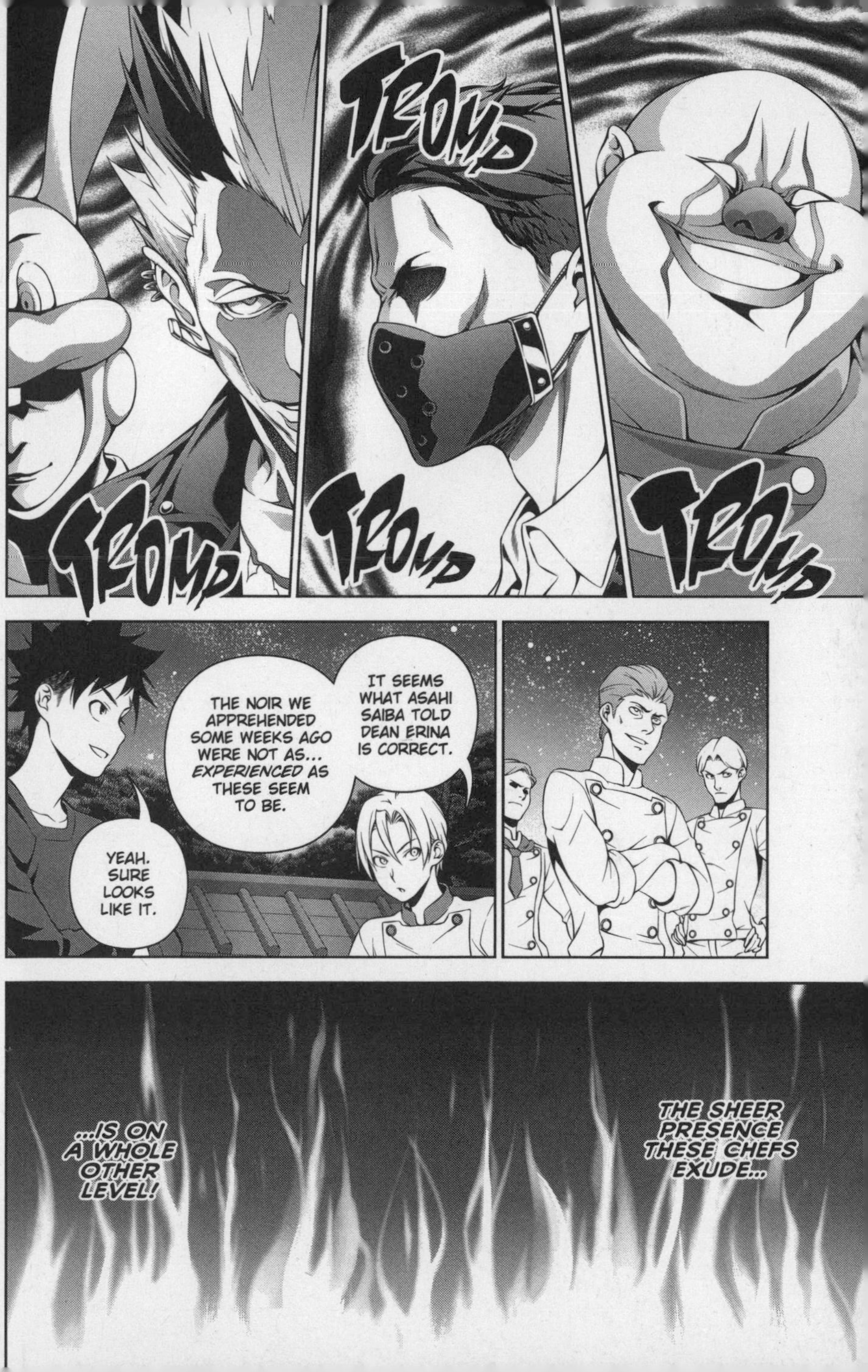
TROMP
TROMP
TROMP
TROMP
TROMP
IT SEEMS WHAT ASAHI SAIBA TOLD DEAN ERINA IS CORRECT.
THE NOIR WE APPREHENDED SOME WEEKS AGO WERE NOT AS... *EXPERIENCED* AS THESE SEEM TO BE.
YEAH. SURE LOOKS LIKE IT.
THE SHEER PRESENCE THESE CHEFS EXUDE...
...IS ON A WHOLE OTHER LEVEL!

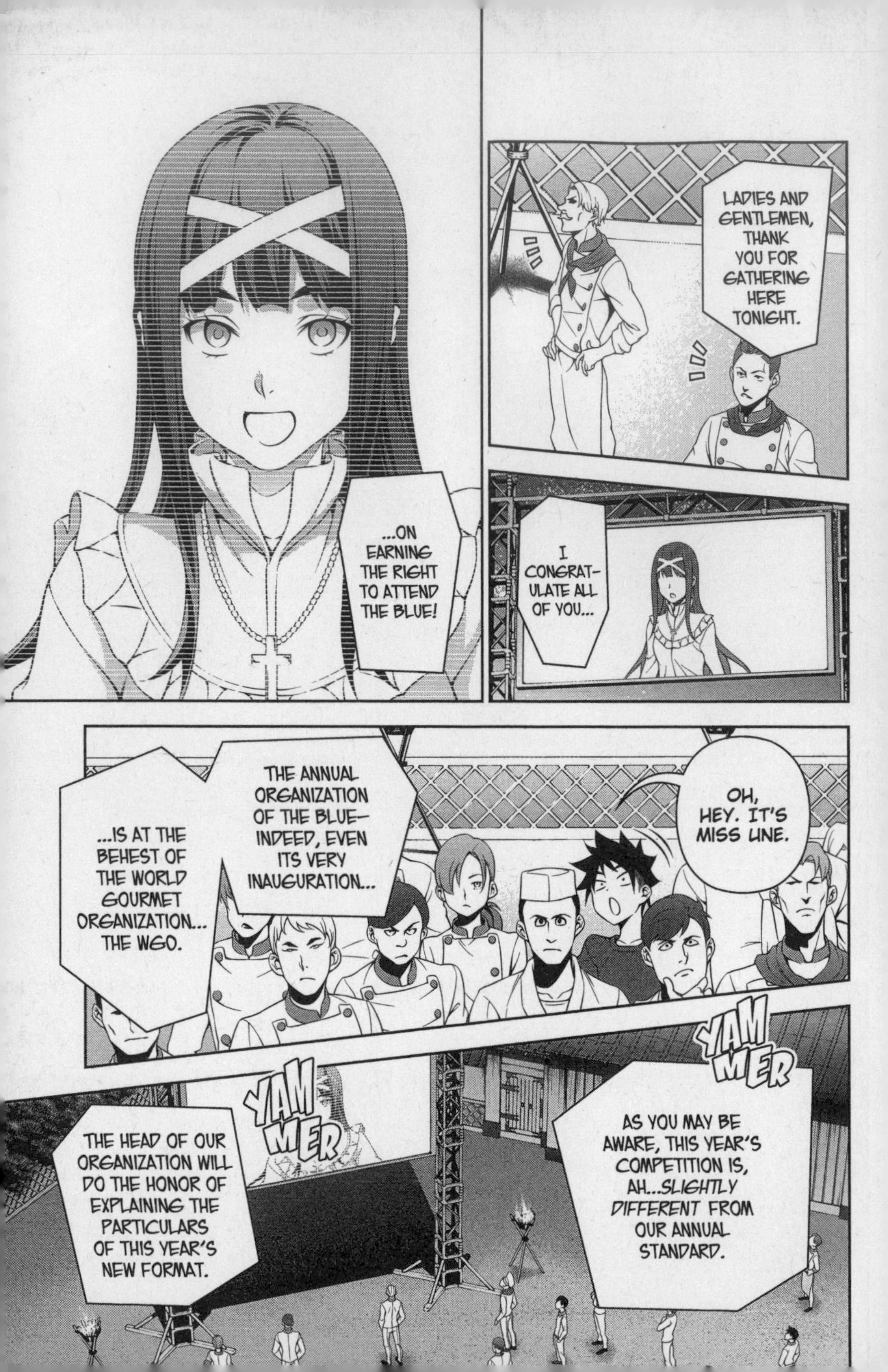
LADIES AND GENTLEMEN, THANK YOU FOR GATHERING HERE TONIGHT.
I CONGRAT-ULATE ALL OF YOU...
...ON EARNING THE RIGHT TO ATTEND THE BLUE!
OH, HEY. IT'S MISS LINE.
THE ANNUAL ORGANIZATION OF THE BLUE—INDEED, EVEN ITS VERY INAUGURATION...
...IS AT THE BEHEST OF THE WORLD GOURMET ORGANIZATION... THE WGO.
YAMMER
AS YOU MAY BE AWARE, THIS YEAR'S COMPETITION IS, AH...SLIGHTLY DIFFERENT FROM OUR ANNUAL STANDARD.
YAMMER
THE HEAD OF OUR ORGANIZATION WILL DO THE HONOR OF EXPLAINING THE PARTICULARS OF THIS YEAR'S NEW FORMAT.

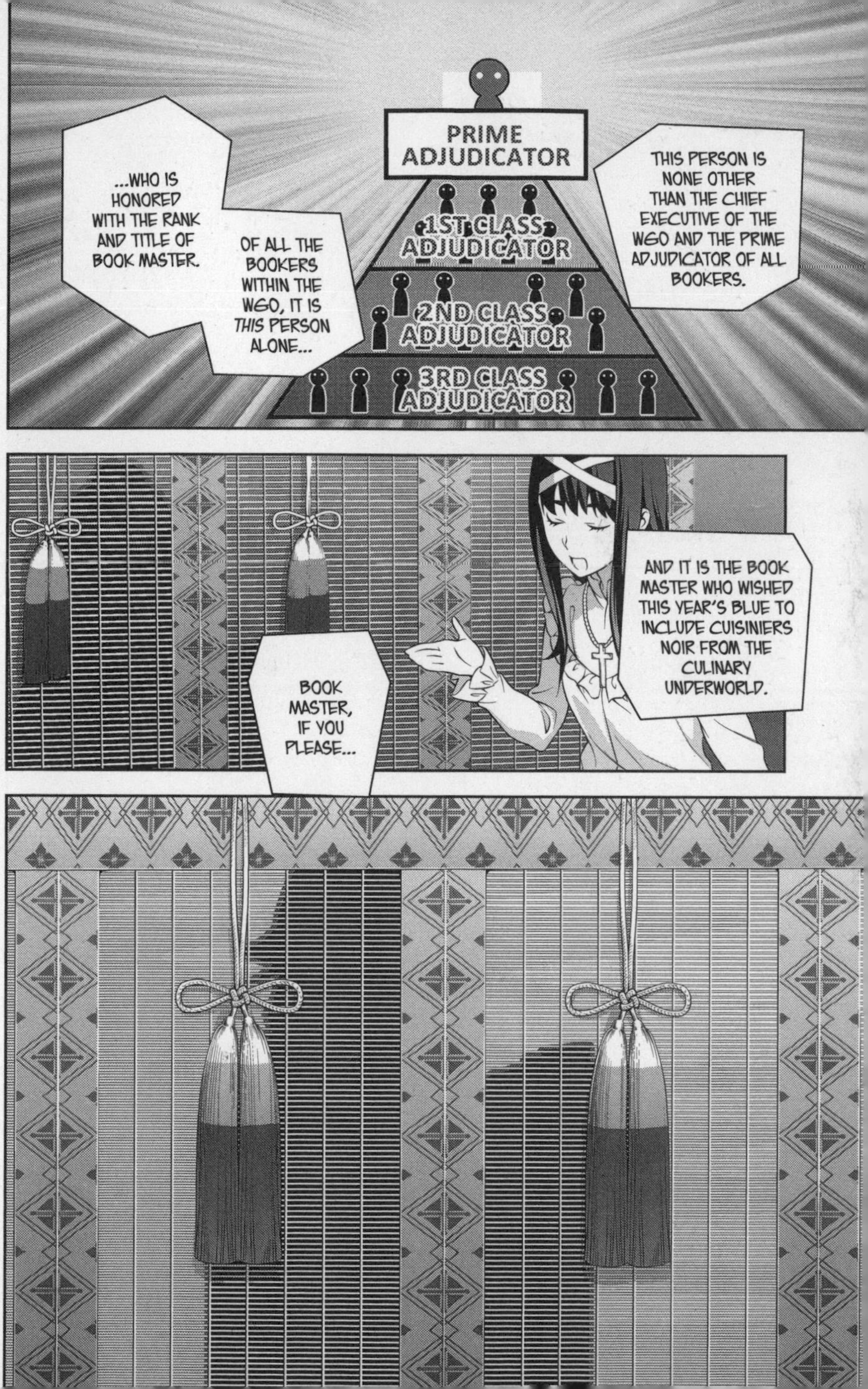
THIS PERSON IS NONE OTHER THAN THE CHIEF EXECUTIVE OF THE WGO AND THE PRIME ADJUDICATOR OF ALL BOOKERS.
PRIME ADJUDICATOR
1ST CLASS ADJUDICATOR
2ND CLASS ADJUDICATOR
3RD CLASS ADJUDICATOR
OF ALL THE BOOKERS WITHIN THE WGO, IT IS THIS PERSON ALONE...
...WHO IS HONORED WITH THE RANK AND TITLE OF BOOK MASTER.
AND IT IS THE BOOK MASTER WHO WISHED THIS YEAR'S BLUE TO INCLUDE CUISINIERS NOIR FROM THE CULINARY UNDERWORLD.
BOOK MASTER, IF YOU PLEASE...

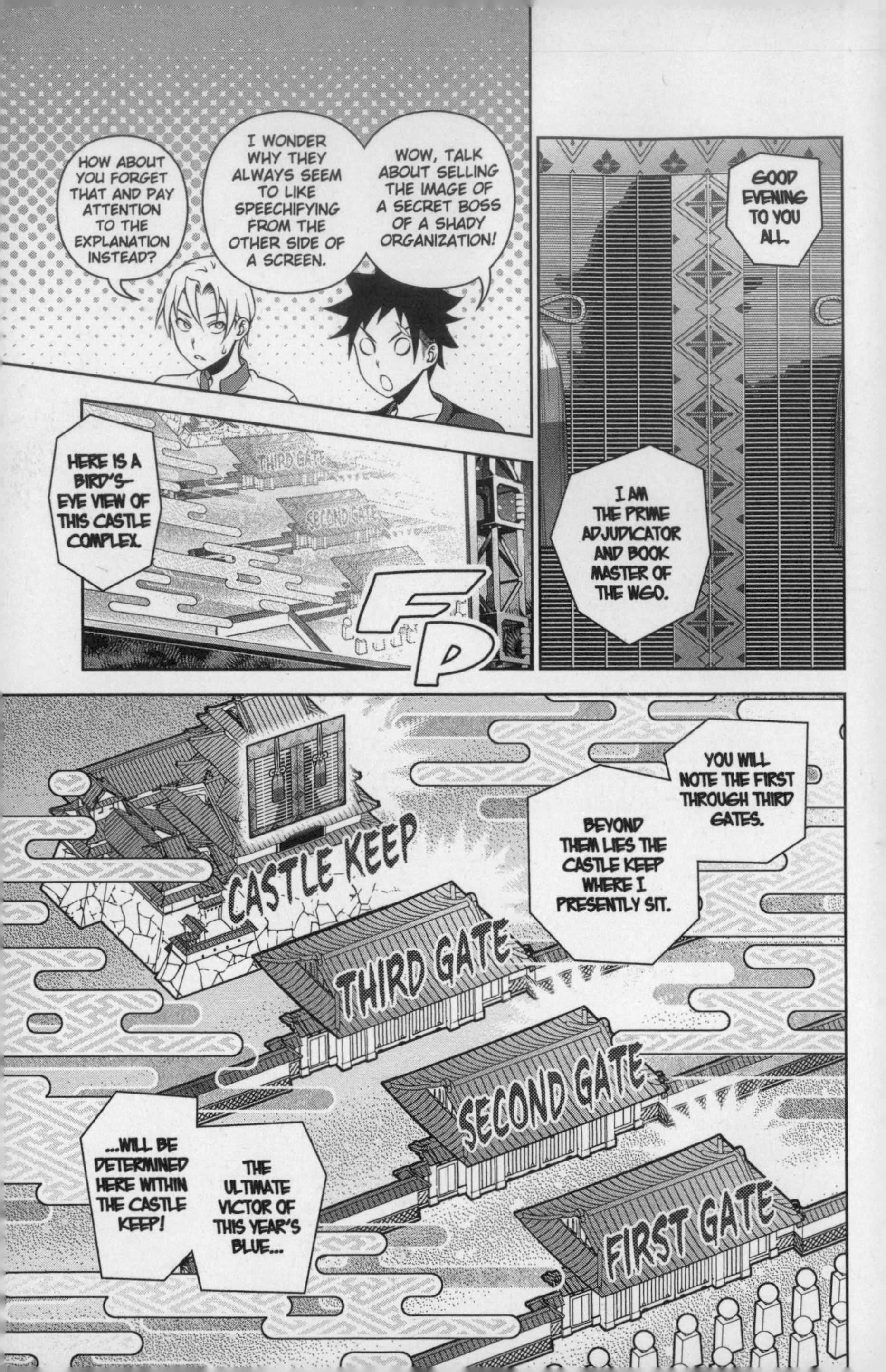
GOOD EVENING TO YOU ALL.
I AM THE PRIME ADJUDICATOR AND BOOK MASTER OF THE WGO.
WOW, TALK ABOUT SELLING THE IMAGE OF A SECRET BOSS OF A SHADY ORGANIZATION!
I WONDER WHY THEY ALWAYS SEEM TO LIKE SPEECHIFYING FROM THE OTHER SIDE OF A SCREEN.
HOW ABOUT YOU FORGET THAT AND PAY ATTENTION TO THE EXPLANATION INSTEAD?
THIRD GATE
SECOND GATE
FP
HERE IS A BIRD'S-EYE VIEW OF THIS CASTLE COMPLEX.
YOU WILL NOTE THE FIRST THROUGH THIRD GATES.
BEYOND THEM LIES THE CASTLE KEEP WHERE I PRESENTLY SIT.
CASTLE KEEP
THIRD GATE
SECOND GATE
FIRST GATE
THE ULTIMATE VICTOR OF THIS YEAR'S BLUE...
...WILL BE DETERMINED HERE WITHIN THE CASTLE KEEP!

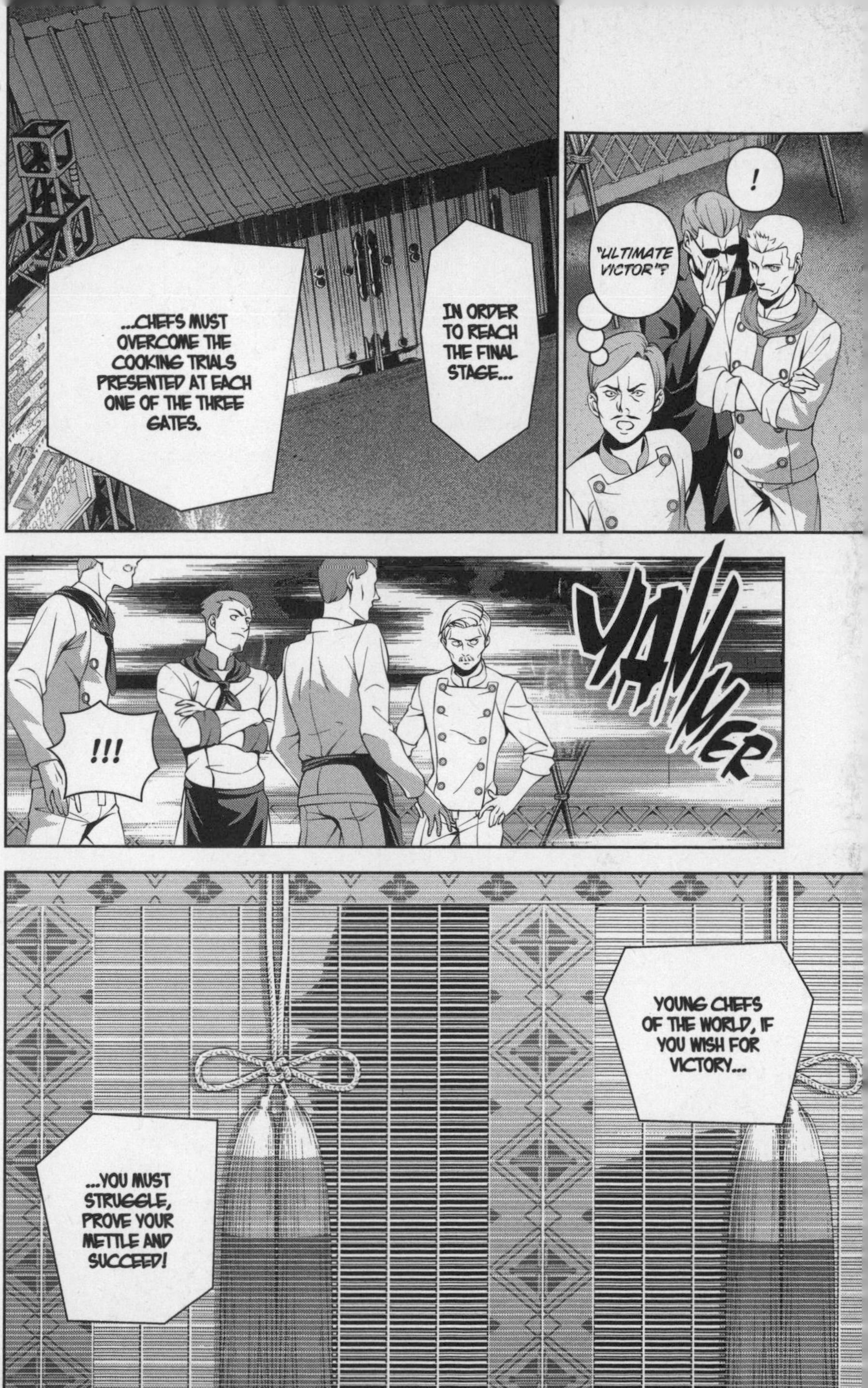
!
"ULTIMATE VICTOR"?
IN ORDER TO REACH THE FINAL STAGE...
...CHEFS MUST OVERCOME THE COOKING TRIALS PRESENTED AT EACH ONE OF THE THREE GATES.
YAMMER
!!!
YOUNG CHEFS OF THE WORLD, IF YOU WISH FOR VICTORY...
...YOU MUST STRUGGLE, PROVE YOUR METTLE AND SUCCEED!

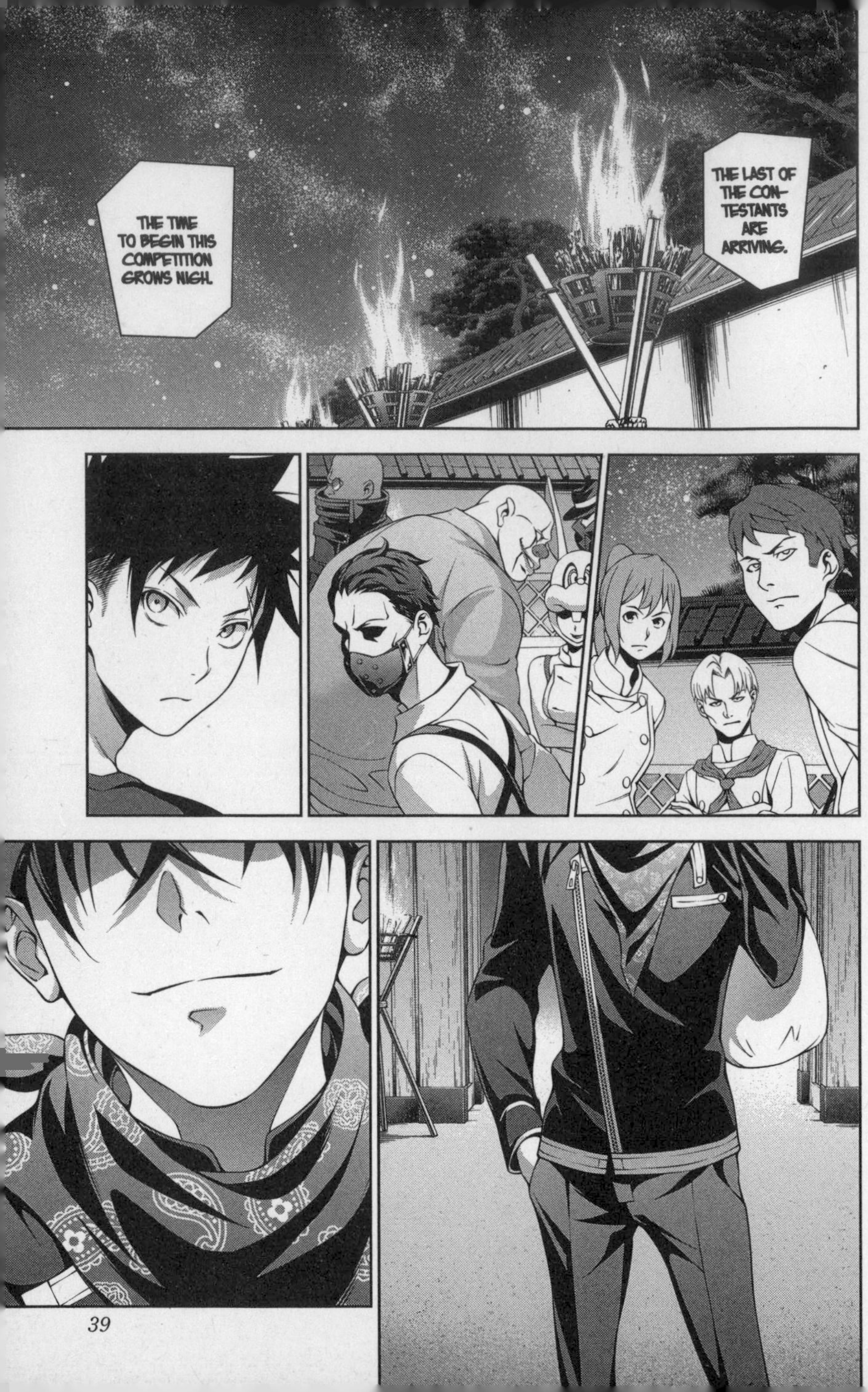
THE LAST OF THE CON-TESTANTS ARE ARRIVING.
THE TIME TO BEGIN THIS COMPETITION GROWS NIGH.

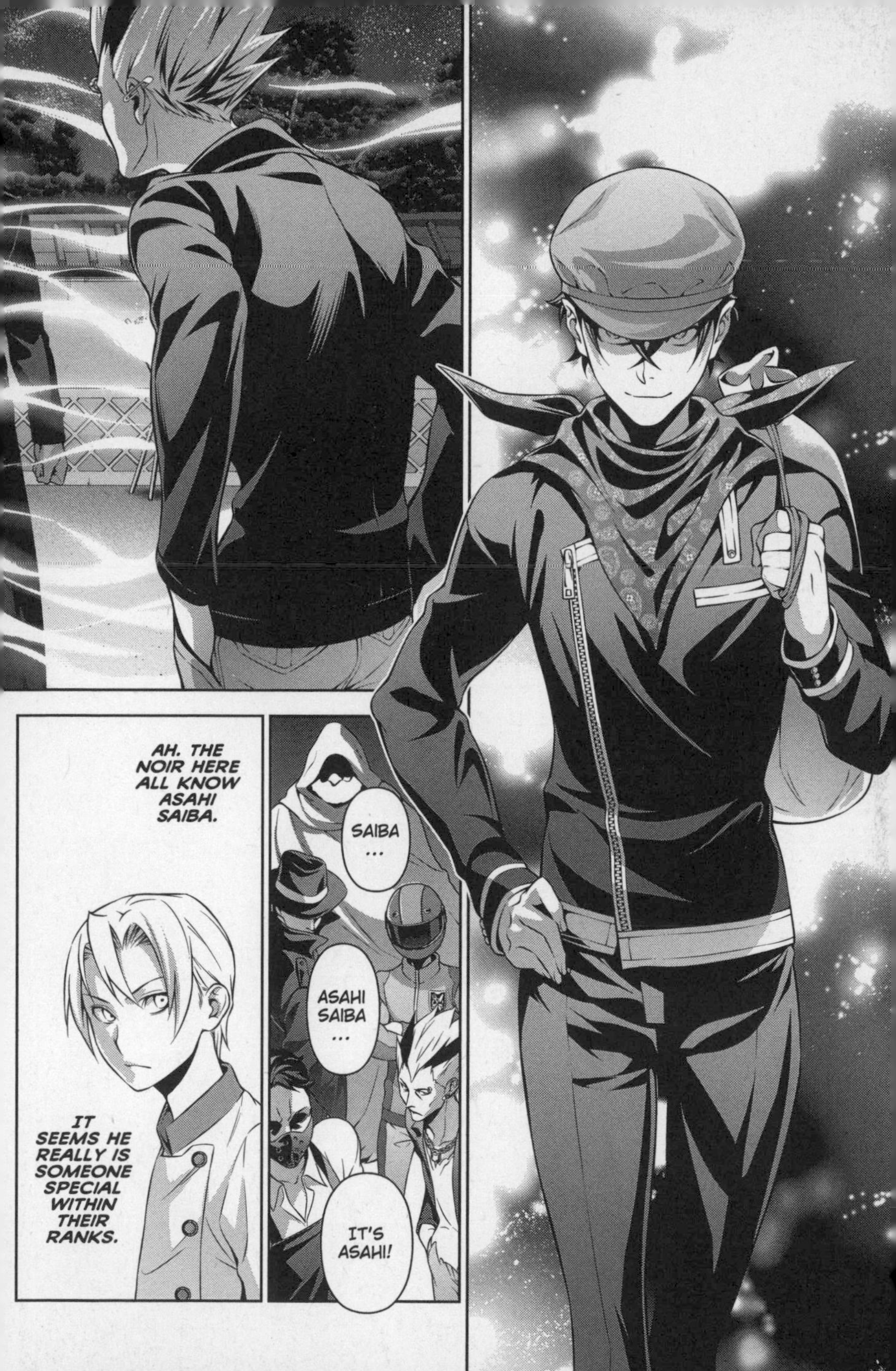
SAIBA...
ASAHI SAIBA...
IT'S ASAHI!
AH. THE NOIR HERE ALL KNOW ASAHI SAIBA.
IT SEEMS HE REALLY IS SOMEONE SPECIAL WITHIN THEIR RANKS.

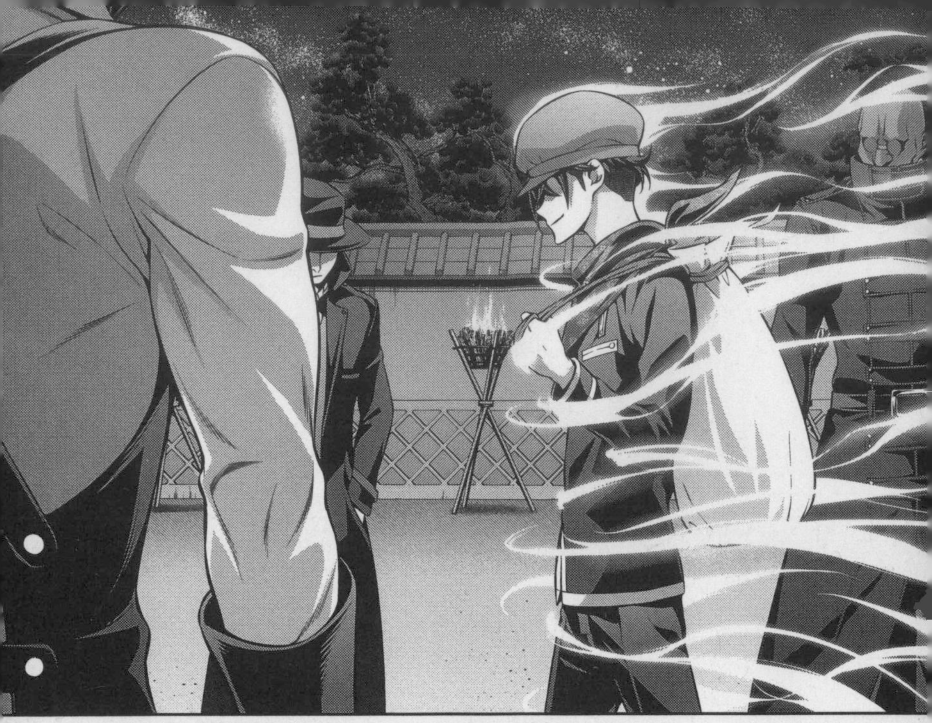

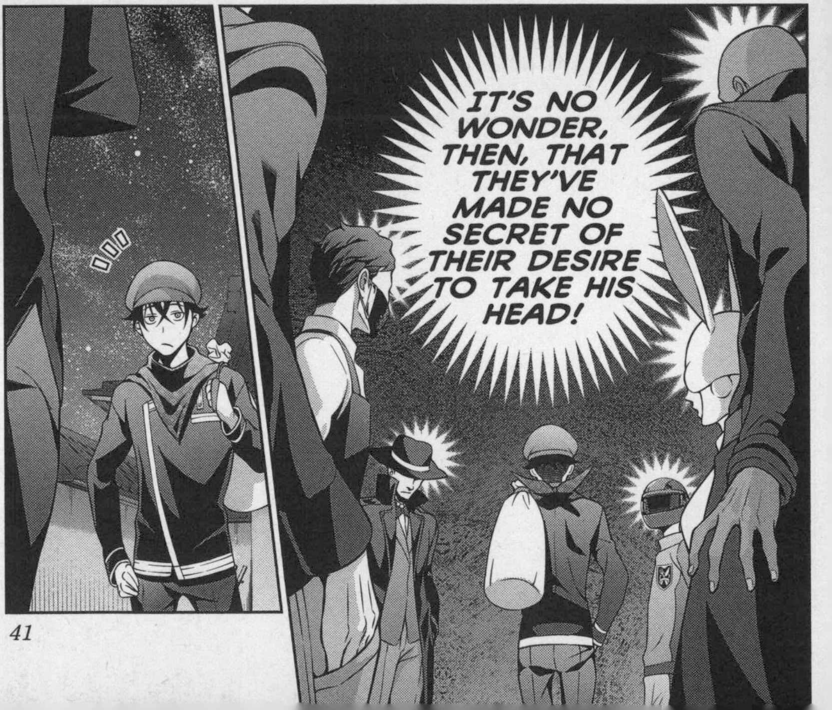
...
IT'S NO WONDER, THEN, THAT THEY'VE MADE NO SECRET OF THEIR DESIRE TO TAKE HIS HEAD!

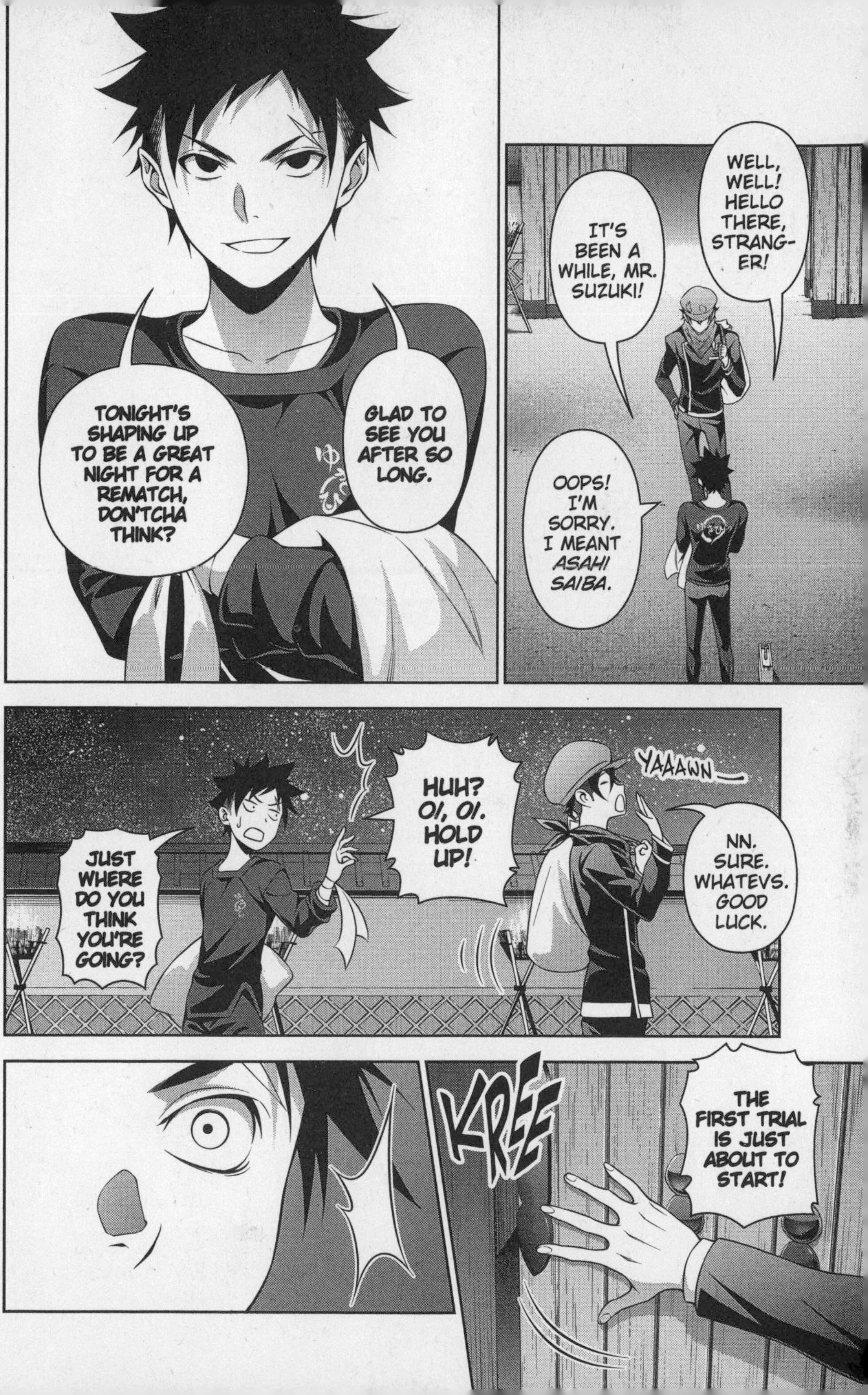
WELL, WELL! HELLO THERE, STRANGER!
IT'S BEEN A WHILE, MR. SUZUKI!
OOPS! I'M SORRY. I MEANT *ASAHI SAIBA.*
GLAD TO SEE YOU AFTER SO LONG.
TONIGHT'S SHAPING UP TO BE A GREAT NIGHT FOR A REMATCH, DON'TCHA THINK?
YAAAWN
NN. SURE. WHATEVS. GOOD LUCK.
HUH? OI, OI. HOLD UP!
JUST WHERE DO YOU THINK YOU'RE GOING?
THE FIRST TRIAL IS JUST ABOUT TO START!
KREE

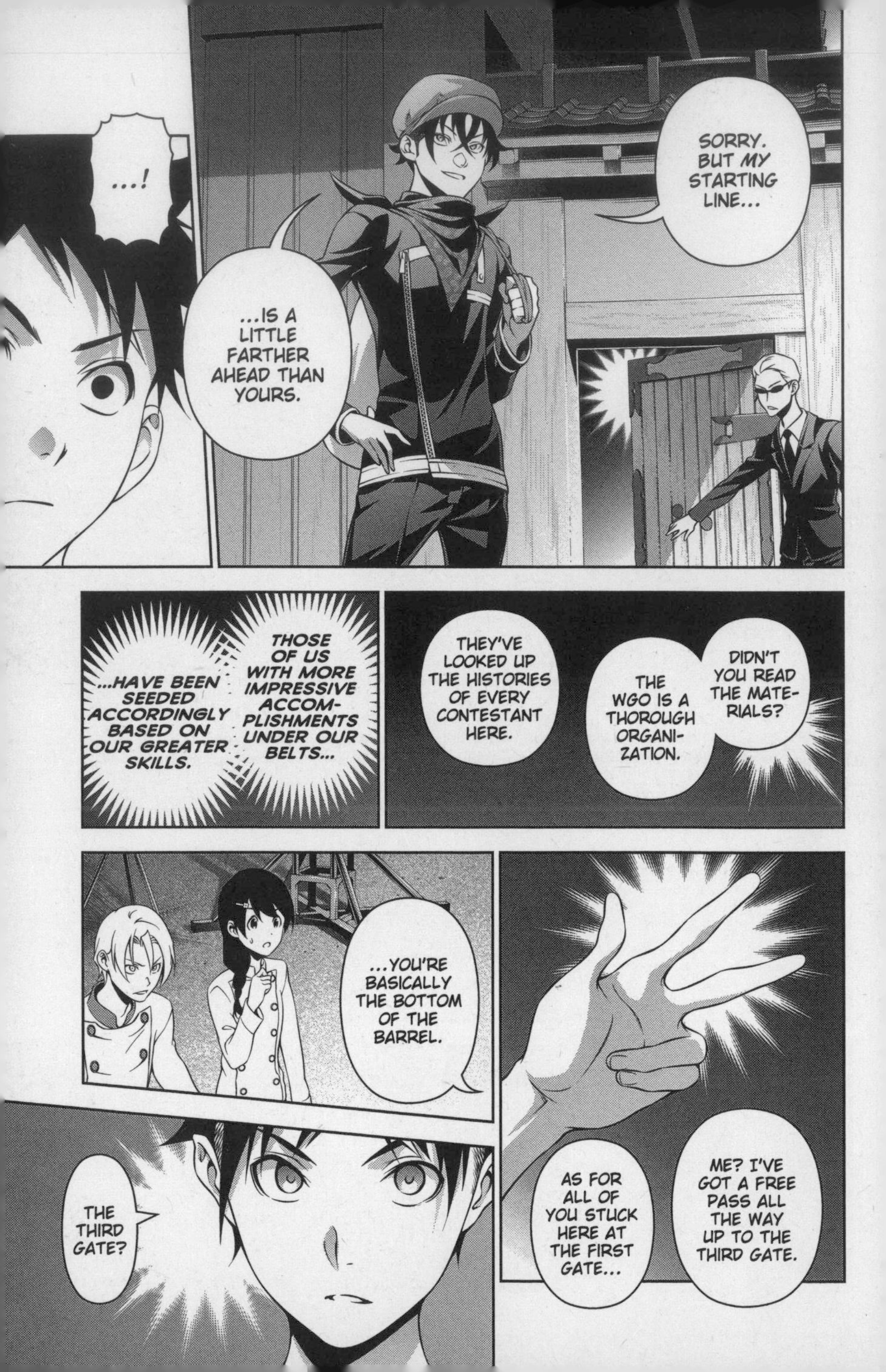
SORRY. BUT MY STARTING LINE...
...IS A LITTLE FARTHER AHEAD THAN YOURS.
...!
DIDN'T YOU READ THE MATE-RIALS?
THE WGO IS A THOROUGH ORGANI-ZATION.
THEY'VE LOOKED UP THE HISTORIES OF EVERY CONTESTANT HERE.
THOSE OF US WITH MORE IMPRESSIVE ACCOM-PLISHMENTS UNDER OUR BELTS...
...HAVE BEEN SEEDED ACCORDINGLY BASED ON OUR GREATER SKILLS.
ME? I'VE GOT A FREE PASS ALL THE WAY UP TO THE THIRD GATE.
AS FOR ALL OF YOU STUCK HERE AT THE FIRST GATE...
...YOU'RE BASICALLY THE BOTTOM OF THE BARREL.
THE THIRD GATE?

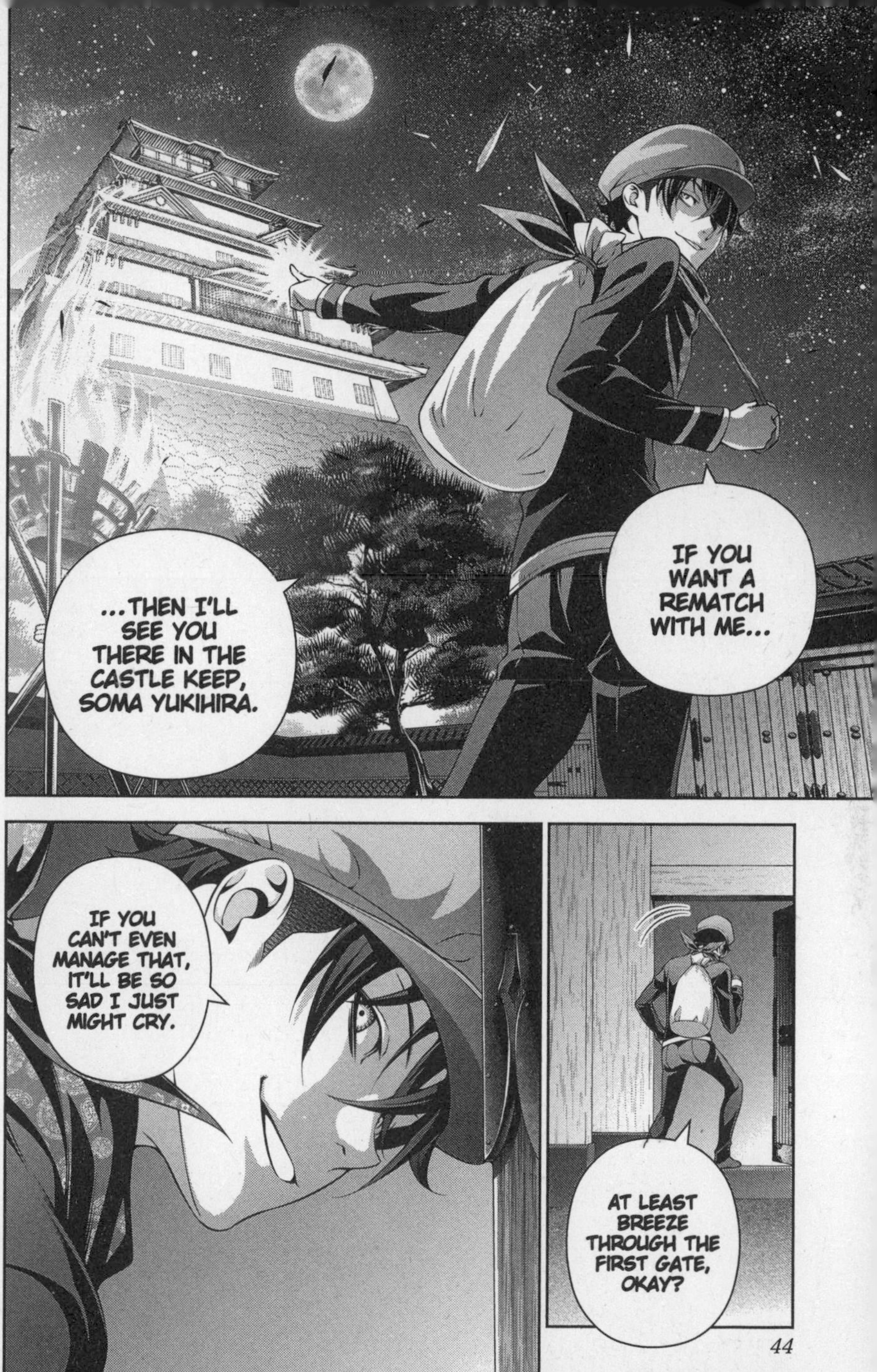
IF YOU WANT A REMATCH WITH ME...
...THEN I'LL SEE YOU THERE IN THE CASTLE KEEP, SOMA YUKIHIRA.
AT LEAST BREEZE THROUGH THE FIRST GATE, OKAY?
IF YOU CAN'T EVEN MANAGE THAT, IT'LL BE SO SAD I JUST MIGHT CRY.

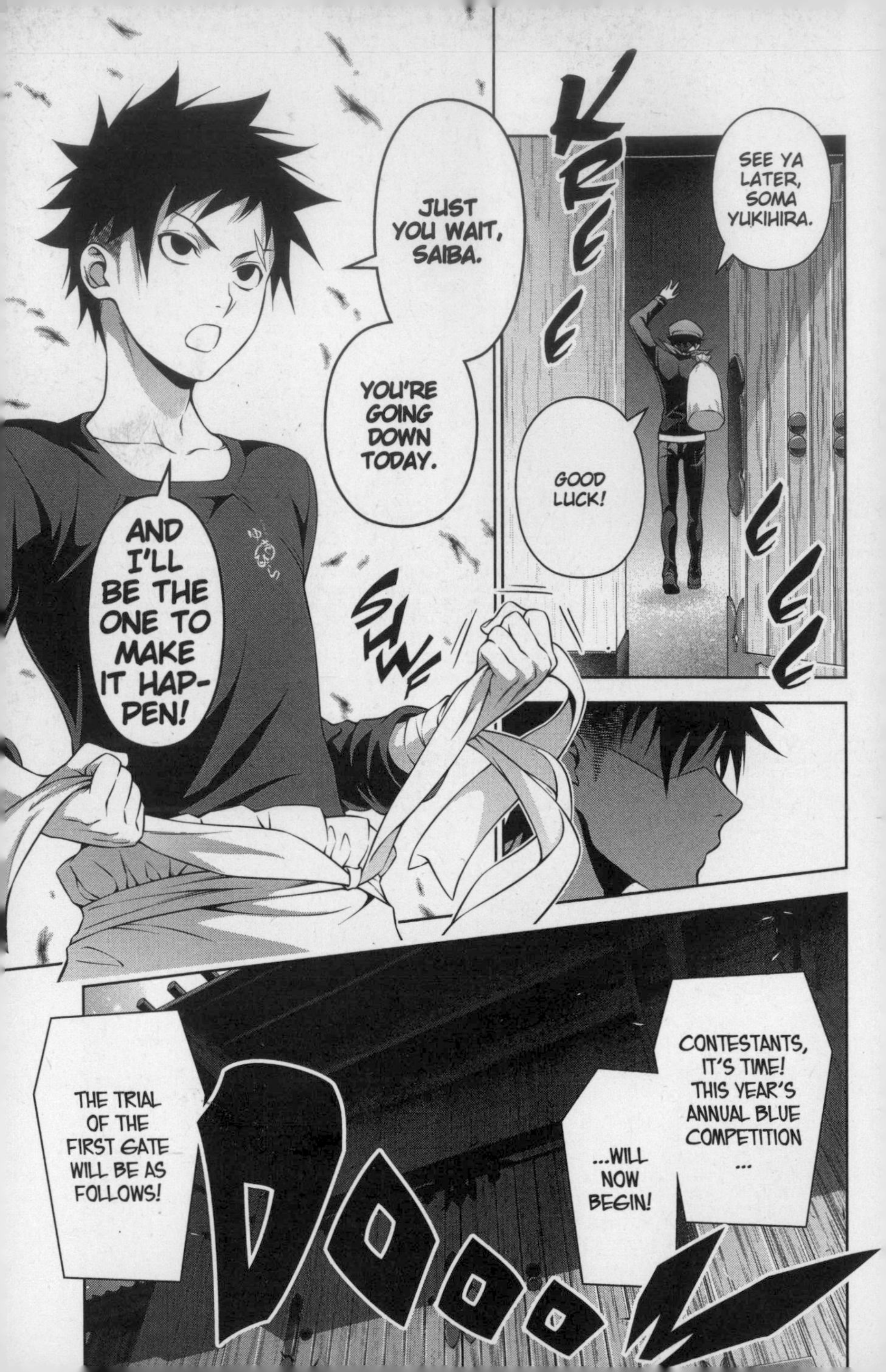
KREEE
SEE YA LATER, SOMA YUKIHIRA.
GOOD LUCK!
EEEE
JUST YOU WAIT, SAIBA.
YOU'RE GOING DOWN TODAY.
AND I'LL BE THE ONE TO MAKE IT HAP-PEN!
SHWF
CONTESTANTS, IT'S TIME! THIS YEAR'S ANNUAL BLUE COMPETITION ...
...WILL NOW BEGIN!
DOOO
THE TRIAL OF THE FIRST GATE WILL BE AS FOLLOWS!

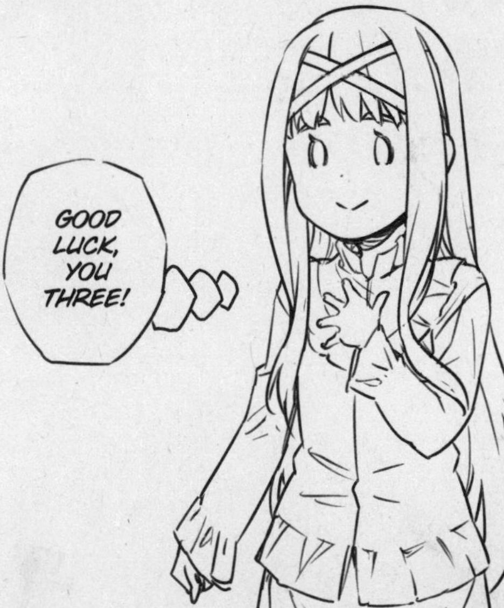
GOOD LUCK, YOU THREE!

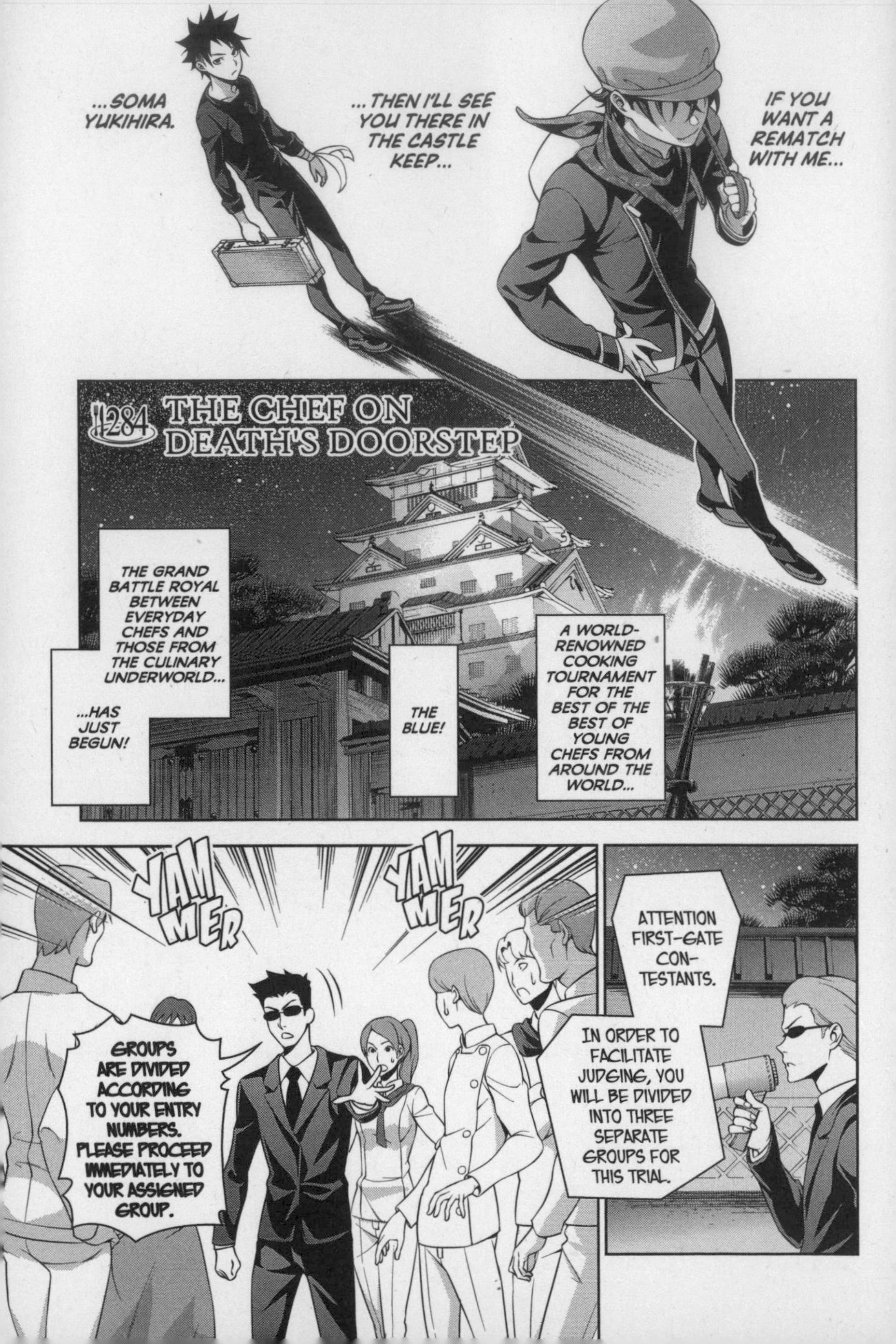
IF YOU WANT A REMATCH WITH ME...
...THEN I'LL SEE YOU THERE IN THE CASTLE KEEP...
...SOMA YUKIHIRA.
284 THE CHEF ON DEATH'S DOORSTEP
A WORLD-RENOWNED COOKING TOURNAMENT FOR THE BEST OF THE BEST OF YOUNG CHEFS FROM AROUND THE WORLD...
THE BLUE!
THE GRAND BATTLE ROYAL BETWEEN EVERYDAY CHEFS AND THOSE FROM THE CULINARY UNDERWORLD...
...HAS JUST BEGUN!
ATTENTION FIRST-GATE CON-TESTANTS.
IN ORDER TO FACILITATE JUDGING, YOU WILL BE DIVIDED INTO THREE SEPARATE GROUPS FOR THIS TRIAL.
YAMMER
YAMMER
GROUPS ARE DIVIDED ACCORDING TO YOUR ENTRY NUMBERS. PLEASE PROCEED IMMEDIATELY TO YOUR ASSIGNED GROUP.

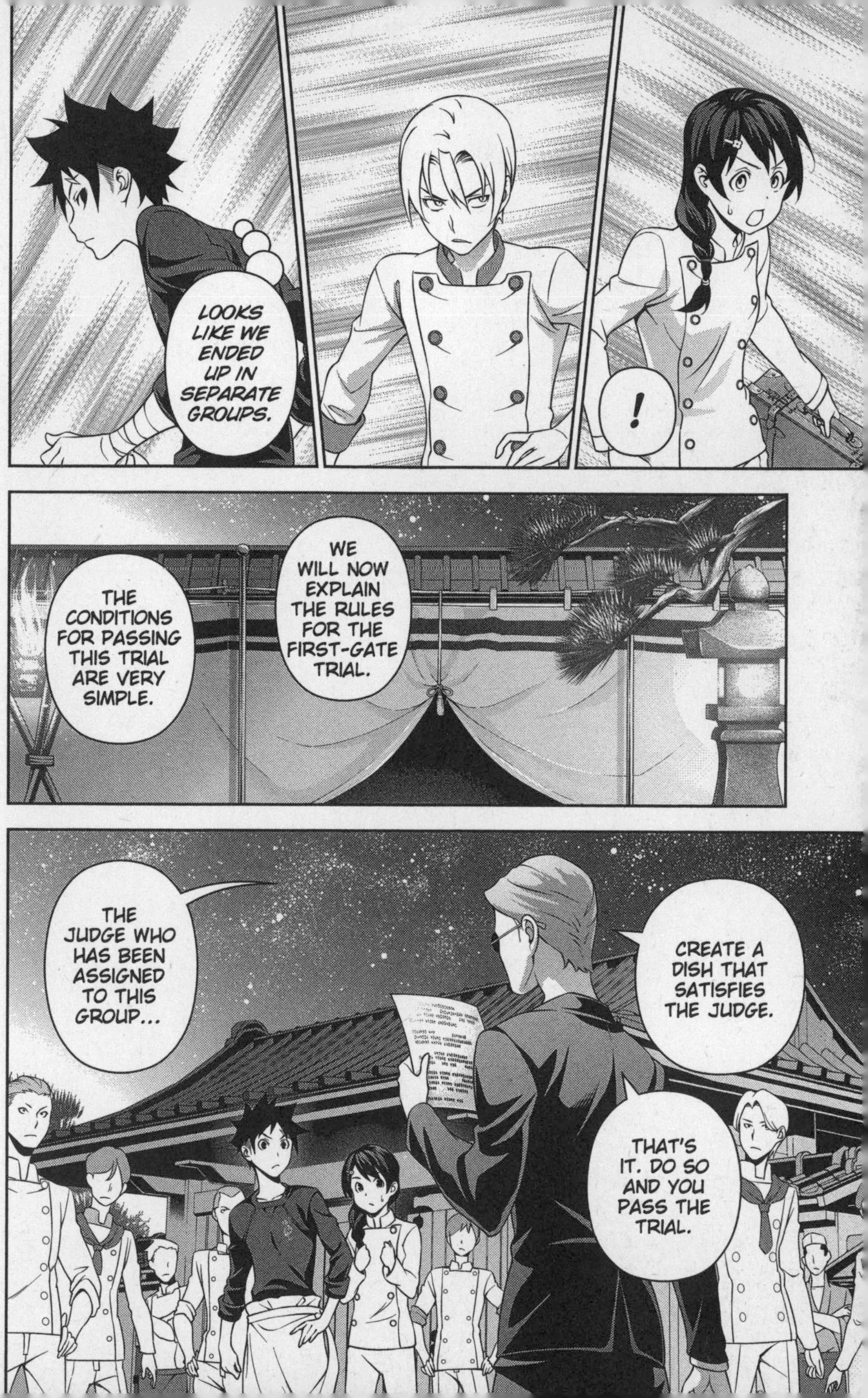
!
LOOKS LIKE WE ENDED UP IN SEPARATE GROUPS.
WE WILL NOW EXPLAIN THE RULES FOR THE FIRST-GATE TRIAL.
THE CONDITIONS FOR PASSING THIS TRIAL ARE VERY SIMPLE.
CREATE A DISH THAT SATISFIES THE JUDGE.
THAT'S IT. DO SO AND YOU PASS THE TRIAL.
THE JUDGE WHO HAS BEEN ASSIGNED TO THIS GROUP...

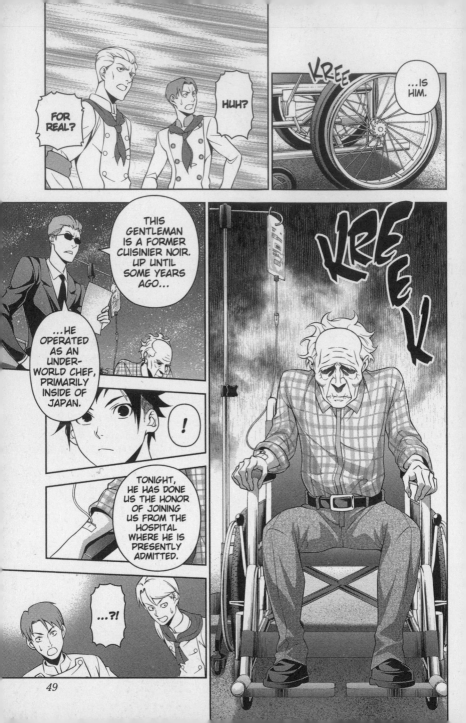

FOR REAL?

HUH?

KR-EE

...IS HIM.

THIS GENTLEMAN IS A FORMER CUISINIER NOIR. UP UNTIL SOME YEARS AGO...

...HE OPERATED AS AN UNDER-WORLD CHEF, PRIMARILY INSIDE OF JAPAN.

!

TONIGHT, HE HAS DONE US THE HONOR OF JOINING US FROM THE HOSPITAL WHERE HE IS PRESENTLY ADMITTED.

KREEK

...?!

49

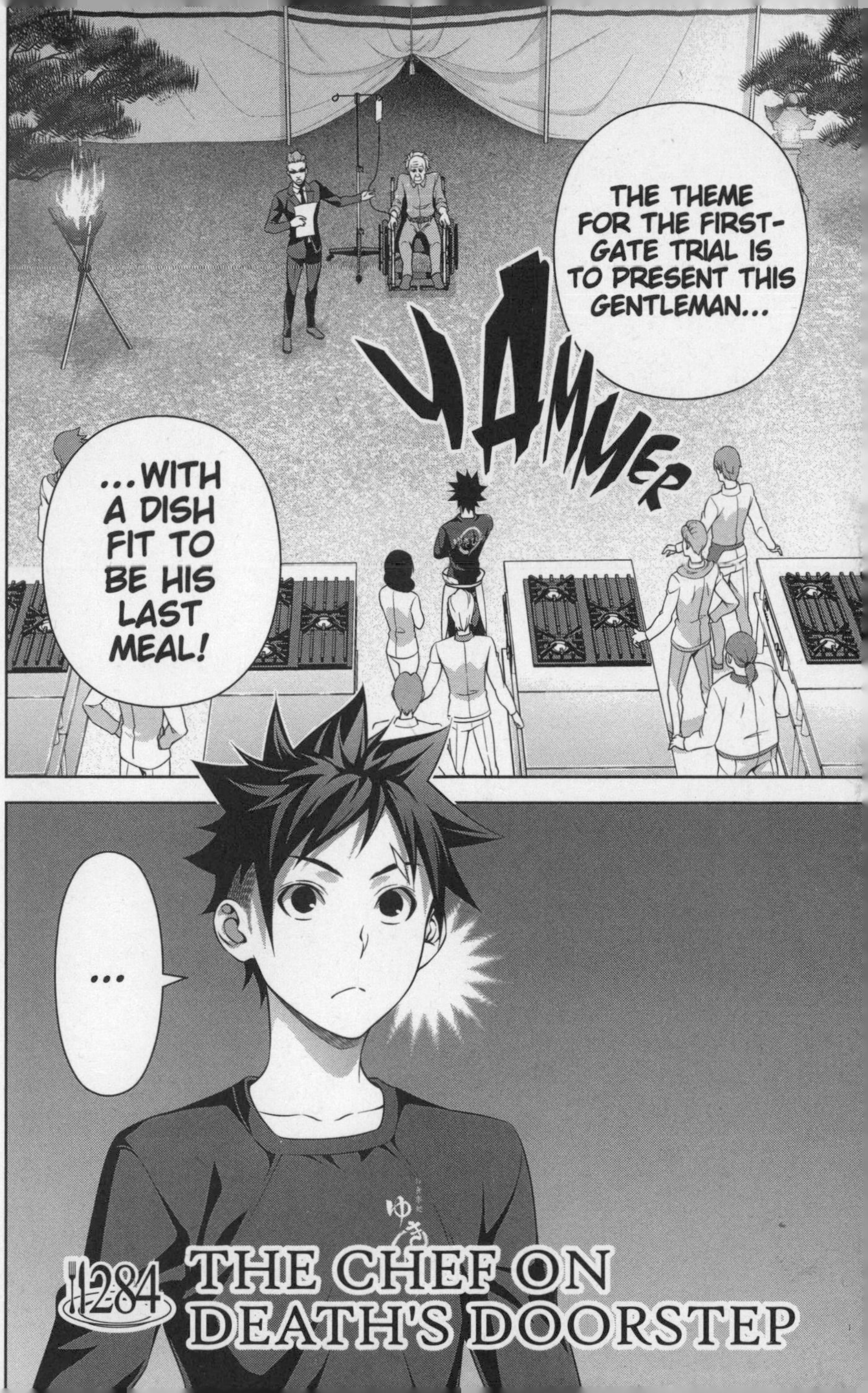
THE THEME FOR THE FIRST-GATE TRIAL IS TO PRESENT THIS GENTLEMAN...
YAMMER
...WITH A DISH FIT TO BE HIS LAST MEAL!
...
284 THE CHEF ON DEATH'S DOORSTEP

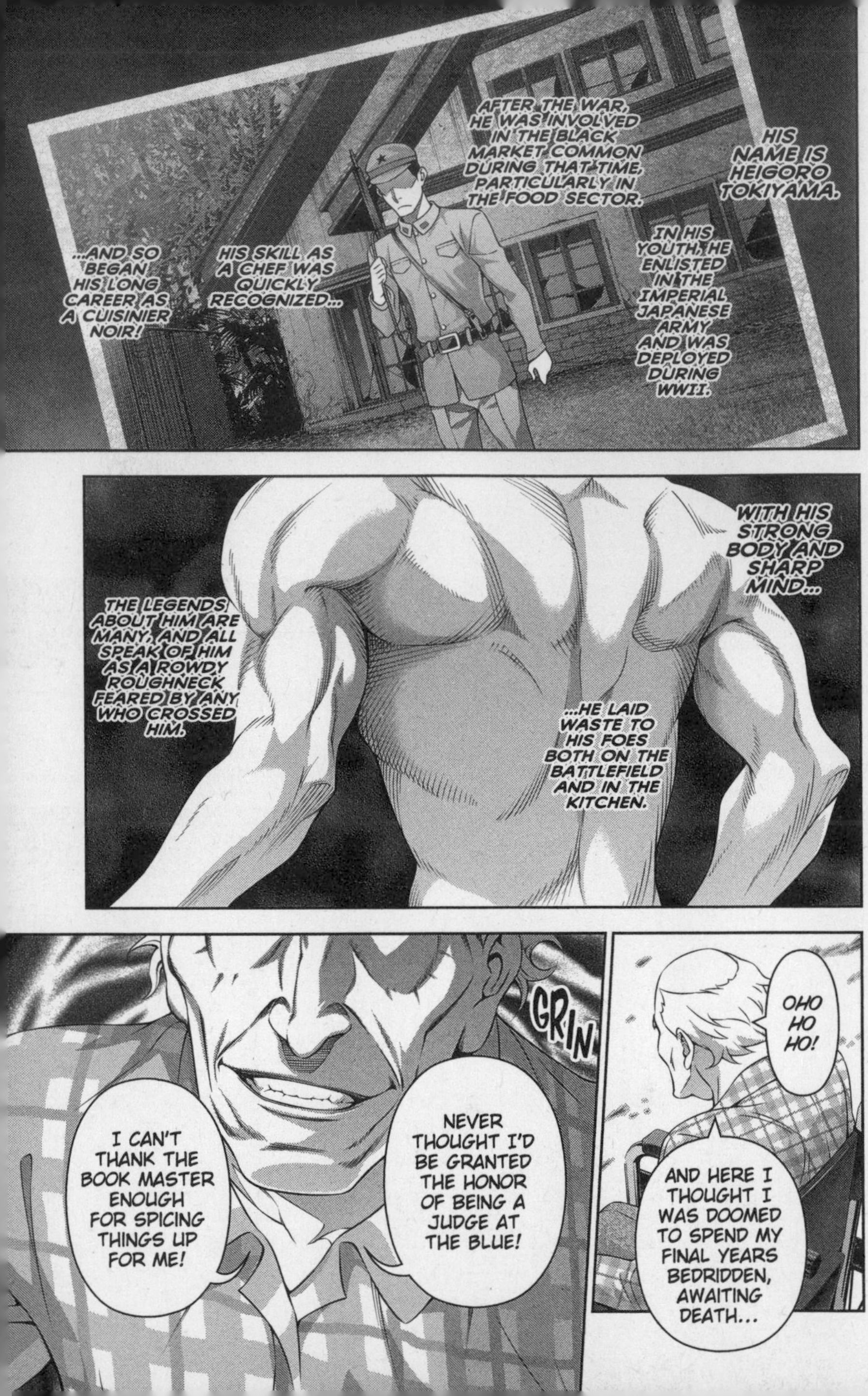
HIS NAME IS HEIGORO TOKIYAMA.
IN HIS YOUTH, HE ENLISTED IN THE IMPERIAL JAPANESE ARMY AND WAS DEPLOYED DURING WWII.
AFTER THE WAR, HE WAS INVOLVED IN THE BLACK MARKET COMMON DURING THAT TIME, PARTICULARLY IN THE FOOD SECTOR.
HIS SKILL AS A CHEF WAS QUICKLY RECOGNIZED...
...AND SO BEGAN HIS LONG CAREER AS A CUISINIER NOIR!
WITH HIS STRONG BODY AND SHARP MIND...
...HE LAID WASTE TO HIS FOES BOTH ON THE BATTLEFIELD AND IN THE KITCHEN.
THE LEGENDS ABOUT HIM ARE MANY, AND ALL SPEAK OF HIM AS A ROWDY ROUGHNECK FEARED BY ANY WHO CROSSED HIM.
OHO HO HO!
AND HERE I THOUGHT I WAS DOOMED TO SPEND MY FINAL YEARS BEDRIDDEN, AWAITING DEATH...
GRIN
NEVER THOUGHT I'D BE GRANTED THE HONOR OF BEING A JUDGE AT THE BLUE!
I CAN'T THANK THE BOOK MASTER ENOUGH FOR SPICING THINGS UP FOR ME!

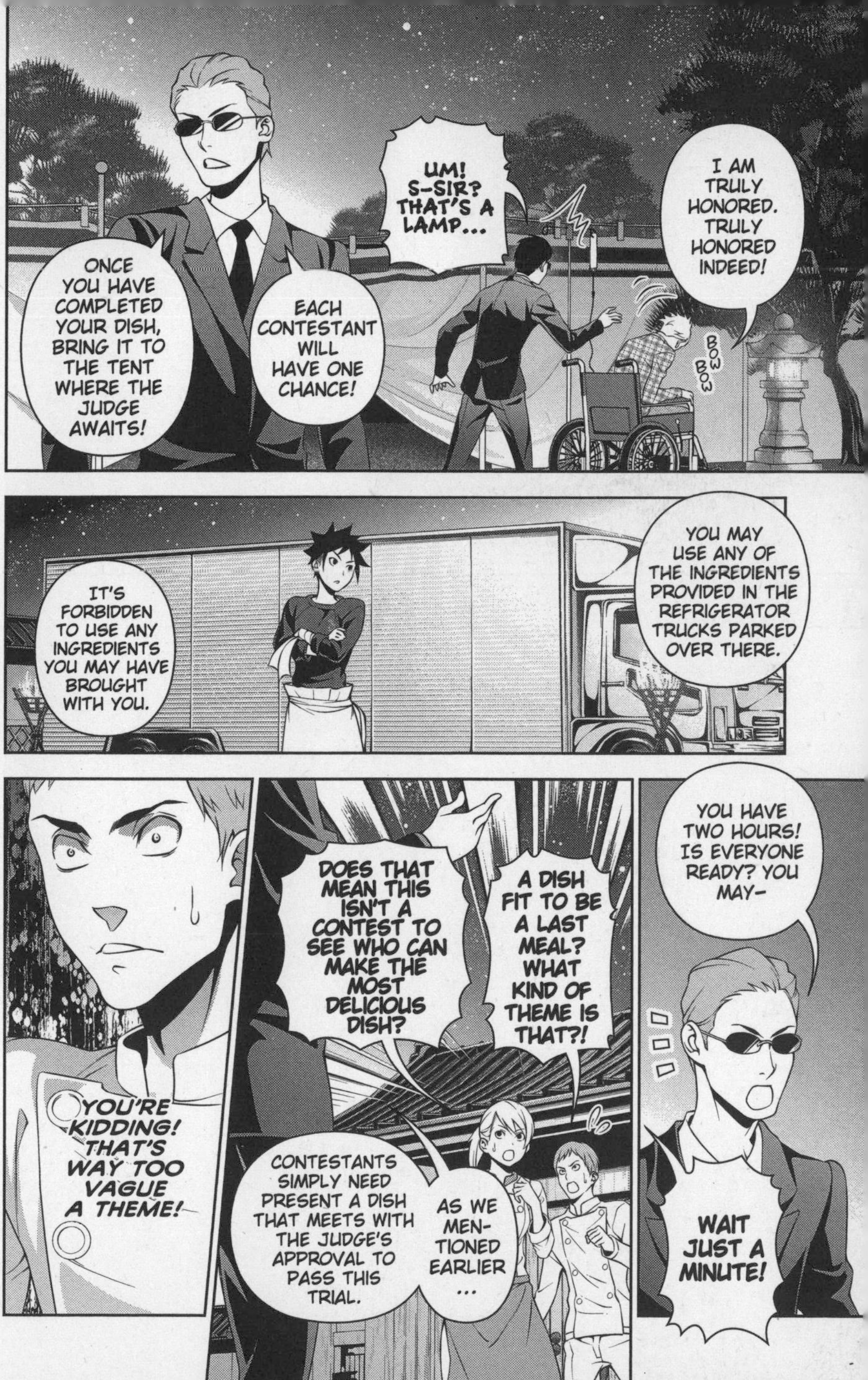
I AM TRULY HONORED. TRULY HONORED INDEED!
BOW BOW
UM! S-SIR? THAT'S A LAMP...
EACH CONTESTANT WILL HAVE ONE CHANCE!
ONCE YOU HAVE COMPLETED YOUR DISH, BRING IT TO THE TENT WHERE THE JUDGE AWAITS!
YOU MAY USE ANY OF THE INGREDIENTS PROVIDED IN THE REFRIGERATOR TRUCKS PARKED OVER THERE.
IT'S FORBIDDEN TO USE ANY INGREDIENTS YOU MAY HAVE BROUGHT WITH YOU.
YOU HAVE TWO HOURS! IS EVERYONE READY? YOU MAY-
WAIT JUST A MINUTE!
A DISH FIT TO BE A LAST MEAL? WHAT KIND OF THEME IS THAT?!
DOES THAT MEAN THIS ISN'T A CONTEST TO SEE WHO CAN MAKE THE MOST DELICIOUS DISH?
AS WE MEN- TIONED EARLIER ...
CONTESTANTS SIMPLY NEED PRESENT A DISH THAT MEETS WITH THE JUDGE'S APPROVAL TO PASS THIS TRIAL.
YOU'RE KIDDING! THAT'S WAY TOO VAGUE A THEME!

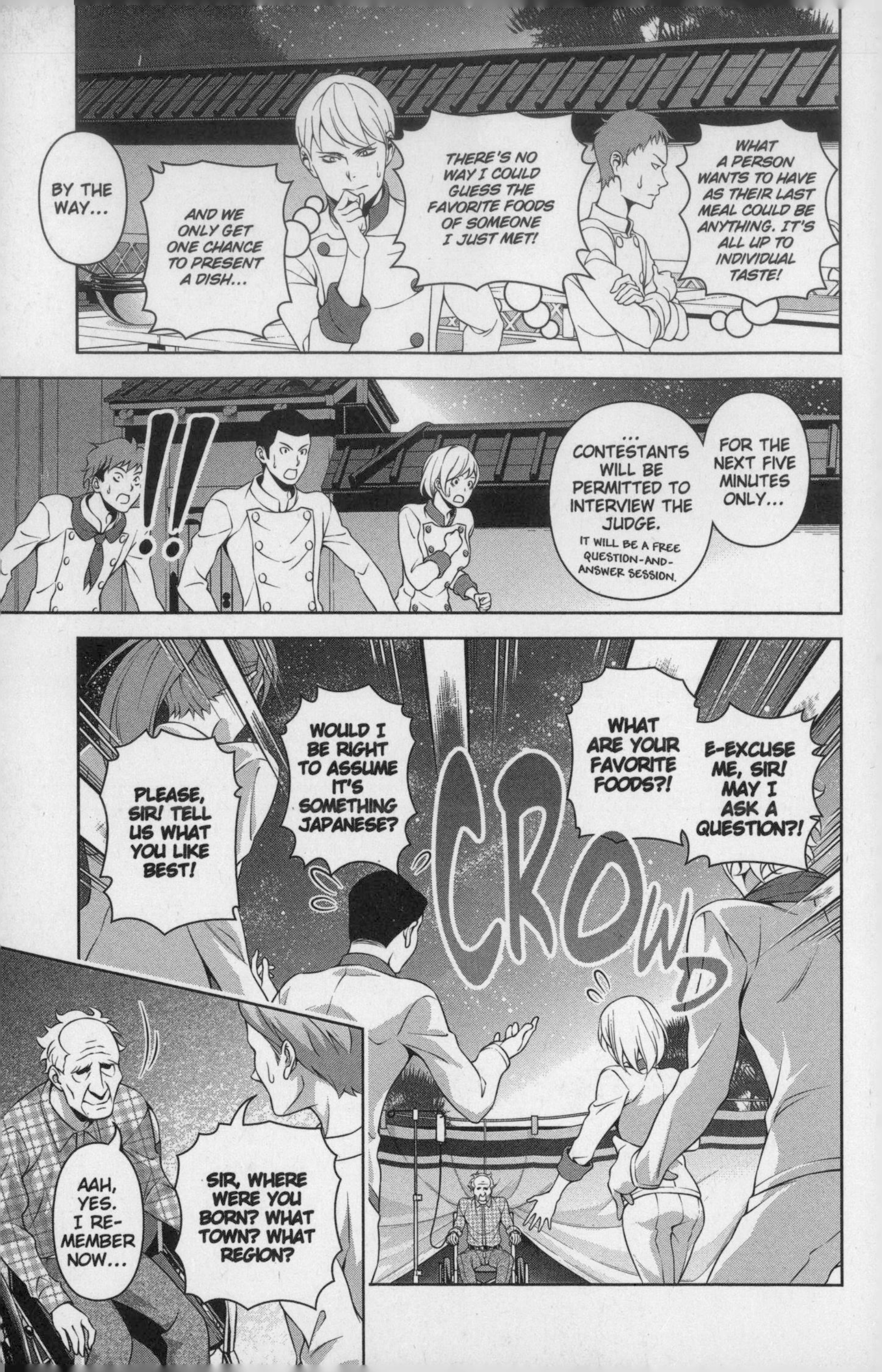
WHAT A PERSON WANTS TO HAVE AS THEIR LAST MEAL COULD BE ANYTHING. IT'S ALL UP TO INDIVIDUAL TASTE!
THERE'S NO WAY I COULD GUESS THE FAVORITE FOODS OF SOMEONE I JUST MET!
AND WE ONLY GET ONE CHANCE TO PRESENT A DISH...
BY THE WAY...
FOR THE NEXT FIVE MINUTES ONLY...
... CONTESTANTS WILL BE PERMITTED TO INTERVIEW THE JUDGE.
IT WILL BE A FREE QUESTION-AND-ANSWER SESSION.
!!
E-EXCUSE ME, SIR! MAY I ASK A QUESTION?!
WHAT ARE YOUR FAVORITE FOODS?!
CROWD
WOULD I BE RIGHT TO ASSUME IT'S SOMETHING JAPANESE?
PLEASE, SIR! TELL US WHAT YOU LIKE BEST!
SIR, WHERE WERE YOU BORN? WHAT TOWN? WHAT REGION?
AAH, YES. I RE-MEMBER NOW...

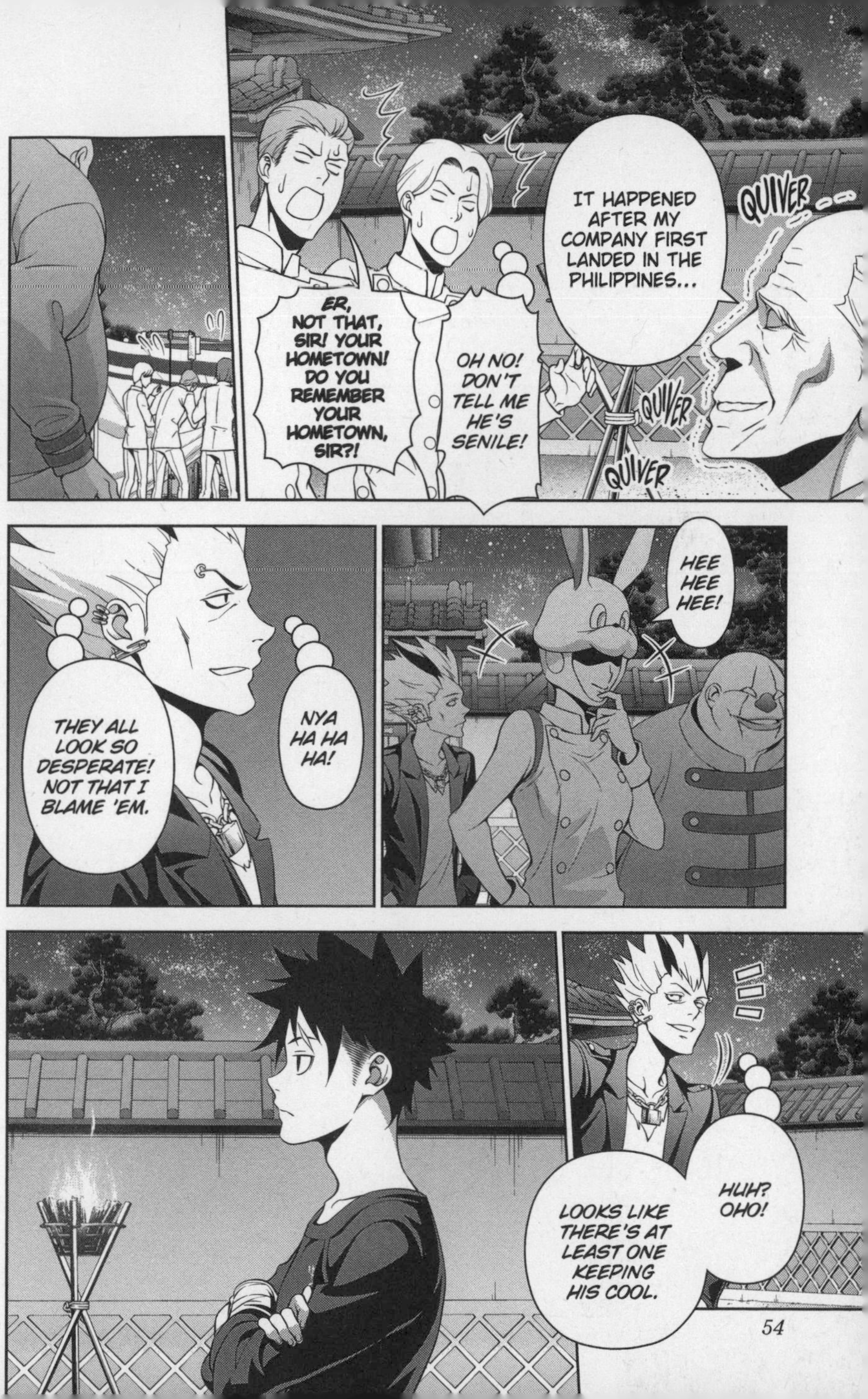
QUIVER
IT HAPPENED AFTER MY COMPANY FIRST LANDED IN THE PHILIPPINES...
QUIVER
QUIVER
OH NO! DON'T TELL ME HE'S SENILE!
ER, NOT THAT, SIR! YOUR HOMETOWN! DO YOU REMEMBER YOUR HOMETOWN, SIR?!
HEE HEE HEE!
NYA HA HA HA!
THEY ALL LOOK SO DESPERATE! NOT THAT I BLAME 'EM.
HUH? OHO!
LOOKS LIKE THERE'S AT LEAST ONE KEEPING HIS COOL.

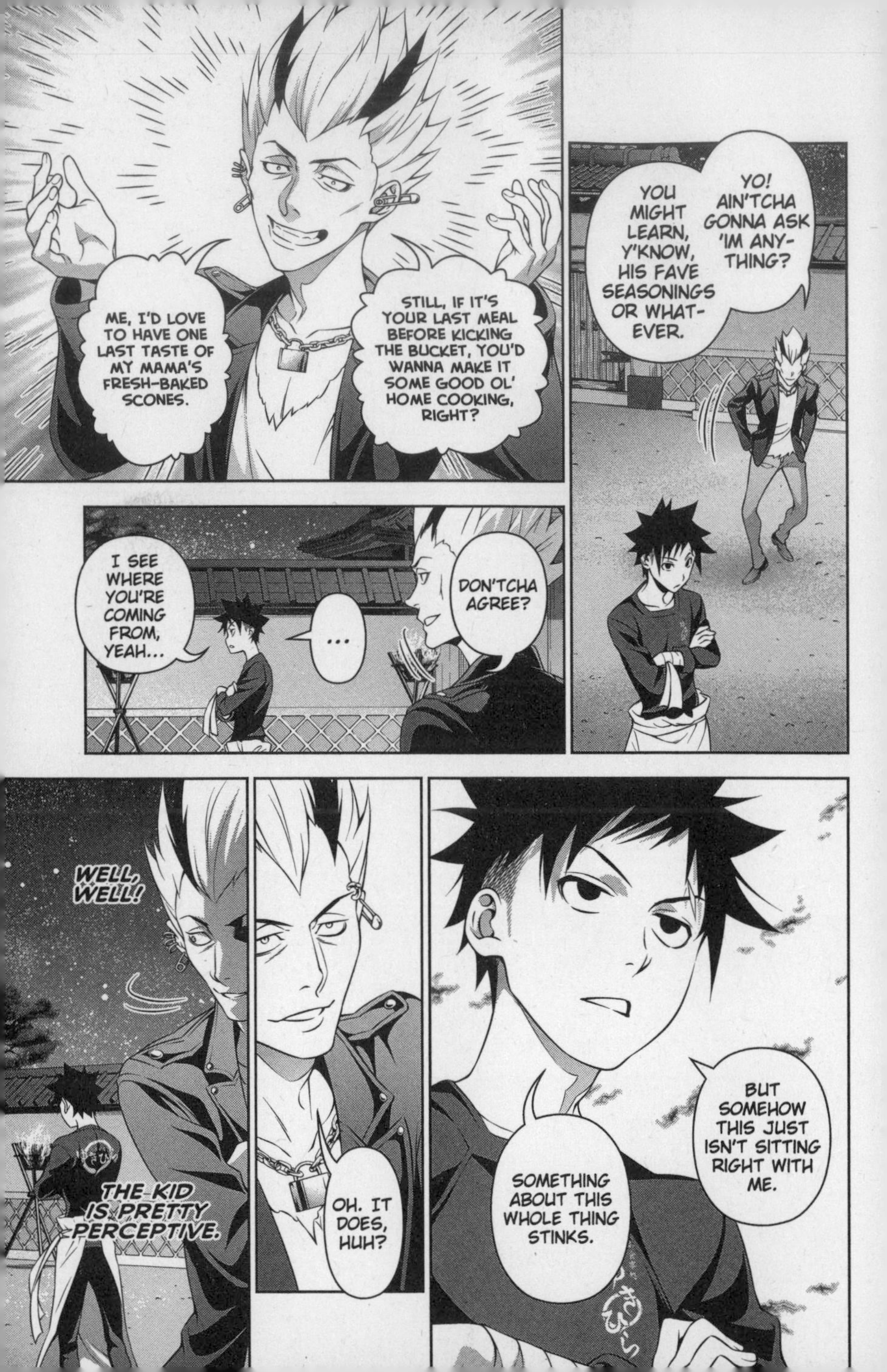
STILL, IF IT'S YOUR LAST MEAL BEFORE KICKING THE BUCKET, YOU'D WANNA MAKE IT SOME GOOD OL' HOME COOKING, RIGHT?
ME, I'D LOVE TO HAVE ONE LAST TASTE OF MY MAMA'S FRESH-BAKED SCONES.
YO! AIN'TCHA GONNA ASK 'IM ANY-THING?
YOU MIGHT LEARN, Y'KNOW, HIS FAVE SEASONINGS OR WHAT-EVER.
DON'TCHA AGREE?
...
I SEE WHERE YOU'RE COMING FROM, YEAH...
BUT SOMEHOW THIS JUST ISN'T SITTING RIGHT WITH ME.
SOMETHING ABOUT THIS WHOLE THING STINKS.
OH. IT DOES, HUH?
WELL, WELL!
THE KID IS PRETTY PERCEPTIVE.

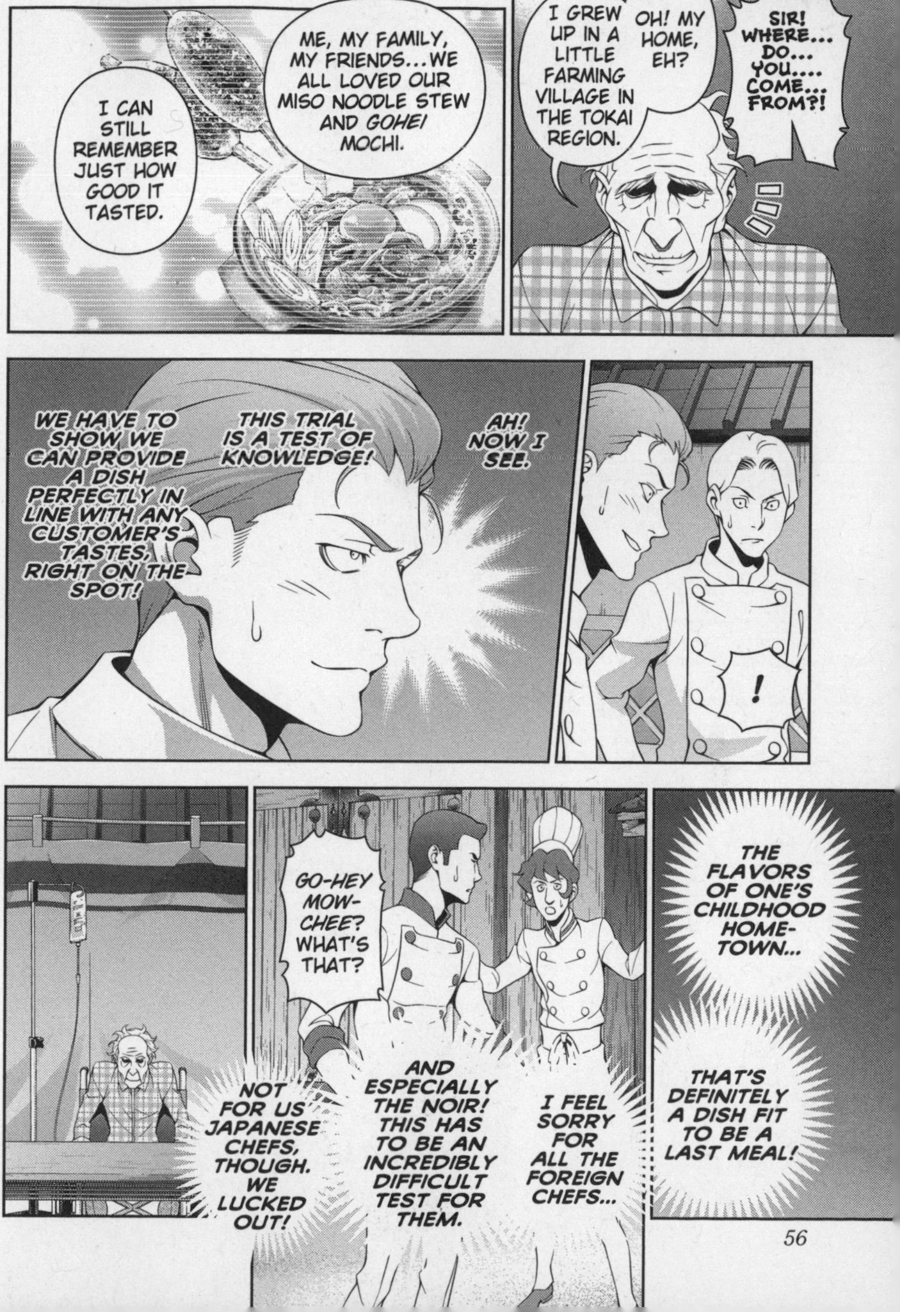
SIR! WHERE... DO... YOU.... COME... FROM?!
OH! MY HOME, EH?
I GREW UP IN A LITTLE FARMING VILLAGE IN THE TOKAI REGION.
ME, MY FAMILY, MY FRIENDS...WE ALL LOVED OUR MISO NOODLE STEW AND *GOHEI* MOCHI.
I CAN STILL REMEMBER JUST HOW GOOD IT TASTED.
!
AH! NOW I SEE.
THIS TRIAL IS A TEST OF KNOWLEDGE!
WE HAVE TO SHOW WE CAN PROVIDE A DISH PERFECTLY IN LINE WITH ANY CUSTOMER'S TASTES, RIGHT ON THE SPOT!
THE FLAVORS OF ONE'S CHILDHOOD HOME-TOWN...
THAT'S DEFINITELY A DISH FIT TO BE A LAST MEAL!
GO-HEY MOW-CHEE? WHAT'S THAT?
I FEEL SORRY FOR ALL THE FOREIGN CHEFS...
AND ESPECIALLY THE NOIR! THIS HAS TO BE AN INCREDIBLY DIFFICULT TEST FOR THEM.
NOT FOR US JAPANESE CHEFS, THOUGH. WE LUCKED OUT!

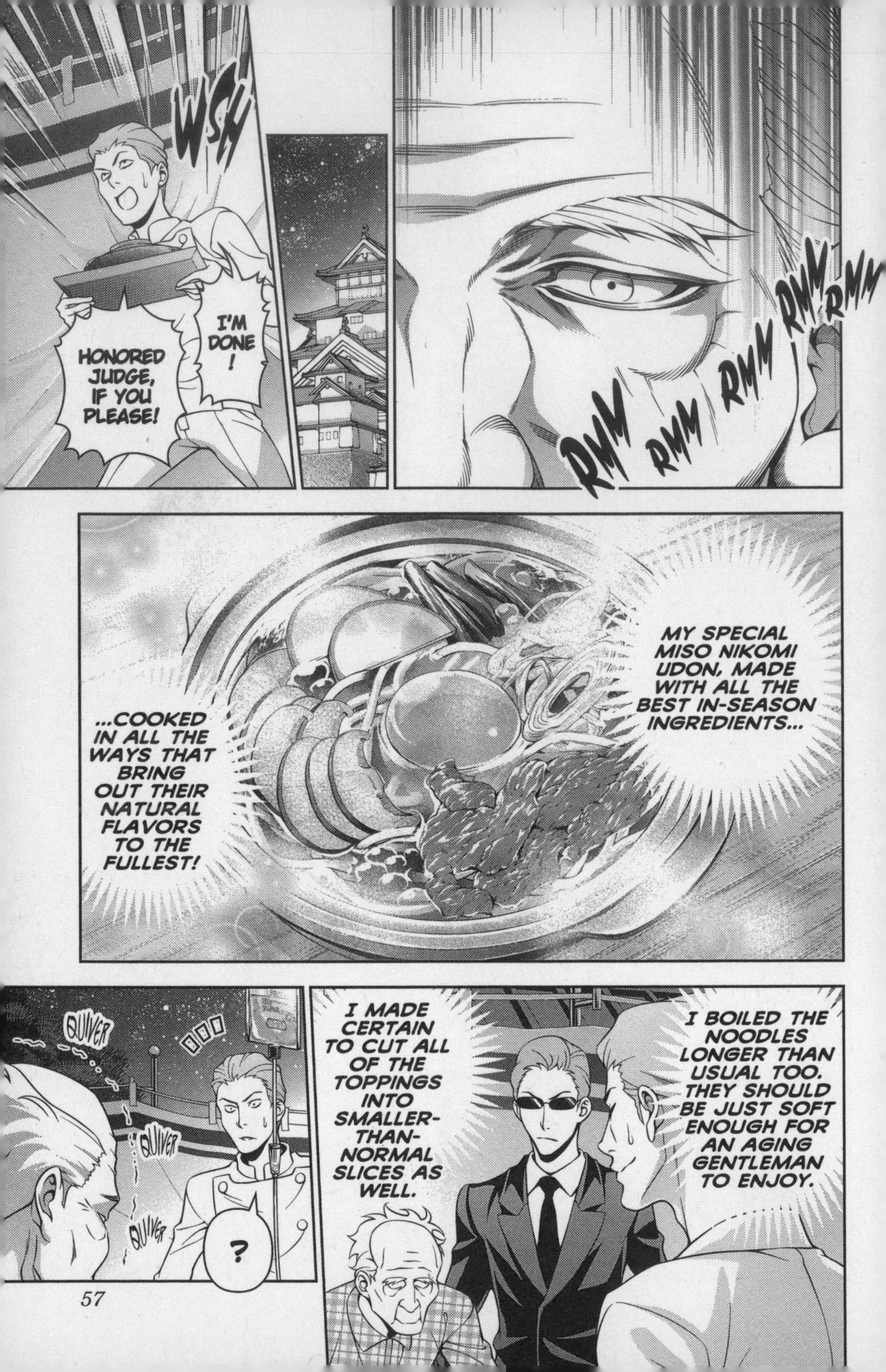
RMM RMM RMM RMM RMM RMM
WSH
I'M DONE!
HONORED JUDGE, IF YOU PLEASE!
MY SPECIAL MISO NIKOMI UDON, MADE WITH ALL THE BEST IN-SEASON INGREDIENTS...
...COOKED IN ALL THE WAYS THAT BRING OUT THEIR NATURAL FLAVORS TO THE FULLEST!
I BOILED THE NOODLES LONGER THAN USUAL TOO. THEY SHOULD BE JUST SOFT ENOUGH FOR AN AGING GENTLEMAN TO ENJOY.
I MADE CERTAIN TO CUT ALL OF THE TOPPINGS INTO SMALLER-THAN-NORMAL SLICES AS WELL.
QUIVER
QUIVER
QUIVER
?

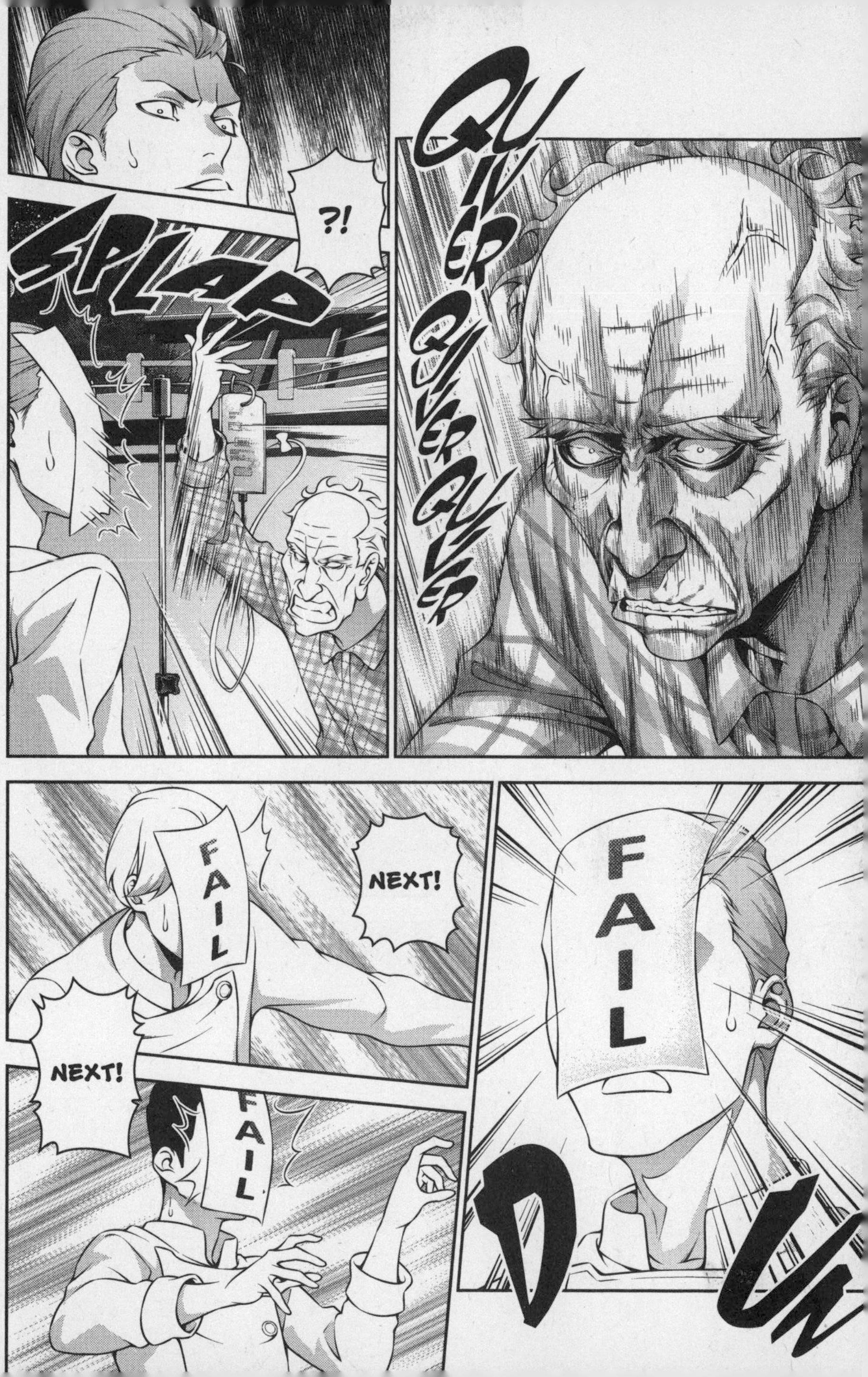
QUIVER QUIVER QUIVER
?!
SPLAP
FAIL
DUN
NEXT!
FAIL
NEXT!
FAIL

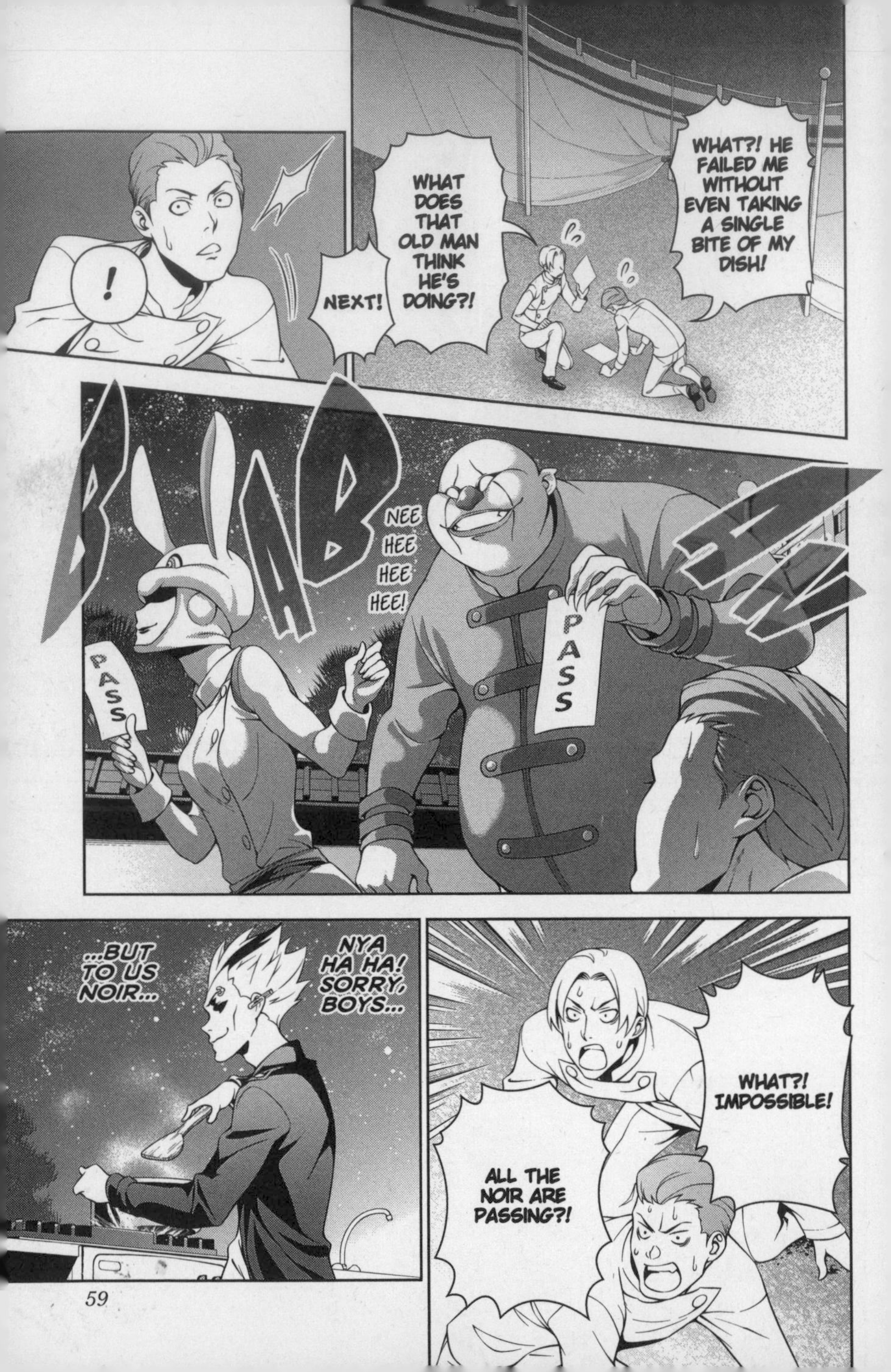
WHAT?! HE FAILED ME WITHOUT EVEN TAKING A SINGLE BITE OF MY DISH!
WHAT DOES THAT OLD MAN THINK HE'S DOING?!
NEXT!
!
NEE HEE HEE HEE!
PASS
PASS
WHAT?! IMPOSSIBLE!
ALL THE NOIR ARE PASSING?!
NYA HA HA! SORRY, BOYS...
...BUT TO US NOIR...

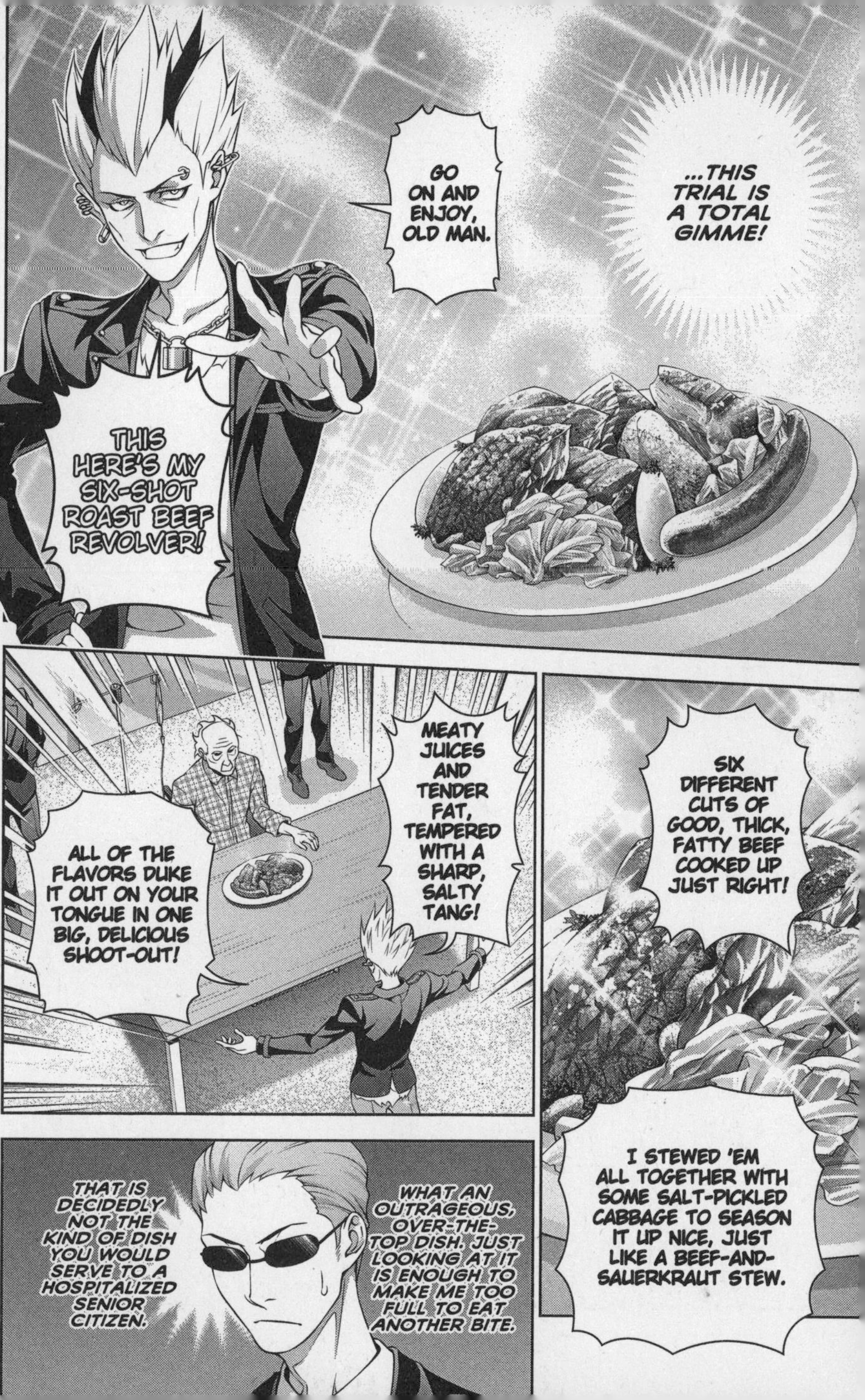
...THIS TRIAL IS A TOTAL GIMME!
GO ON AND ENJOY, OLD MAN.
THIS HERE'S MY SIX-SHOT ROAST BEEF REVOLVER!
SIX DIFFERENT CUTS OF GOOD, THICK, FATTY BEEF COOKED UP JUST RIGHT!
I STEWED 'EM ALL TOGETHER WITH SOME SALT-PICKLED CABBAGE TO SEASON IT UP NICE, JUST LIKE A BEEF-AND-SAUERKRAUT STEW.
MEATY JUICES AND TENDER FAT, TEMPERED WITH A SHARP, SALTY TANG!
ALL OF THE FLAVORS DUKE IT OUT ON YOUR TONGUE IN ONE BIG, DELICIOUS SHOOT-OUT!
WHAT AN OUTRAGEOUS, OVER-THE-TOP DISH. JUST LOOKING AT IT IS ENOUGH TO MAKE ME TOO FULL TO EAT ANOTHER BITE.
THAT IS DECIDEDLY NOT THE KIND OF DISH YOU WOULD SERVE TO A HOSPITALIZED SENIOR CITIZEN.

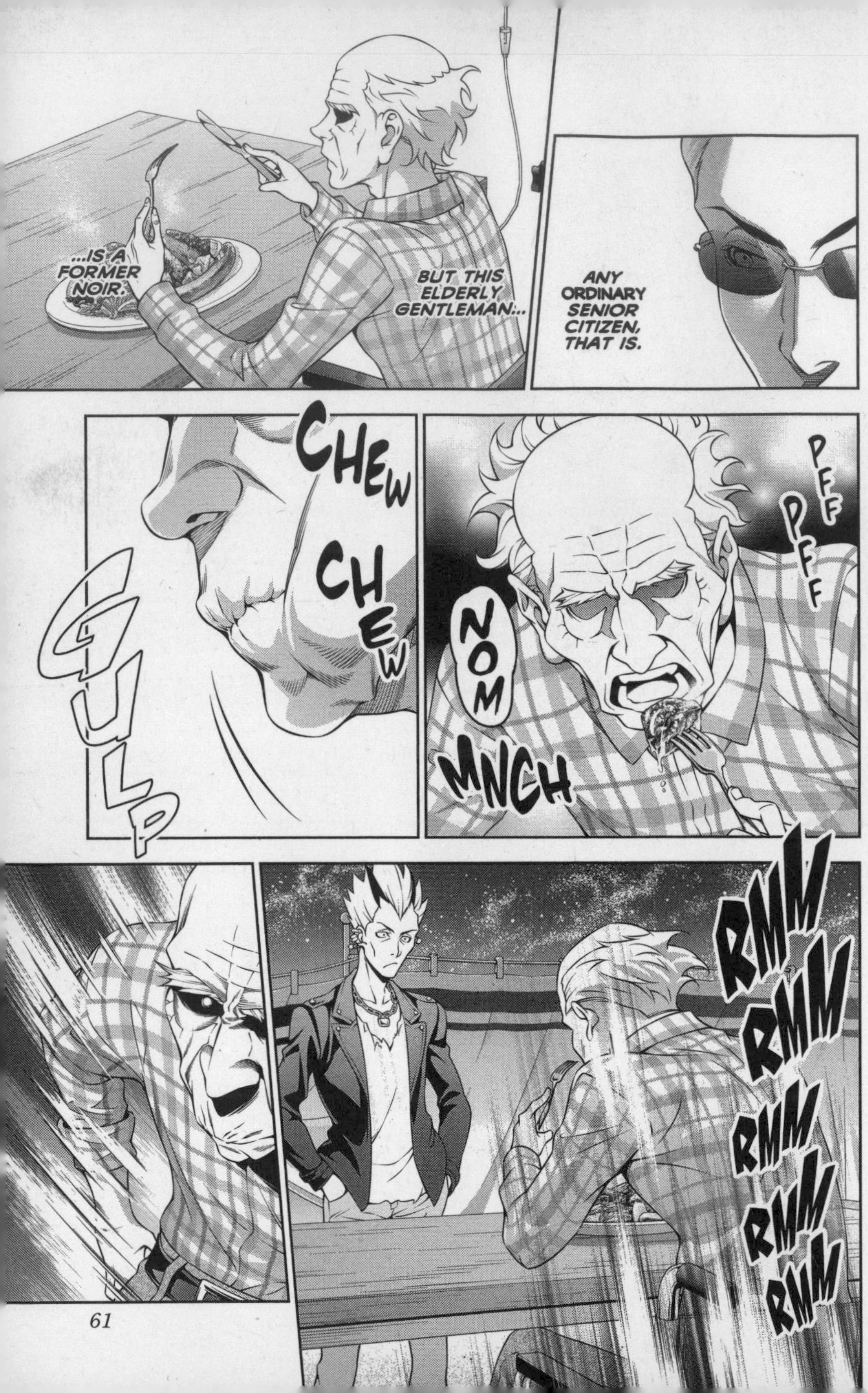
ANY ORDINARY SENIOR CITIZEN, THAT IS.
BUT THIS ELDERLY GENTLEMAN:...
...IS A FORMER NOIR.
PFF PFF
NOM
MNCH
CHEW CHEW CHEW
GULP
RMM RMM RMM RMM RMM RMM RMM

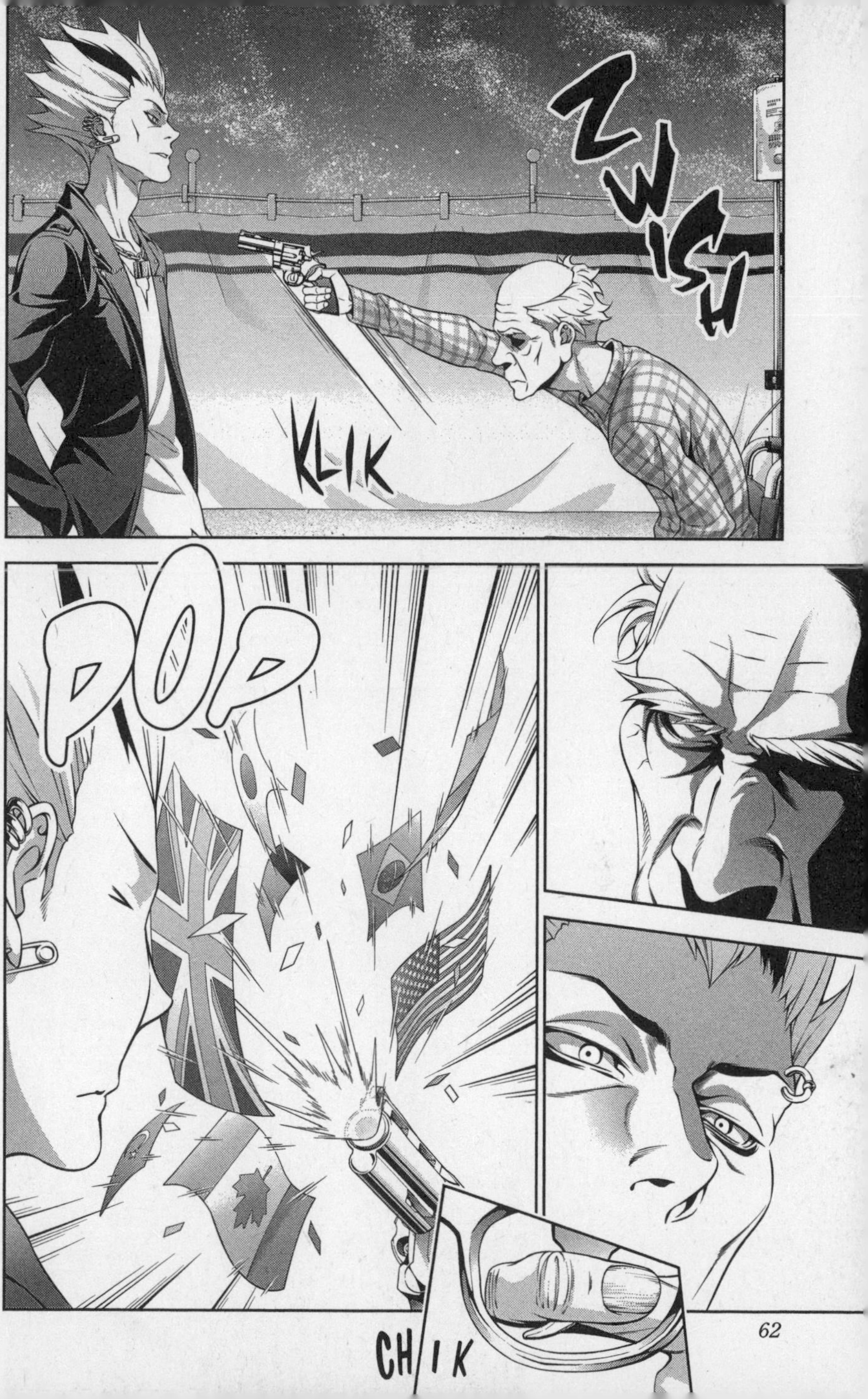
ZWISH
KLIK
POP
CHIK

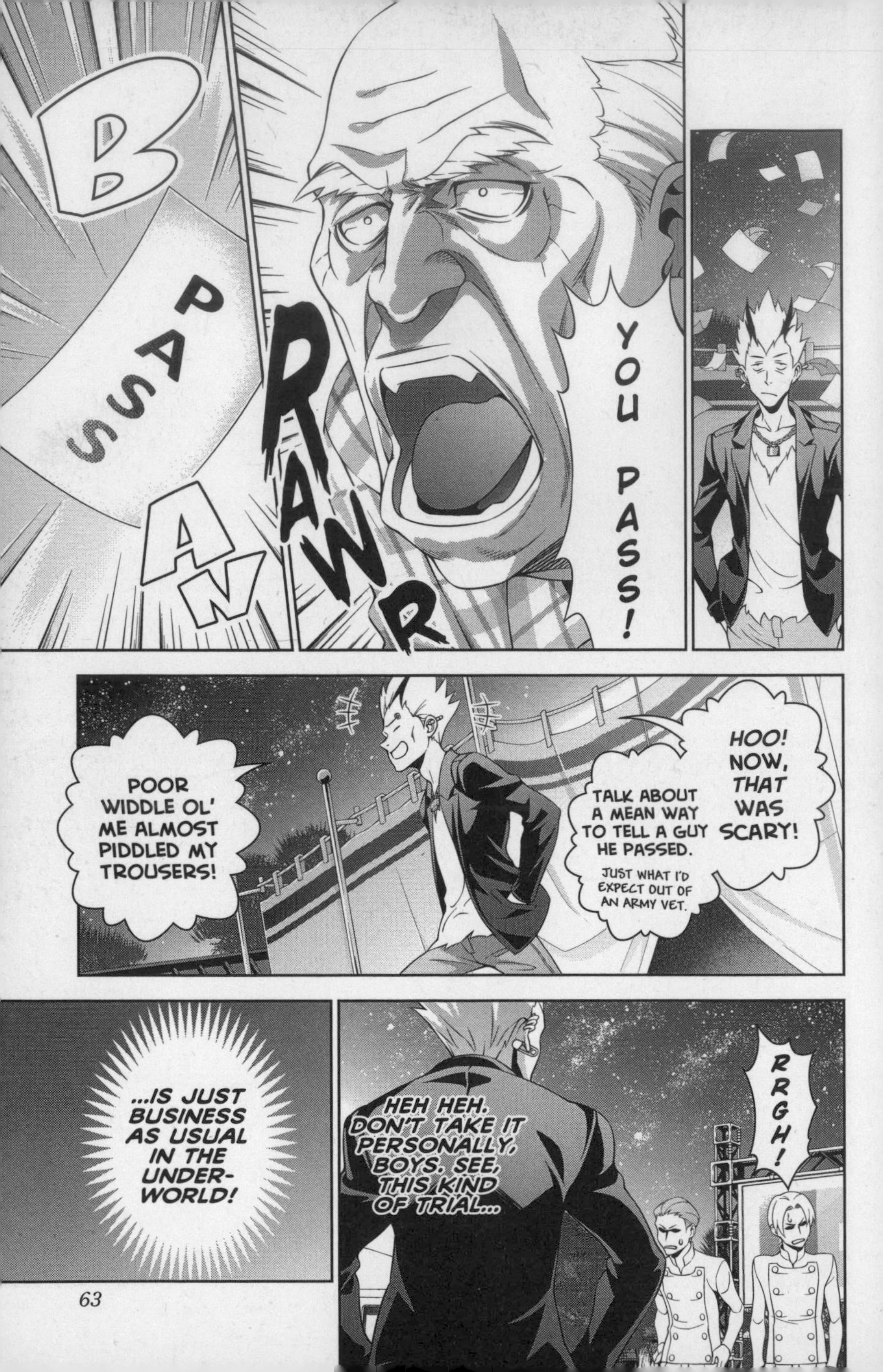
YOU PASS!
RAWR
B
PASS
AN
HOO! NOW, THAT WAS SCARY!
TALK ABOUT A MEAN WAY TO TELL A GUY HE PASSED.
JUST WHAT I'D EXPECT OUT OF AN ARMY VET.
POOR WIDDLE OL' ME ALMOST PIDDLED MY TROUSERS!
RRGH!
HEH HEH. DON'T TAKE IT PERSONALLY, BOYS. SEE, THIS KIND OF TRIAL...
...IS JUST BUSINESS AS USUAL IN THE UNDERWORLD!

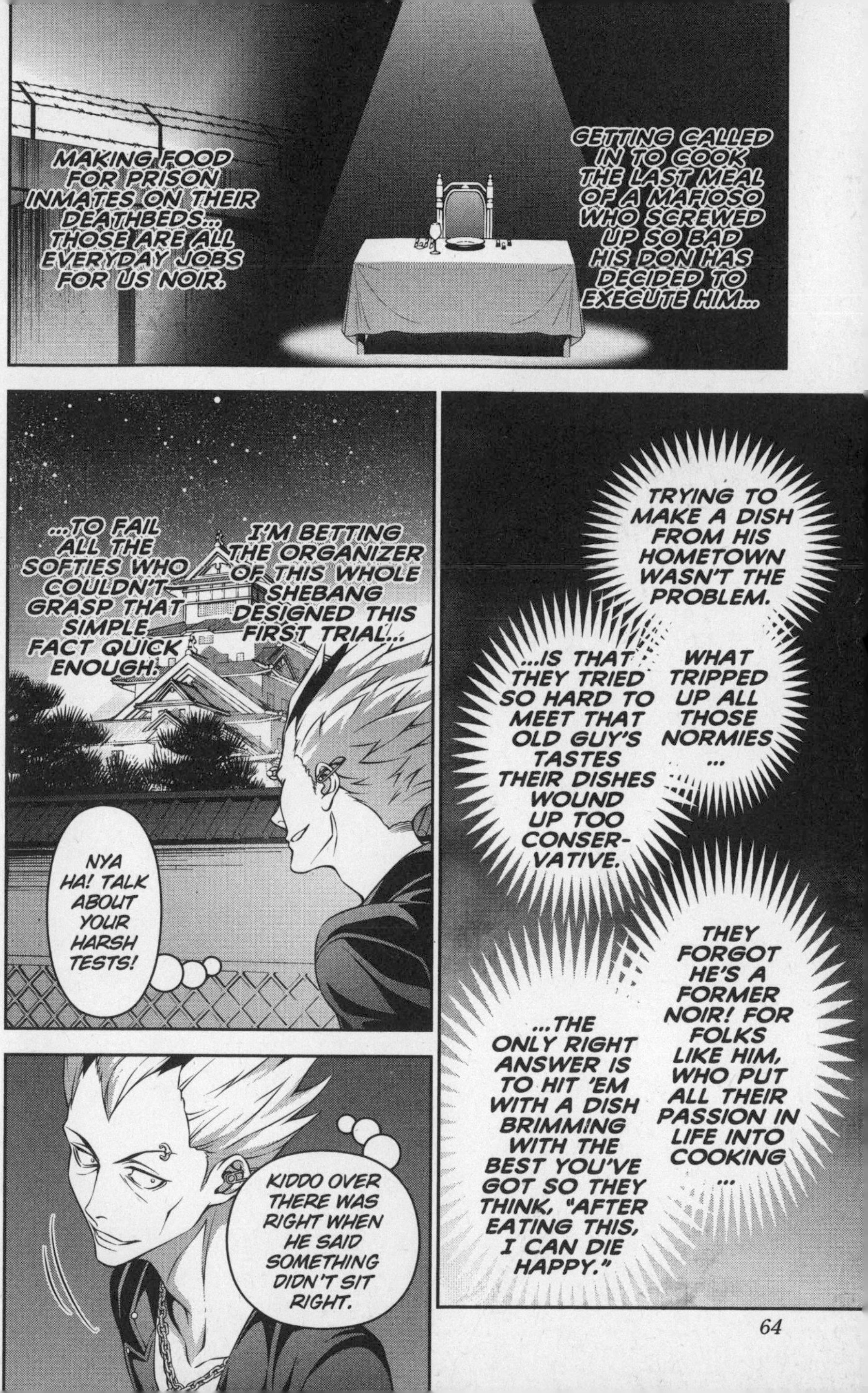
GETTING CALLED IN TO COOK THE LAST MEAL OF A MAFIOSO WHO SCREWED UP SO BAD HIS DON HAS DECIDED TO EXECUTE HIM...
MAKING FOOD FOR PRISON INMATES ON THEIR DEATHBEDS... THOSE ARE ALL EVERYDAY JOBS FOR US NOIR.
TRYING TO MAKE A DISH FROM HIS HOMETOWN WASN'T THE PROBLEM.
WHAT TRIPPED UP ALL THOSE NORMIES...
...IS THAT THEY TRIED SO HARD TO MEET THAT OLD GUY'S TASTES THEIR DISHES WOUND UP TOO CONSER-VATIVE.
THEY FORGOT HE'S A FORMER NOIR! FOR FOLKS LIKE HIM, WHO PUT ALL THEIR PASSION IN LIFE INTO COOKING...
...THE ONLY RIGHT ANSWER IS TO HIT 'EM WITH A DISH BRIMMING WITH THE BEST YOU'VE GOT SO THEY THINK, "AFTER EATING THIS, I CAN DIE HAPPY."
I'M BETTING THE ORGANIZER OF THIS WHOLE SHEBANG DESIGNED THIS FIRST TRIAL...
...TO FAIL ALL THE SOFTIES WHO COULDN'T GRASP THAT SIMPLE FACT QUICK ENOUGH.
NYA HA! TALK ABOUT YOUR HARSH TESTS!
KIDDO OVER THERE WAS RIGHT WHEN HE SAID SOMETHING DIDN'T SIT RIGHT.

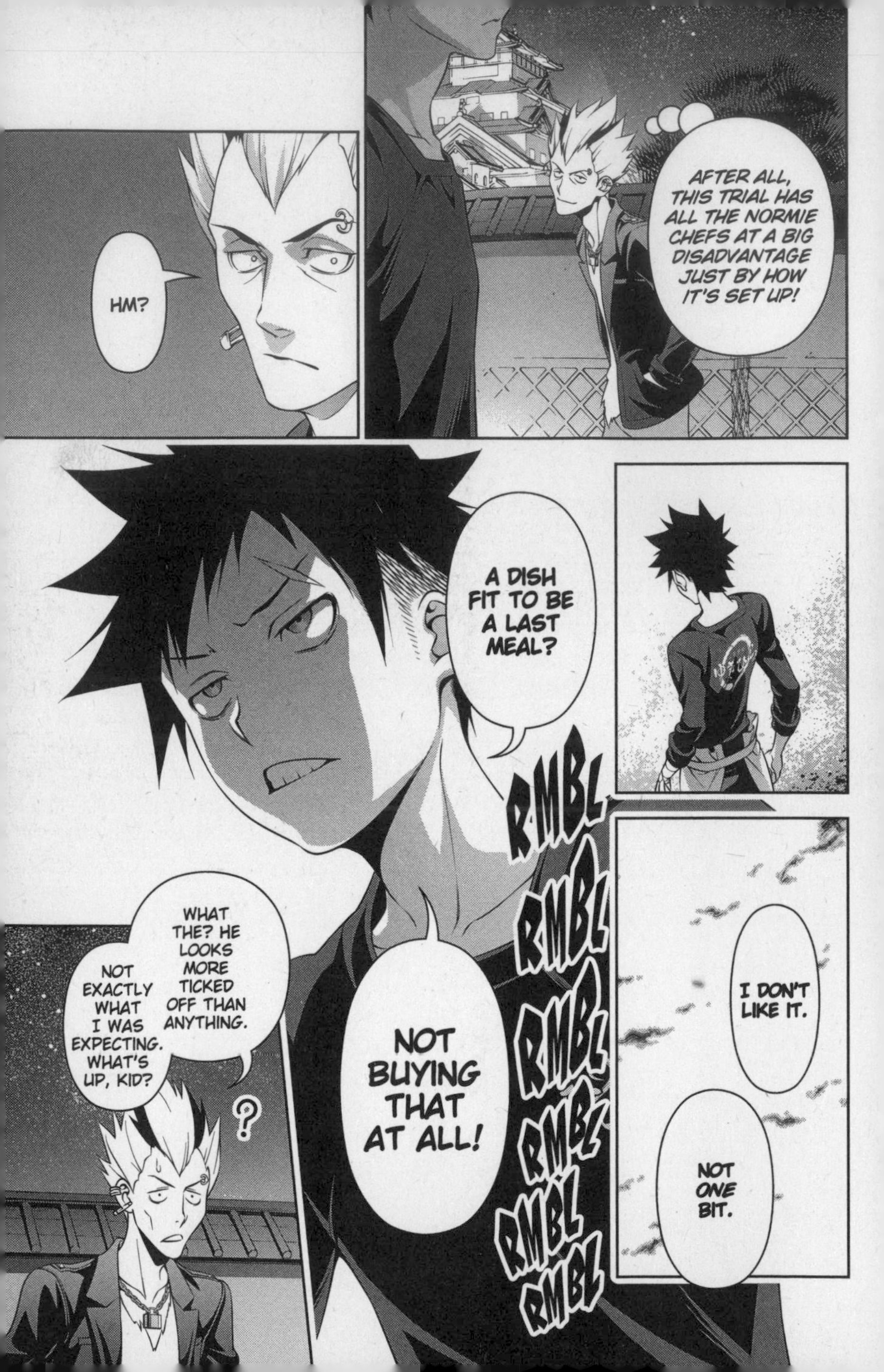
AFTER ALL, THIS TRIAL HAS ALL THE NORMIE CHEFS AT A BIG DISADVANTAGE JUST BY HOW IT'S SET UP!
HM?
A DISH FIT TO BE A LAST MEAL?
I DON'T LIKE IT.
NOT ONE BIT.
RMBL RMBL RMBL RMBL RMBL RMBL
NOT BUYING THAT AT ALL!
WHAT THE? HE LOOKS MORE TICKED OFF THAN ANYTHING.
NOT EXACTLY WHAT I WAS EXPECTING. WHAT'S UP, KID?
?

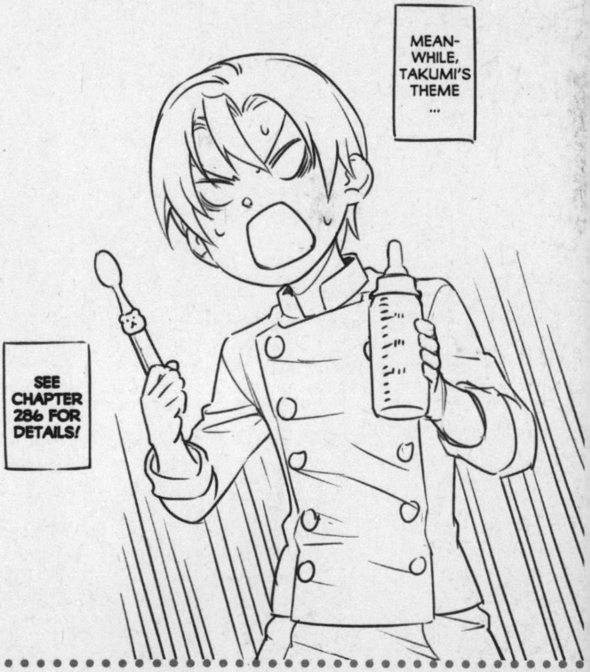
MEAN-WHILE, TAKUMI'S THEME ...
SEE CHAPTER 286 FOR DETAILS!

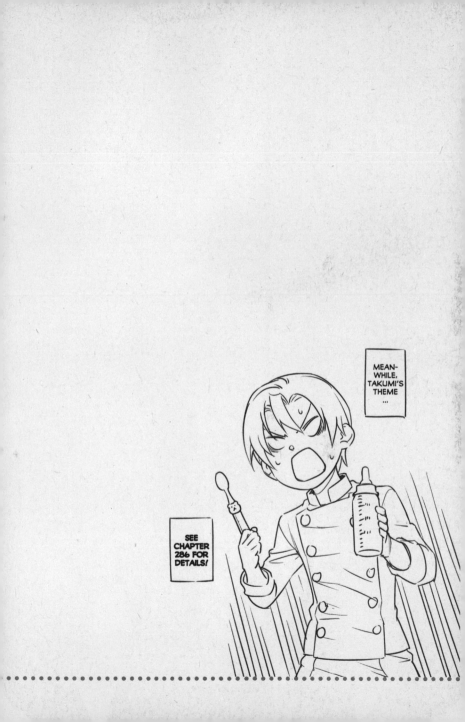

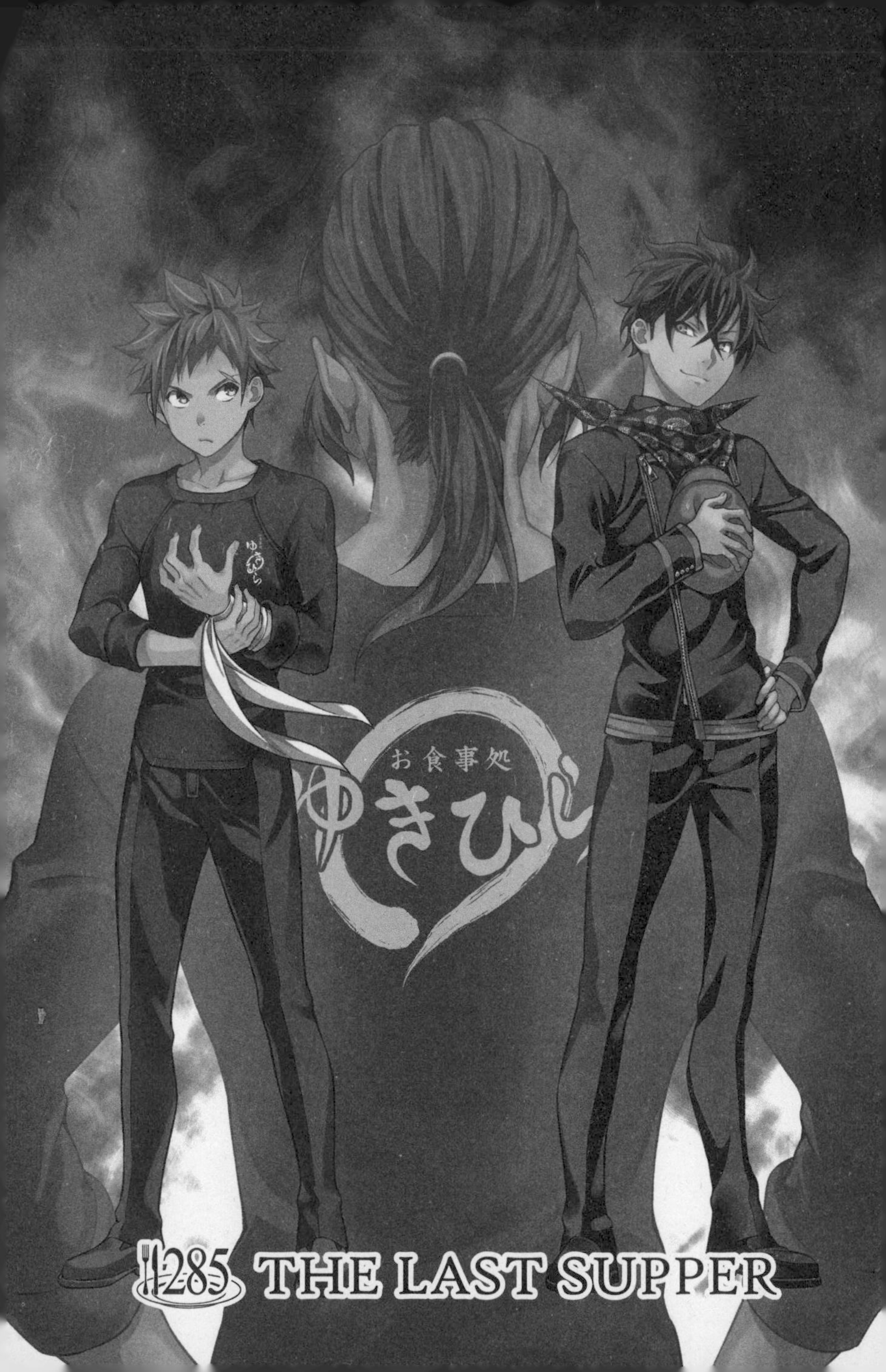
お食事処
285 THE LAST SUPPER

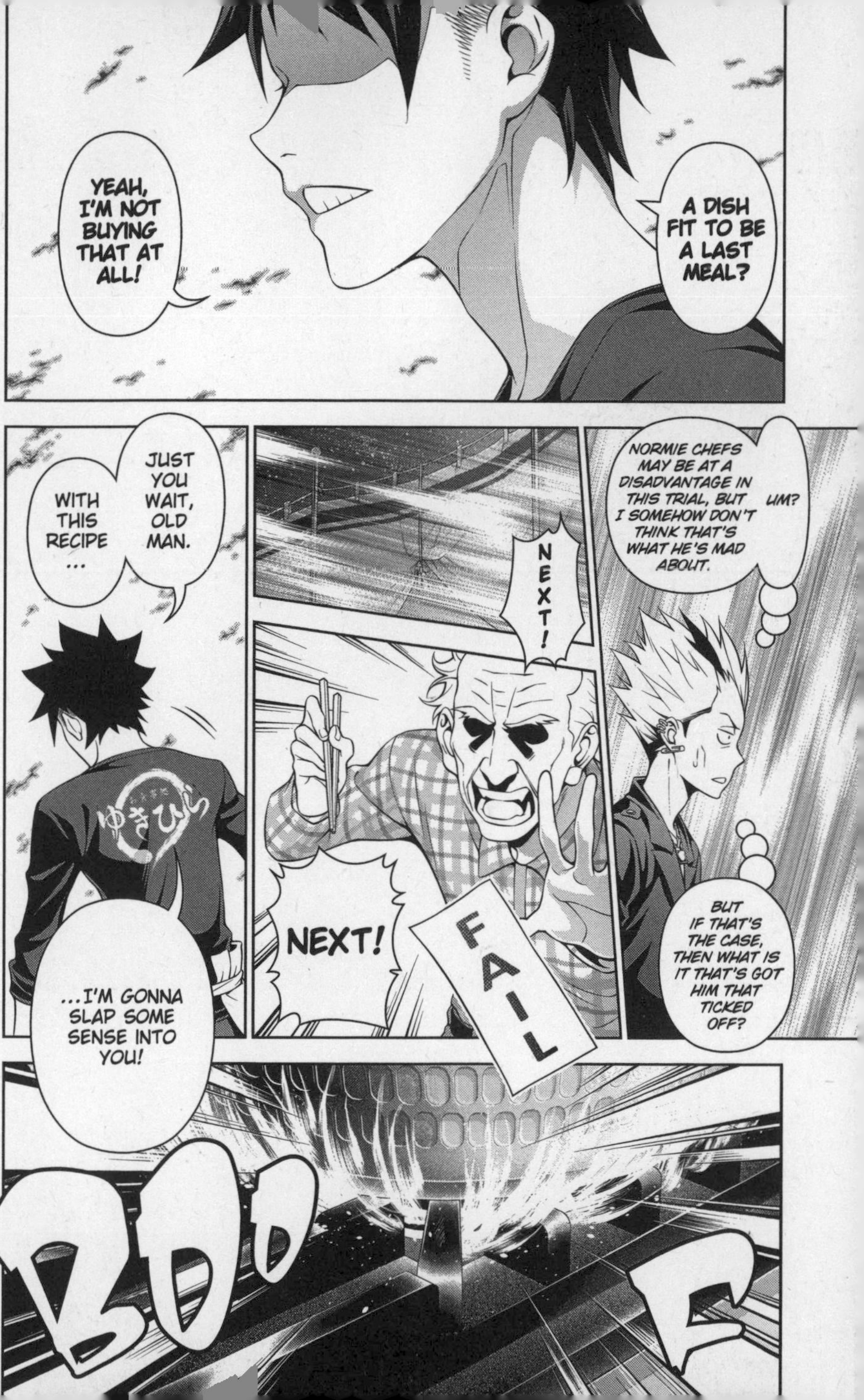
A DISH FIT TO BE A LAST MEAL?
YEAH, I'M NOT BUYING THAT AT ALL!
NORMIE CHEFS MAY BE AT A DISADVANTAGE IN THIS TRIAL, BUT I SOMEHOW DON'T THINK THAT'S WHAT HE'S MAD ABOUT.
UM?
BUT IF THAT'S THE CASE, THEN WHAT IS IT THAT'S GOT HIM THAT TICKED OFF?
NEXT!
NEXT!
FAIL
JUST YOU WAIT, OLD MAN.
WITH THIS RECIPE...
...I'M GONNA SLAP SOME SENSE INTO YOU!
BOOF

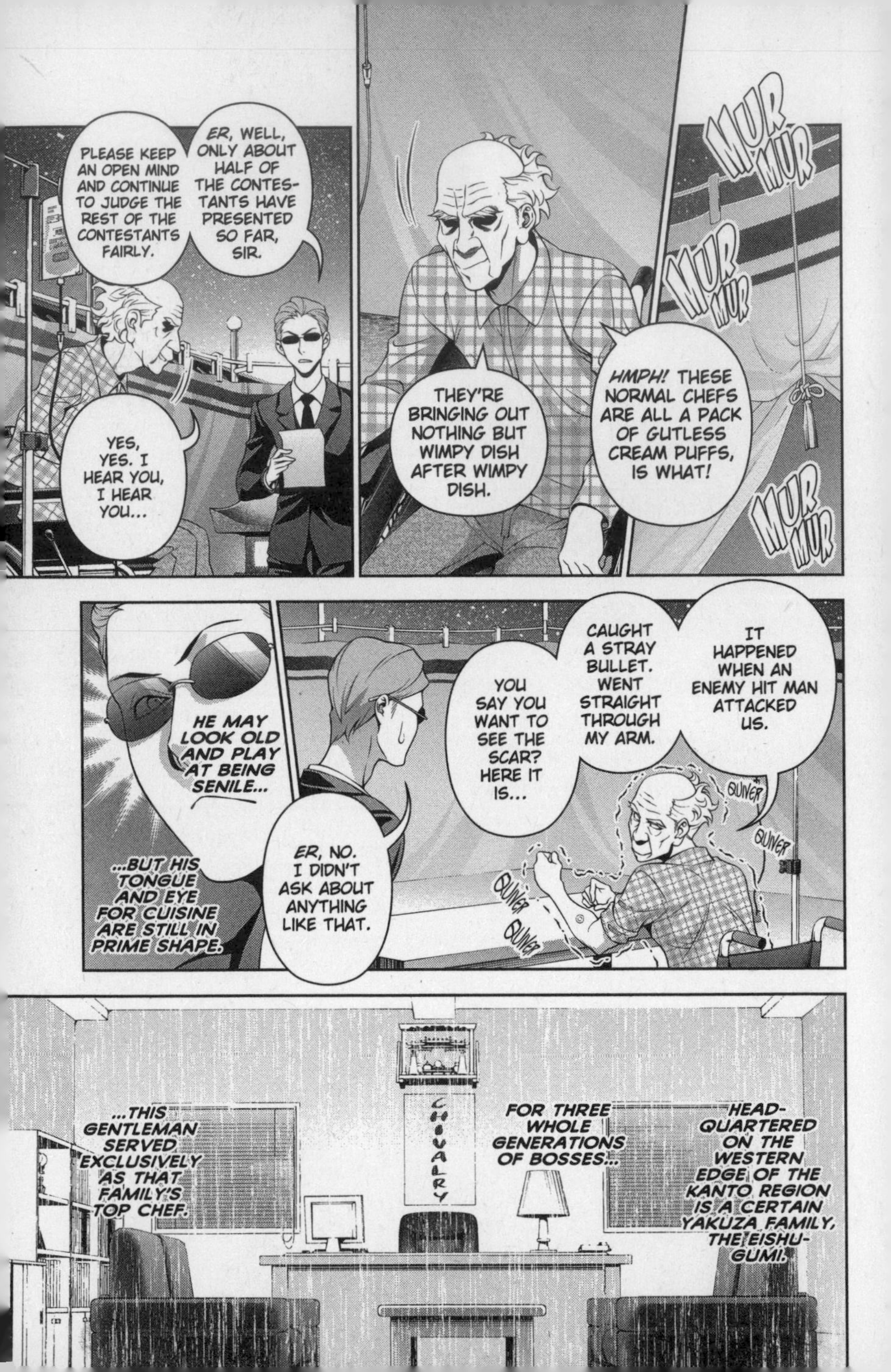
MUR MUR
MUR MUR
HMPH! THESE NORMAL CHEFS ARE ALL A PACK OF GUTLESS CREAM PUFFS, IS WHAT!
MUR MUR
THEY'RE BRINGING OUT NOTHING BUT WIMPY DISH AFTER WIMPY DISH.
ER, WELL, ONLY ABOUT HALF OF THE CONTESTANTS HAVE PRESENTED SO FAR, SIR.
PLEASE KEEP AN OPEN MIND AND CONTINUE TO JUDGE THE REST OF THE CONTESTANTS FAIRLY.
YES, YES. I HEAR YOU, I HEAR YOU...
IT HAPPENED WHEN AN ENEMY HIT MAN ATTACKED US.
CAUGHT A STRAY BULLET. WENT STRAIGHT THROUGH MY ARM.
YOU SAY YOU WANT TO SEE THE SCAR? HERE IT IS...
QUIVER
QUIVER
QUIVER
QUIVER
ER, NO. I DIDN'T ASK ABOUT ANYTHING LIKE THAT.
HE MAY LOOK OLD AND PLAY AT BEING SENILE...
...BUT HIS TONGUE AND EYE FOR CUISINE ARE STILL IN PRIME SHAPE.
HEADQUARTERED ON THE WESTERN EDGE OF THE KANTO REGION IS A CERTAIN YAKUZA FAMILY, THE EISHU-GUMI.
CHIVALRY
FOR THREE WHOLE GENERATIONS OF BOSSES...
...THIS GENTLEMAN SERVED EXCLUSIVELY AS THAT FAMILY'S TOP CHEF.

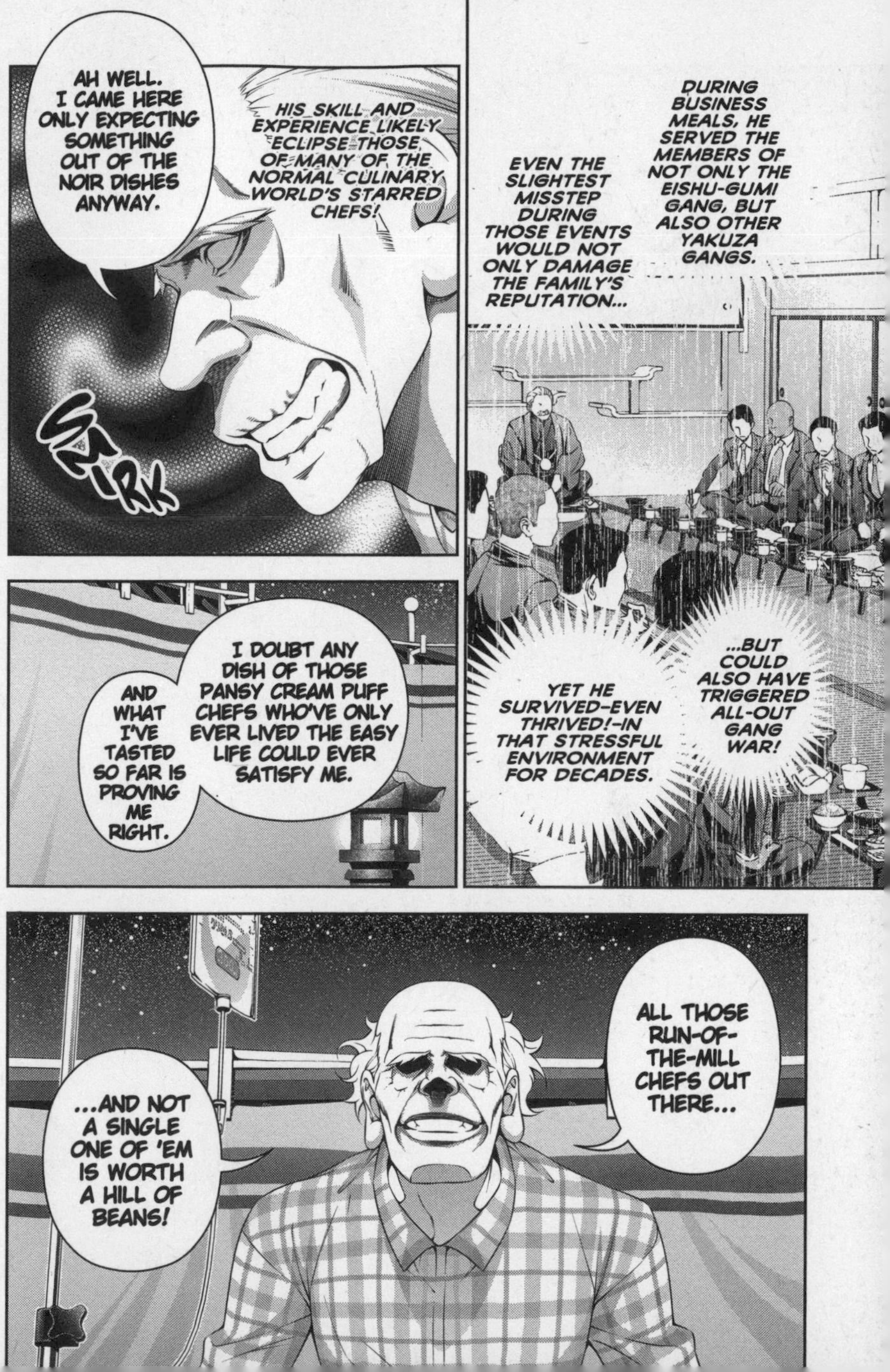
DURING BUSINESS MEALS, HE SERVED THE MEMBERS OF NOT ONLY THE EISHU-GUMI GANG, BUT ALSO OTHER YAKUZA GANGS.
EVEN THE SLIGHTEST MISSTEP DURING THOSE EVENTS WOULD NOT ONLY DAMAGE THE FAMILY'S REPUTATION...
...BUT COULD ALSO HAVE TRIGGERED ALL-OUT GANG WAR!
YET HE SURVIVED–EVEN THRIVED!–IN THAT STRESSFUL ENVIRONMENT FOR DECADES.
HIS SKILL AND EXPERIENCE LIKELY ECLIPSE THOSE OF MANY OF THE NORMAL CULINARY WORLD'S STARRED CHEFS!
AH WELL. I CAME HERE ONLY EXPECTING SOMETHING OUT OF THE NOIR DISHES ANYWAY.
SMIRK
I DOUBT ANY DISH OF THOSE PANSY CREAM PUFF CHEFS WHO'VE ONLY EVER LIVED THE EASY LIFE COULD EVER SATISFY ME.
AND WHAT I'VE TASTED SO FAR IS PROVING ME RIGHT.
ALL THOSE RUN-OF-THE-MILL CHEFS OUT THERE...
...AND NOT A SINGLE ONE OF 'EM IS WORTH A HILL OF BEANS!

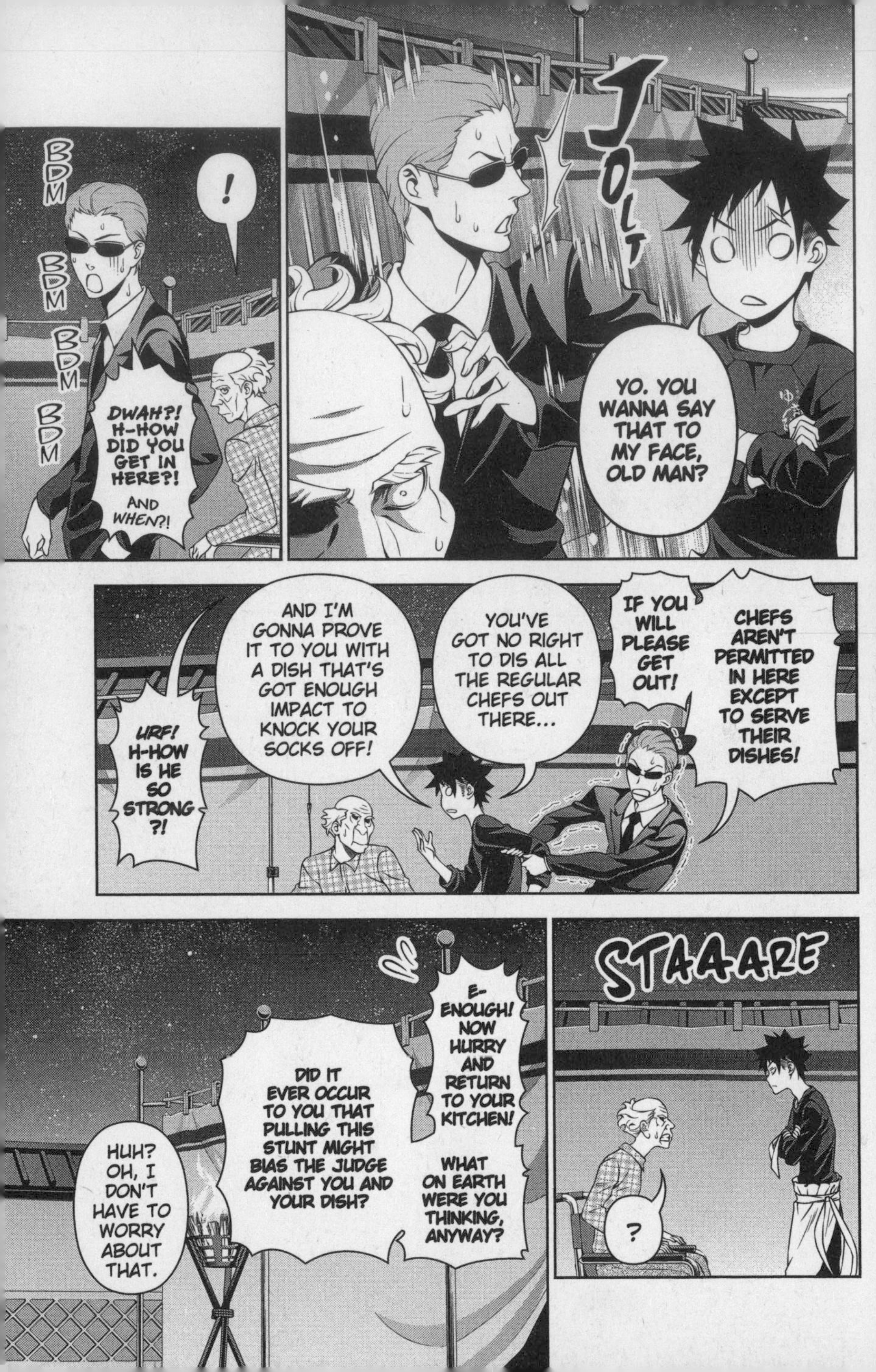
JOLT
YO. YOU WANNA SAY THAT TO MY FACE, OLD MAN?
!
BDM BDM BDM BDM
DWAH?! H-HOW DID YOU GET IN HERE?!
AND WHEN?!
CHEFS AREN'T PERMITTED IN HERE EXCEPT TO SERVE THEIR DISHES!
IF YOU WILL PLEASE GET OUT!
YOU'VE GOT NO RIGHT TO DIS ALL THE REGULAR CHEFS OUT THERE...
AND I'M GONNA PROVE IT TO YOU WITH A DISH THAT'S GOT ENOUGH IMPACT TO KNOCK YOUR SOCKS OFF!
URF! H-HOW IS HE SO STRONG?!
STAAARE
?
E-ENOUGH! NOW HURRY AND RETURN TO YOUR KITCHEN!
WHAT ON EARTH WERE YOU THINKING, ANYWAY?
DID IT EVER OCCUR TO YOU THAT PULLING THIS STUNT MIGHT BIAS THE JUDGE AGAINST YOU AND YOUR DISH?
HUH? OH, I DON'T HAVE TO WORRY ABOUT THAT.

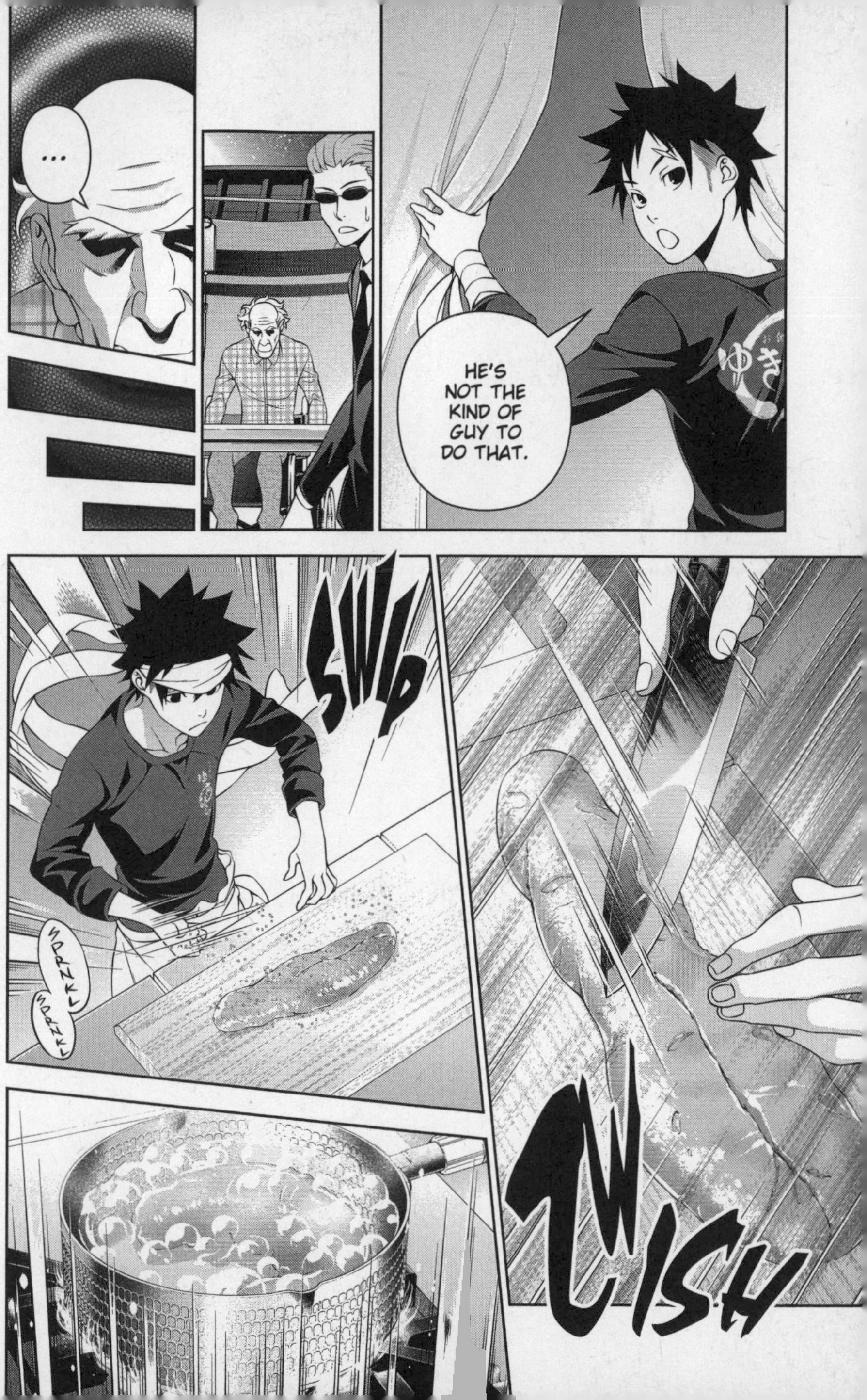
HE'S NOT THE KIND OF GUY TO DO THAT.
...
WISH
SWIP
SPRNKL
SPRNKL

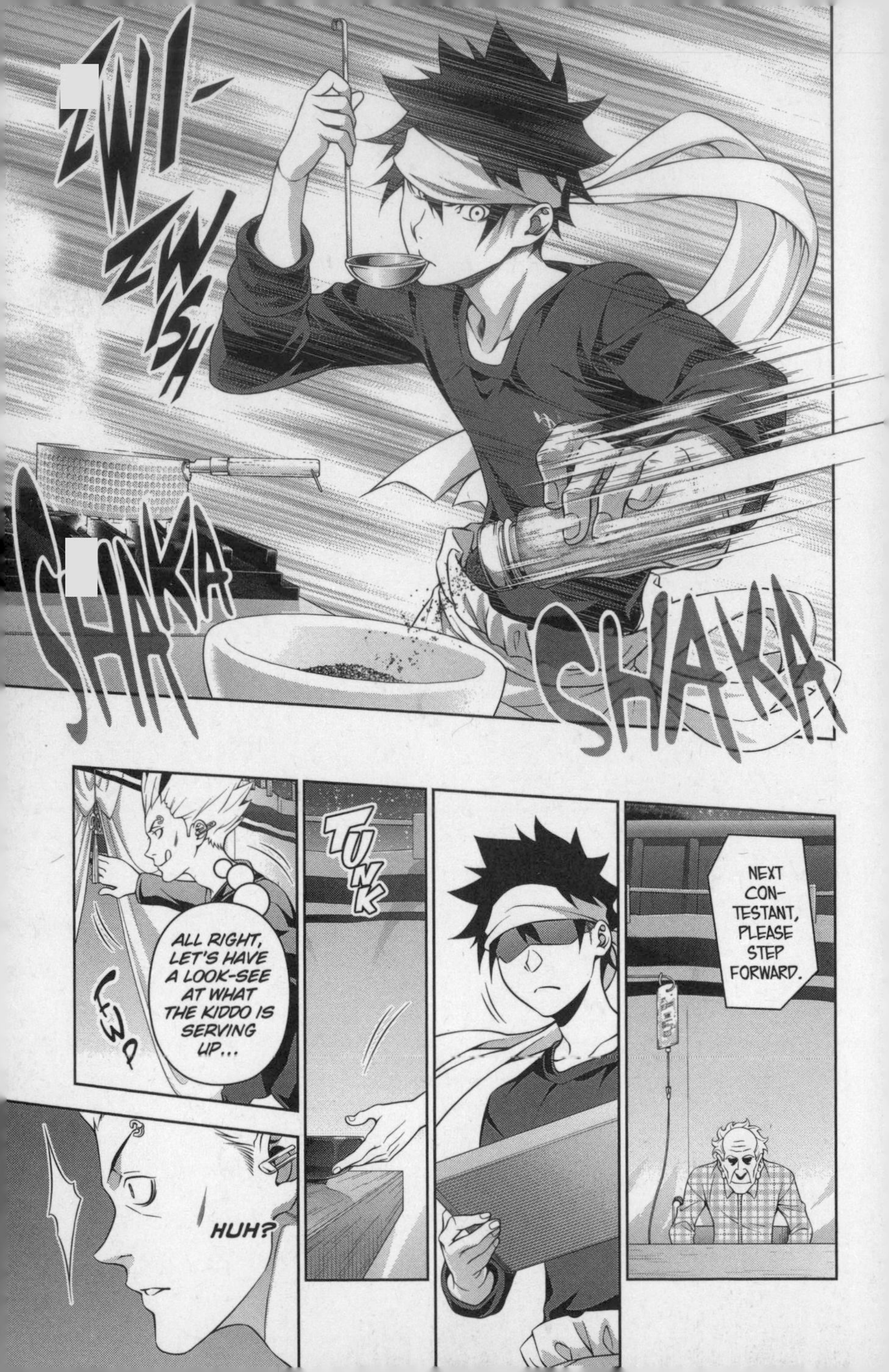
ZWI-ZWISH
SHAKA
SHAKA
NEXT CON-TESTANT, PLEASE STEP FORWARD.
TUNK
ALL RIGHT, LET'S HAVE A LOOK-SEE AT WHAT THE KIDDO IS SERVING UP...
FWP
HUH?

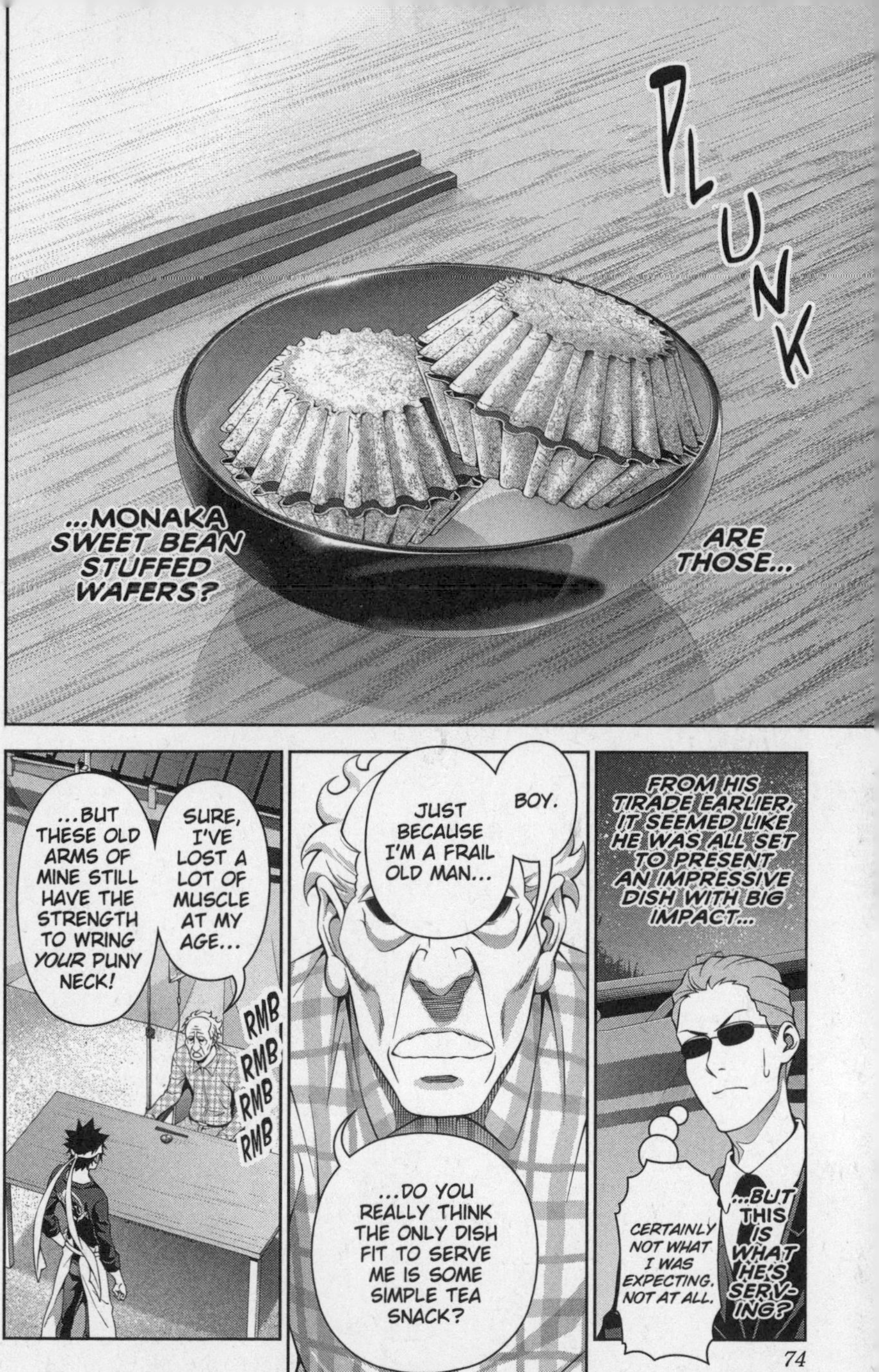
PLUNK
ARE THOSE...
...MONAKA SWEET BEAN STUFFED WAFERS?
FROM HIS TIRADE EARLIER, IT SEEMED LIKE HE WAS ALL SET TO PRESENT AN IMPRESSIVE DISH WITH BIG IMPACT...
...BUT THIS IS WHAT HE'S SERV-ING?
CERTAINLY NOT WHAT I WAS EXPECTING. NOT AT ALL.
BOY.
JUST BECAUSE I'M A FRAIL OLD MAN...
...DO YOU REALLY THINK THE ONLY DISH FIT TO SERVE ME IS SOME SIMPLE TEA SNACK?
SURE, I'VE LOST A LOT OF MUSCLE AT MY AGE...
...BUT THESE OLD ARMS OF MINE STILL HAVE THE STRENGTH TO WRING *YOUR* PUNY NECK!
RMB RMB RMB RMB

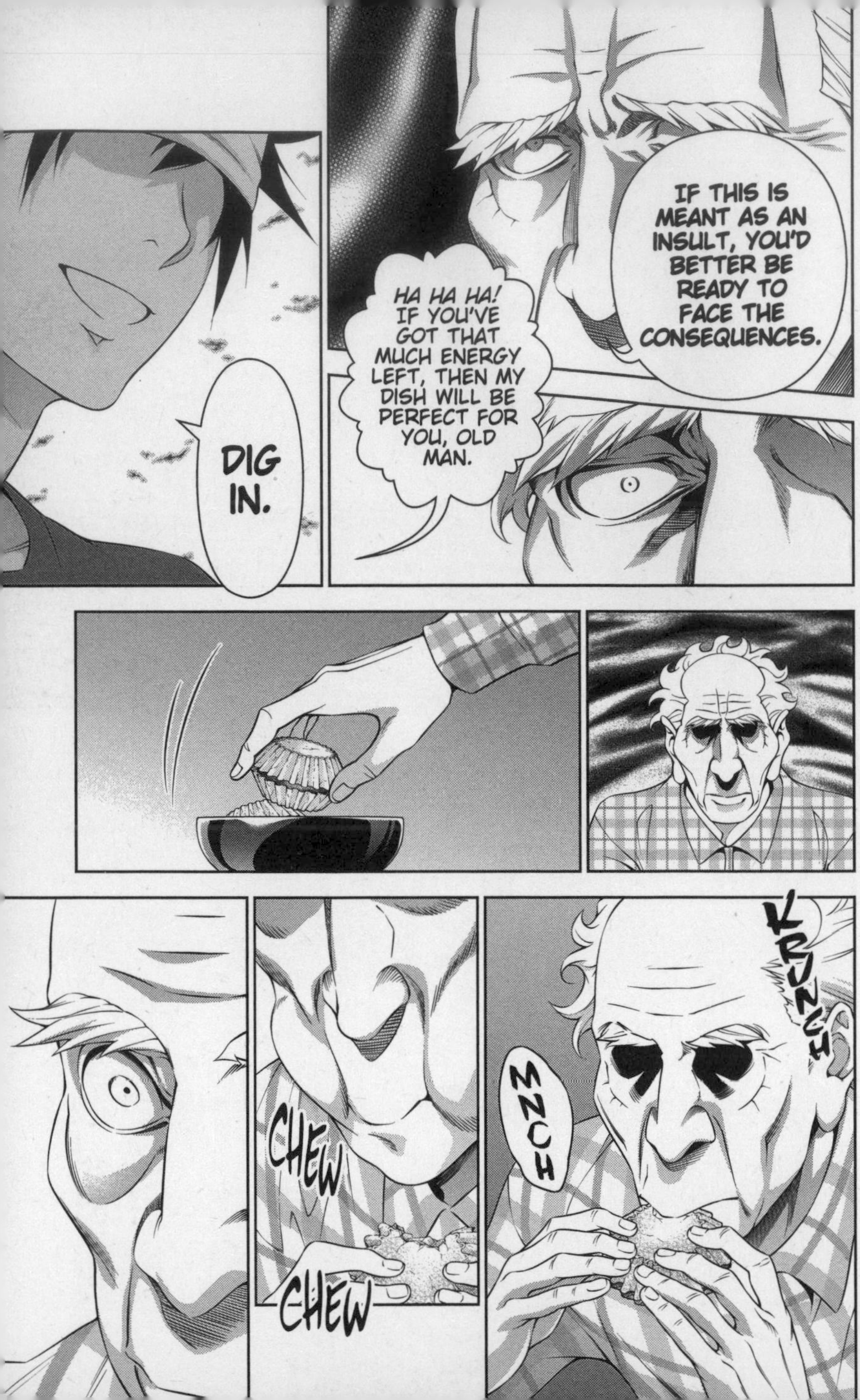
IF THIS IS MEANT AS AN INSULT, YOU'D BETTER BE READY TO FACE THE CONSEQUENCES.
HA HA HA! IF YOU'VE GOT THAT MUCH ENERGY LEFT, THEN MY DISH WILL BE PERFECT FOR YOU, OLD MAN.
DIG IN.
KRUNCH
MNCH
CHEW
CHEW

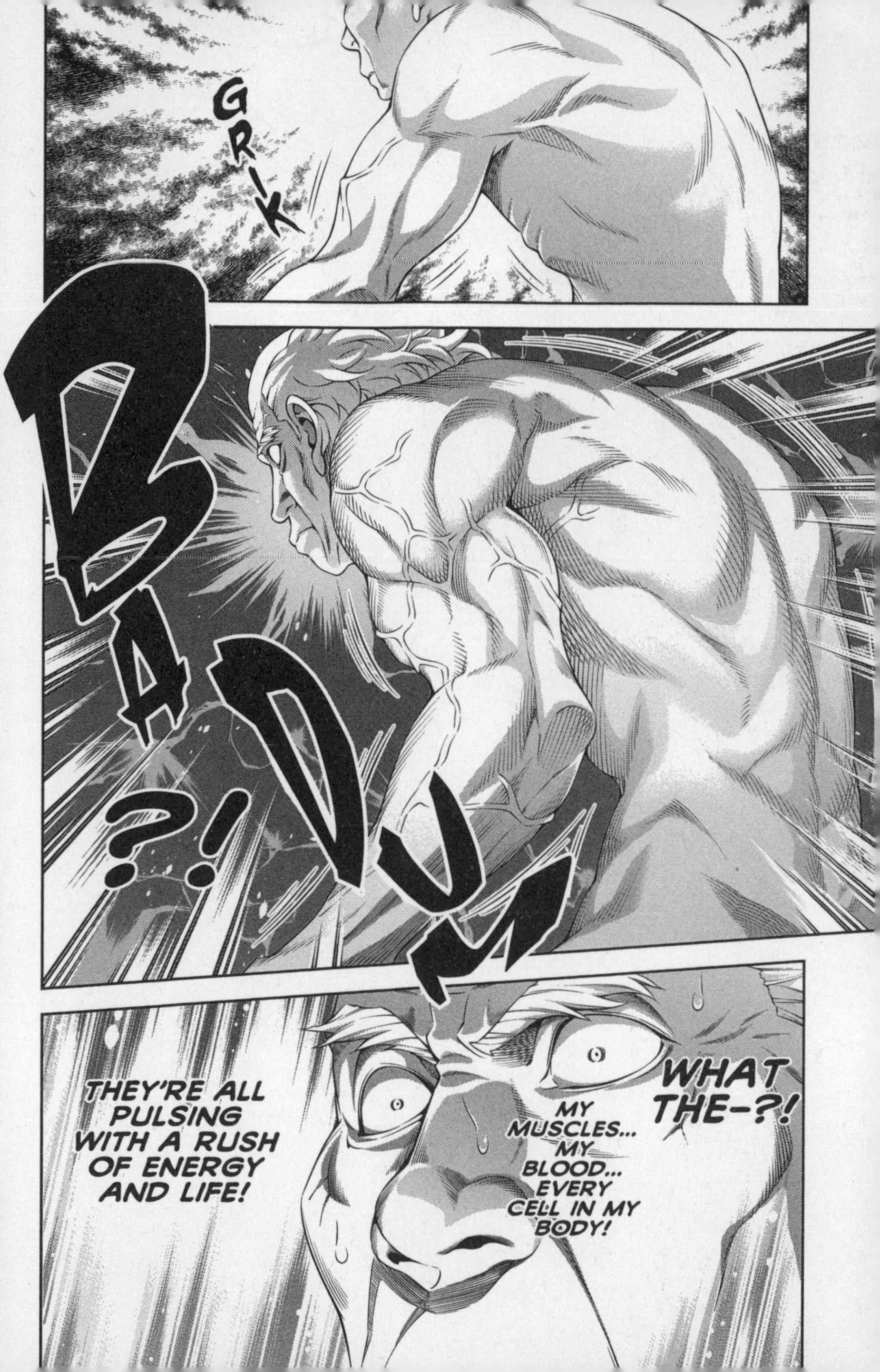
GRIK
BADUM
?!
WHAT THE-?!
MY MUSCLES... MY BLOOD... EVERY CELL IN MY BODY!
THEY'RE ALL PULSING WITH A RUSH OF ENERGY AND LIFE!

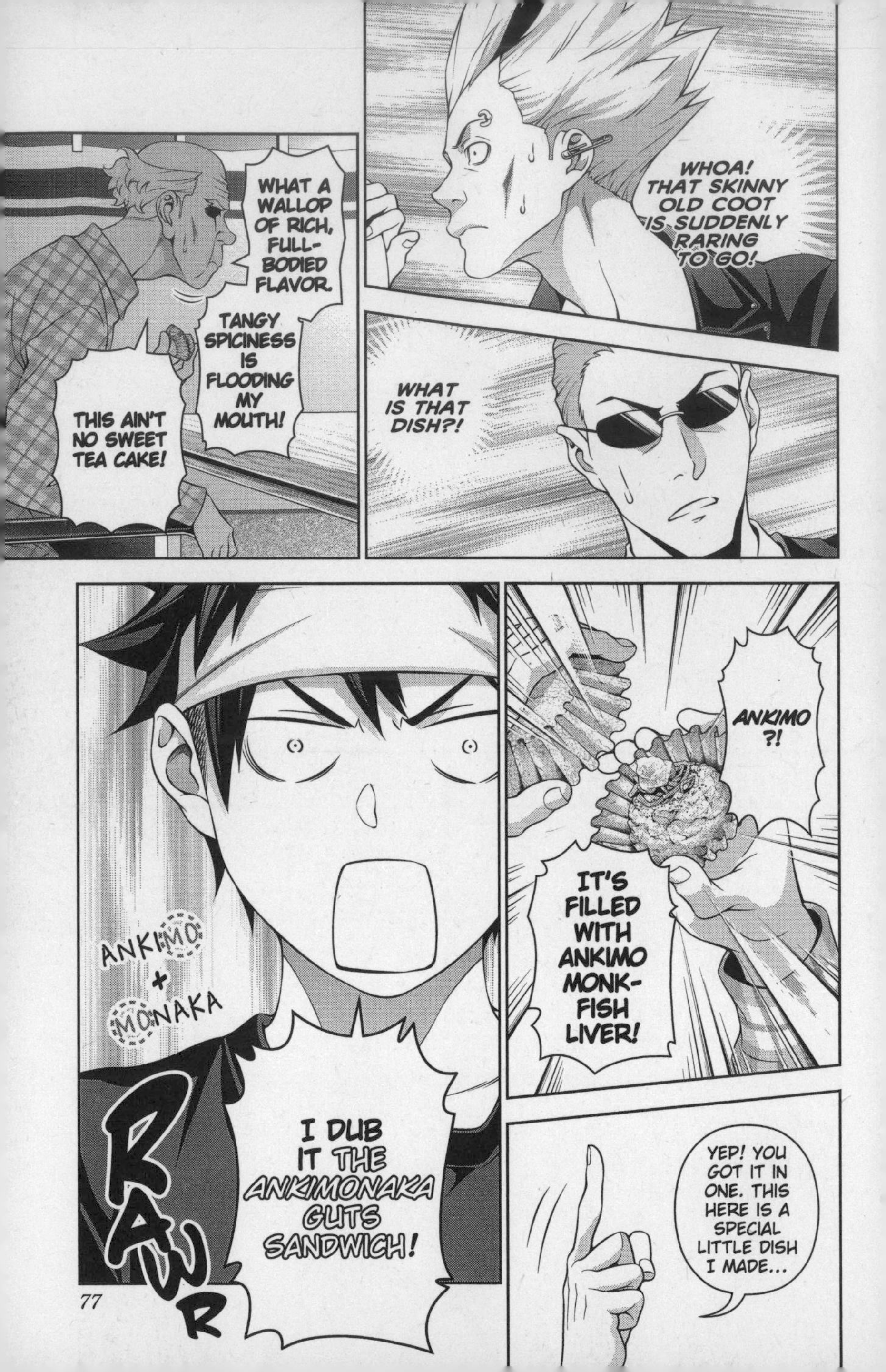
WHOA! THAT SKINNY OLD COOT IS SUDDENLY RARING TO GO!
WHAT IS THAT DISH?!
WHAT A WALLOP OF RICH, FULL-BODIED FLAVOR.
TANGY SPICINESS IS FLOODING MY MOUTH!
THIS AIN'T NO SWEET TEA CAKE!
ANKIMO ?!
IT'S FILLED WITH ANKIMO MONK-FISH LIVER!
YEP! YOU GOT IT IN ONE. THIS HERE IS A SPECIAL LITTLE DISH I MADE...
ANKIMO + MONAKA
I DUB IT THE ANKIMONAKA GUTS SANDWICH!
RAWR

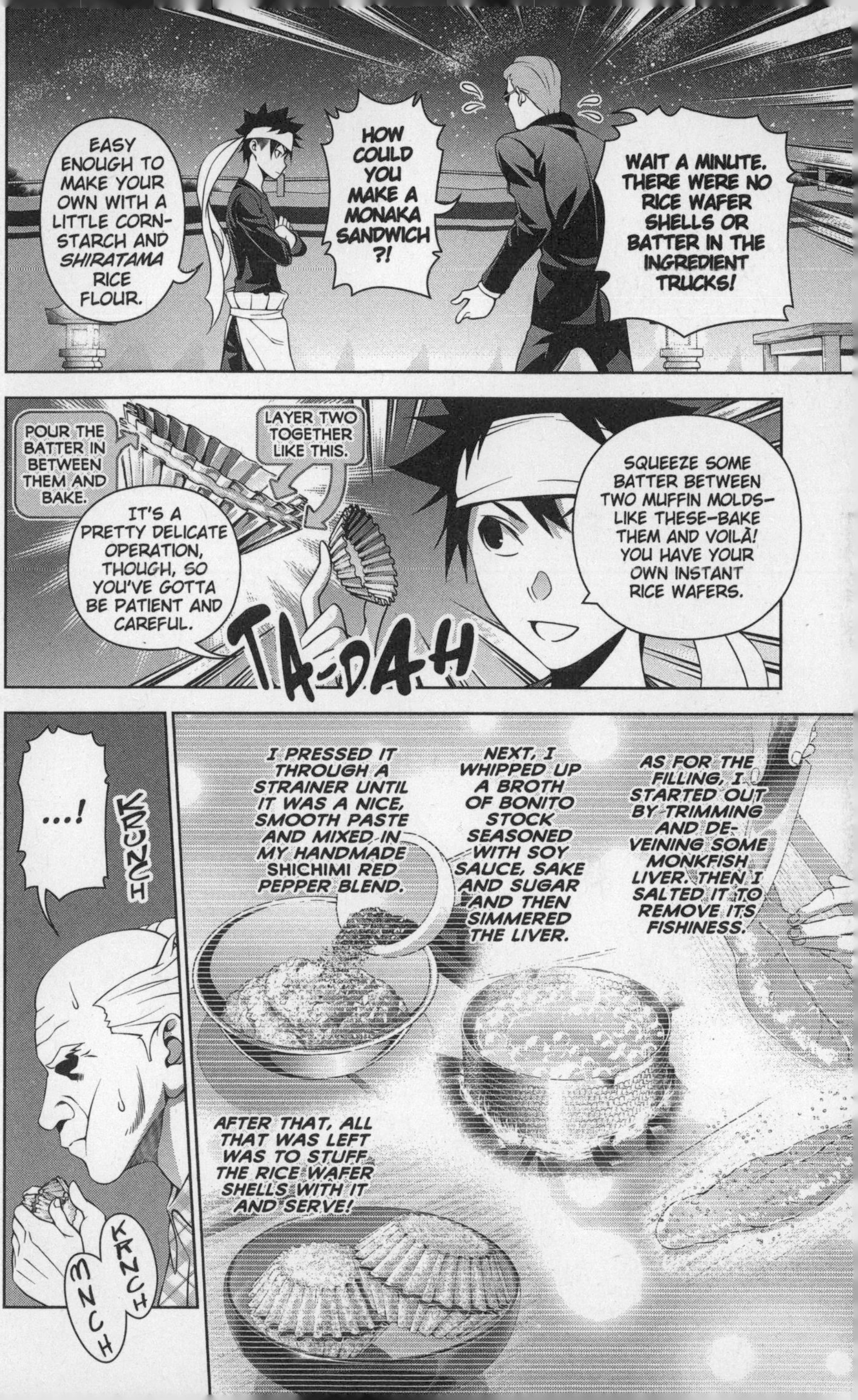
WAIT A MINUTE. THERE WERE NO RICE WAFER SHELLS OR BATTER IN THE INGREDIENT TRUCKS!
HOW COULD YOU MAKE A MONAKA SANDWICH ?!
EASY ENOUGH TO MAKE YOUR OWN WITH A LITTLE CORN-STARCH AND *SHIRATAMA* RICE FLOUR.
SQUEEZE SOME BATTER BETWEEN TWO MUFFIN MOLDS–LIKE THESE–BAKE THEM AND VOILÀ! YOU HAVE YOUR OWN INSTANT RICE WAFERS.
LAYER TWO TOGETHER LIKE THIS.
POUR THE BATTER IN BETWEEN THEM AND BAKE.
IT'S A PRETTY DELICATE OPERATION, THOUGH, SO YOU'VE GOTTA BE PATIENT AND CAREFUL.
TA-DAH
AS FOR THE FILLING, I STARTED OUT BY TRIMMING AND DE-VEINING SOME MONKFISH LIVER. THEN I SALTED IT TO REMOVE ITS FISHINESS.
NEXT, I WHIPPED UP A BROTH OF BONITO STOCK SEASONED WITH SOY SAUCE, SAKE AND SUGAR AND THEN SIMMERED THE LIVER.
I PRESSED IT THROUGH A STRAINER UNTIL IT WAS A NICE, SMOOTH PASTE AND MIXED IN MY HANDMADE SHICHIMI RED PEPPER BLEND.
AFTER THAT, ALL THAT WAS LEFT WAS TO STUFF THE RICE WAFER SHELLS WITH IT AND SERVE!
...!
KRUNCH
KRNCH
MNCH

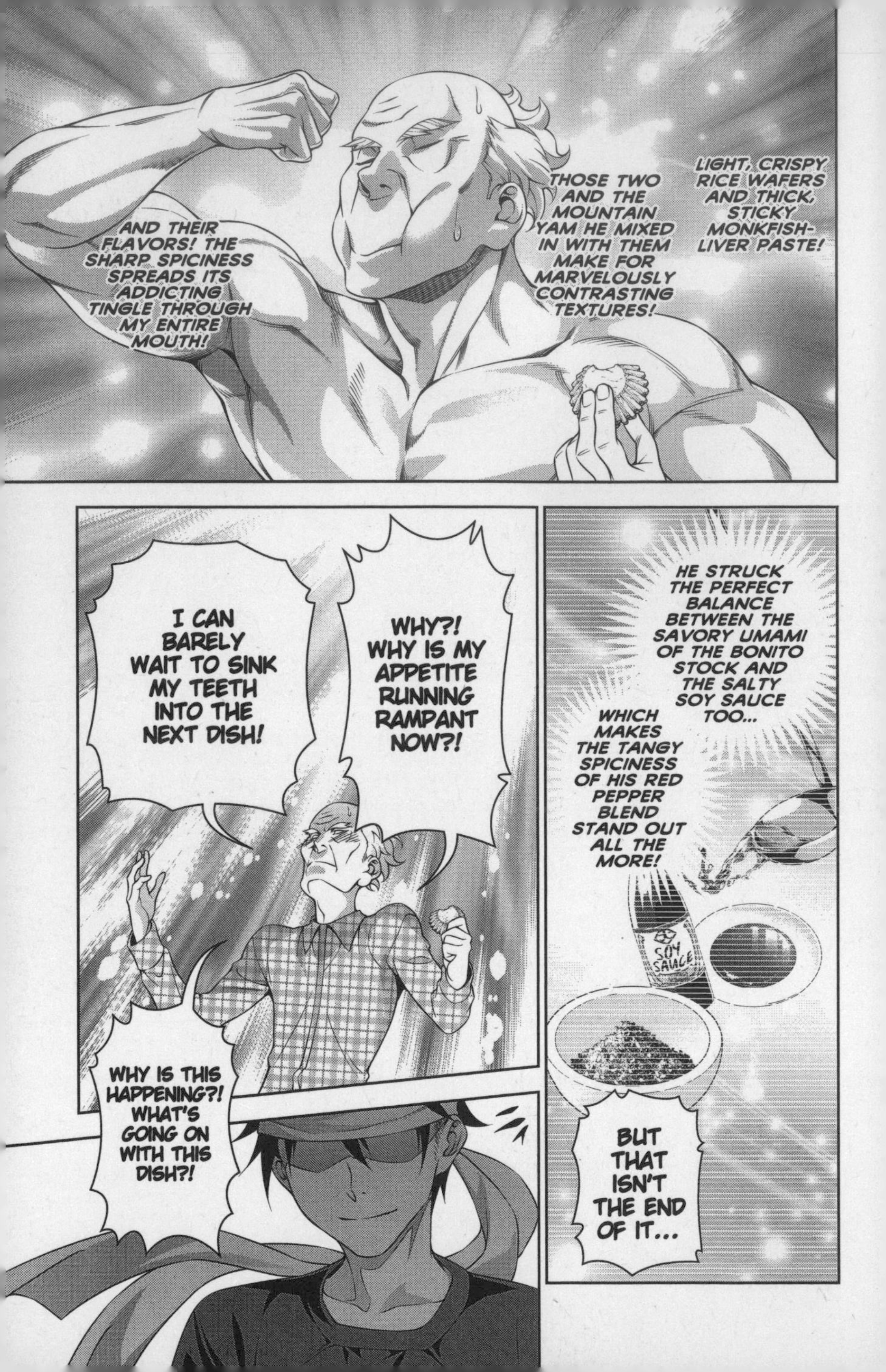
LIGHT, CRISPY RICE WAFERS AND THICK, STICKY MONKFISH-LIVER PASTE!
THOSE TWO AND THE MOUNTAIN YAM HE MIXED IN WITH THEM MAKE FOR MARVELOUSLY CONTRASTING TEXTURES!
AND THEIR FLAVORS! THE SHARP SPICINESS SPREADS ITS ADDICTING TINGLE THROUGH MY ENTIRE MOUTH!
HE STRUCK THE PERFECT BALANCE BETWEEN THE SAVORY UMAMI OF THE BONITO STOCK AND THE SALTY SOY SAUCE TOO...
WHICH MAKES THE TANGY SPICINESS OF HIS RED PEPPER BLEND STAND OUT ALL THE MORE!
SOY SAUCE
BUT THAT ISN'T THE END OF IT...
WHY?! WHY IS MY APPETITE RUNNING RAMPANT NOW?!
I CAN BARELY WAIT TO SINK MY TEETH INTO THE NEXT DISH!
WHY IS THIS HAPPENING?! WHAT'S GOING ON WITH THIS DISH?!

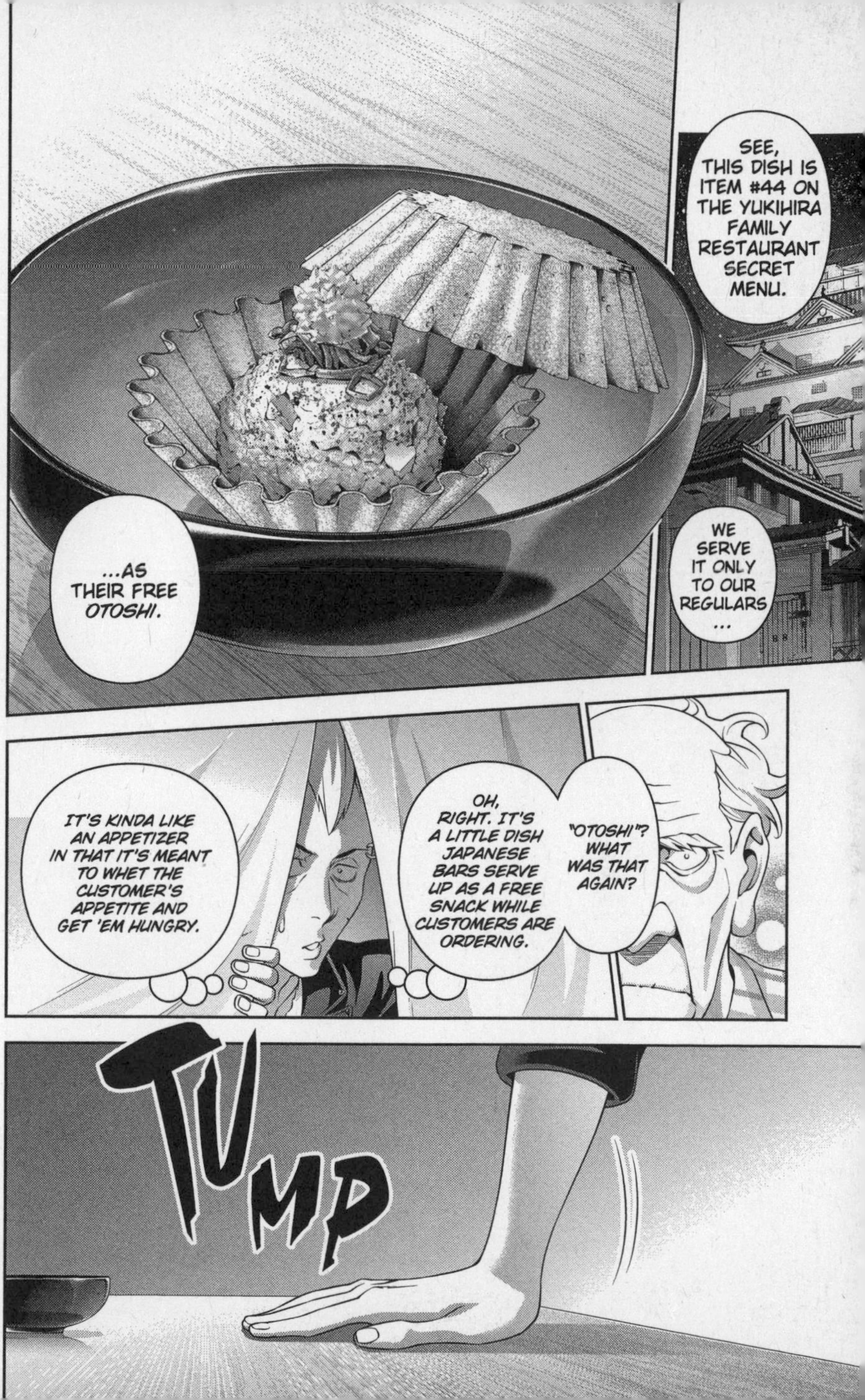
SEE, THIS DISH IS ITEM #44 ON THE YUKIHIRA FAMILY RESTAURANT SECRET MENU.
WE SERVE IT ONLY TO OUR REGULARS...
...AS THEIR FREE *OTOSHI*.
"OTOSHI"? WHAT WAS THAT AGAIN?
OH, RIGHT. IT'S A LITTLE DISH JAPANESE BARS SERVE UP AS A FREE SNACK WHILE CUSTOMERS ARE ORDERING.
IT'S KINDA LIKE AN APPETIZER IN THAT IT'S MEANT TO WHET THE CUSTOMER'S APPETITE AND GET 'EM HUNGRY.
TUMP

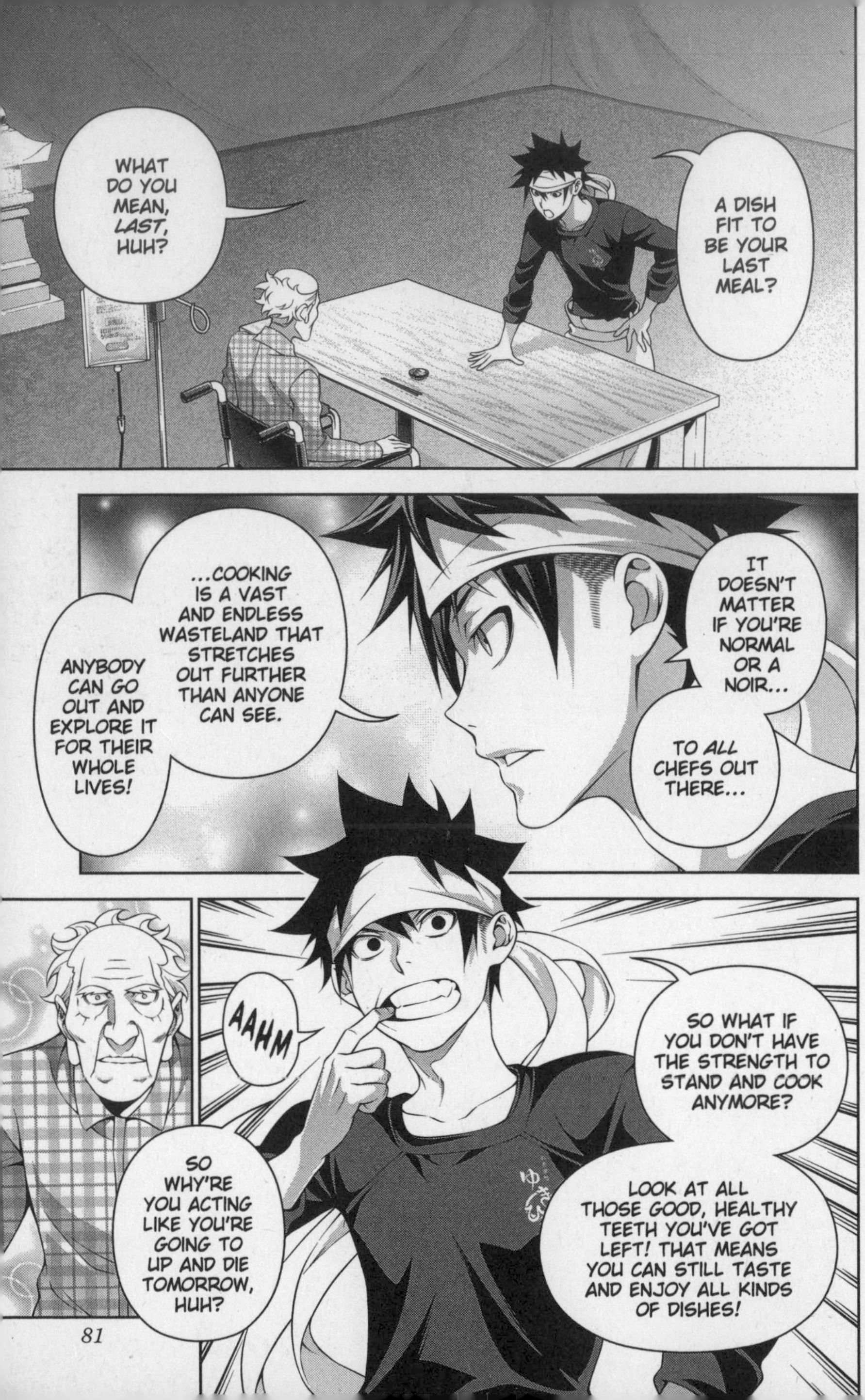
A DISH FIT TO BE YOUR LAST MEAL?
WHAT DO YOU MEAN, *LAST*, HUH?
IT DOESN'T MATTER IF YOU'RE NORMAL OR A NOIR...
TO *ALL* CHEFS OUT THERE...
...COOKING IS A VAST AND ENDLESS WASTELAND THAT STRETCHES OUT FURTHER THAN ANYONE CAN SEE.
ANYBODY CAN GO OUT AND EXPLORE IT FOR THEIR WHOLE LIVES!
SO WHAT IF YOU DON'T HAVE THE STRENGTH TO STAND AND COOK ANYMORE?
AAHM
LOOK AT ALL THOSE GOOD, HEALTHY TEETH YOU'VE GOT LEFT! THAT MEANS YOU CAN STILL TASTE AND ENJOY ALL KINDS OF DISHES!
SO WHY'RE YOU ACTING LIKE YOU'RE GOING TO UP AND DIE TOMORROW, HUH?

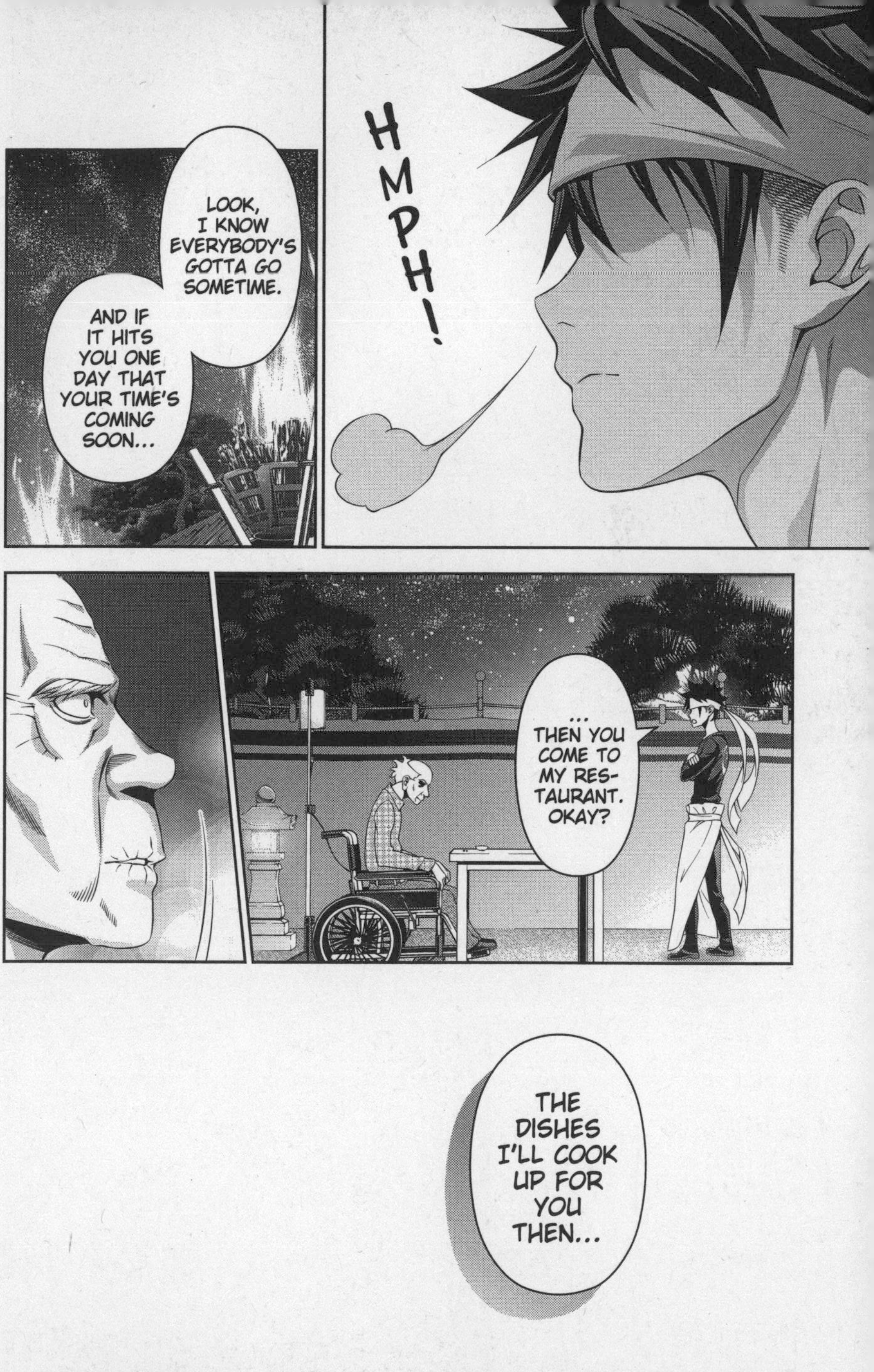
HMPH!
LOOK, I KNOW EVERYBODY'S GOTTA GO SOMETIME.
AND IF IT HITS YOU ONE DAY THAT YOUR TIME'S COMING SOON...
... THEN YOU COME TO MY RES- TAURANT. OKAY?
THE DISHES I'LL COOK UP FOR YOU THEN...

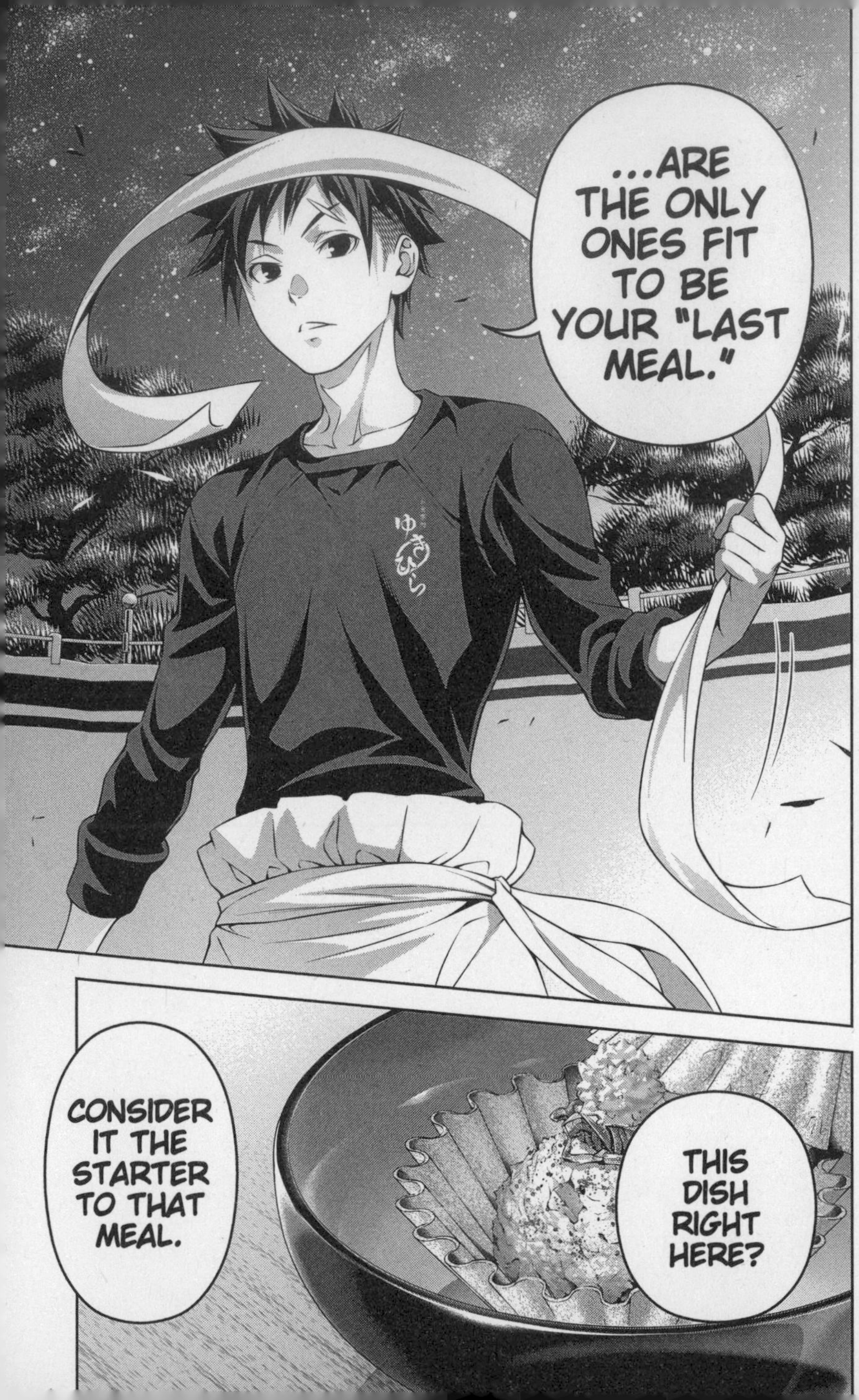
...ARE THE ONLY ONES FIT TO BE YOUR "LAST MEAL."
THIS DISH RIGHT HERE?
CONSIDER IT THE STARTER TO THAT MEAL.

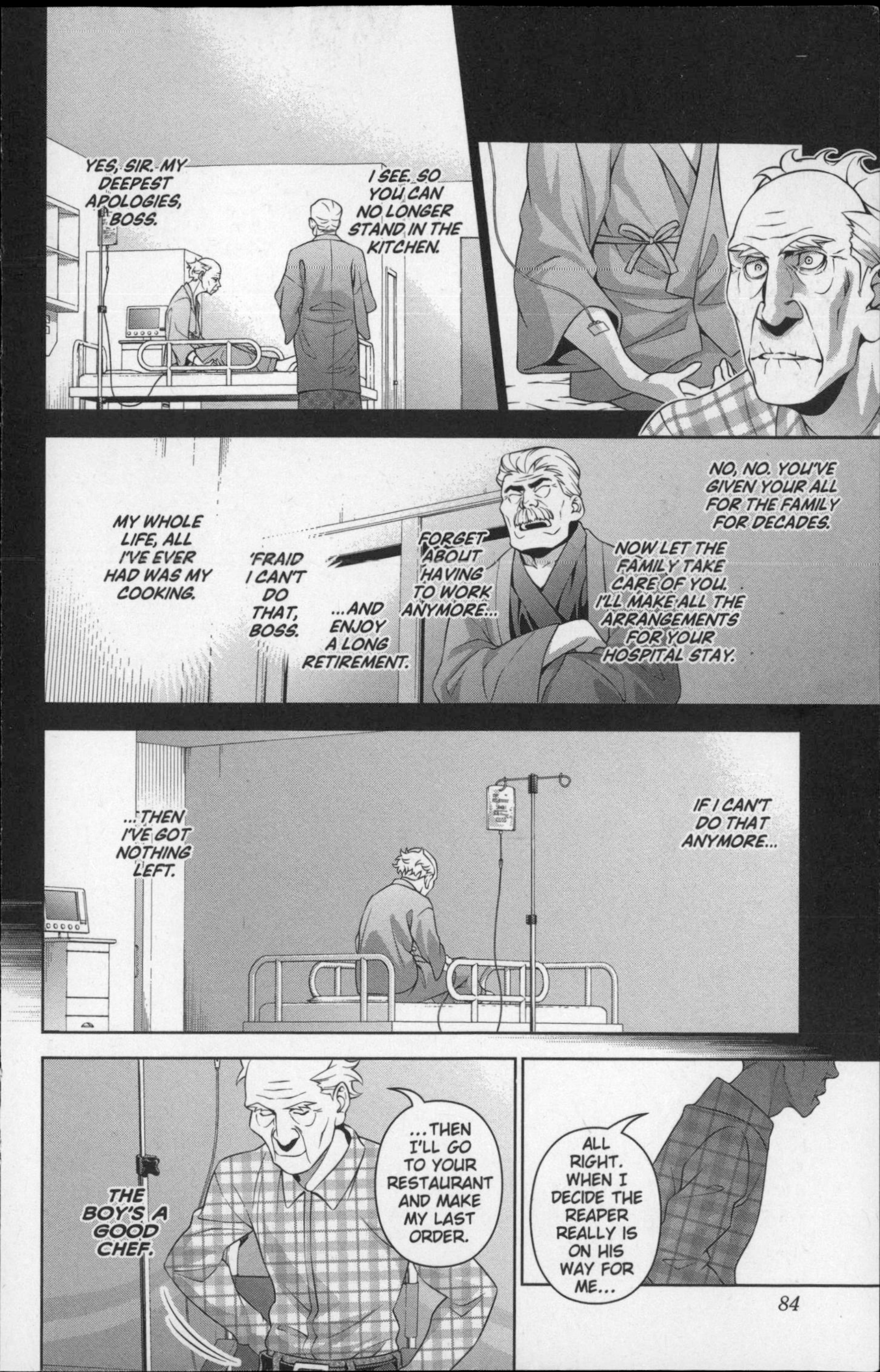
I SEE. SO YOU CAN NO LONGER STAND IN THE KITCHEN.
YES, SIR. MY DEEPEST APOLOGIES, BOSS.
NO, NO. YOU'VE GIVEN YOUR ALL FOR THE FAMILY FOR DECADES.
NOW LET THE FAMILY TAKE CARE OF YOU. I'LL MAKE ALL THE ARRANGEMENTS FOR YOUR HOSPITAL STAY.
FORGET ABOUT HAVING TO WORK ANYMORE...
...AND ENJOY A LONG RETIREMENT.
'FRAID I CAN'T DO THAT, BOSS.
MY WHOLE LIFE, ALL I'VE EVER HAD WAS MY COOKING.
IF I CAN'T DO THAT ANYMORE...
...THEN I'VE GOT NOTHING LEFT.
ALL RIGHT. WHEN I DECIDE THE REAPER REALLY IS ON HIS WAY FOR ME...
...THEN I'LL GO TO YOUR RESTAURANT AND MAKE MY LAST ORDER.
THE BOY'S A GOOD CHEF.

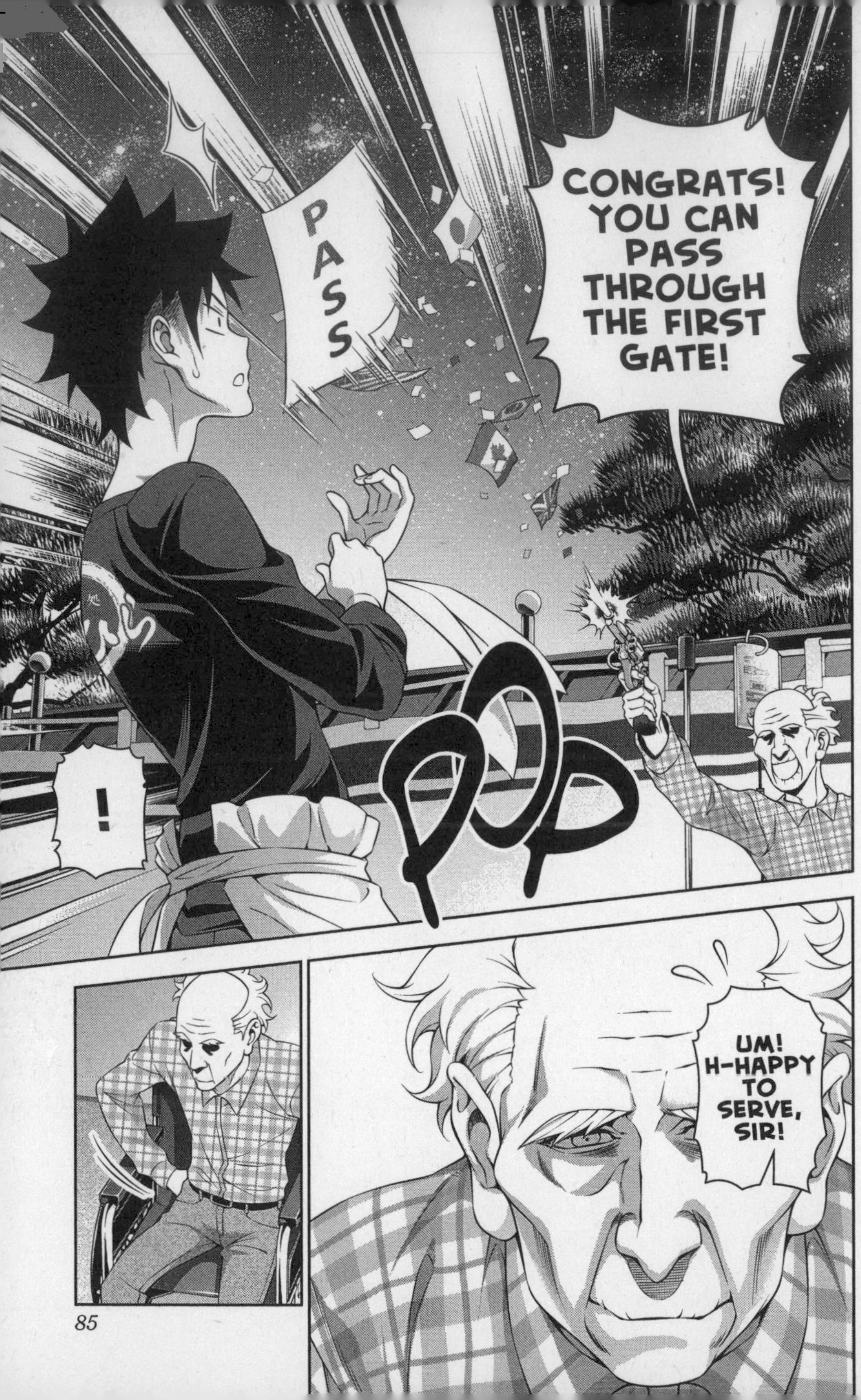
CONGRATS! YOU CAN PASS THROUGH THE FIRST GATE!
PASS
POP
!
UM! H-HAPPY TO SERVE, SIR!

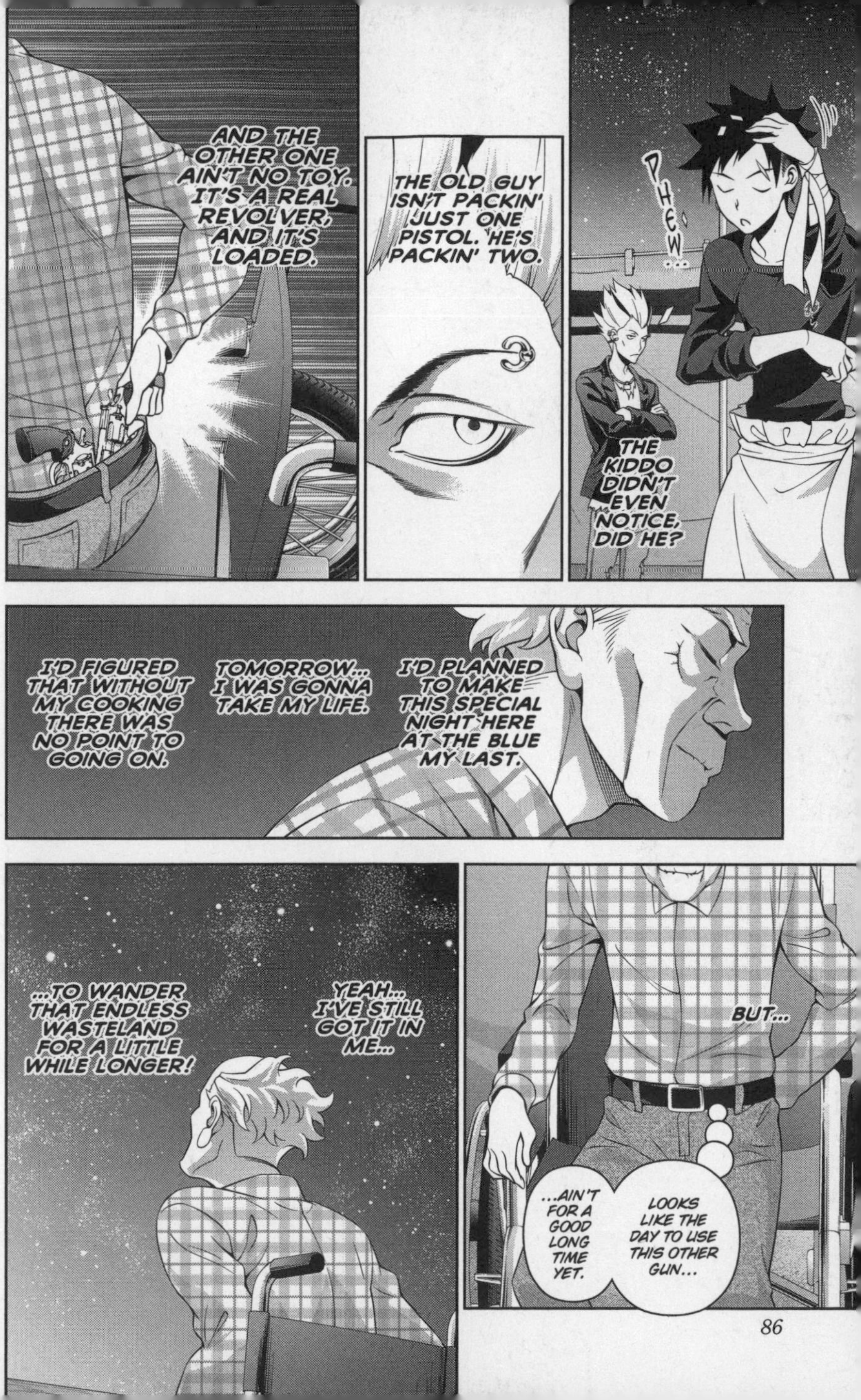
PHEW...
THE KIDDO DIDN'T EVEN NOTICE, DID HE?
THE OLD GUY ISN'T PACKIN' JUST ONE PISTOL. HE'S PACKIN' TWO.
AND THE OTHER ONE AIN'T NO TOY. IT'S A REAL REVOLVER, AND IT'S LOADED.
I'D PLANNED TO MAKE THIS SPECIAL NIGHT HERE AT THE BLUE MY LAST.
TOMORROW... I WAS GONNA TAKE MY LIFE.
I'D FIGURED THAT WITHOUT MY COOKING THERE WAS NO POINT TO GOING ON.
BUT...
LOOKS LIKE THE DAY TO USE THIS OTHER GUN...
...AIN'T FOR A GOOD LONG TIME YET.
YEAH... I'VE STILL GOT IT IN ME...
...TO WANDER THAT ENDLESS WASTELAND FOR A LITTLE WHILE LONGER!

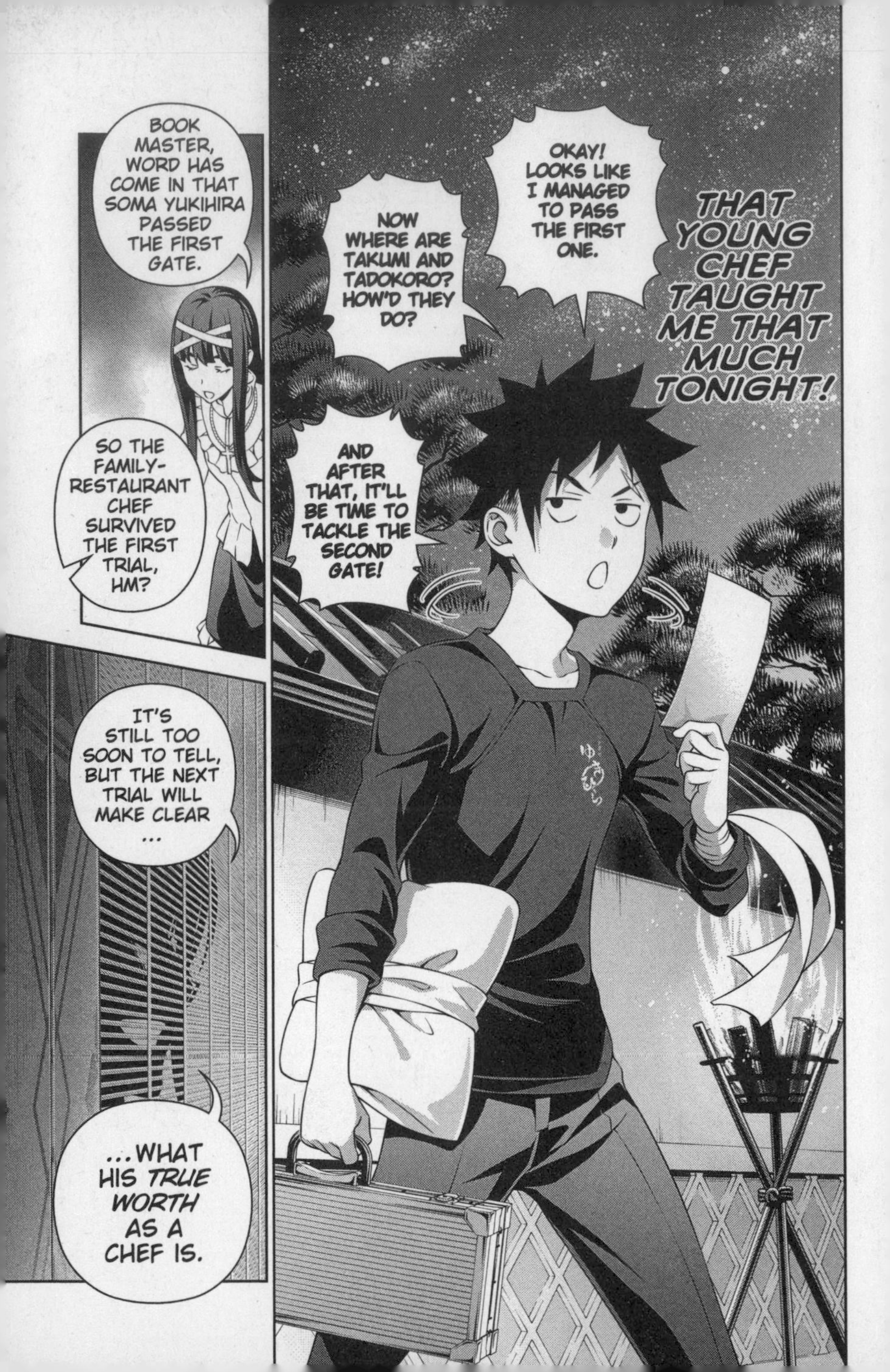
THAT YOUNG CHEF TAUGHT ME THAT MUCH TONIGHT!
OKAY! LOOKS LIKE I MANAGED TO PASS THE FIRST ONE.
NOW WHERE ARE TAKUMI AND TADOKORO? HOW'D THEY DO?
AND AFTER THAT, IT'LL BE TIME TO TACKLE THE SECOND GATE!
BOOK MASTER, WORD HAS COME IN THAT SOMA YUKIHIRA PASSED THE FIRST GATE.
SO THE FAMILY-RESTAURANT CHEF SURVIVED THE FIRST TRIAL, HM?
IT'S STILL TOO SOON TO TELL, BUT THE NEXT TRIAL WILL MAKE CLEAR ...
...WHAT HIS *TRUE WORTH* AS A CHEF IS.

ARTIST: YUTO TSUKUDA   RECIPE BY: YUKI MORISAKI

VOLUME 33
SPECIAL SUPPLEMENT!

PRACTICAL RECIPE #1

IT'S TOTALLY OKAY TO USE PREPACKAGED SHELLS FOR THE MONAKA!

YUKIHIRA FAMILY RESTAURANT SECRET MENU ITEM #44
ANKIMONAKA GUTS SANDWICH

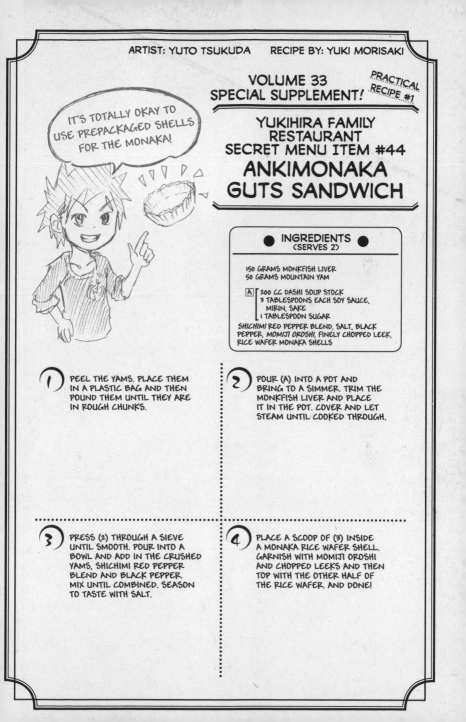

● INGREDIENTS ●
(SERVES 2)

150 GRAMS MONKFISH LIVER
50 GRAMS MOUNTAIN YAM

A ⎡ 200 CC DASHI SOUP STOCK
⎢ 3 TABLESPOONS EACH SOY SAUCE,
⎢ MIRIN, SAKE
⎣ 1 TABLESPOON SUGAR

SHICHIMI RED PEPPER BLEND, SALT, BLACK PEPPER, MOMIJI OROSHI, FINELY CHOPPED LEEK, RICE WAFER MONAKA SHELLS

1) PEEL THE YAMS. PLACE THEM IN A PLASTIC BAG AND THEN POUND THEM UNTIL THEY ARE IN ROUGH CHUNKS.

2) POUR (A) INTO A POT AND BRING TO A SIMMER. TRIM THE MONKFISH LIVER AND PLACE IT IN THE POT. COVER AND LET STEAM UNTIL COOKED THROUGH.

3) PRESS (2) THROUGH A SIEVE UNTIL SMOOTH. POUR INTO A BOWL AND ADD IN THE CRUSHED YAMS, SHICHIMI RED PEPPER BLEND AND BLACK PEPPER. MIX UNTIL COMBINED. SEASON TO TASTE WITH SALT.

4) PLACE A SCOOP OF (3) INSIDE A MONAKA RICE WAFER SHELL. GARNISH WITH MOMIJI OROSHI AND CHOPPED LEEKS AND THEN TOP WITH THE OTHER HALF OF THE RICE WAFER. AND DONE!

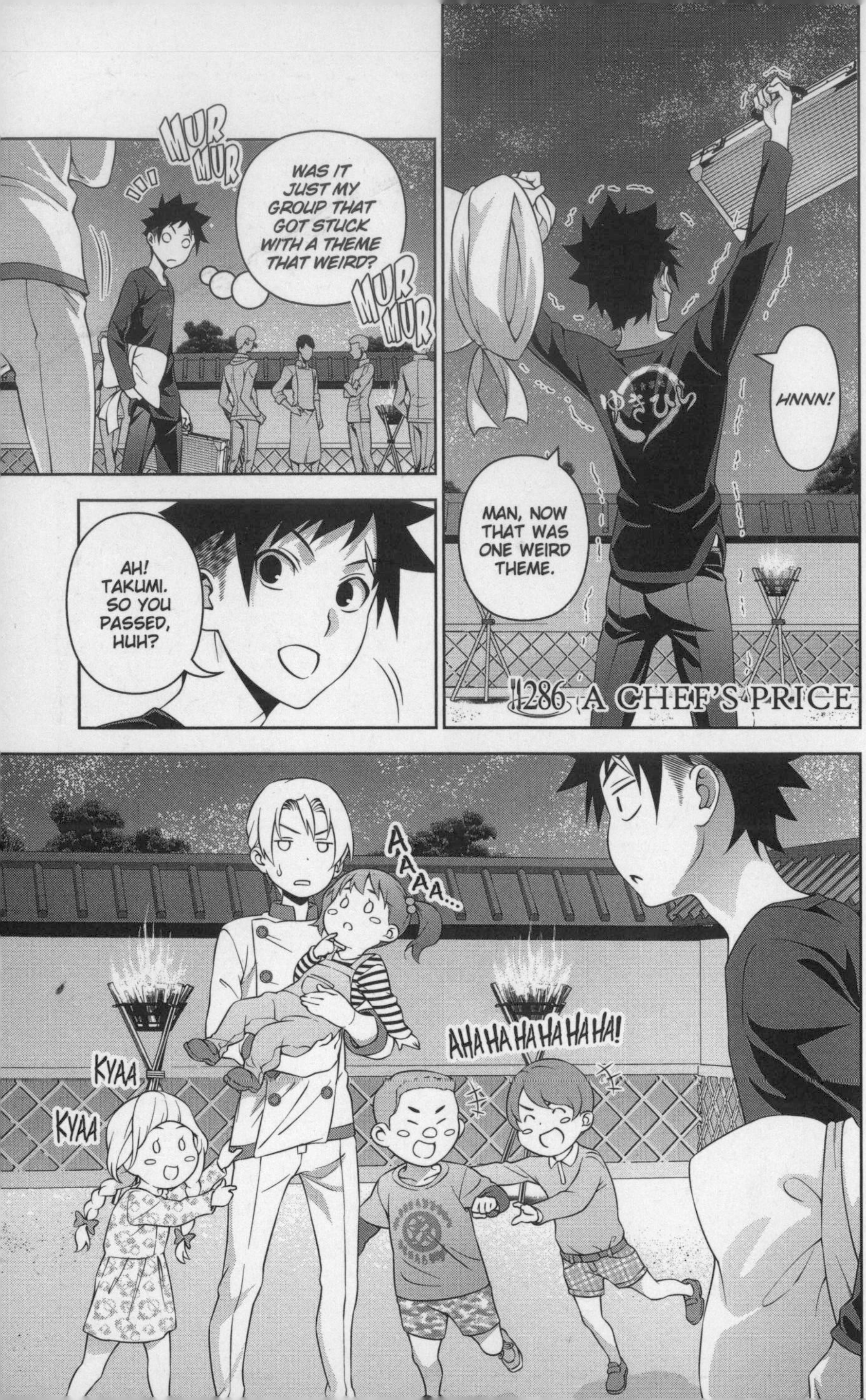
HNNN!
MAN, NOW THAT WAS ONE WEIRD THEME.
286 A CHEF'S PRICE
MUR MUR
WAS IT JUST MY GROUP THAT GOT STUCK WITH A THEME THAT WEIRD?
MUR MUR
AH! TAKUMI. SO YOU PASSED, HUH?
AAAA...
AHAHAHAHAHAHAHA!
KYAA
KYAA

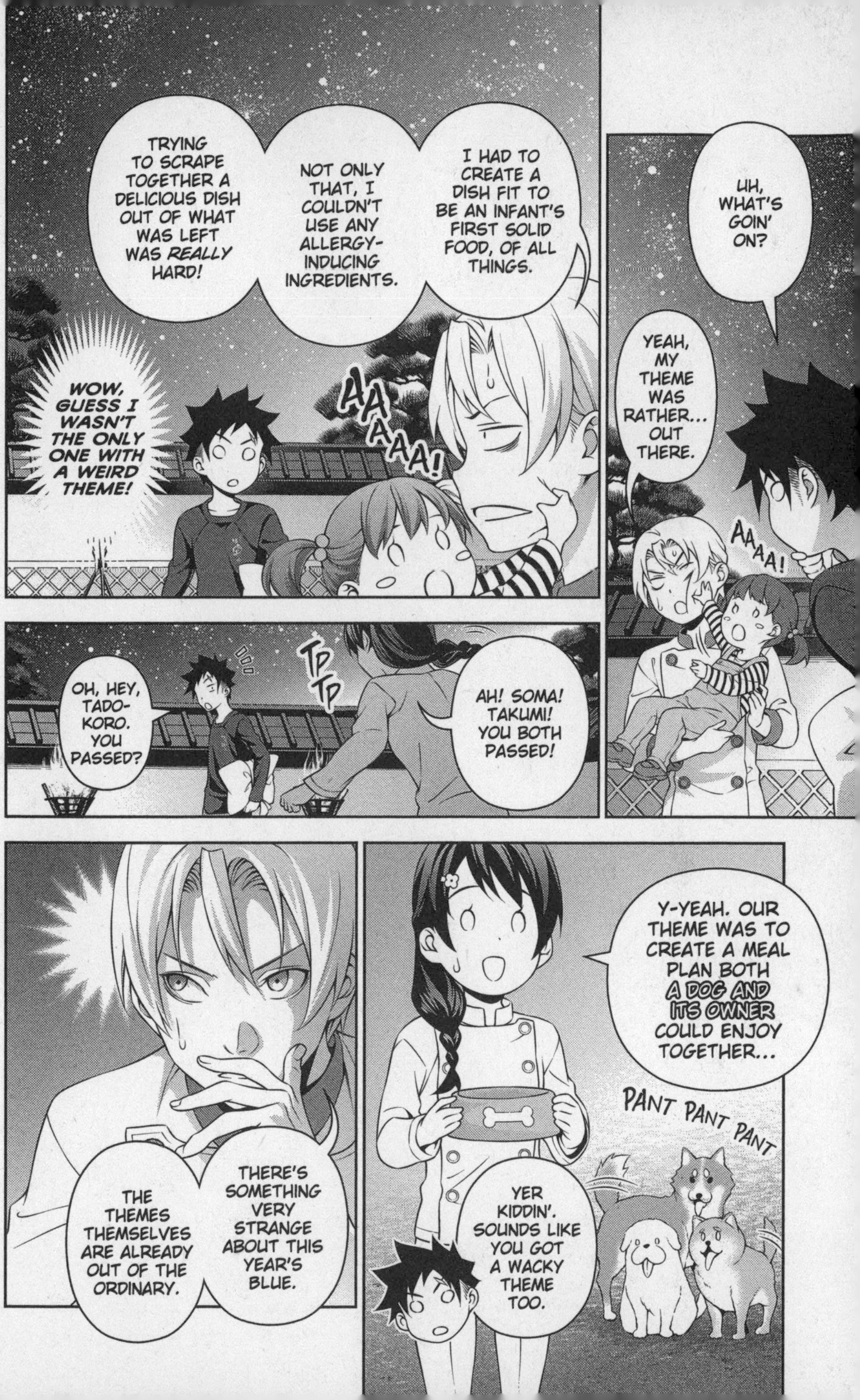
UH, WHAT'S GOIN' ON?
YEAH, MY THEME WAS RATHER... OUT THERE.
AAAA!
I HAD TO CREATE A DISH FIT TO BE AN INFANT'S FIRST SOLID FOOD, OF ALL THINGS.
NOT ONLY THAT, I COULDN'T USE ANY ALLERGY-INDUCING INGREDIENTS.
TRYING TO SCRAPE TOGETHER A DELICIOUS DISH OUT OF WHAT WAS LEFT WAS *REALLY* HARD!
AAAAAA!
WOW, GUESS I WASN'T THE ONLY ONE WITH A WEIRD THEME!
TP TP
AH! SOMA! TAKUMI! YOU BOTH PASSED!
OH, HEY, TADOKORO. YOU PASSED?
Y-YEAH. OUR THEME WAS TO CREATE A MEAL PLAN BOTH A DOG AND ITS OWNER COULD ENJOY TOGETHER...
PANT PANT PANT
YER KIDDIN'. SOUNDS LIKE YOU GOT A WACKY THEME TOO.
THERE'S SOMETHING VERY STRANGE ABOUT THIS YEAR'S BLUE.
THE THEMES THEMSELVES ARE ALREADY OUT OF THE ORDINARY.

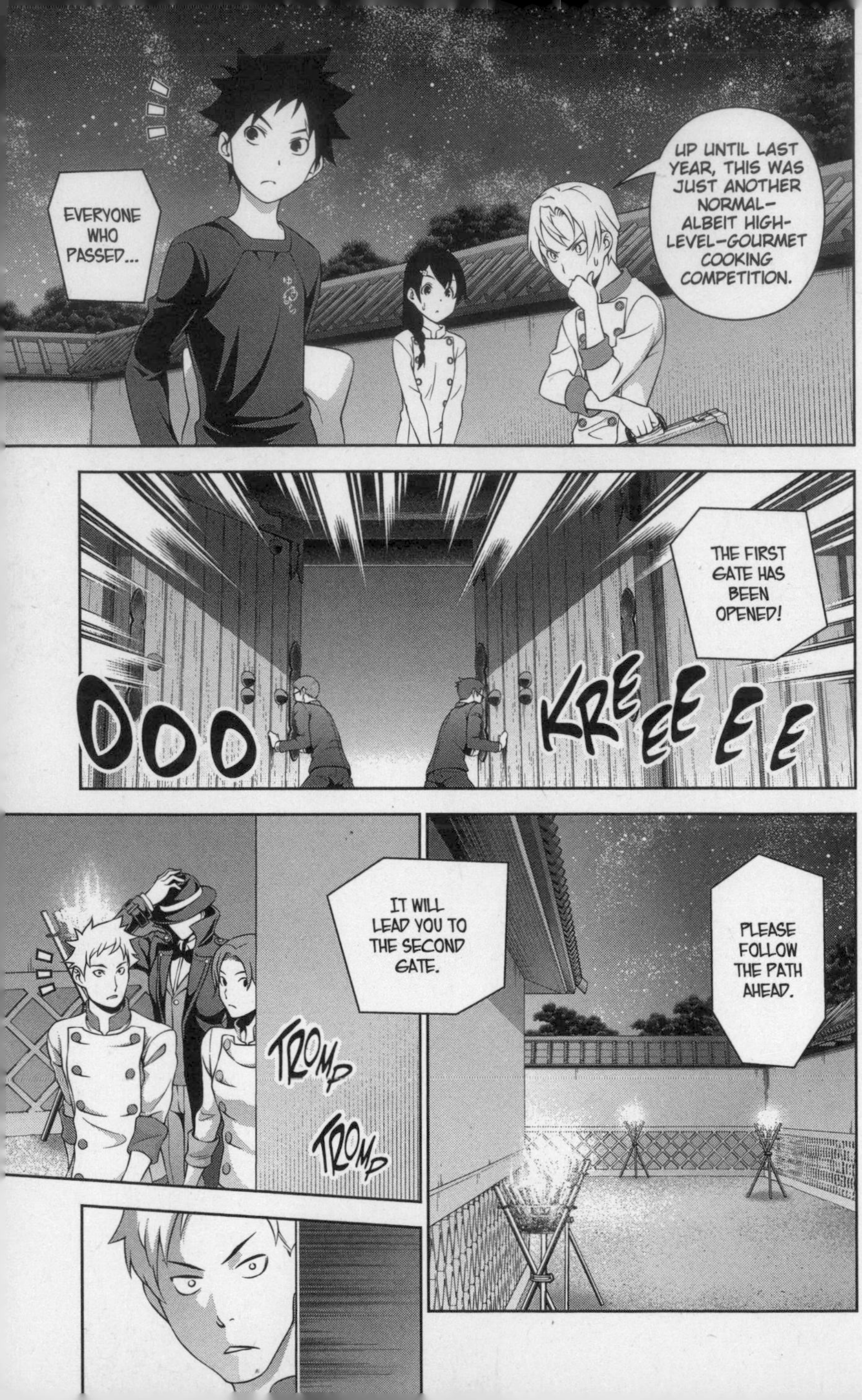
UP UNTIL LAST YEAR, THIS WAS JUST ANOTHER NORMAL—ALBEIT HIGH-LEVEL—GOURMET COOKING COMPETITION.
EVERYONE WHO PASSED...
THE FIRST GATE HAS BEEN OPENED!
DOOO KREEEEE
PLEASE FOLLOW THE PATH AHEAD.
IT WILL LEAD YOU TO THE SECOND GATE.
TROMP
TROMP

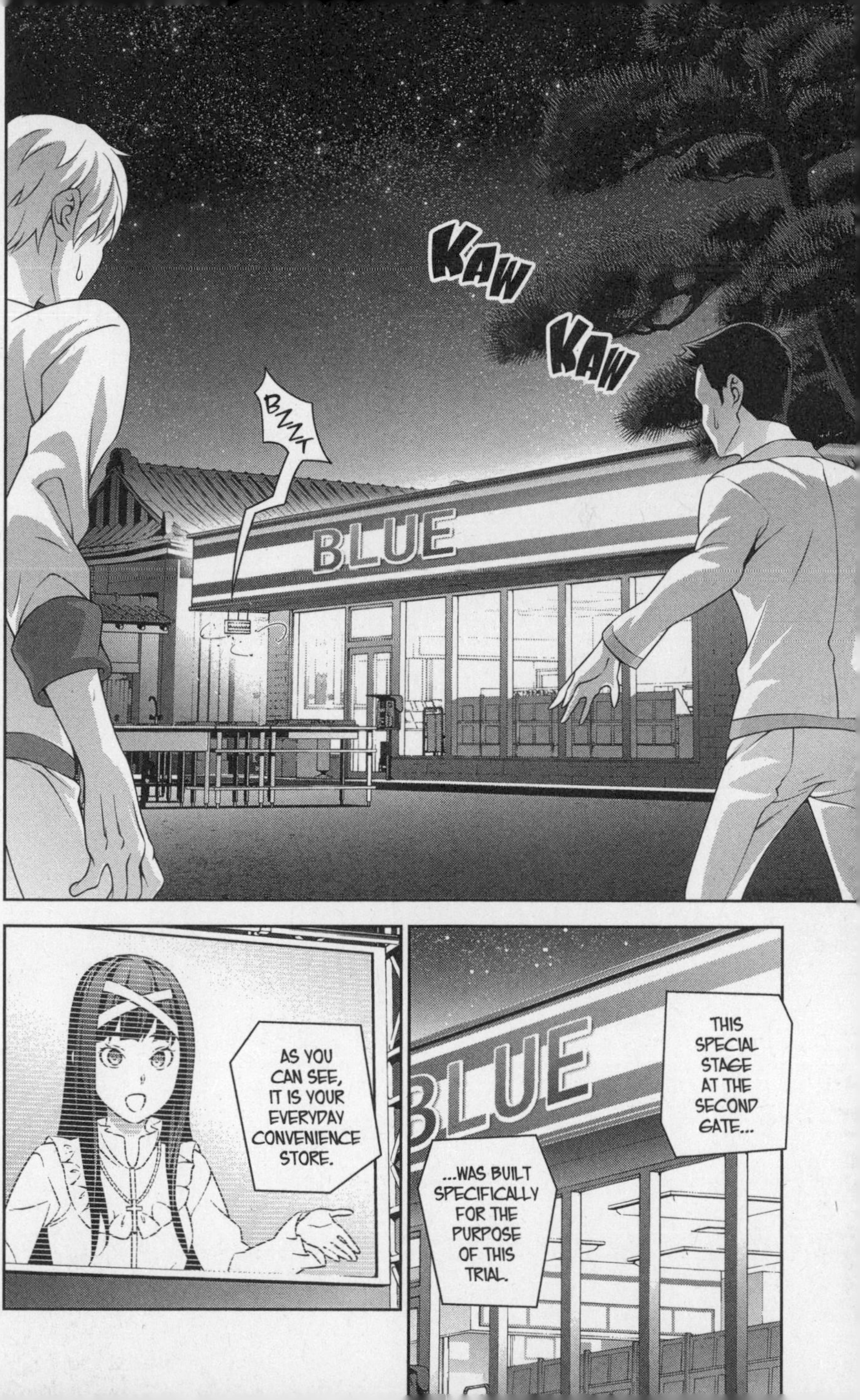
KAW
KAW
BZZZT
BLUE
BLUE
THIS SPECIAL STAGE AT THE SECOND GATE...
...WAS BUILT SPECIFICALLY FOR THE PURPOSE OF THIS TRIAL.
AS YOU CAN SEE, IT IS YOUR EVERYDAY CONVENIENCE STORE.

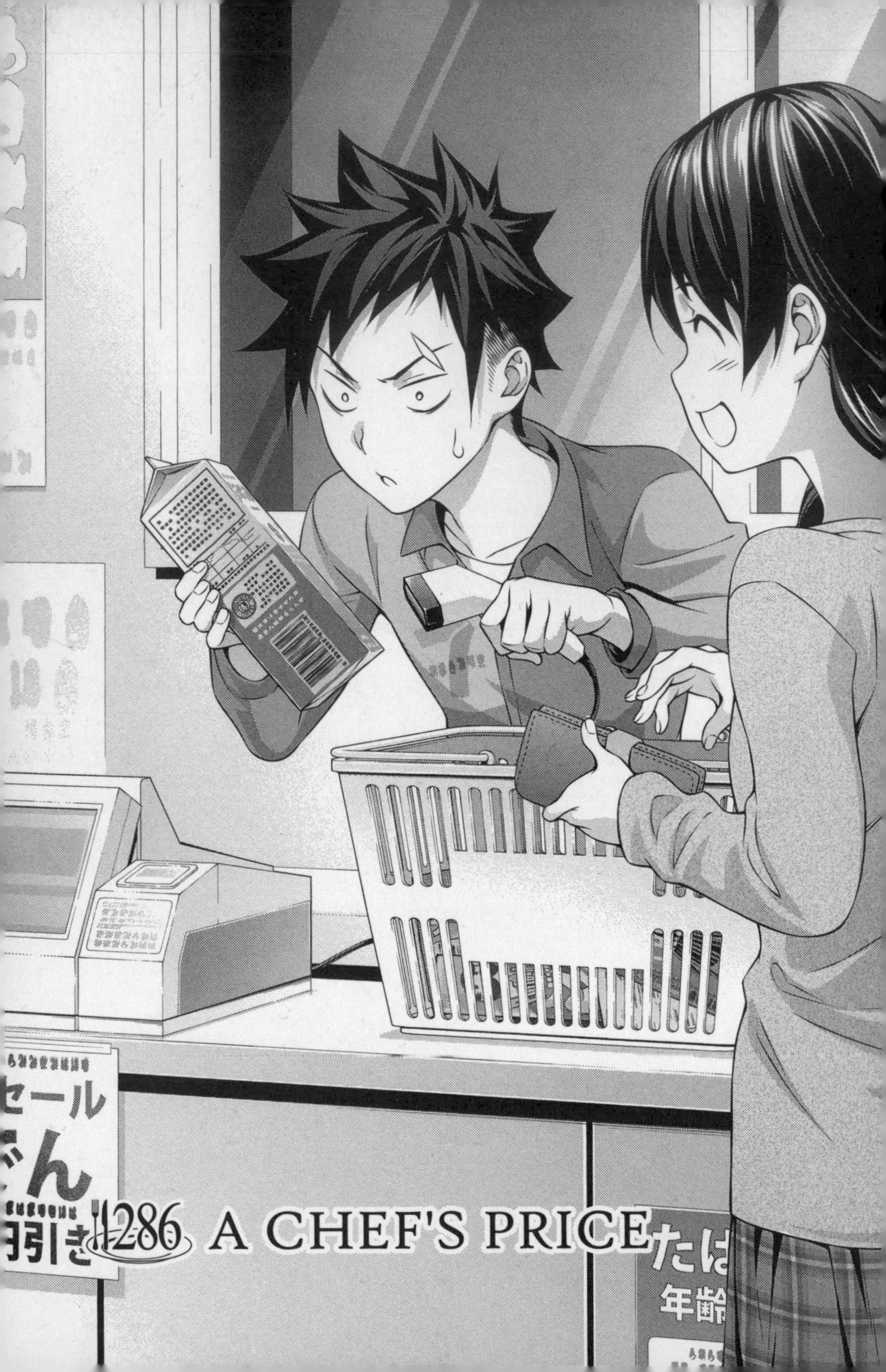
セール
ん
引き
286 A CHEF'S PRICE
たは
年齢

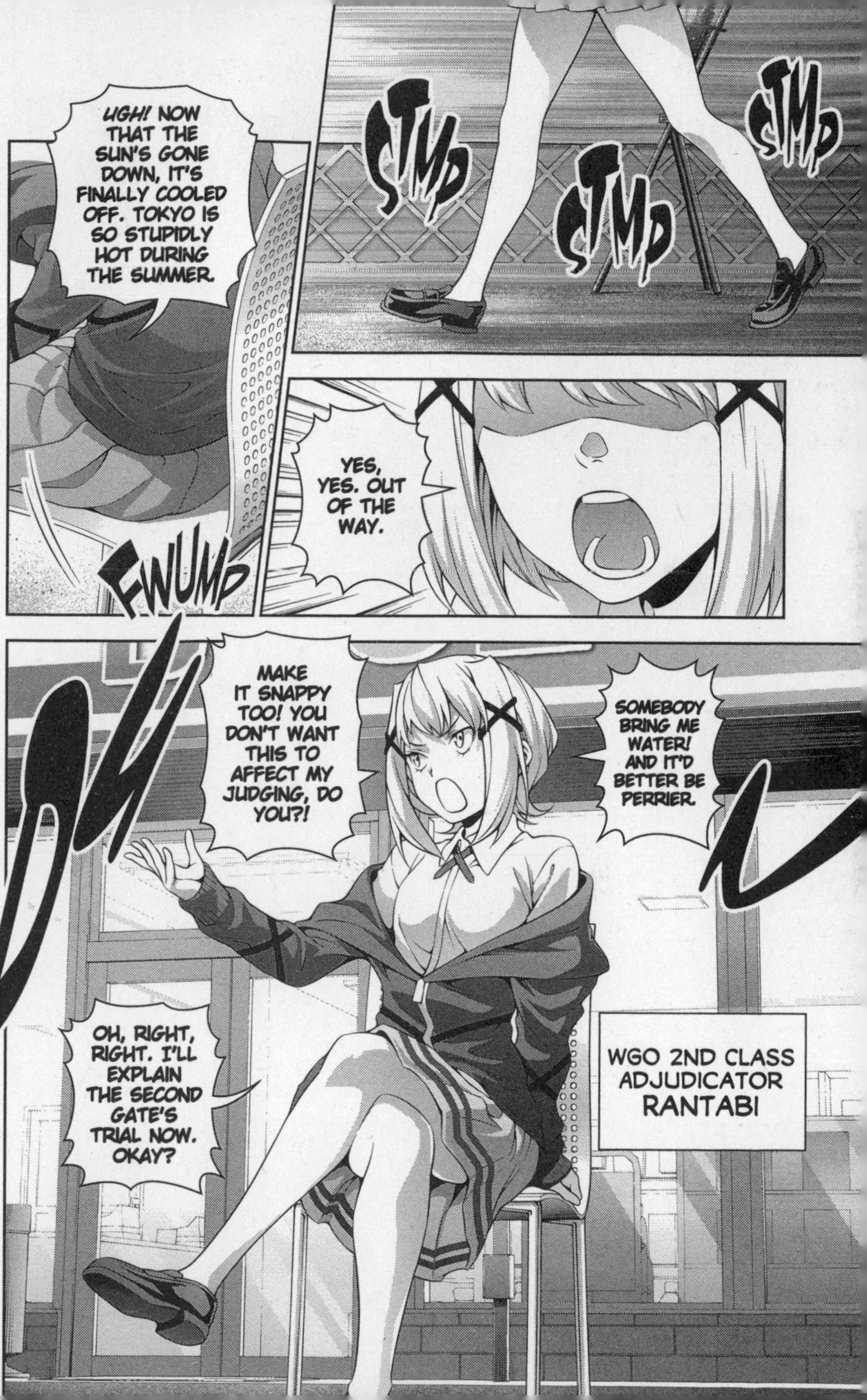
STMP
STMP
STMP
YES, YES. OUT OF THE WAY.
UGH! NOW THAT THE SUN'S GONE DOWN, IT'S FINALLY COOLED OFF. TOKYO IS SO STUPIDLY HOT DURING THE SUMMER.
FWUMP
SOMEBODY BRING ME WATER! AND IT'D BETTER BE PERRIER.
MAKE IT SNAPPY TOO! YOU DON'T WANT THIS TO AFFECT MY JUDGING, DO YOU?!
WGO 2ND CLASS ADJUDICATOR RANTABI
OH, RIGHT, RIGHT. I'LL EXPLAIN THE SECOND GATE'S TRIAL NOW. OKAY?

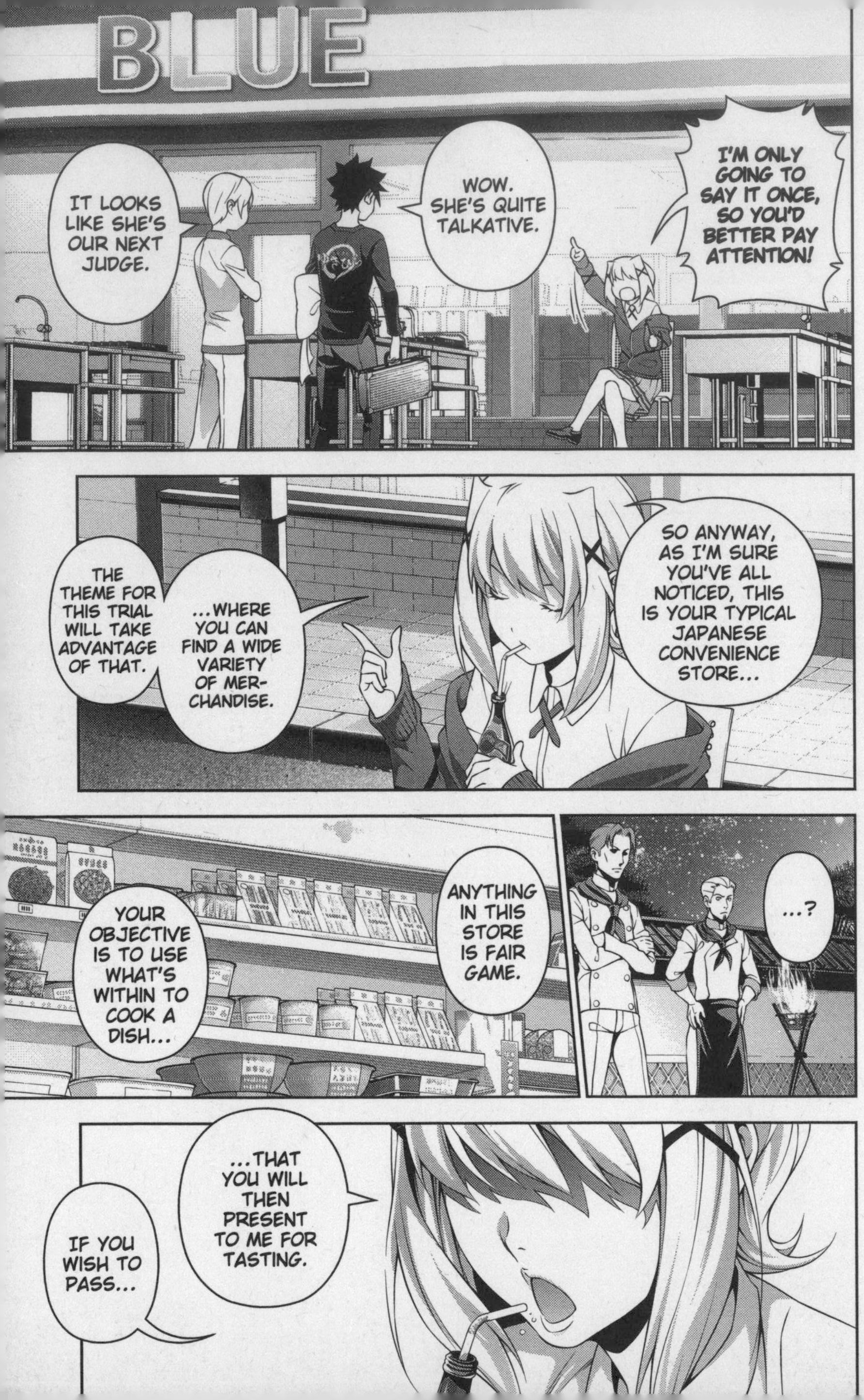
BLUE
I'M ONLY GOING TO SAY IT ONCE, SO YOU'D BETTER PAY ATTENTION!
WOW. SHE'S QUITE TALKATIVE.
IT LOOKS LIKE SHE'S OUR NEXT JUDGE.
SO ANYWAY, AS I'M SURE YOU'VE ALL NOTICED, THIS IS YOUR TYPICAL JAPANESE CONVENIENCE STORE...
...WHERE YOU CAN FIND A WIDE VARIETY OF MER-CHANDISE.
THE THEME FOR THIS TRIAL WILL TAKE ADVANTAGE OF THAT.
...?
ANYTHING IN THIS STORE IS FAIR GAME.
YOUR OBJECTIVE IS TO USE WHAT'S WITHIN TO COOK A DISH...
...THAT YOU WILL THEN PRESENT TO ME FOR TASTING.
IF YOU WISH TO PASS...

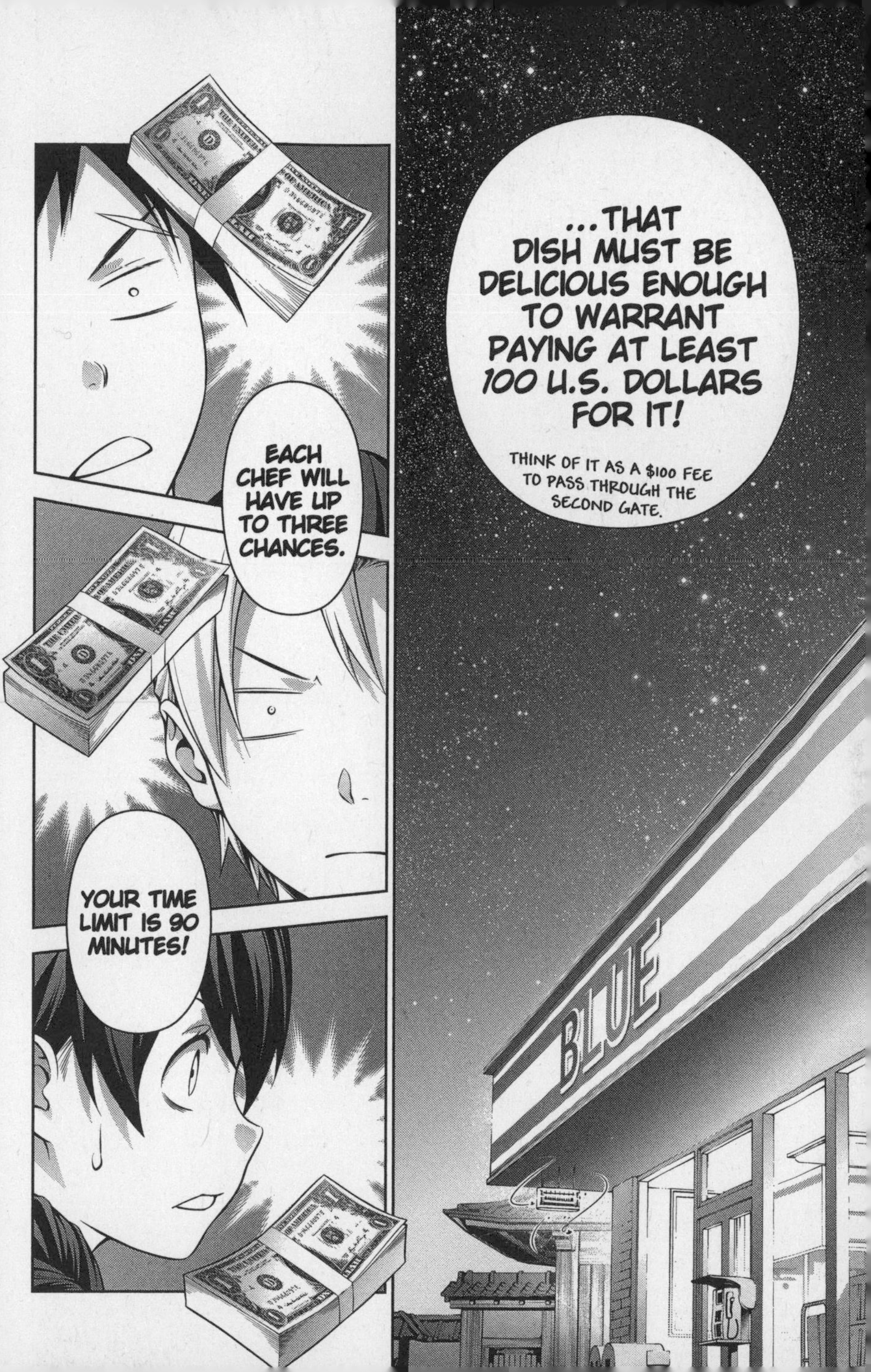
...THAT DISH MUST BE DELICIOUS ENOUGH TO WARRANT PAYING AT LEAST 100 U.S. DOLLARS FOR IT!
THINK OF IT AS A $100 FEE TO PASS THROUGH THE SECOND GATE.
BLUE
EACH CHEF WILL HAVE UP TO THREE CHANCES.
YOUR TIME LIMIT IS 90 MINUTES!

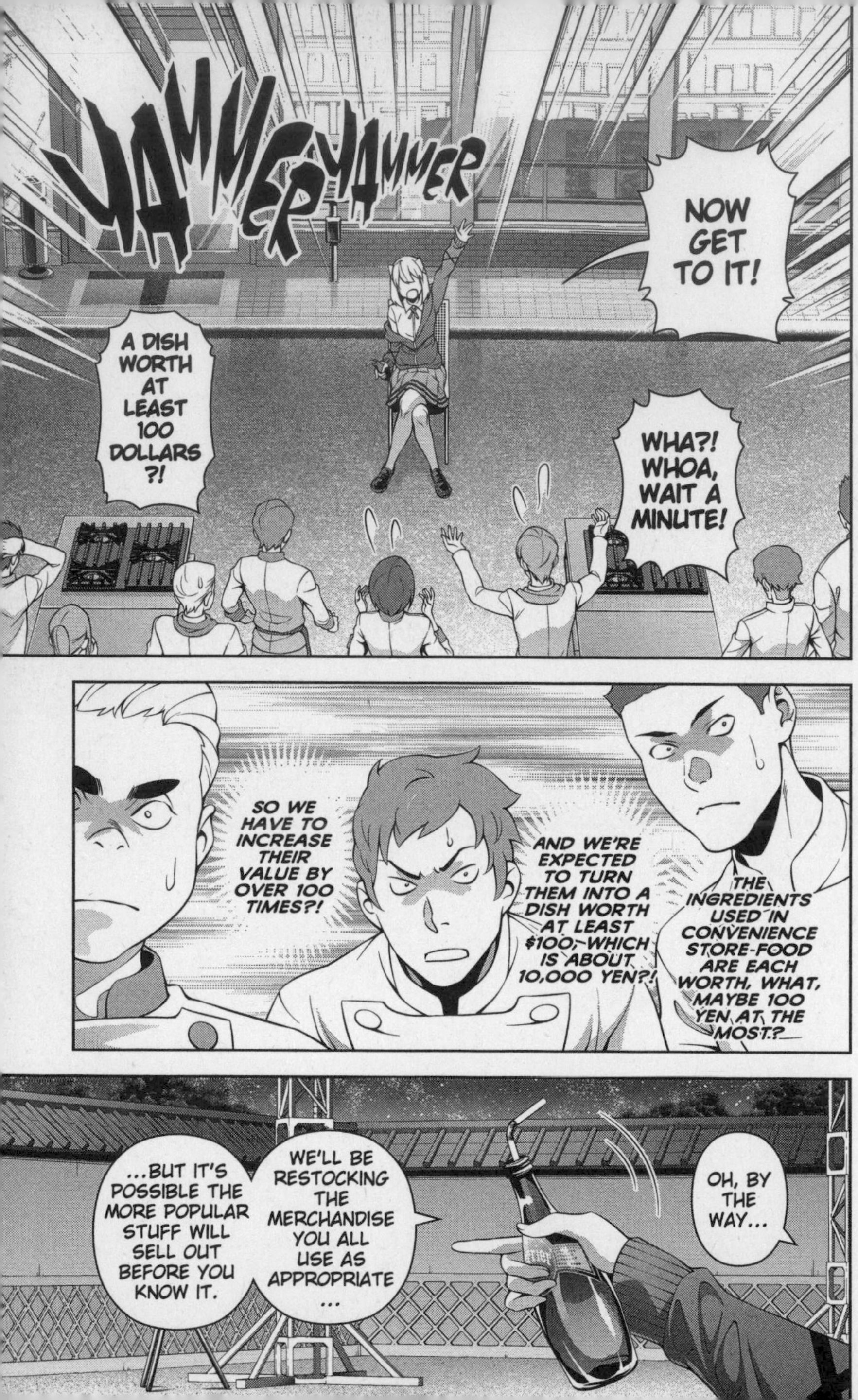
NOW GET TO IT!
YAMMER YAMMER
WHA?! WHOA, WAIT A MINUTE!
A DISH WORTH AT LEAST 100 DOLLARS?!
THE INGREDIENTS USED IN CONVENIENCE STORE-FOOD ARE EACH WORTH, WHAT, MAYBE 100 YEN AT THE MOST?
AND WE'RE EXPECTED TO TURN THEM INTO A DISH WORTH AT LEAST $100, WHICH IS ABOUT 10,000 YEN?!
SO WE HAVE TO INCREASE THEIR VALUE BY OVER 100 TIMES?!
OH, BY THE WAY...
WE'LL BE RESTOCKING THE MERCHANDISE YOU ALL USE AS APPROPRIATE...
...BUT IT'S POSSIBLE THE MORE POPULAR STUFF WILL SELL OUT BEFORE YOU KNOW IT.

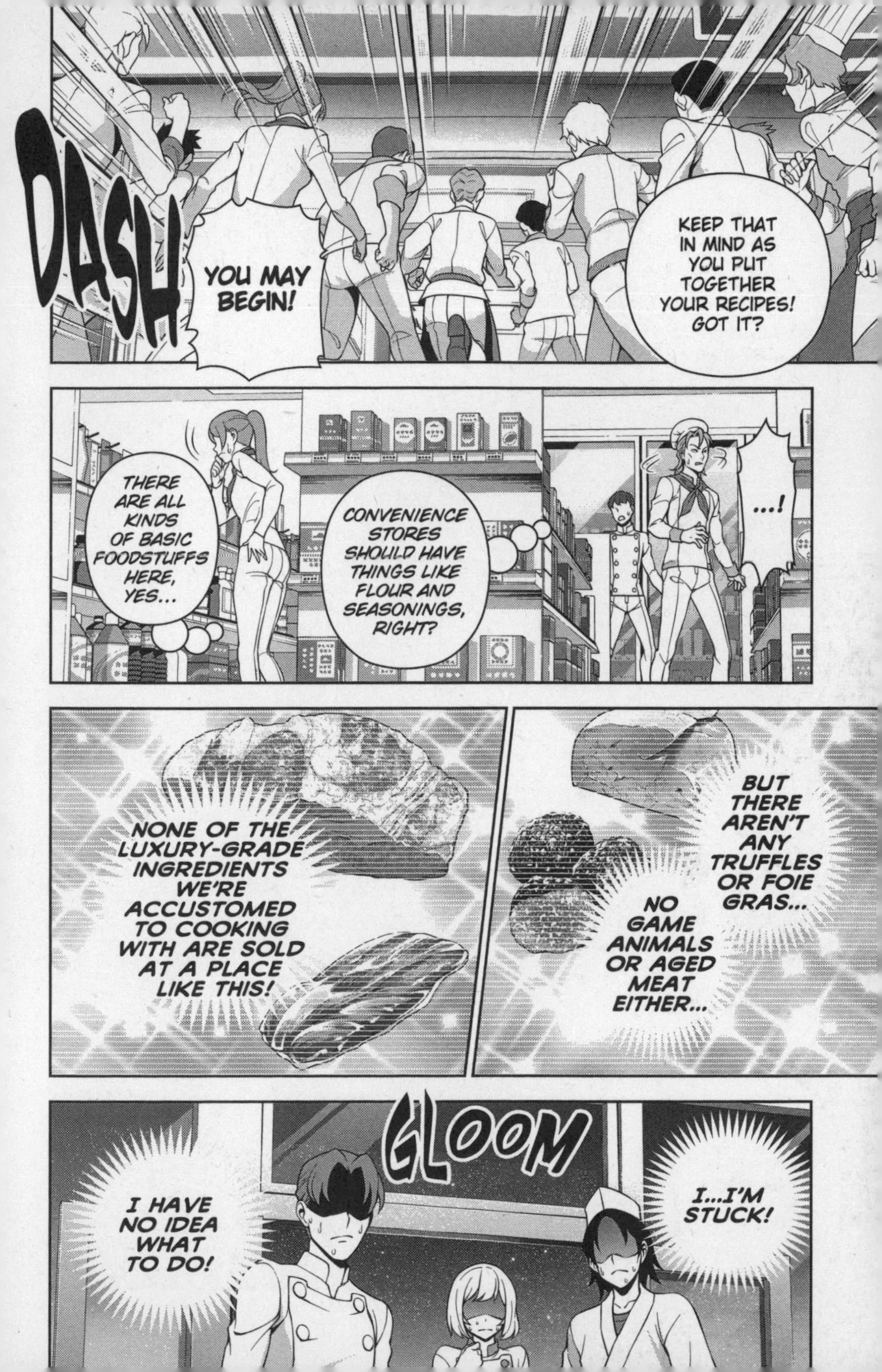
KEEP THAT IN MIND AS YOU PUT TOGETHER YOUR RECIPES! GOT IT?
YOU MAY BEGIN!
DASH
...!
CONVENIENCE STORES SHOULD HAVE THINGS LIKE FLOUR AND SEASONINGS, RIGHT?
THERE ARE ALL KINDS OF BASIC FOODSTUFFS HERE, YES...
BUT THERE AREN'T ANY TRUFFLES OR FOIE GRAS...
NO GAME ANIMALS OR AGED MEAT EITHER...
NONE OF THE LUXURY-GRADE INGREDIENTS WE'RE ACCUSTOMED TO COOKING WITH ARE SOLD AT A PLACE LIKE THIS!
GLOOM
I...I'M STUCK!
I HAVE NO IDEA WHAT TO DO!

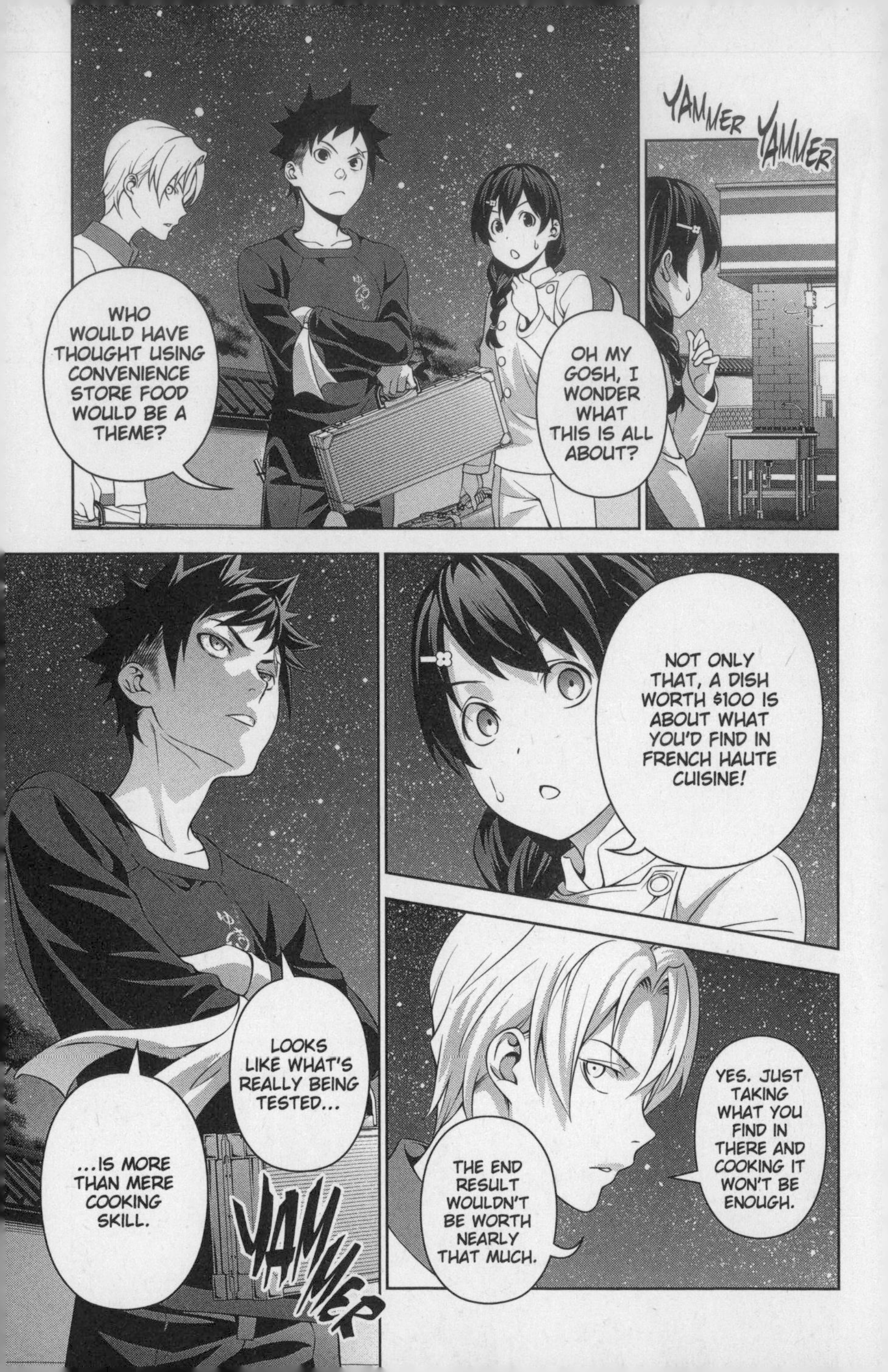
YAMMER YAMMER
OH MY GOSH, I WONDER WHAT THIS IS ALL ABOUT?
WHO WOULD HAVE THOUGHT USING CONVENIENCE STORE FOOD WOULD BE A THEME?
NOT ONLY THAT, A DISH WORTH $100 IS ABOUT WHAT YOU'D FIND IN FRENCH HAUTE CUISINE!
YES. JUST TAKING WHAT YOU FIND IN THERE AND COOKING IT WON'T BE ENOUGH.
THE END RESULT WOULDN'T BE WORTH NEARLY THAT MUCH.
LOOKS LIKE WHAT'S REALLY BEING TESTED...
...IS MORE THAN MERE COOKING SKILL.
YAMMER

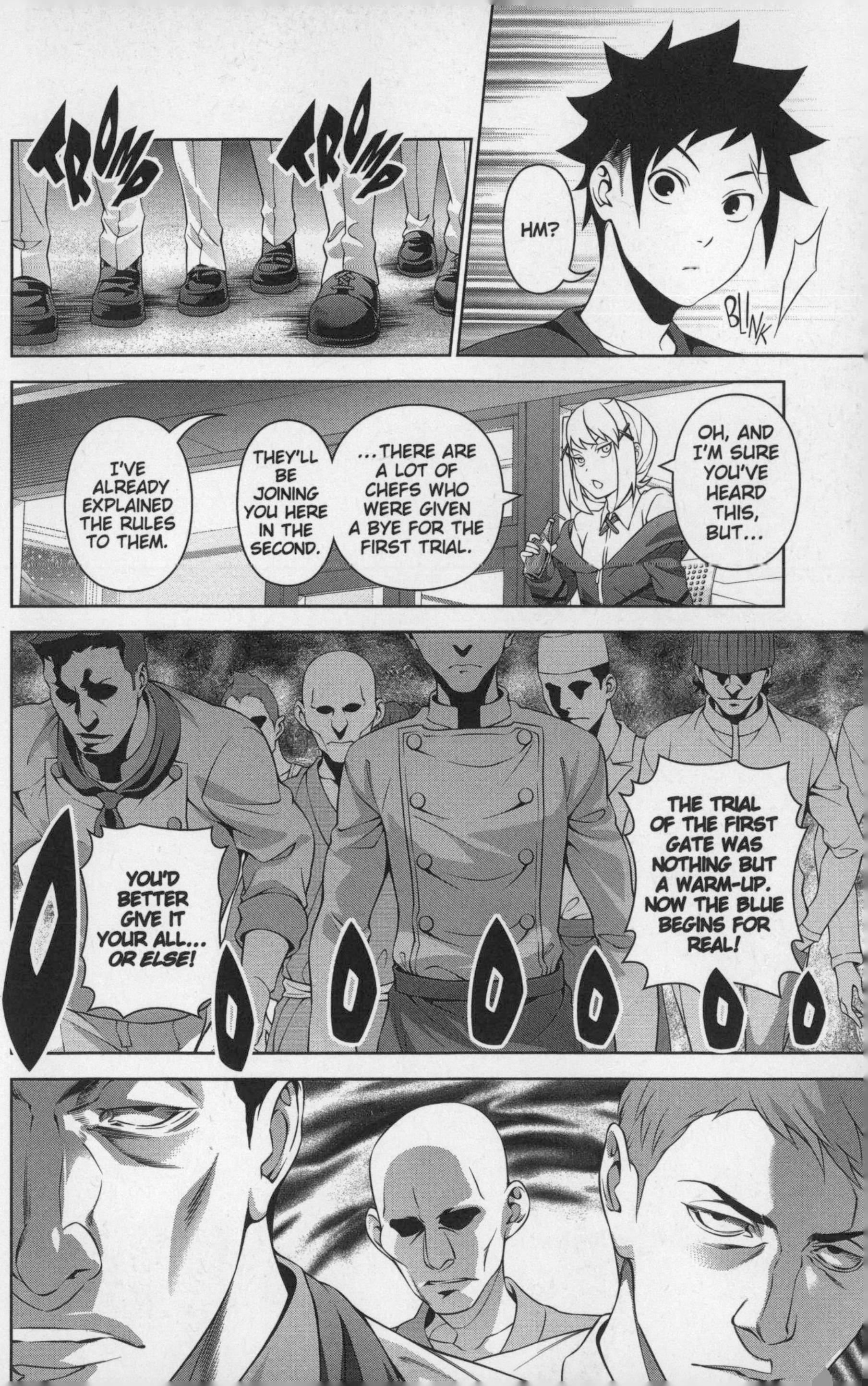
HM?
BLINK
TROMP
TROMP
OH, AND I'M SURE YOU'VE HEARD THIS, BUT...
...THERE ARE A LOT OF CHEFS WHO WERE GIVEN A BYE FOR THE FIRST TRIAL.
THEY'LL BE JOINING YOU HERE IN THE SECOND.
I'VE ALREADY EXPLAINED THE RULES TO THEM.
THE TRIAL OF THE FIRST GATE WAS NOTHING BUT A WARM-UP. NOW THE BLUE BEGINS FOR REAL!
YOU'D BETTER GIVE IT YOUR ALL... OR ELSE!

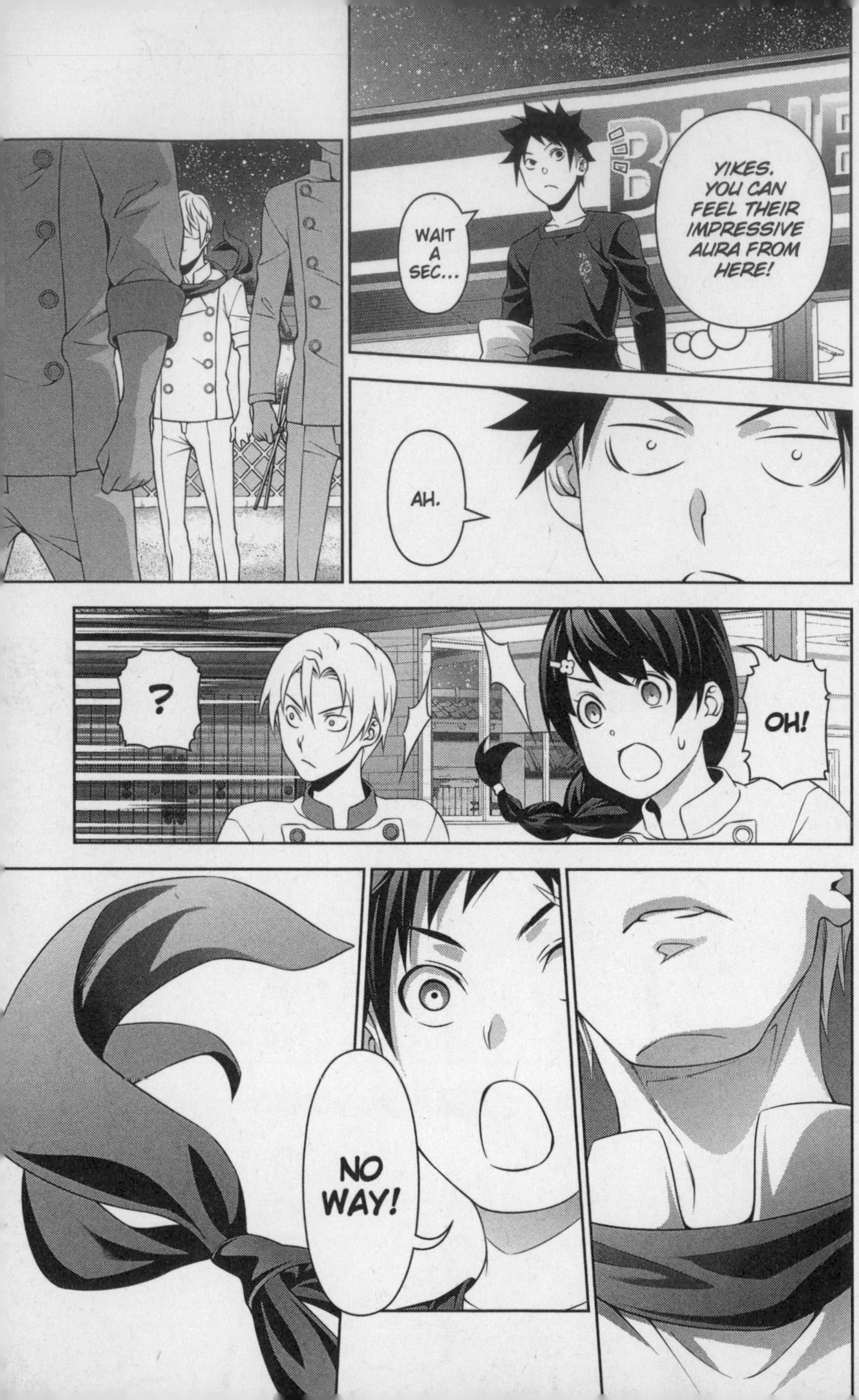
YIKES. YOU CAN FEEL THEIR IMPRESSIVE AURA FROM HERE!
WAIT A SEC...
AH.
OH!
?
NO WAY!

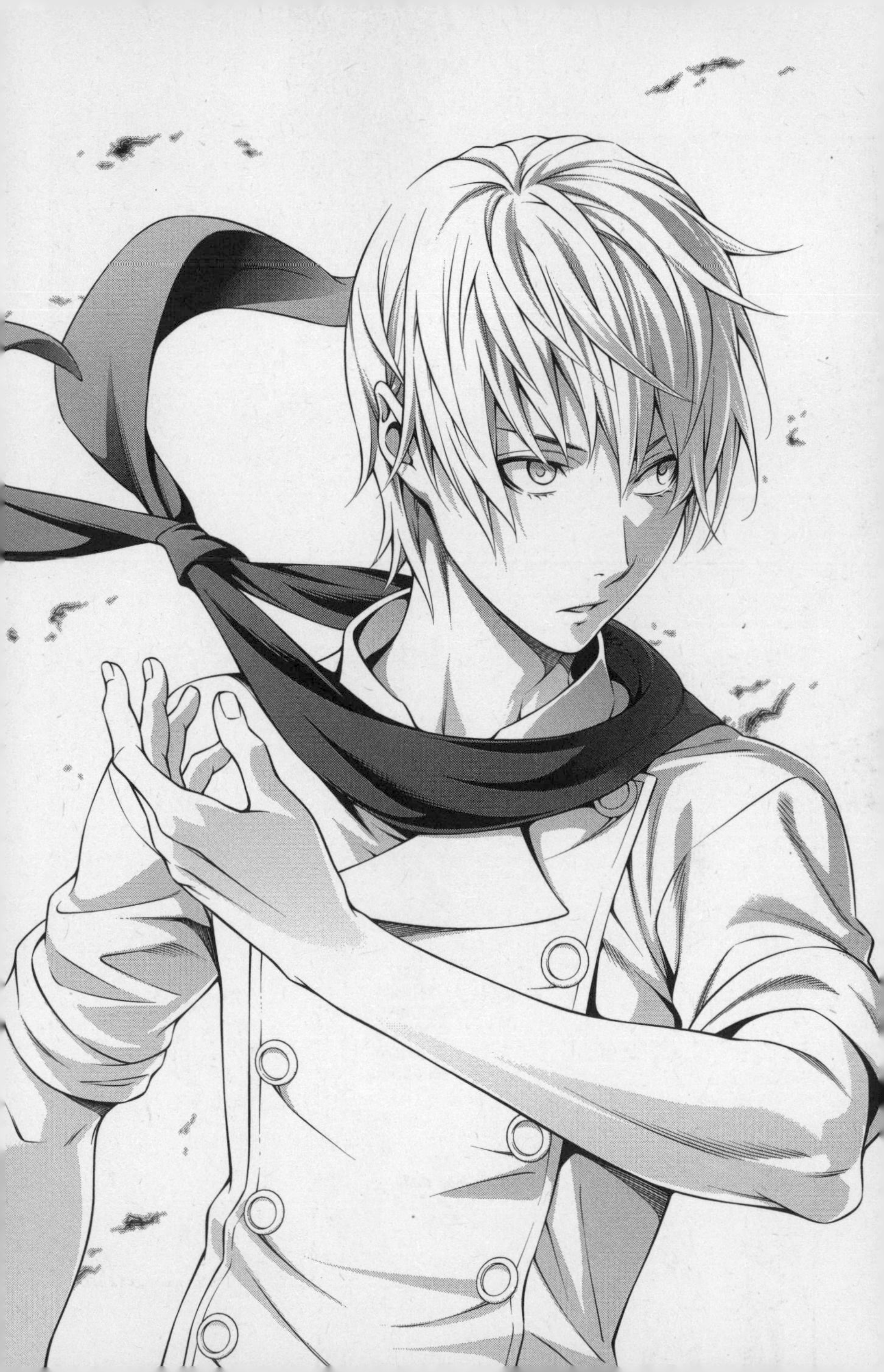

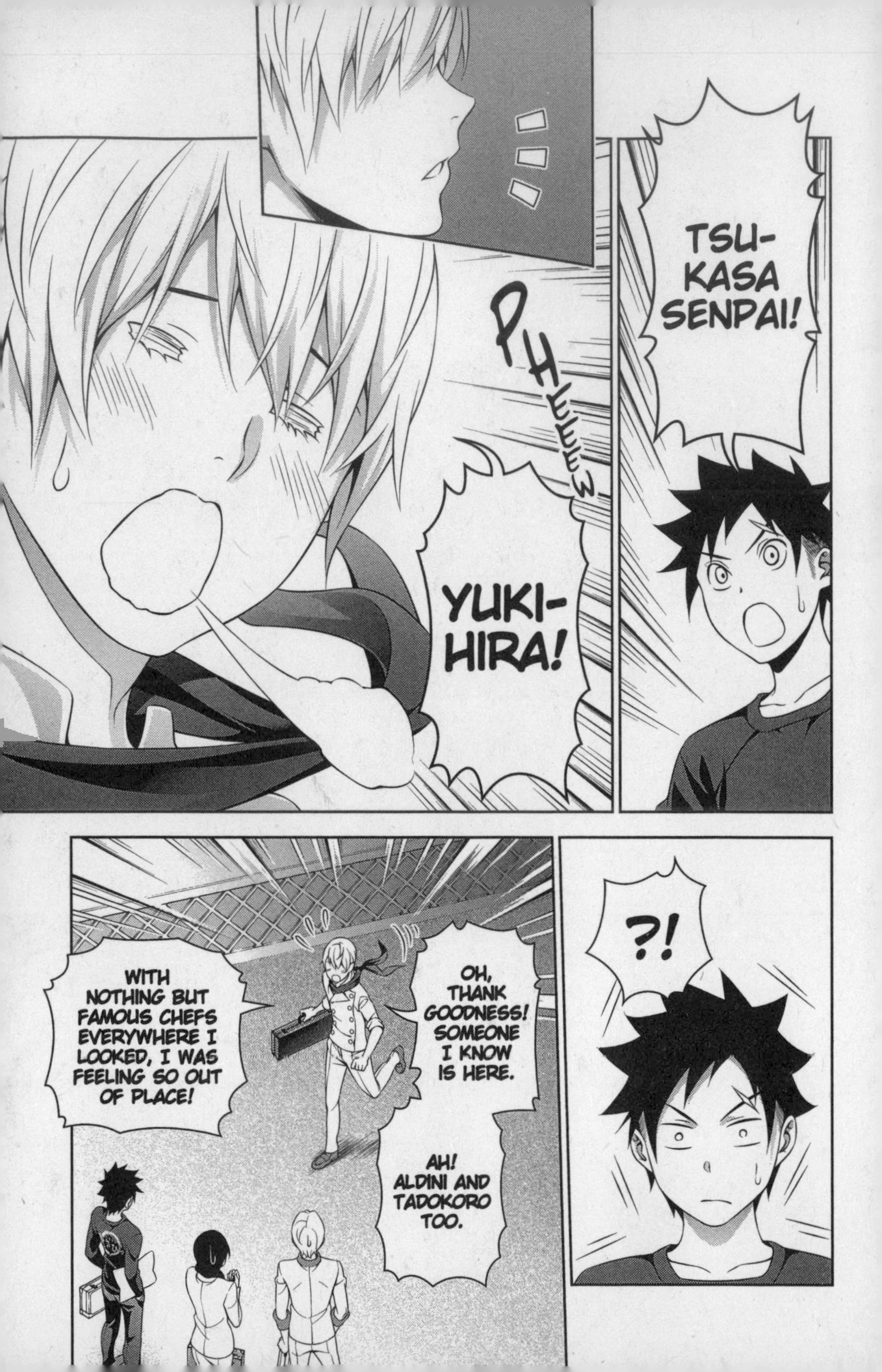
TSU-
KASA
SENPAI!
...
PHEEEW
YUKI-
HIRA!
?!
OH, THANK GOODNESS! SOMEONE I KNOW IS HERE.
WITH NOTHING BUT FAMOUS CHEFS EVERYWHERE I LOOKED, I WAS FEELING SO OUT OF PLACE!
AH! ALDINI AND TADOKORO TOO.

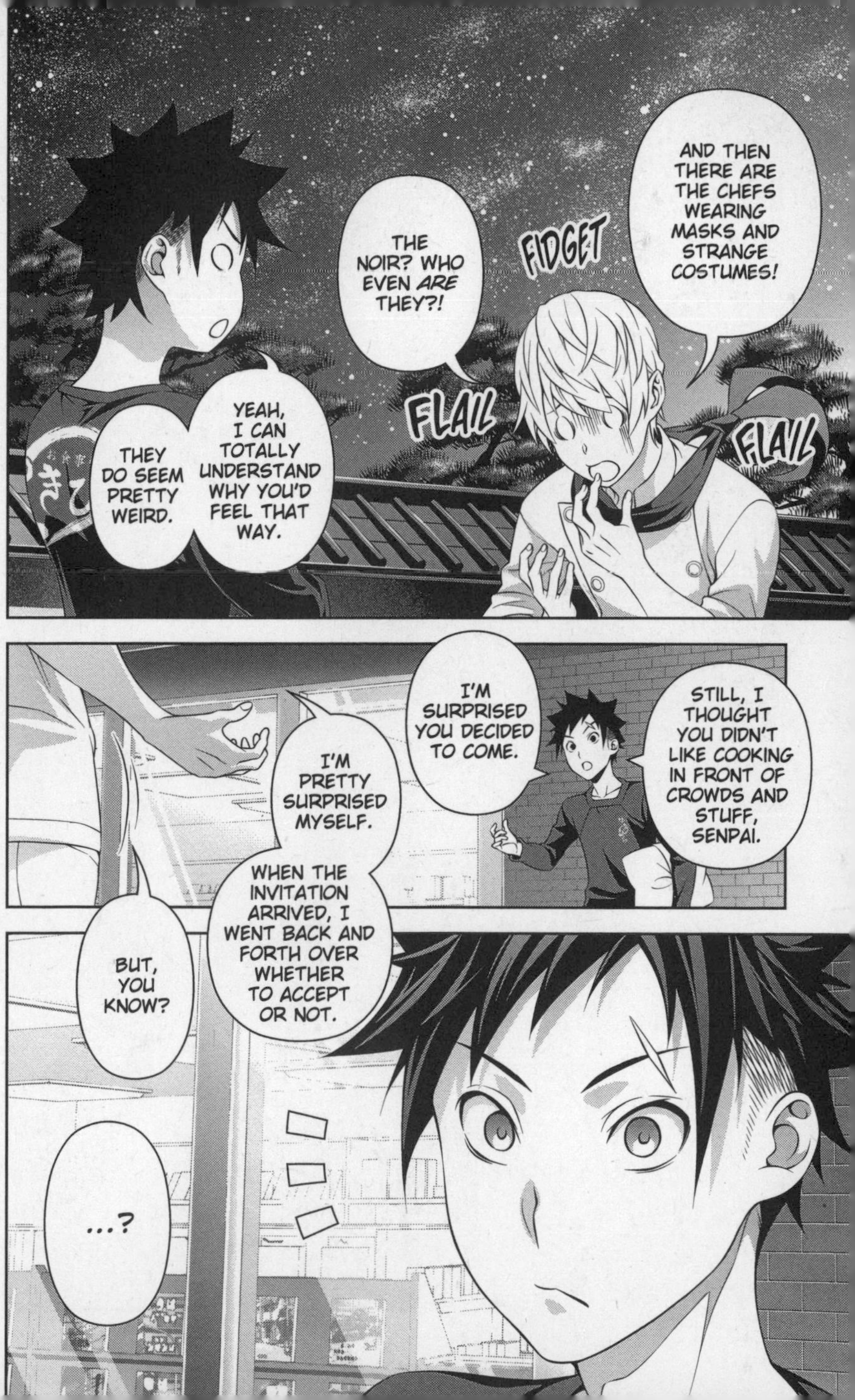
AND THEN THERE ARE THE CHEFS WEARING MASKS AND STRANGE COSTUMES!
FIDGET
FLAIL
THE NOIR? WHO EVEN *ARE* THEY?!
FLAIL
YEAH, I CAN TOTALLY UNDERSTAND WHY YOU'D FEEL THAT WAY.
THEY DO SEEM PRETTY WEIRD.
STILL, I THOUGHT YOU DIDN'T LIKE COOKING IN FRONT OF CROWDS AND STUFF, SENPAI.
I'M SURPRISED YOU DECIDED TO COME.
I'M PRETTY SURPRISED MYSELF.
WHEN THE INVITATION ARRIVED, I WENT BACK AND FORTH OVER WHETHER TO ACCEPT OR NOT.
BUT, YOU KNOW?
...?

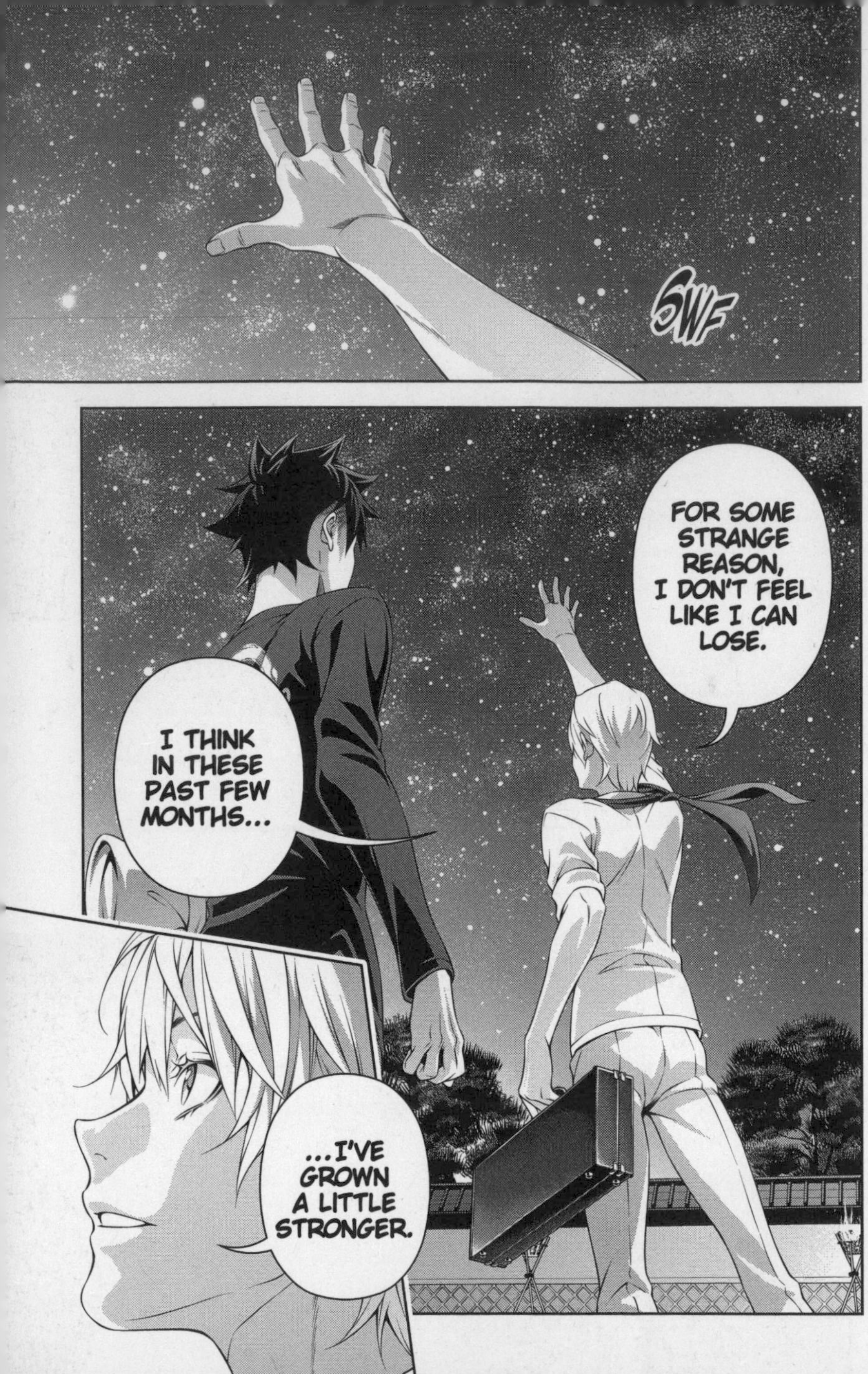
SWF
FOR SOME STRANGE REASON, I DON'T FEEL LIKE I CAN LOSE.
I THINK IN THESE PAST FEW MONTHS...
...I'VE GROWN A LITTLE STRONGER.

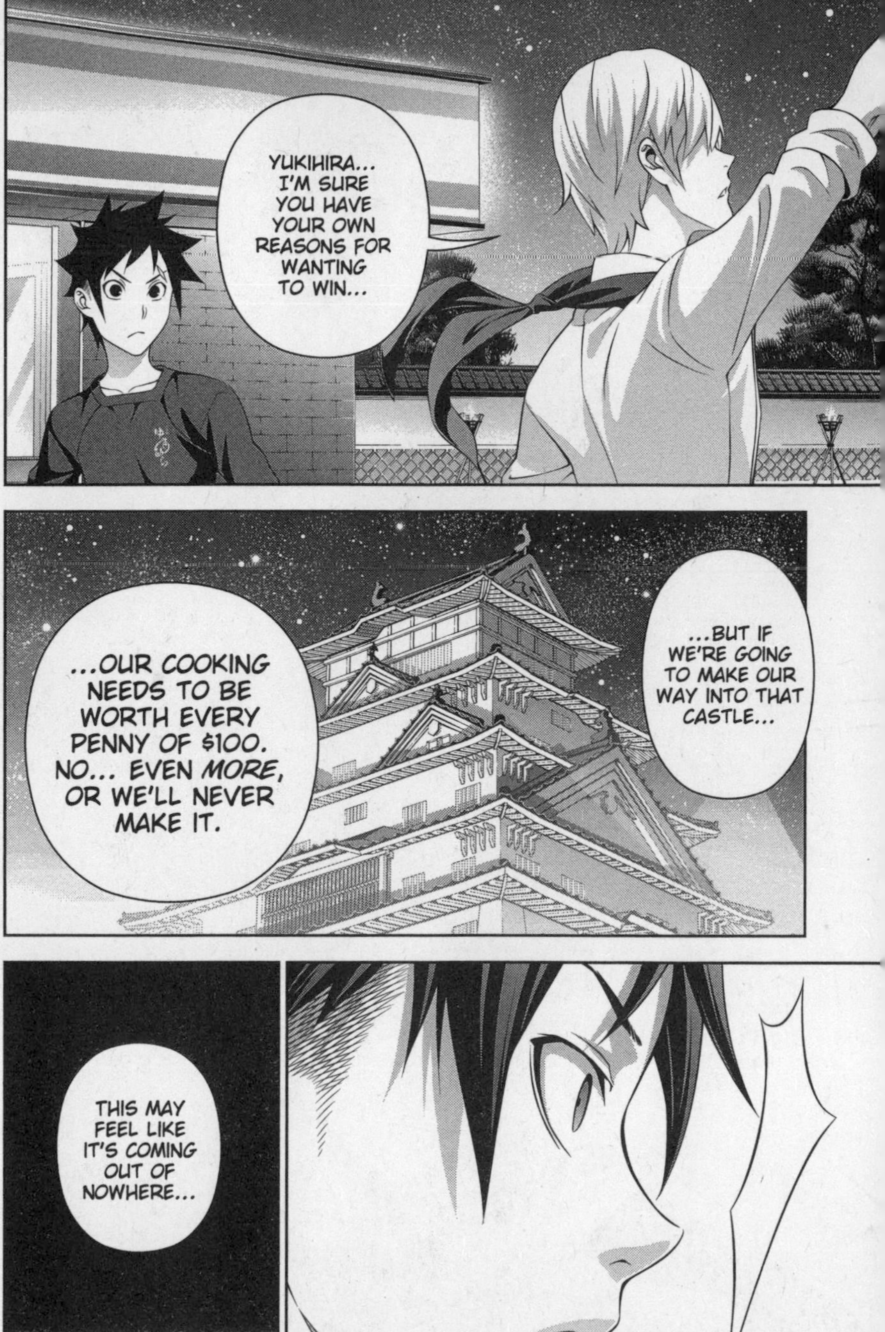
YUKIHIRA... I'M SURE YOU HAVE YOUR OWN REASONS FOR WANTING TO WIN...
...BUT IF WE'RE GOING TO MAKE OUR WAY INTO THAT CASTLE...
...OUR COOKING NEEDS TO BE WORTH EVERY PENNY OF $100. NO... EVEN *MORE*, OR WE'LL NEVER MAKE IT.
THIS MAY FEEL LIKE IT'S COMING OUT OF NOWHERE...

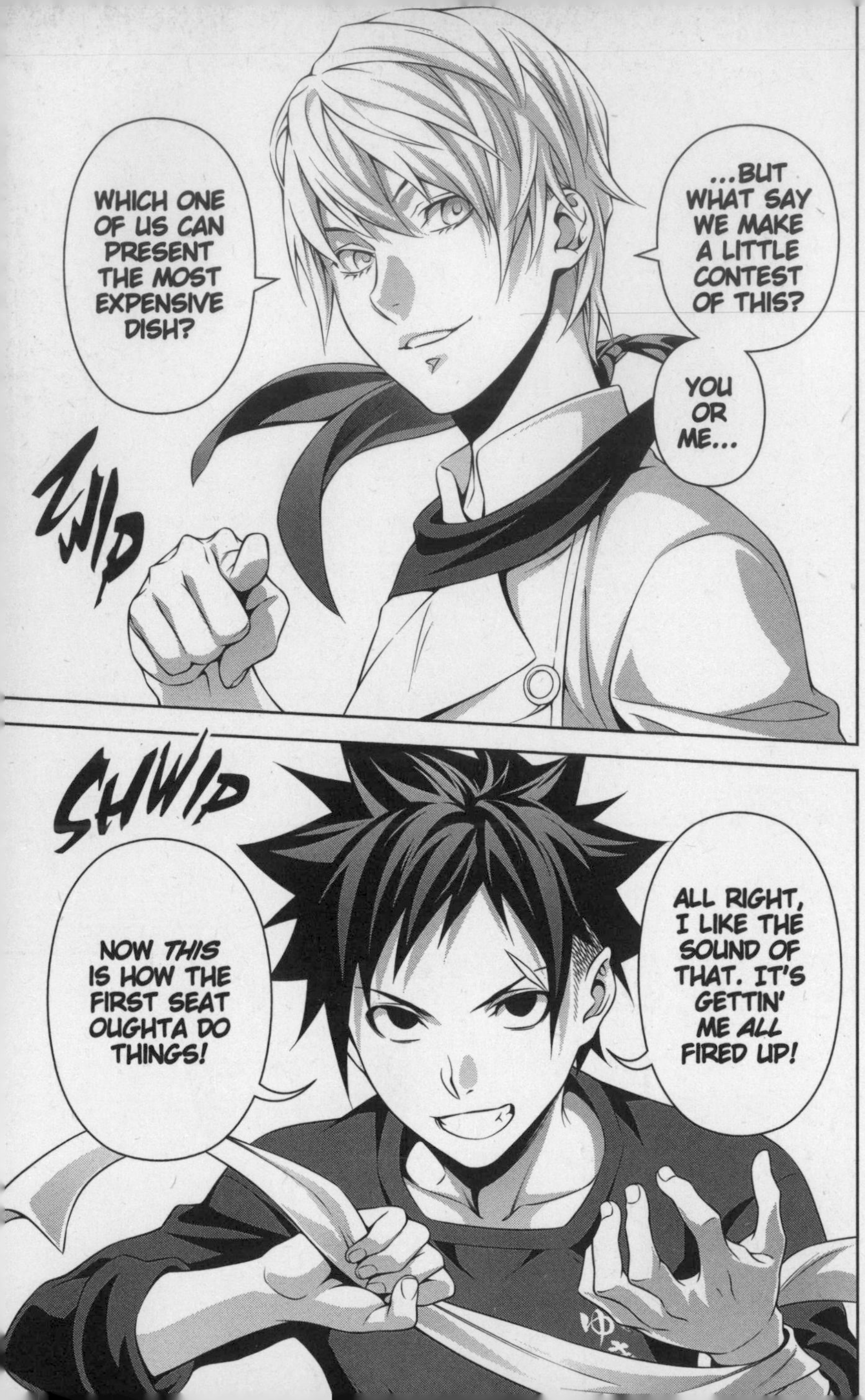
...BUT WHAT SAY WE MAKE A LITTLE CONTEST OF THIS?
YOU OR ME...
WHICH ONE OF US CAN PRESENT THE MOST EXPENSIVE DISH?
ZWIP
ALL RIGHT, I LIKE THE SOUND OF THAT. IT'S GETTIN' ME *ALL* FIRED UP!
SHWIP
NOW *THIS* IS HOW THE FIRST SEAT OUGHTA DO THINGS!

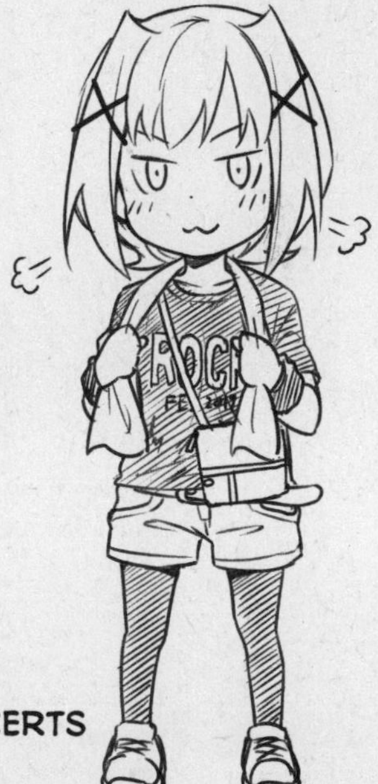
ROCK

MISS RANTABI (24)

HOBBIES: ATTENDING ROCK CONCERTS

287 CONVENIENCE STORE BRAWL

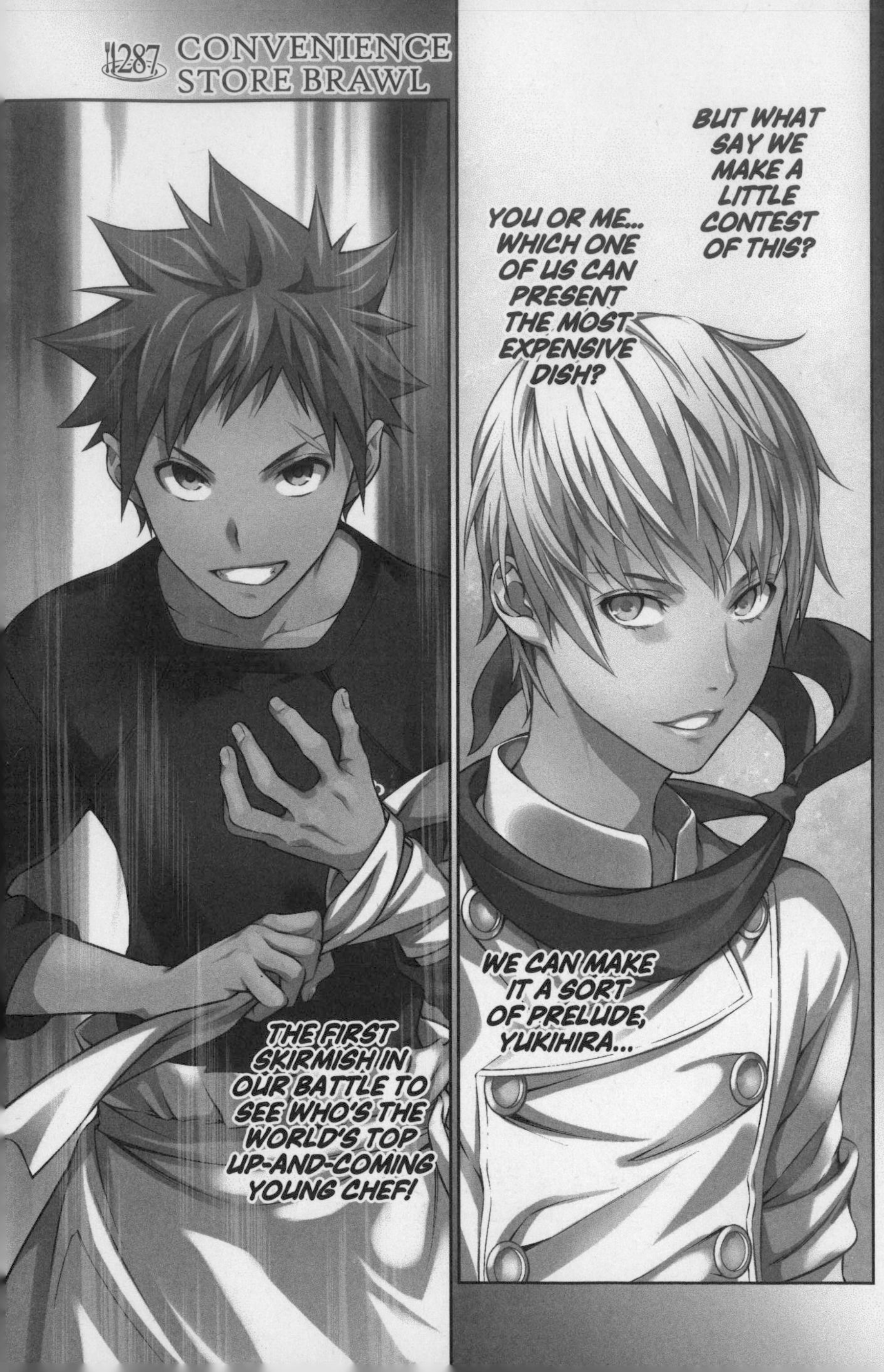
BUT WHAT SAY WE MAKE A LITTLE CONTEST OF THIS?
YOU OR ME... WHICH ONE OF US CAN PRESENT THE MOST EXPENSIVE DISH?
WE CAN MAKE IT A SORT OF PRELUDE, YUKIHIRA...
THE FIRST SKIRMISH IN OUR BATTLE TO SEE WHO'S THE WORLD'S TOP UP-AND-COMING YOUNG CHEF!

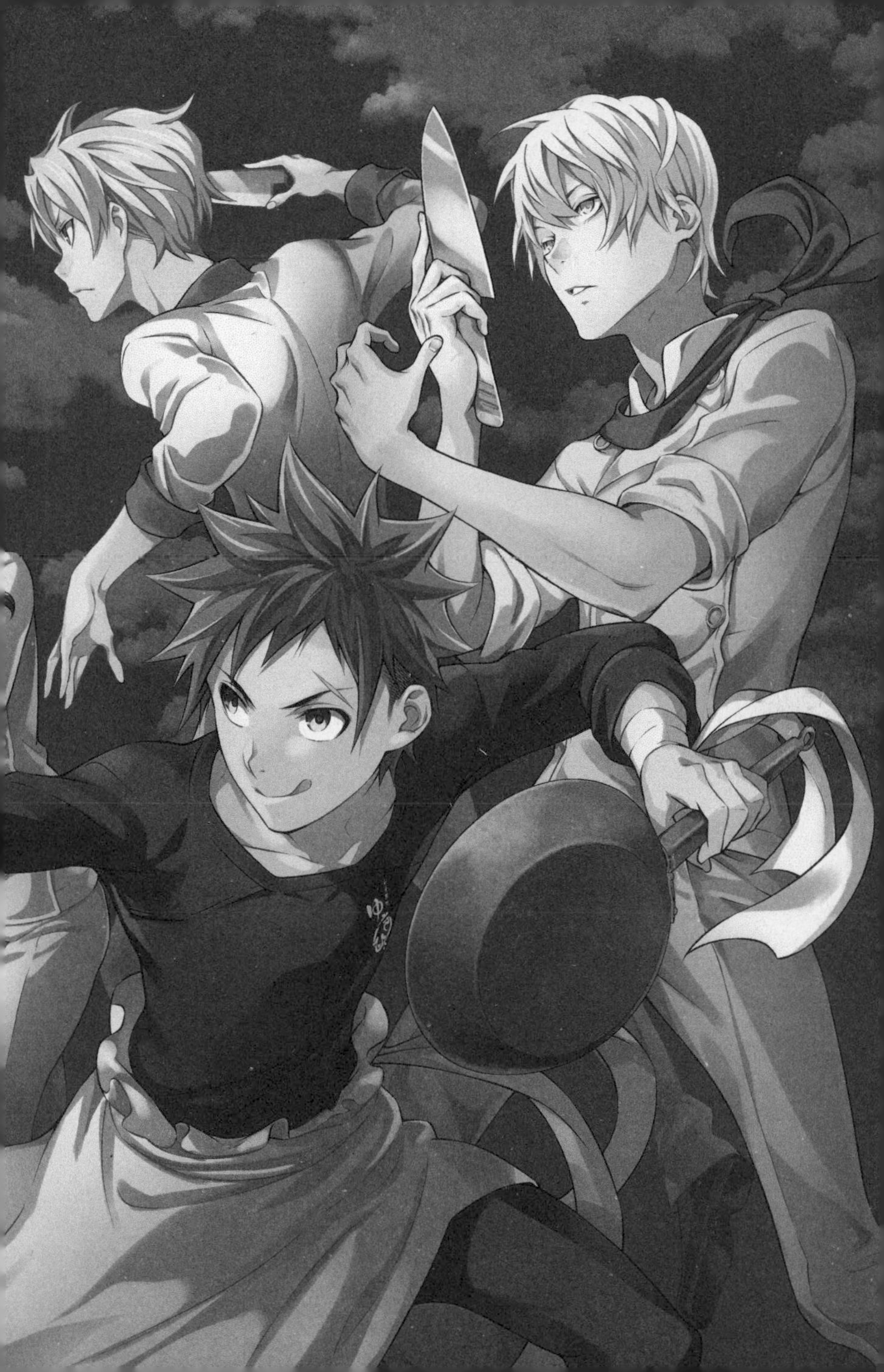

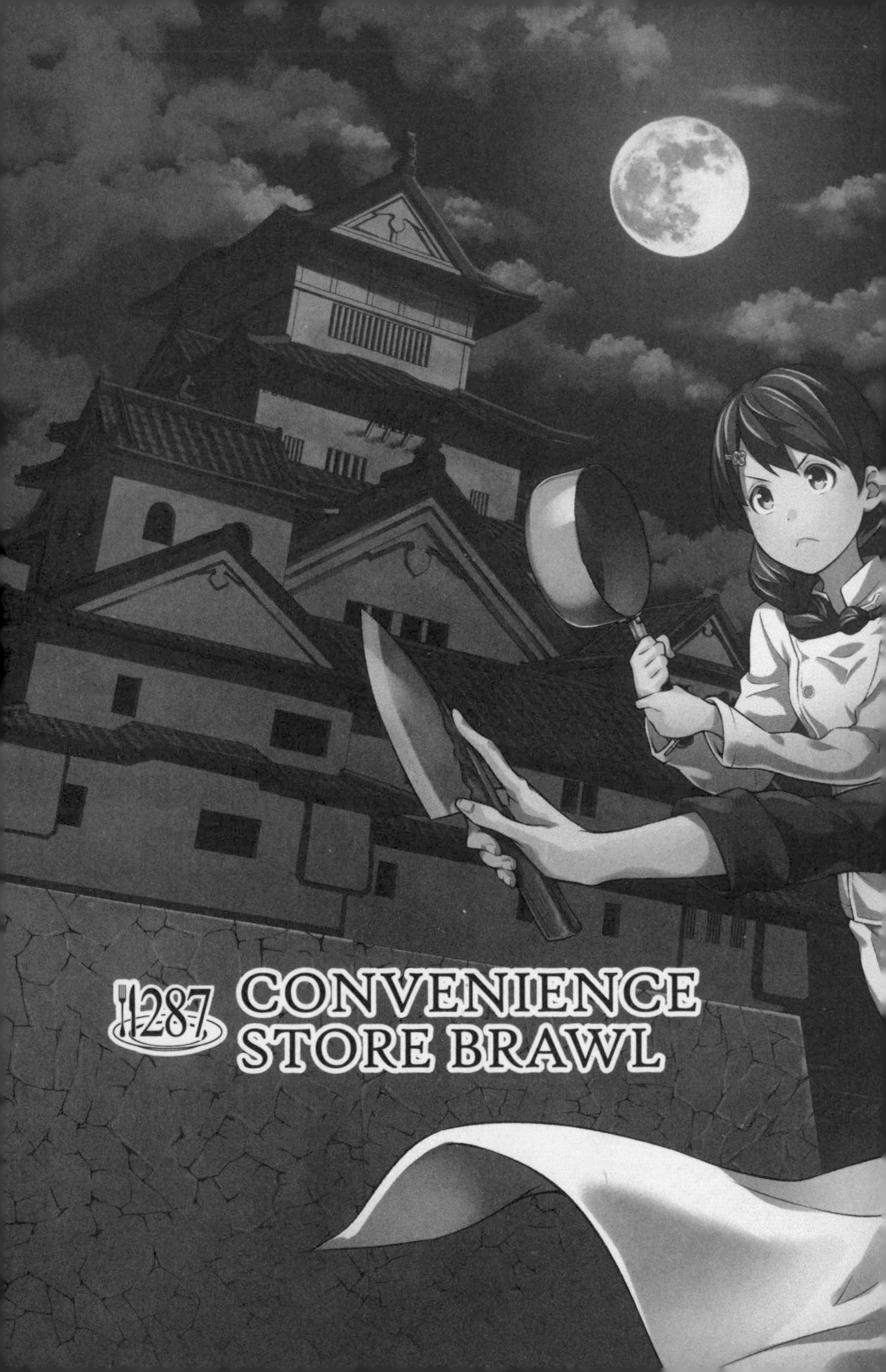
287
CONVENIENCE STORE BRAWL

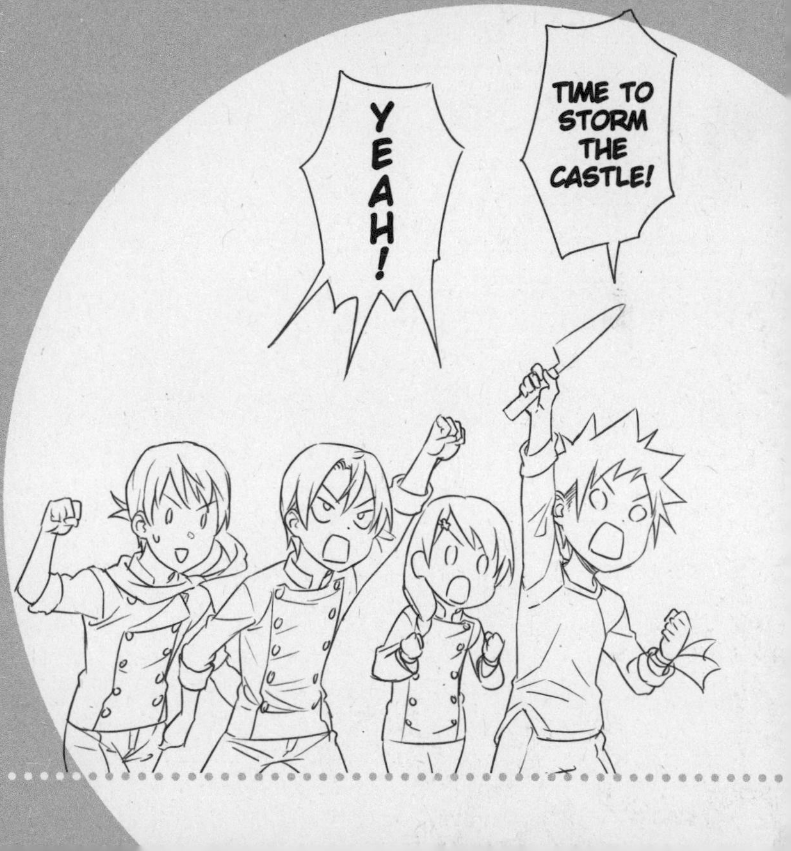
TIME TO STORM THE CASTLE!
YEAH!

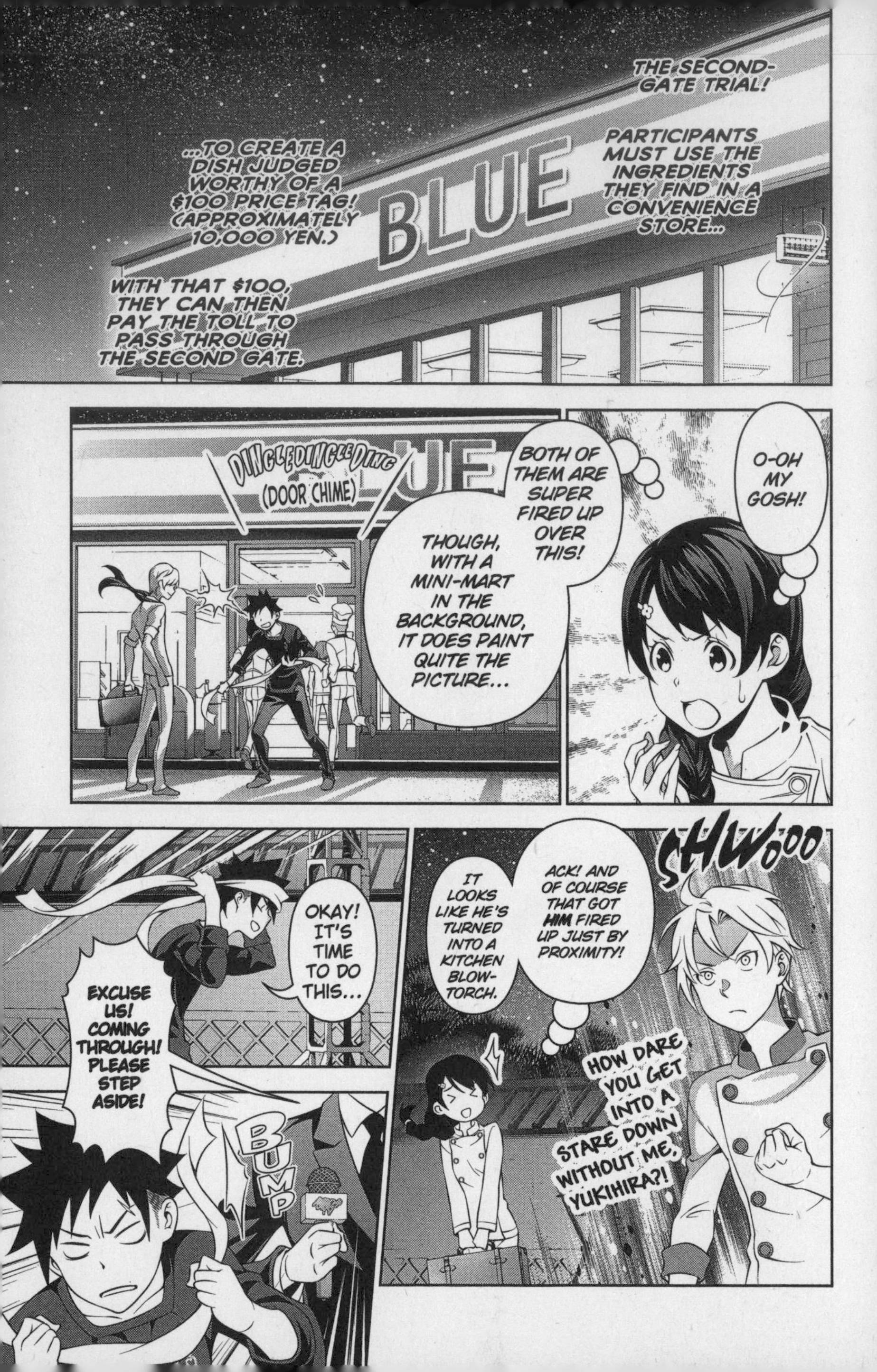
THE SECOND-GATE TRIAL!
PARTICIPANTS MUST USE THE INGREDIENTS THEY FIND IN A CONVENIENCE STORE...
BLUE
...TO CREATE A DISH JUDGED WORTHY OF A $100 PRICE TAG! (APPROXIMATELY 10,000 YEN.)
WITH THAT $100, THEY CAN THEN PAY THE TOLL TO PASS THROUGH THE SECOND GATE.
O-OH MY GOSH!
BOTH OF THEM ARE SUPER FIRED UP OVER THIS!
THOUGH, WITH A MINI-MART IN THE BACKGROUND, IT DOES PAINT QUITE THE PICTURE...
DINGLEDINGLEDING
(DOOR CHIME)
SHWOOO
ACK! AND OF COURSE THAT GOT HIM FIRED UP JUST BY PROXIMITY!
IT LOOKS LIKE HE'S TURNED INTO A KITCHEN BLOW-TORCH.
HOW DARE YOU GET INTO A STARE DOWN WITHOUT ME, YUKIHIRA?!
OKAY! IT'S TIME TO DO THIS...
EXCUSE US! COMING THROUGH! PLEASE STEP ASIDE!
BUMP

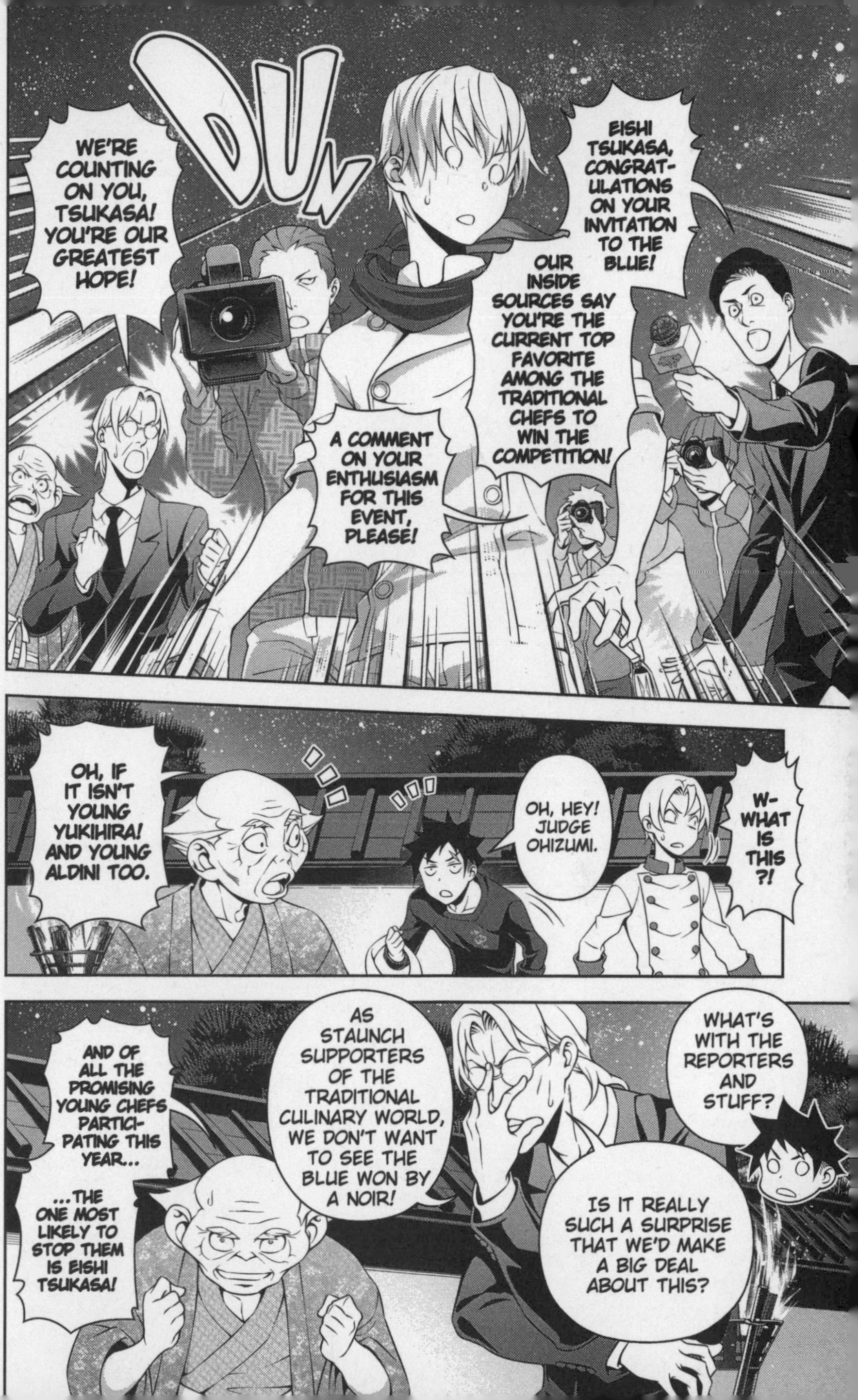
EISHI TSUKASA, CONGRATULATIONS ON YOUR INVITATION TO THE BLUE!
OUR INSIDE SOURCES SAY YOU'RE THE CURRENT TOP FAVORITE AMONG THE TRADITIONAL CHEFS TO WIN THE COMPETITION!
DUN
WE'RE COUNTING ON YOU, TSUKASA! YOU'RE OUR GREATEST HOPE!
A COMMENT ON YOUR ENTHUSIASM FOR THIS EVENT, PLEASE!
W-WHAT IS THIS?!
OH, HEY! JUDGE OHIZUMI.
OH, IF IT ISN'T YOUNG YUKIHIRA! AND YOUNG ALDINI TOO.
WHAT'S WITH THE REPORTERS AND STUFF?
AS STAUNCH SUPPORTERS OF THE TRADITIONAL CULINARY WORLD, WE DON'T WANT TO SEE THE BLUE WON BY A NOIR!
IS IT REALLY SUCH A SURPRISE THAT WE'D MAKE A BIG DEAL ABOUT THIS?
AND OF ALL THE PROMISING YOUNG CHEFS PARTICI-PATING THIS YEAR...
...THE ONE MOST LIKELY TO STOP THEM IS EISHI TSUKASA!

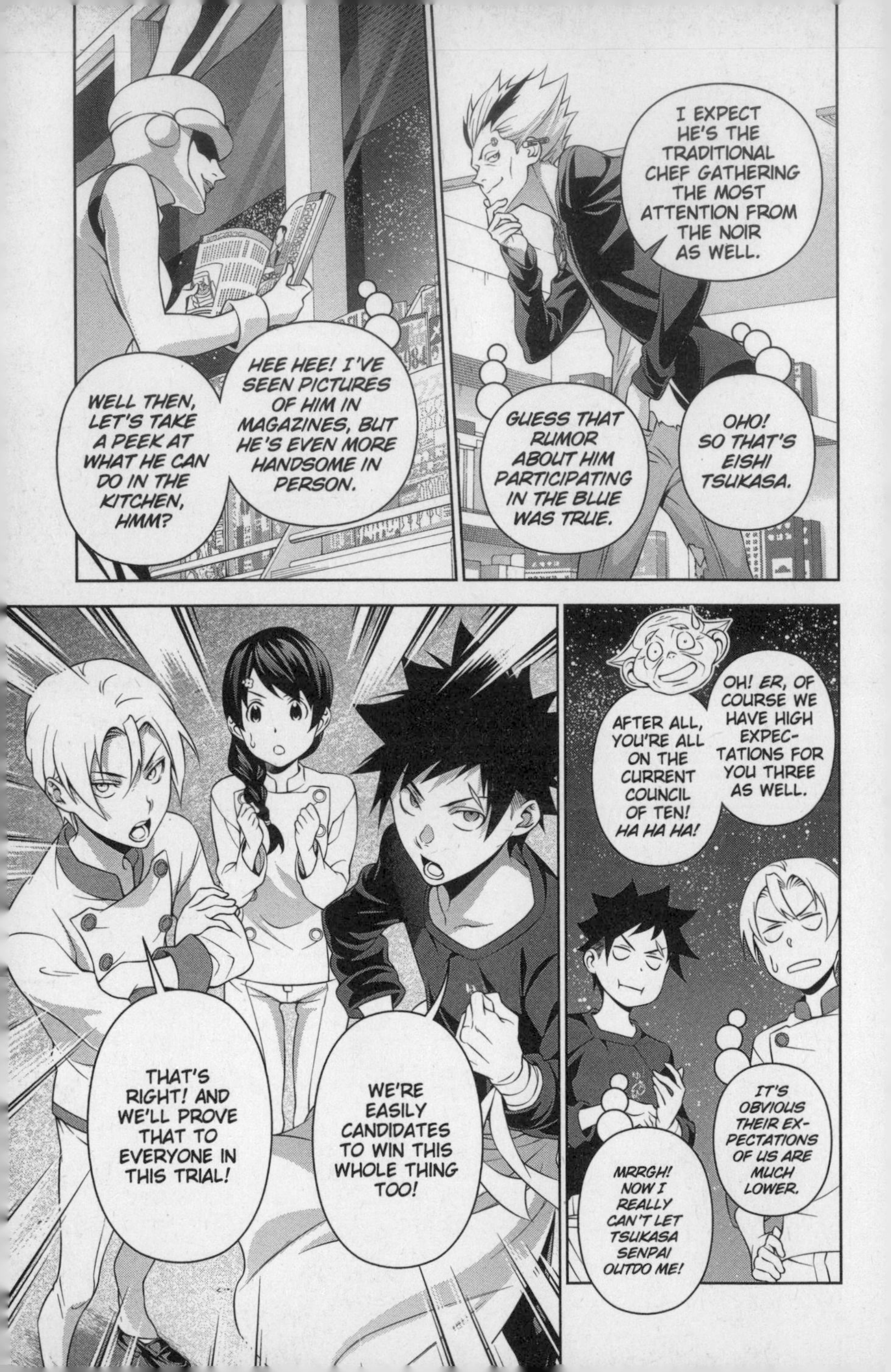

I EXPECT HE'S THE TRADITIONAL CHEF GATHERING THE MOST ATTENTION FROM THE NOIR AS WELL.
OHO! SO THAT'S EISHI TSUKASA.
GUESS THAT RUMOR ABOUT HIM PARTICIPATING IN THE BLUE WAS TRUE.
HEE HEE! I'VE SEEN PICTURES OF HIM IN MAGAZINES, BUT HE'S EVEN MORE HANDSOME IN PERSON.
WELL THEN, LET'S TAKE A PEEK AT WHAT HE CAN DO IN THE KITCHEN, HMM?
OH! ER, OF COURSE WE HAVE HIGH EXPEC-TATIONS FOR YOU THREE AS WELL.
AFTER ALL, YOU'RE ALL ON THE CURRENT COUNCIL OF TEN! HA HA HA!
IT'S OBVIOUS THEIR EX-PECTATIONS OF US ARE MUCH LOWER.
MRRGH! NOW I REALLY CAN'T LET TSUKASA SENPAI OUTDO ME!
WE'RE EASILY CANDIDATES TO WIN THIS WHOLE THING TOO!
THAT'S RIGHT! AND WE'LL PROVE THAT TO EVERYONE IN THIS TRIAL!

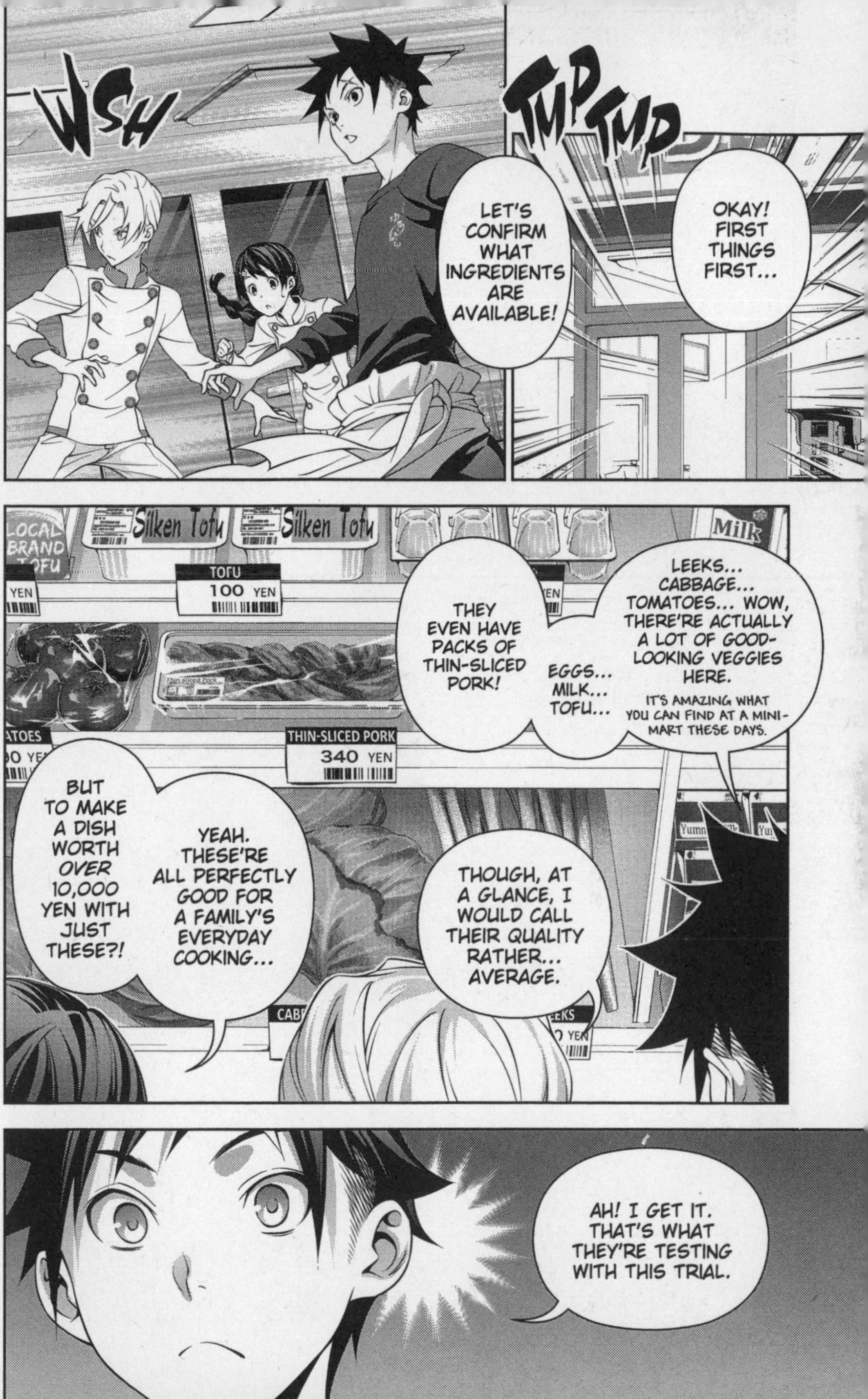
TMP TMP
OKAY! FIRST THINGS FIRST...
WSH
LET'S CONFIRM WHAT INGREDIENTS ARE AVAILABLE!
Milk
Silken Tofu
Silken Tofu
LOCAL BRAND TOFU
TOFU 100 YEN
THIN-SLICED PORK 340 YEN
LEEKS... CABBAGE... TOMATOES... WOW, THERE'RE ACTUALLY A LOT OF GOOD-LOOKING VEGGIES HERE.
IT'S AMAZING WHAT YOU CAN FIND AT A MINI-MART THESE DAYS.
EGGS... MILK... TOFU...
THEY EVEN HAVE PACKS OF THIN-SLICED PORK!
THOUGH, AT A GLANCE, I WOULD CALL THEIR QUALITY RATHER... AVERAGE.
YEAH. THESE'RE ALL PERFECTLY GOOD FOR A FAMILY'S EVERYDAY COOKING...
BUT TO MAKE A DISH WORTH OVER 10,000 YEN WITH JUST THESE?!
AH! I GET IT. THAT'S WHAT THEY'RE TESTING WITH THIS TRIAL.

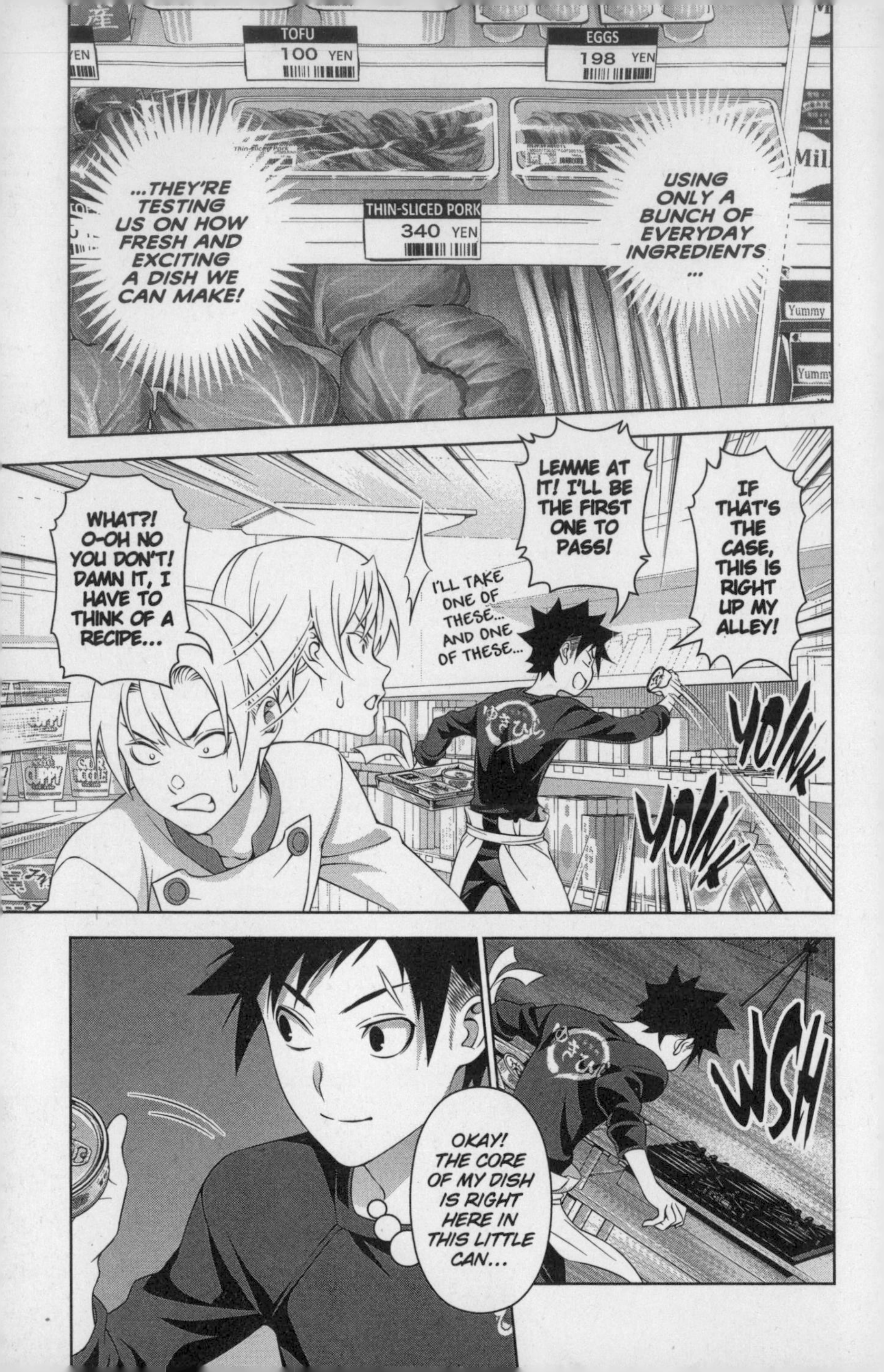
EGGS
198 YEN
TOFU
100 YEN
USING ONLY A BUNCH OF EVERYDAY INGREDIENTS...
THIN-SLICED PORK
340 YEN
...THEY'RE TESTING US ON HOW FRESH AND EXCITING A DISH WE CAN MAKE!
Milk
Yummy
Yummy
IF THAT'S THE CASE, THIS IS RIGHT UP MY ALLEY!
LEMME AT IT! I'LL BE THE FIRST ONE TO PASS!
YOINK
YOINK
I'LL TAKE ONE OF THESE... AND ONE OF THESE...
WHAT?! O-OH NO YOU DON'T! DAMN IT, I HAVE TO THINK OF A RECIPE...
WSH
OKAY! THE CORE OF MY DISH IS RIGHT HERE IN THIS LITTLE CAN...

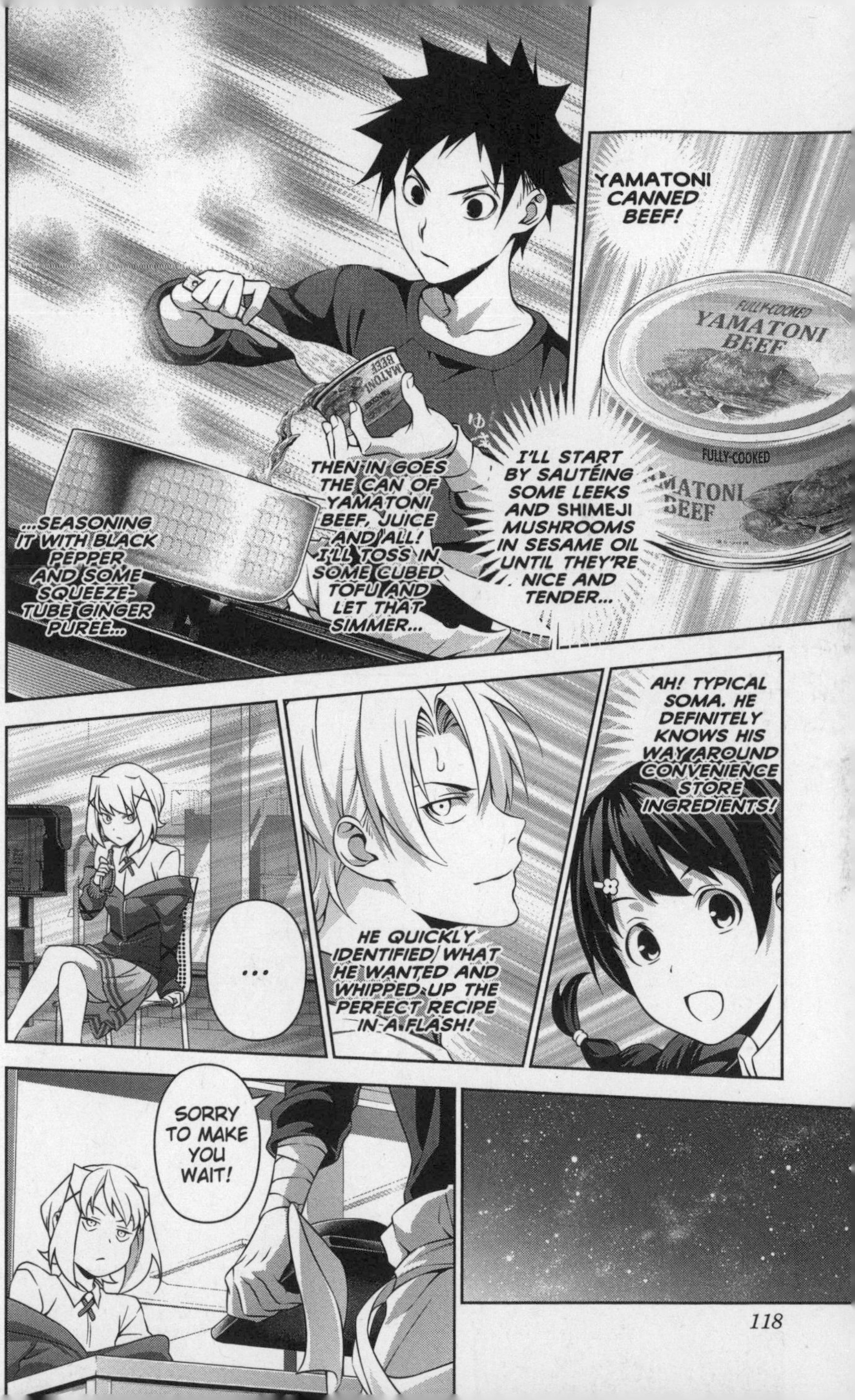
YAMATONI CANNED BEEF!
FULLY-COOKED YAMATONI BEEF
FULLY-COOKED YAMATONI BEEF
I'LL START BY SAUTÉING SOME LEEKS AND SHIMEJI MUSHROOMS IN SESAME OIL UNTIL THEY'RE NICE AND TENDER...
THEN IN GOES THE CAN OF YAMATONI BEEF, JUICE AND ALL! I'LL TOSS IN SOME CUBED TOFU AND LET THAT SIMMER...
...SEASONING IT WITH BLACK PEPPER AND SOME SQUEEZE-TUBE GINGER PUREE...
AH! TYPICAL SOMA. HE DEFINITELY KNOWS HIS WAY AROUND CONVENIENCE STORE INGREDIENTS!
HE QUICKLY IDENTIFIED WHAT HE WANTED AND WHIPPED UP THE PERFECT RECIPE IN A FLASH!
...
SORRY TO MAKE YOU WAIT!

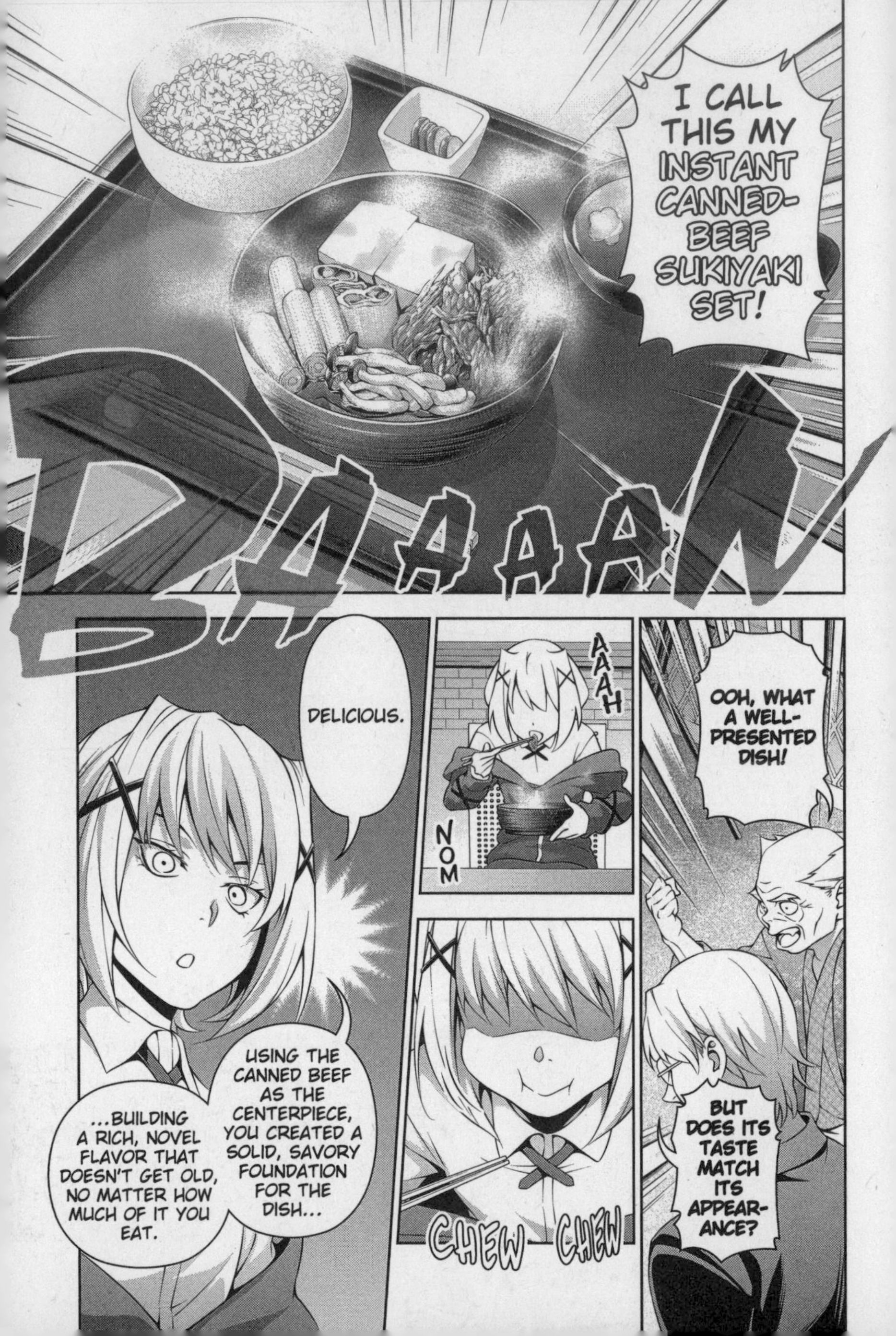
I CALL THIS MY INSTANT CANNED-BEEF SUKIYAKI SET!
DAAAAN
OOH, WHAT A WELL-PRESENTED DISH!
BUT DOES ITS TASTE MATCH ITS APPEARANCE?
AAAH
NOM
CHEW CHEW
DELICIOUS.
USING THE CANNED BEEF AS THE CENTERPIECE, YOU CREATED A SOLID, SAVORY FOUNDATION FOR THE DISH...
...BUILDING A RICH, NOVEL FLAVOR THAT DOESN'T GET OLD, NO MATTER HOW MUCH OF IT YOU EAT.

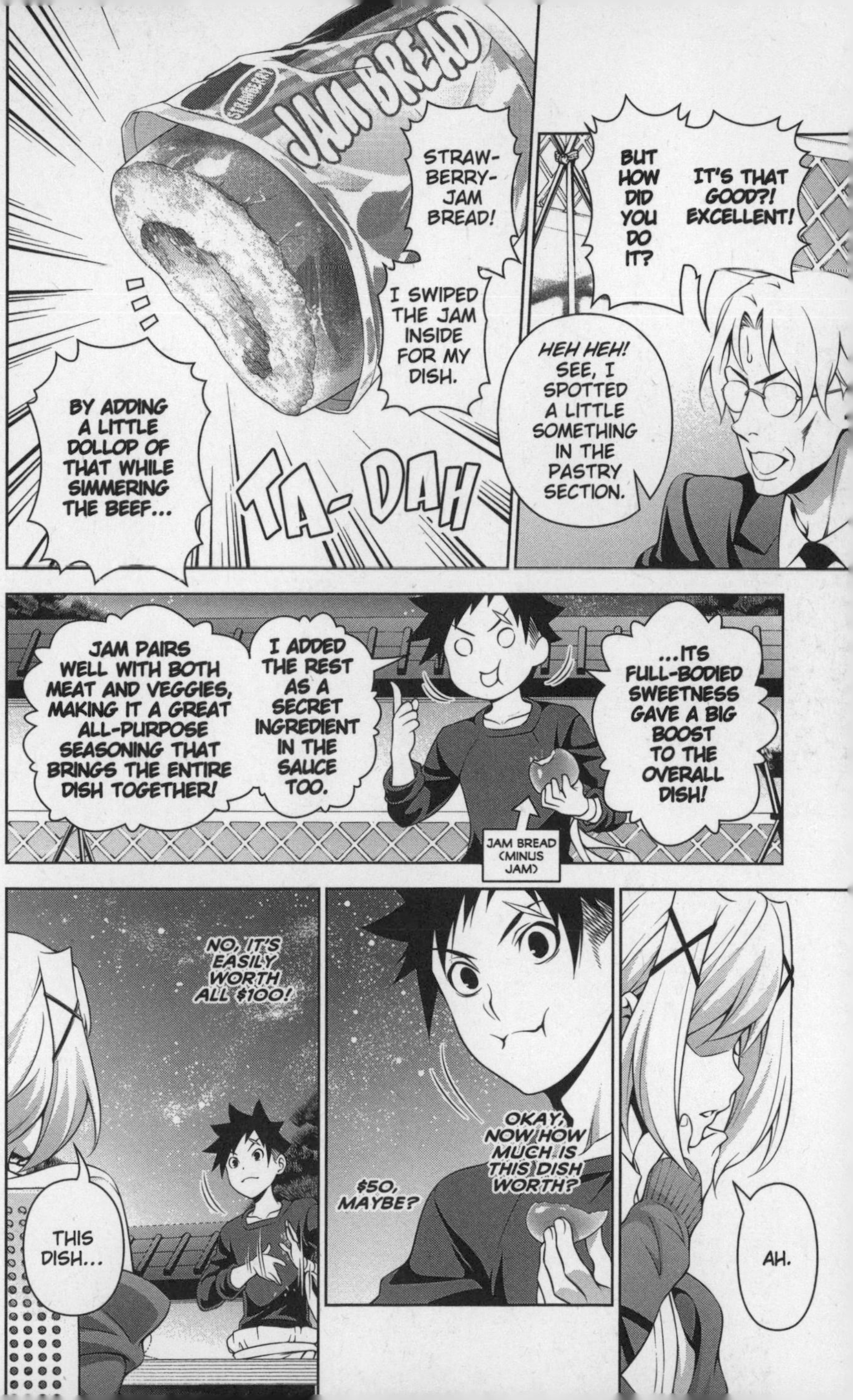
IT'S THAT GOOD?! EXCELLENT!
BUT HOW DID YOU DO IT?
HEH HEH! SEE, I SPOTTED A LITTLE SOMETHING IN THE PASTRY SECTION.
JAM BREAD
STRAW-BERRY-JAM BREAD!
I SWIPED THE JAM INSIDE FOR MY DISH.
TA-DAH
BY ADDING A LITTLE DOLLOP OF THAT WHILE SIMMERING THE BEEF...
...ITS FULL-BODIED SWEETNESS GAVE A BIG BOOST TO THE OVERALL DISH!
JAM BREAD (MINUS JAM)
I ADDED THE REST AS A SECRET INGREDIENT IN THE SAUCE TOO.
JAM PAIRS WELL WITH BOTH MEAT AND VEGGIES, MAKING IT A GREAT ALL-PURPOSE SEASONING THAT BRINGS THE ENTIRE DISH TOGETHER!
AH.
OKAY, NOW HOW MUCH IS THIS DISH WORTH?
$50, MAYBE?
NO, IT'S EASILY WORTH ALL $100!
THIS DISH...

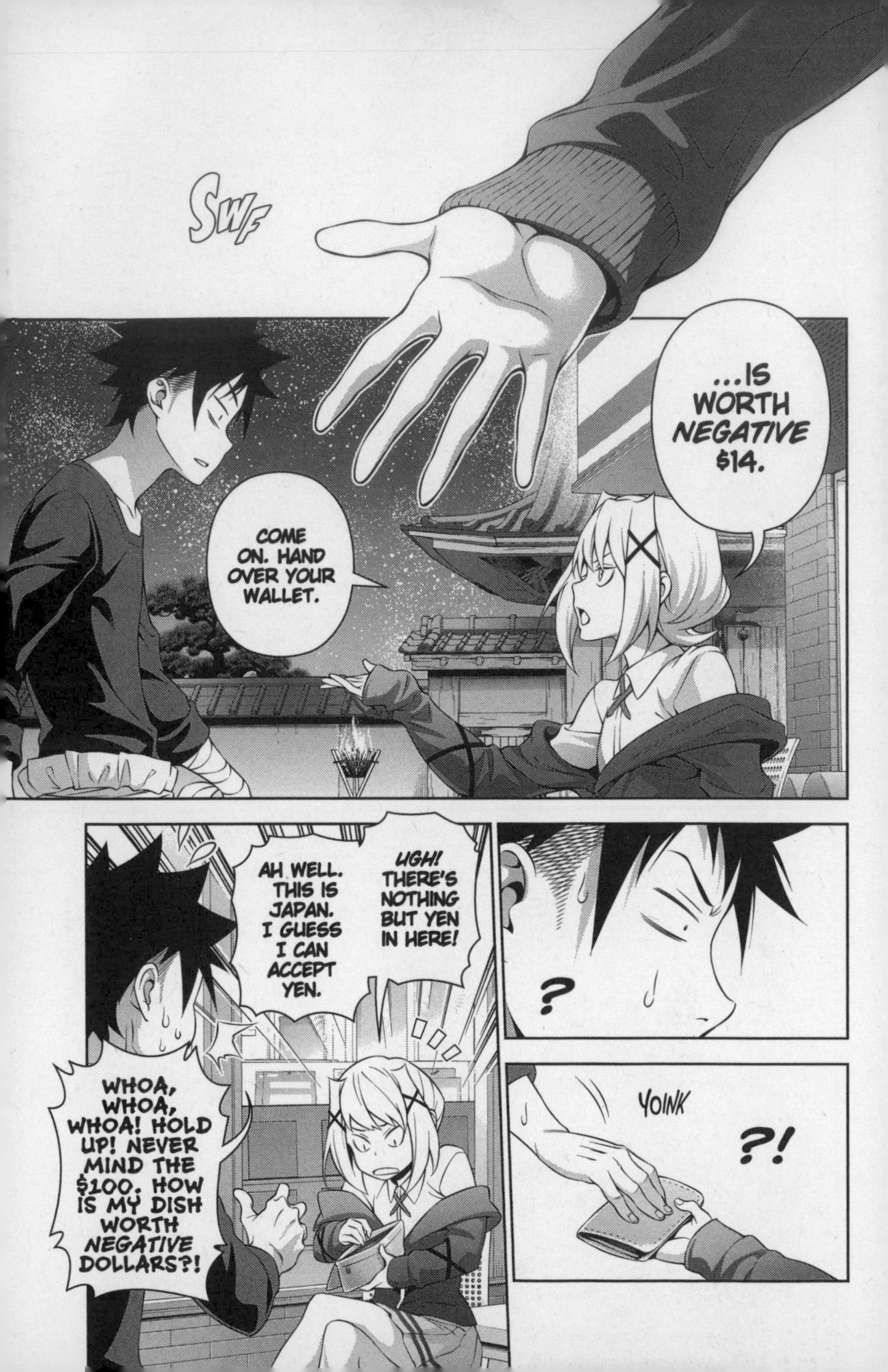
...IS WORTH NEGATIVE $14.
SWF
COME ON. HAND OVER YOUR WALLET.
?
YOINK
?!
UGH! THERE'S NOTHING BUT YEN IN HERE!
AH WELL. THIS IS JAPAN. I GUESS I CAN ACCEPT YEN.
WHOA, WHOA, WHOA! HOLD UP! NEVER MIND THE $100. HOW IS MY DISH WORTH NEGATIVE DOLLARS?!

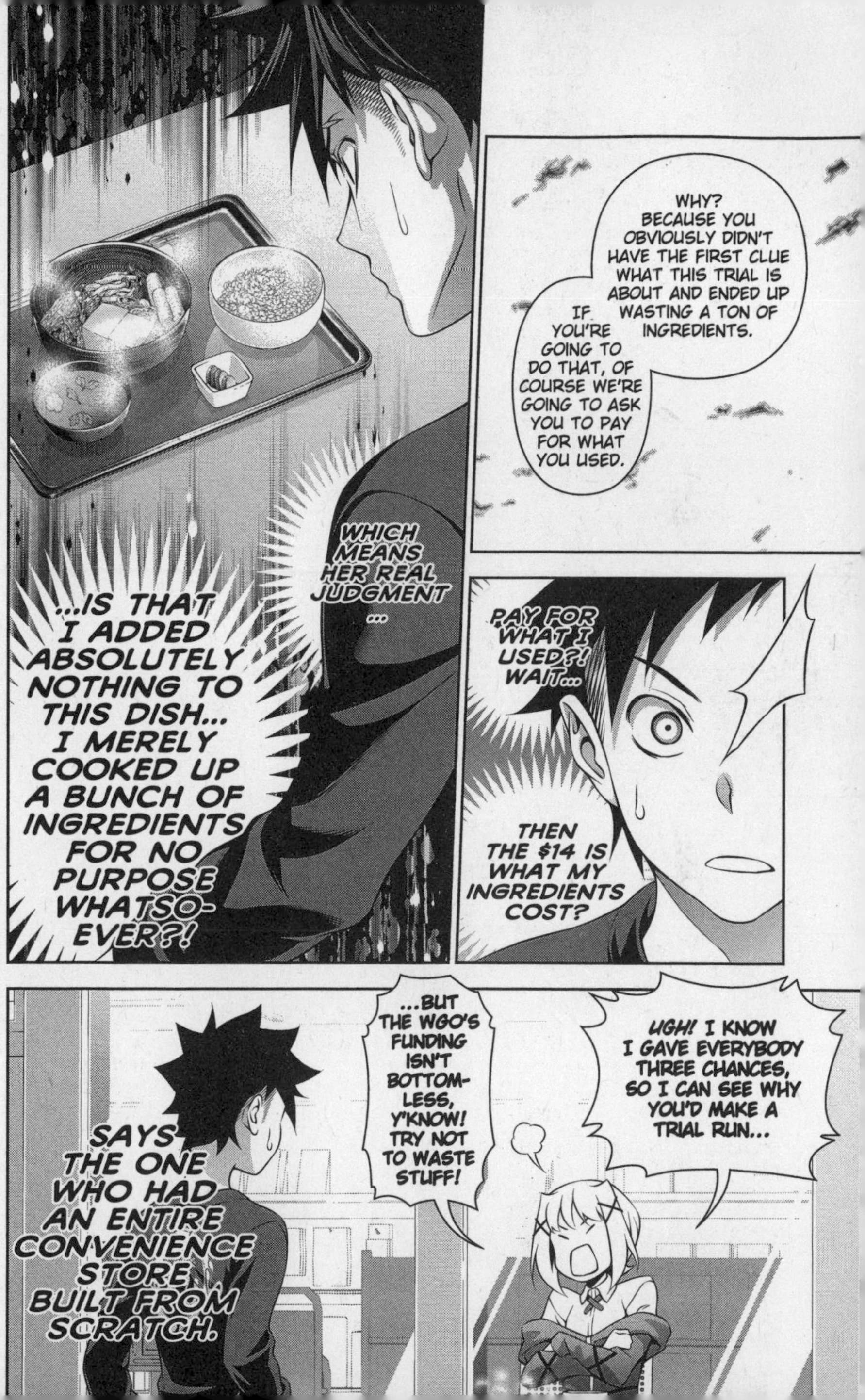
WHY? BECAUSE YOU OBVIOUSLY DIDN'T HAVE THE FIRST CLUE WHAT THIS TRIAL IS ABOUT AND ENDED UP WASTING A TON OF INGREDIENTS.
IF YOU'RE GOING TO DO THAT, OF COURSE WE'RE GOING TO ASK YOU TO PAY FOR WHAT YOU USED.
PAY FOR WHAT I USED?! WAIT...
THEN THE $14 IS WHAT MY INGREDIENTS COST?
WHICH MEANS HER REAL JUDGMENT...
...IS THAT I ADDED ABSOLUTELY NOTHING TO THIS DISH... I MERELY COOKED UP A BUNCH OF INGREDIENTS FOR NO PURPOSE WHATSO-EVER?!
UGH! I KNOW I GAVE EVERYBODY THREE CHANCES, SO I CAN SEE WHY YOU'D MAKE A TRIAL RUN...
...BUT THE WGO'S FUNDING ISN'T BOTTOM-LESS, Y'KNOW! TRY NOT TO WASTE STUFF!
SAYS THE ONE WHO HAD AN ENTIRE CONVENIENCE STORE BUILT FROM SCRATCH.

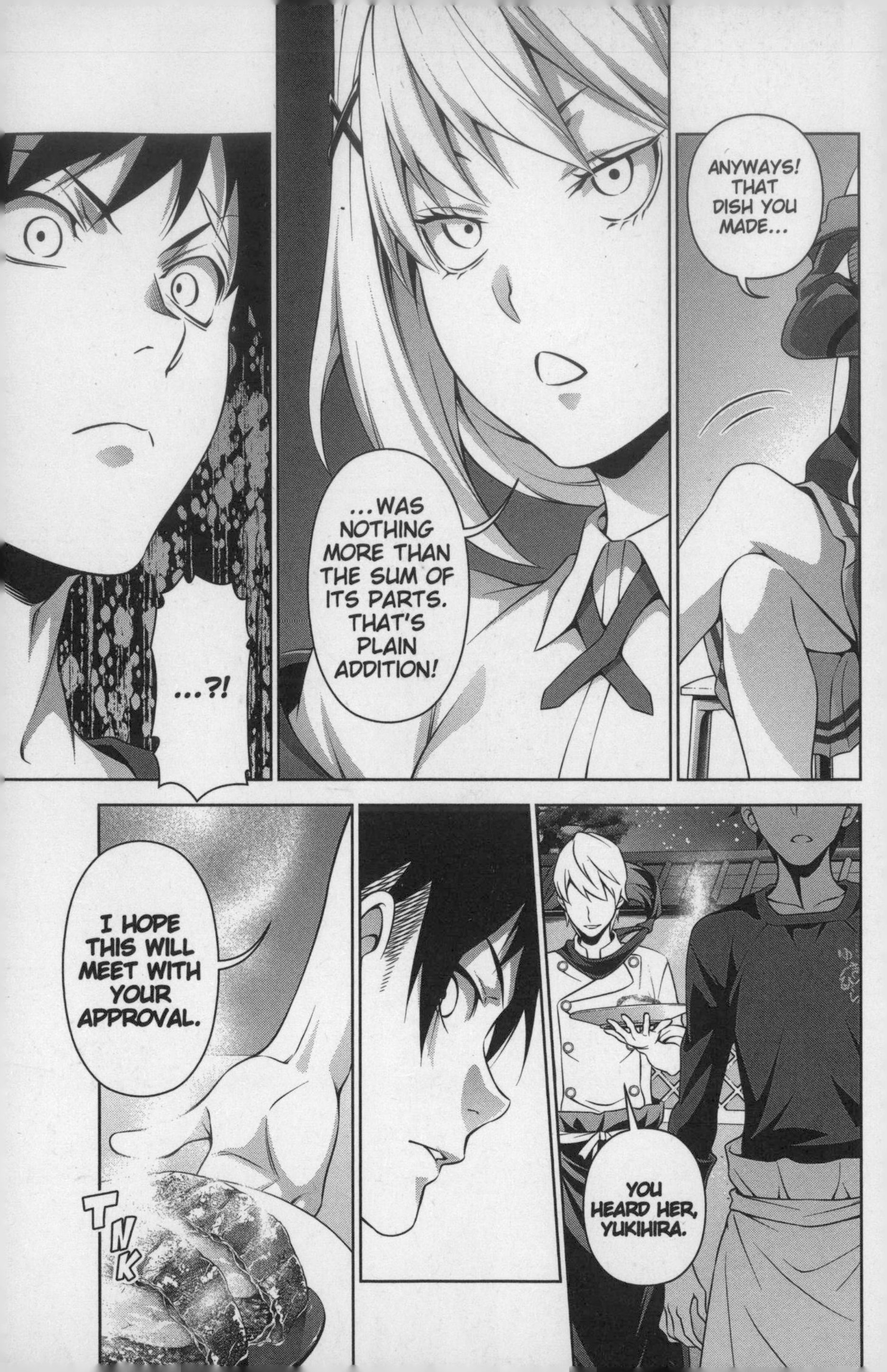
ANYWAYS! THAT DISH YOU MADE...
...WAS NOTHING MORE THAN THE SUM OF ITS PARTS. THAT'S PLAIN ADDITION!
...?!
YOU HEARD HER, YUKIHIRA.
I HOPE THIS WILL MEET WITH YOUR APPROVAL.
TNK

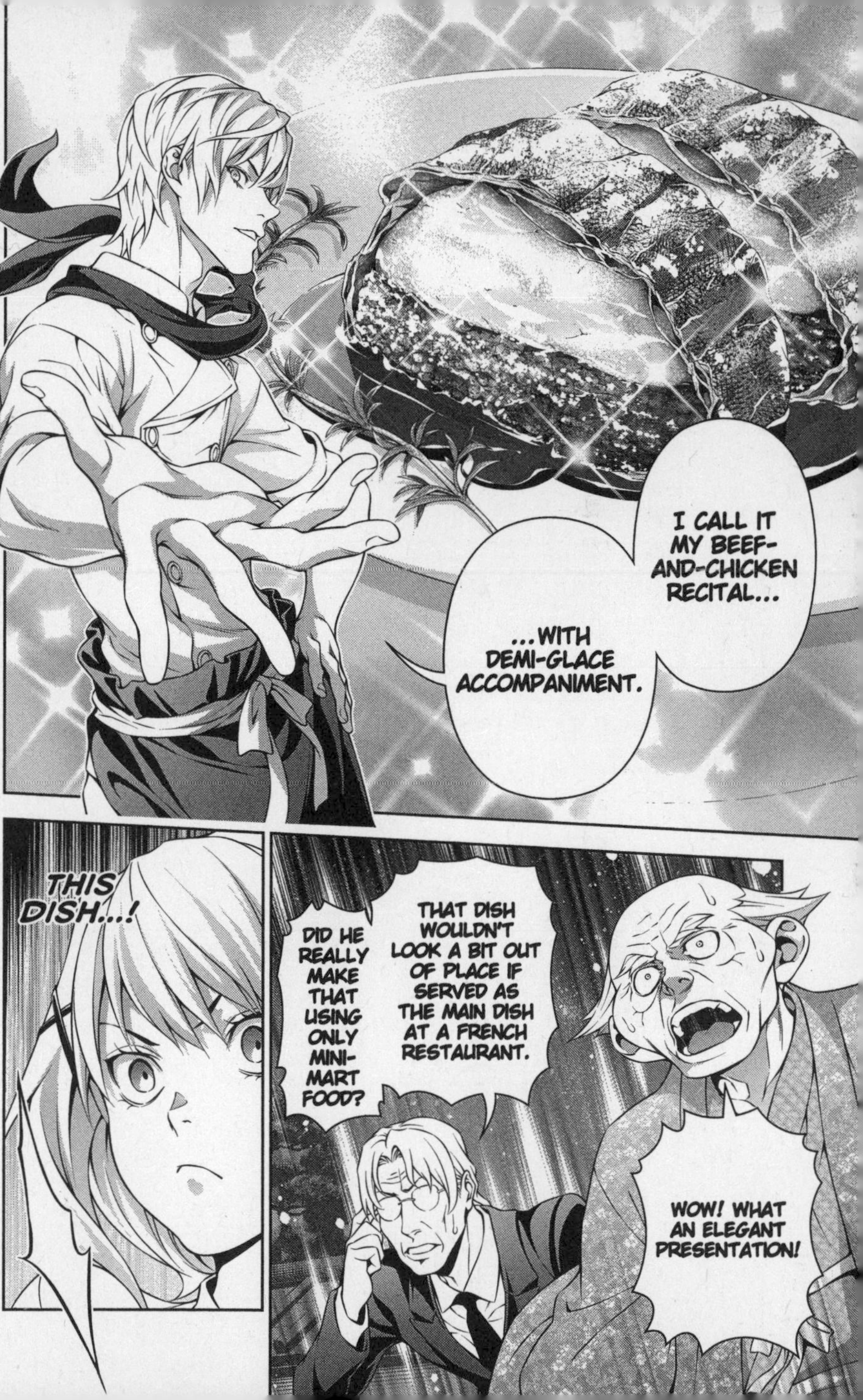
I CALL IT MY BEEF-AND-CHICKEN RECITAL...
...WITH DEMI-GLACE ACCOMPANIMENT.
THAT DISH WOULDN'T LOOK A BIT OUT OF PLACE IF SERVED AS THE MAIN DISH AT A FRENCH RESTAURANT.
DID HE REALLY MAKE THAT USING ONLY MINI-MART FOOD?
WOW! WHAT AN ELEGANT PRESENTATION!
THIS DISH...!

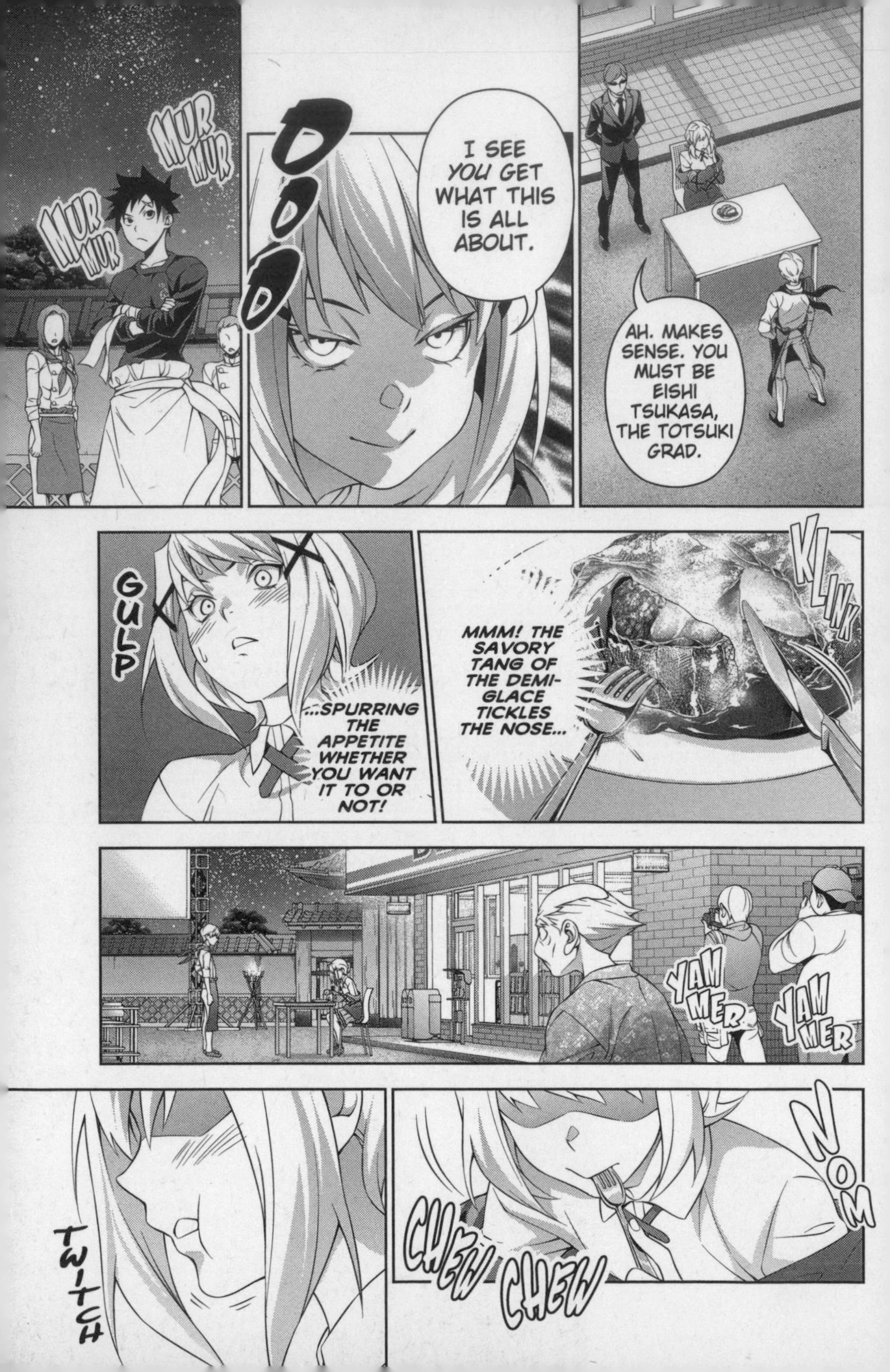

AH. MAKES SENSE. YOU MUST BE EISHI TSUKASA, THE TOTSUKI GRAD.
I SEE YOU GET WHAT THIS IS ALL ABOUT.
MUR MUR
MUR MUR
KLINK
MMM! THE SAVORY TANG OF THE DEMI-GLACE TICKLES THE NOSE...
...SPURRING THE APPETITE WHETHER YOU WANT IT TO OR NOT!
GULP
YAM MER
YAM MER
NOM
CHEW CHEW
TWITCH

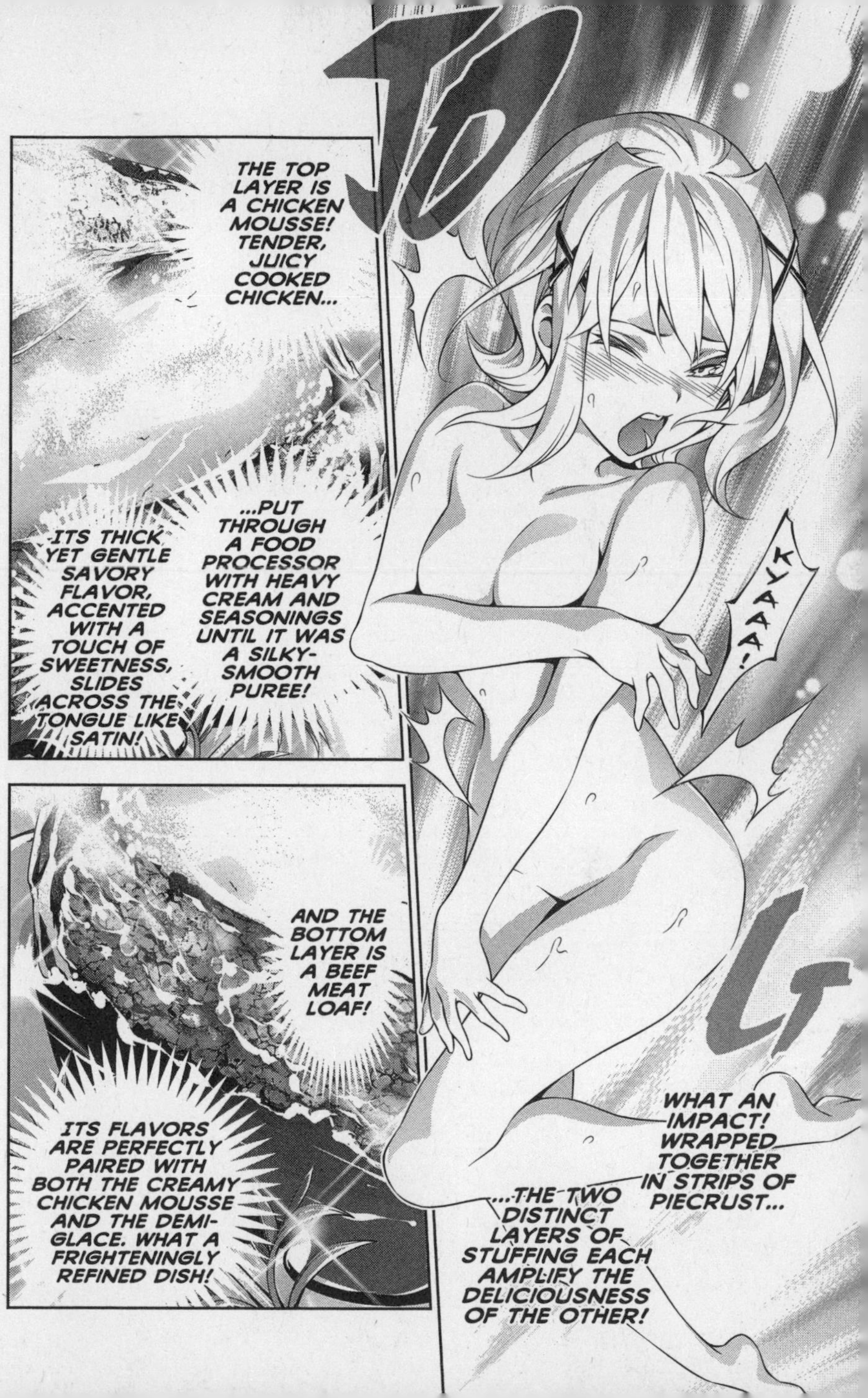
KYAAA!
WHAT AN IMPACT! WRAPPED TOGETHER IN STRIPS OF PIECRUST...
...THE TWO DISTINCT LAYERS OF STUFFING EACH AMPLIFY THE DELICIOUSNESS OF THE OTHER!
THE TOP LAYER IS A CHICKEN MOUSSE! TENDER, JUICY COOKED CHICKEN...
...PUT THROUGH A FOOD PROCESSOR WITH HEAVY CREAM AND SEASONINGS UNTIL IT WAS A SILKY-SMOOTH PUREE!
ITS THICK YET GENTLE SAVORY FLAVOR, ACCENTED WITH A TOUCH OF SWEETNESS, SLIDES ACROSS THE TONGUE LIKE SATIN!
AND THE BOTTOM LAYER IS A BEEF MEAT LOAF!
ITS FLAVORS ARE PERFECTLY PAIRED WITH BOTH THE CREAMY CHICKEN MOUSSE AND THE DEMI-GLACE. WHAT A FRIGHTENINGLY REFINED DISH!

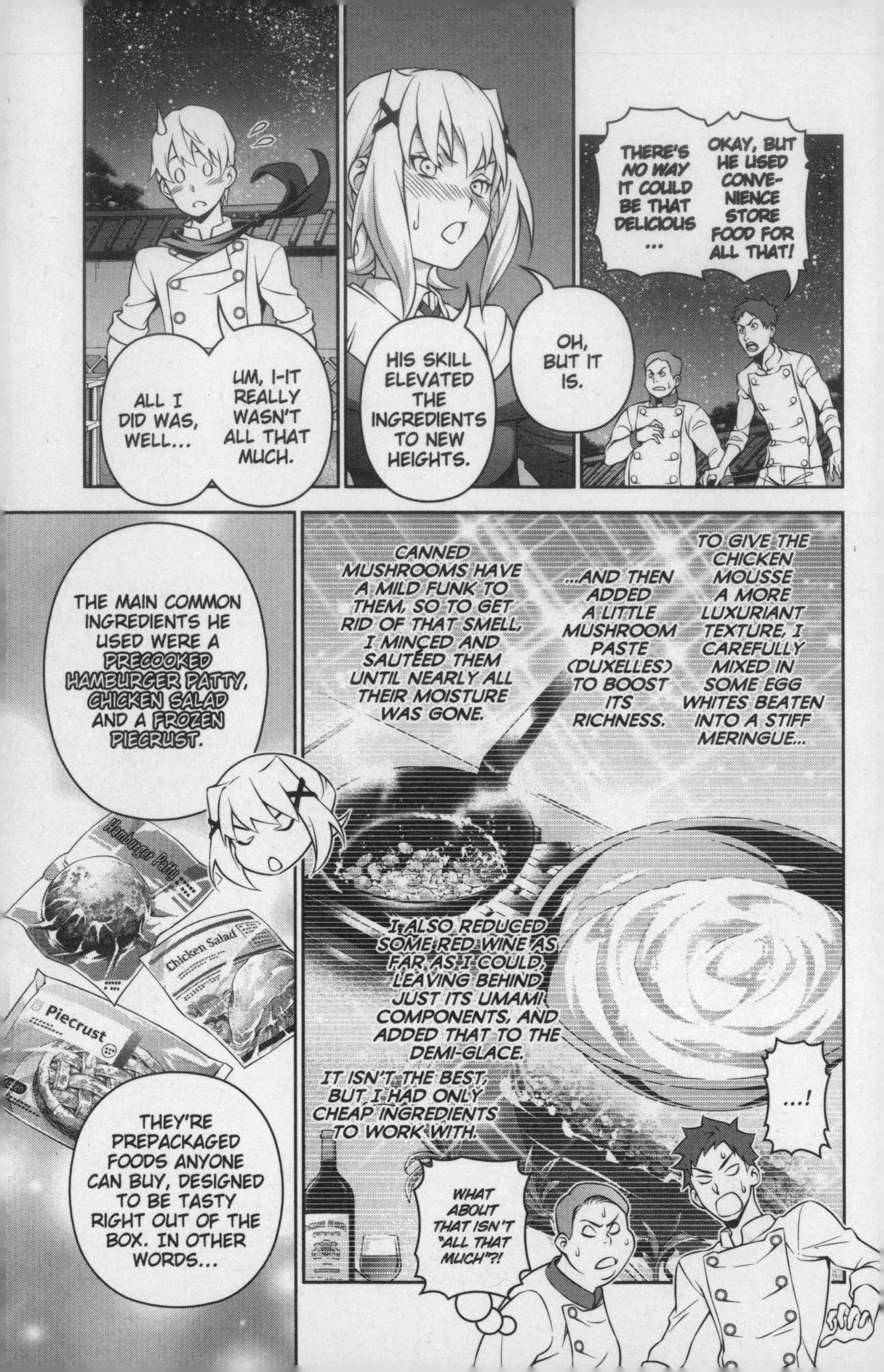
OKAY, BUT HE USED CONVENIENCE STORE FOOD FOR ALL THAT!
THERE'S NO WAY IT COULD BE THAT DELICIOUS...
OH, BUT IT IS.
HIS SKILL ELEVATED THE INGREDIENTS TO NEW HEIGHTS.
UM, I-IT REALLY WASN'T ALL THAT MUCH.
ALL I DID WAS, WELL...
CANNED MUSHROOMS HAVE A MILD FUNK TO THEM, SO TO GET RID OF THAT SMELL, I MINCED AND SAUTÉED THEM UNTIL NEARLY ALL THEIR MOISTURE WAS GONE.
...AND THEN ADDED A LITTLE MUSHROOM PASTE (DUXELLES) TO BOOST ITS RICHNESS.
TO GIVE THE CHICKEN MOUSSE A MORE LUXURIANT TEXTURE, I CAREFULLY MIXED IN SOME EGG WHITES BEATEN INTO A STIFF MERINGUE...
I ALSO REDUCED SOME RED WINE AS FAR AS I COULD, LEAVING BEHIND JUST ITS UMAMI COMPONENTS, AND ADDED THAT TO THE DEMI-GLACE.
IT ISN'T THE BEST, BUT I HAD ONLY CHEAP INGREDIENTS TO WORK WITH.
...!
WHAT ABOUT THAT ISN'T "ALL THAT MUCH"?!
THE MAIN COMMON INGREDIENTS HE USED WERE A PRECOOKED HAMBURGER PATTY, CHICKEN SALAD AND A FROZEN PIECRUST.
Hamburger Patty
Chicken Salad
Piecrust
THEY'RE PREPACKAGED FOODS ANYONE CAN BUY, DESIGNED TO BE TASTY RIGHT OUT OF THE BOX. IN OTHER WORDS...

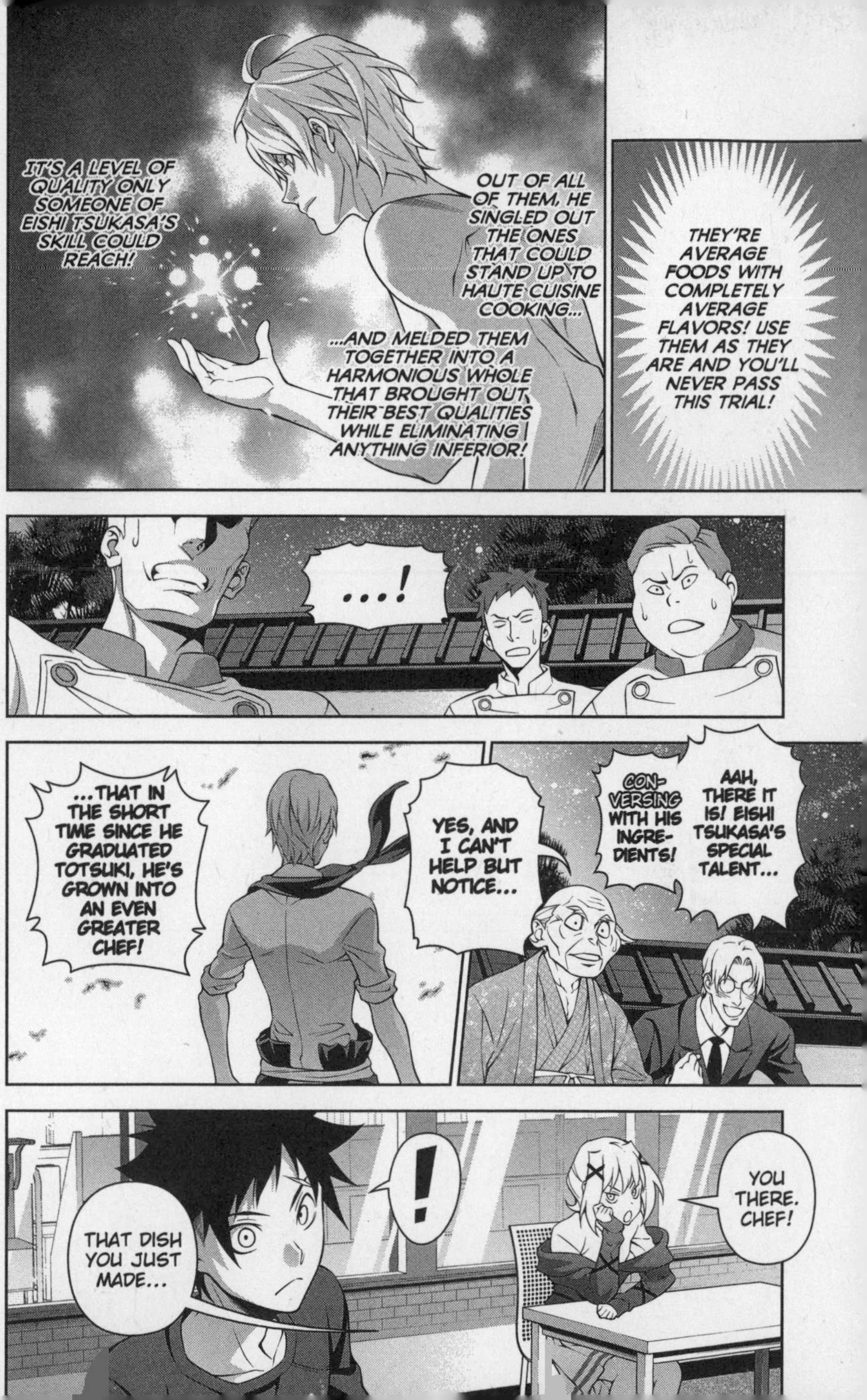
THEY'RE AVERAGE FOODS WITH COMPLETELY AVERAGE FLAVORS! USE THEM AS THEY ARE AND YOU'LL NEVER PASS THIS TRIAL!
OUT OF ALL OF THEM, HE SINGLED OUT THE ONES THAT COULD STAND UP TO HAUTE CUISINE COOKING...
...AND MELDED THEM TOGETHER INTO A HARMONIOUS WHOLE THAT BROUGHT OUT THEIR BEST QUALITIES WHILE ELIMINATING ANYTHING INFERIOR!
IT'S A LEVEL OF QUALITY ONLY SOMEONE OF EISHI TSUKASA'S SKILL COULD REACH!
...!
AAH, THERE IT IS! EISHI TSUKASA'S SPECIAL TALENT...
CON-VERSING WITH HIS INGRE-DIENTS!
YES, AND I CAN'T HELP BUT NOTICE...
...THAT IN THE SHORT TIME SINCE HE GRADUATED TOTSUKI, HE'S GROWN INTO AN EVEN GREATER CHEF!
YOU THERE. CHEF!
!
THAT DISH YOU JUST MADE...

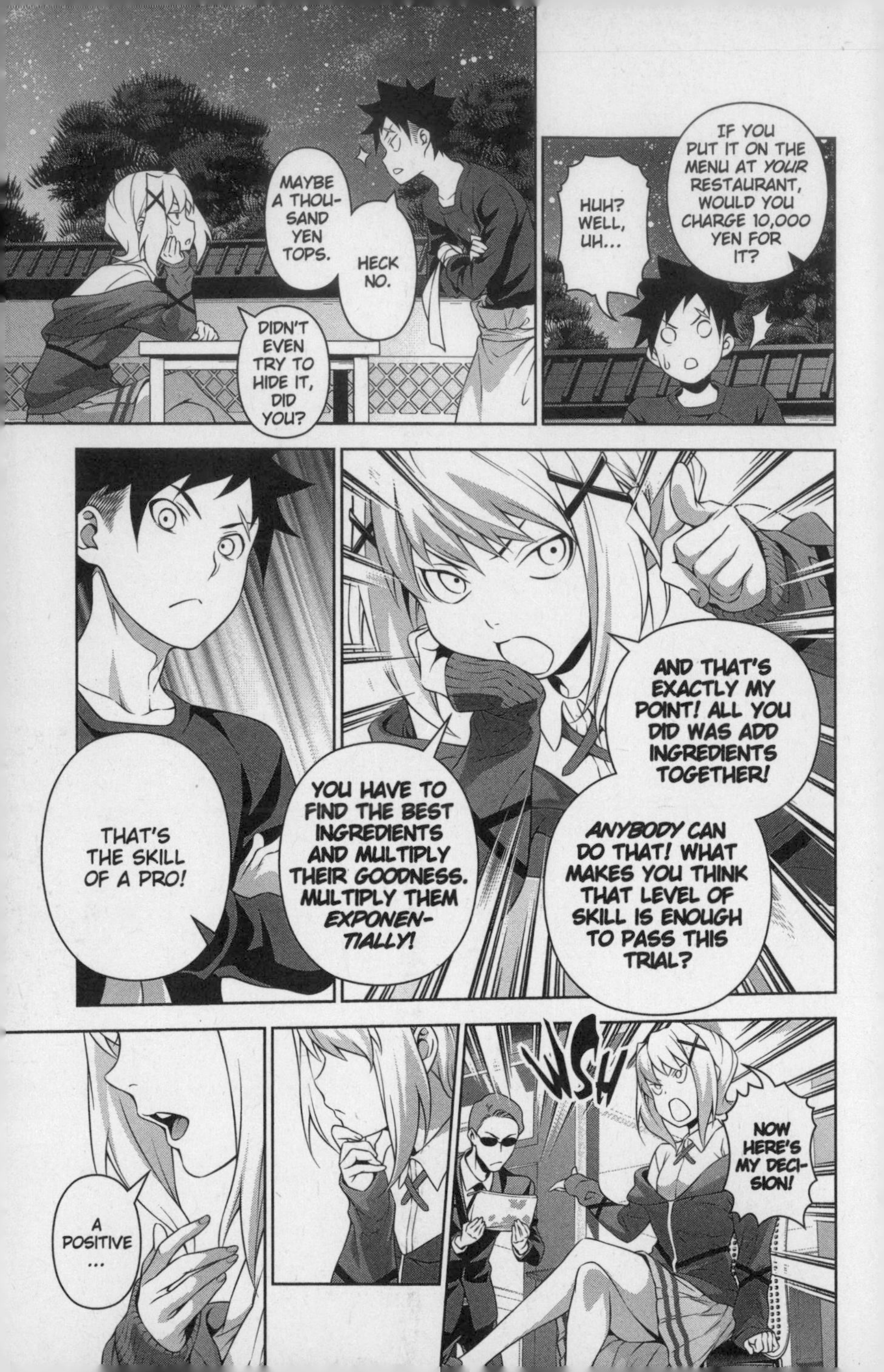
IF YOU PUT IT ON THE MENU AT *YOUR* RESTAURANT, WOULD YOU CHARGE 10,000 YEN FOR IT?
HUH? WELL, UH...
MAYBE A THOUSAND YEN TOPS.
HECK NO.
DIDN'T EVEN TRY TO HIDE IT, DID YOU?
AND THAT'S EXACTLY MY POINT! ALL YOU DID WAS ADD INGREDIENTS TOGETHER!
ANYBODY CAN DO THAT! WHAT MAKES YOU THINK THAT LEVEL OF SKILL IS ENOUGH TO PASS THIS TRIAL?
YOU HAVE TO FIND THE BEST INGREDIENTS AND MULTIPLY THEIR GOODNESS. MULTIPLY THEM *EXPONENTIALLY!*
THAT'S THE SKILL OF A PRO!
WSH
NOW HERE'S MY DECISION!
A POSITIVE ...

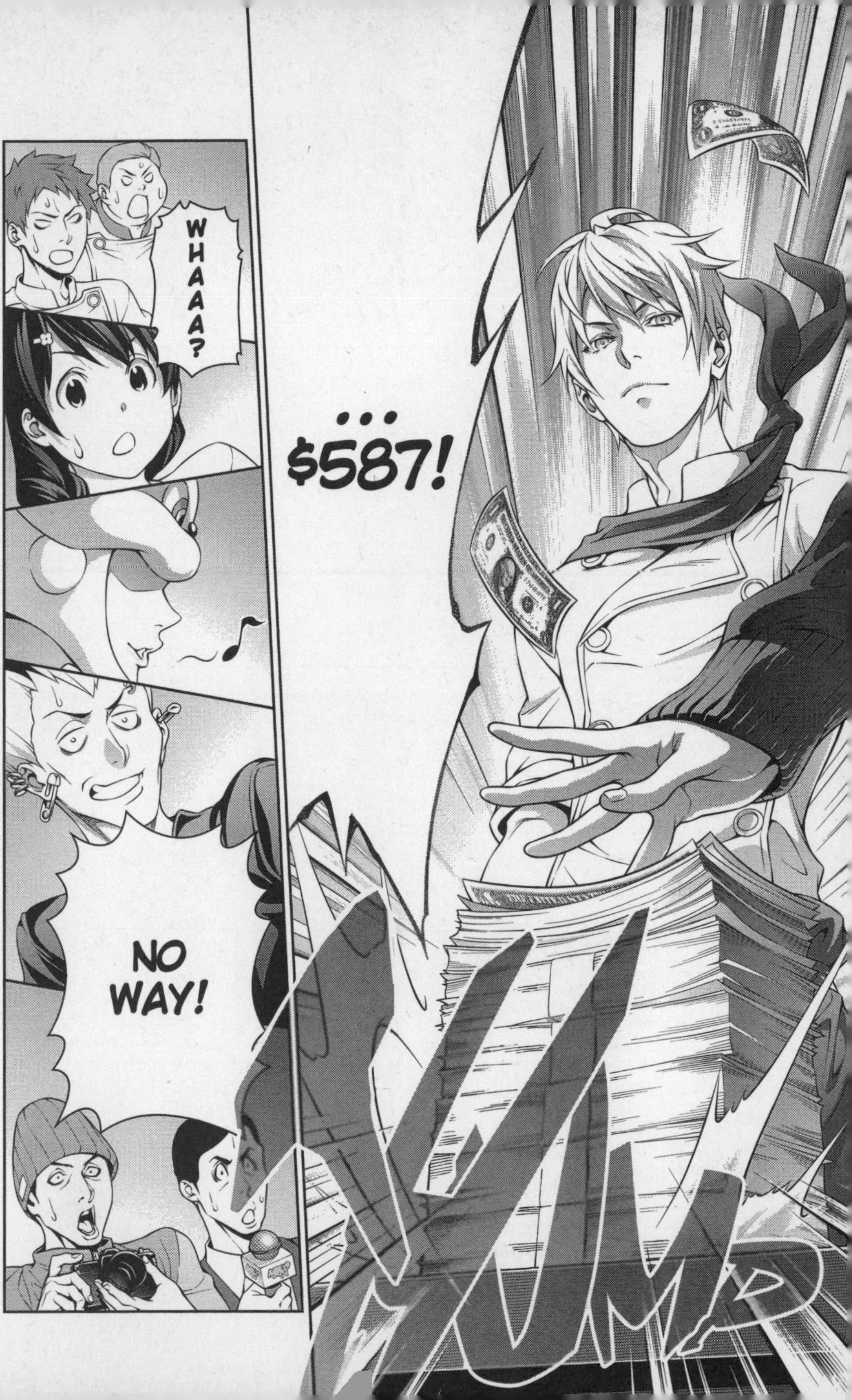
...
$587!
WHAAAA?
NO WAY!

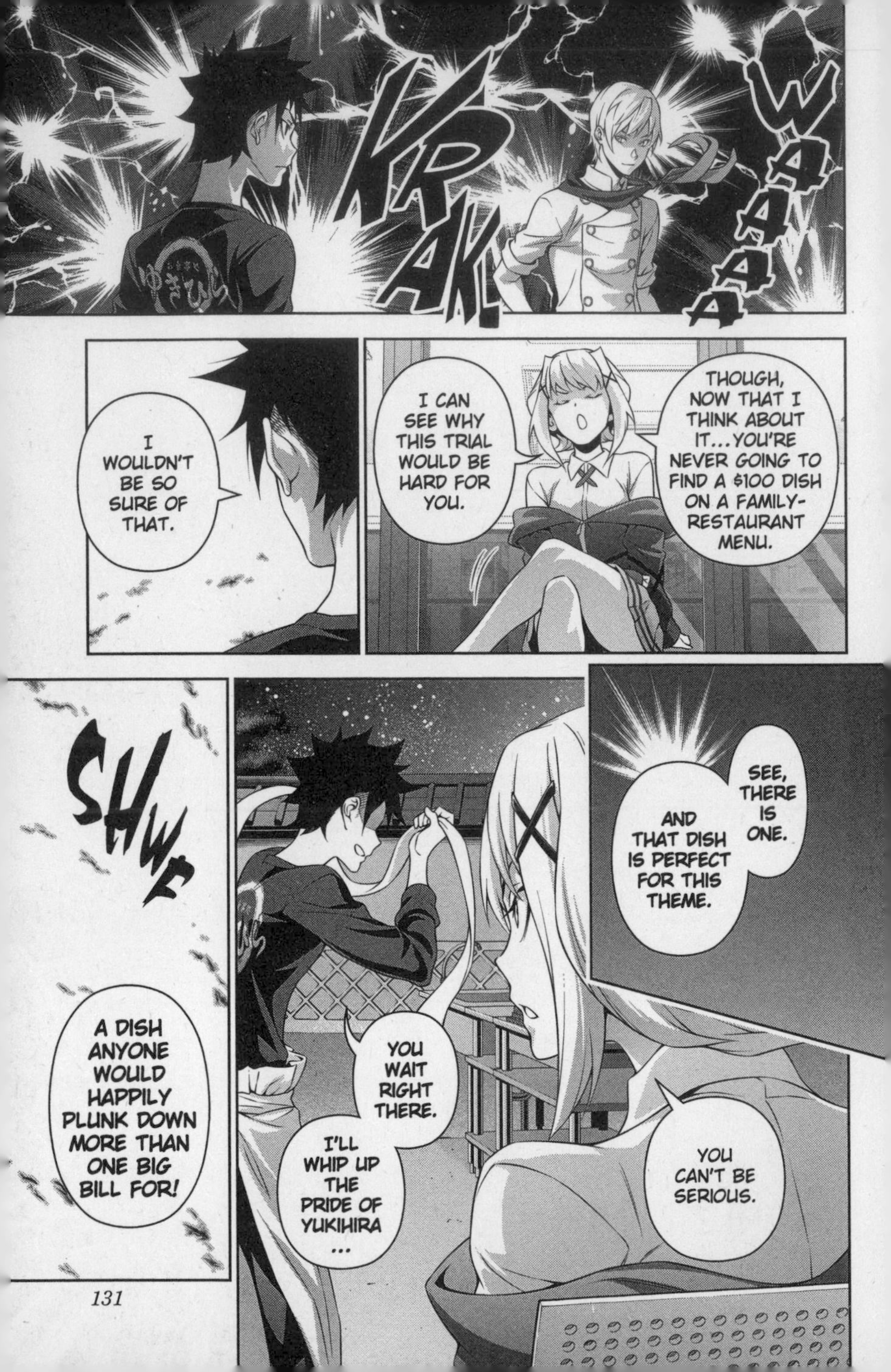
WAAAAA
KRAKL
THOUGH, NOW THAT I THINK ABOUT IT...YOU'RE NEVER GOING TO FIND A $100 DISH ON A FAMILY-RESTAURANT MENU.
I CAN SEE WHY THIS TRIAL WOULD BE HARD FOR YOU.
I WOULDN'T BE SO SURE OF THAT.
SEE, THERE IS ONE.
AND THAT DISH IS PERFECT FOR THIS THEME.
YOU CAN'T BE SERIOUS.
YOU WAIT RIGHT THERE.
I'LL WHIP UP THE PRIDE OF YUKIHIRA...
SHWF
A DISH ANYONE WOULD HAPPILY PLUNK DOWN MORE THAN ONE BIG BILL FOR!

ARTIST: YUTO TSUKUDA RECIPE BY: YUKI MORISAKI

VOLUME 33
SPECIAL SUPPLEMENT!

PRACTICAL RECIPE #2

INSTANT CANNED BEEF JOKE SUKIYAKI

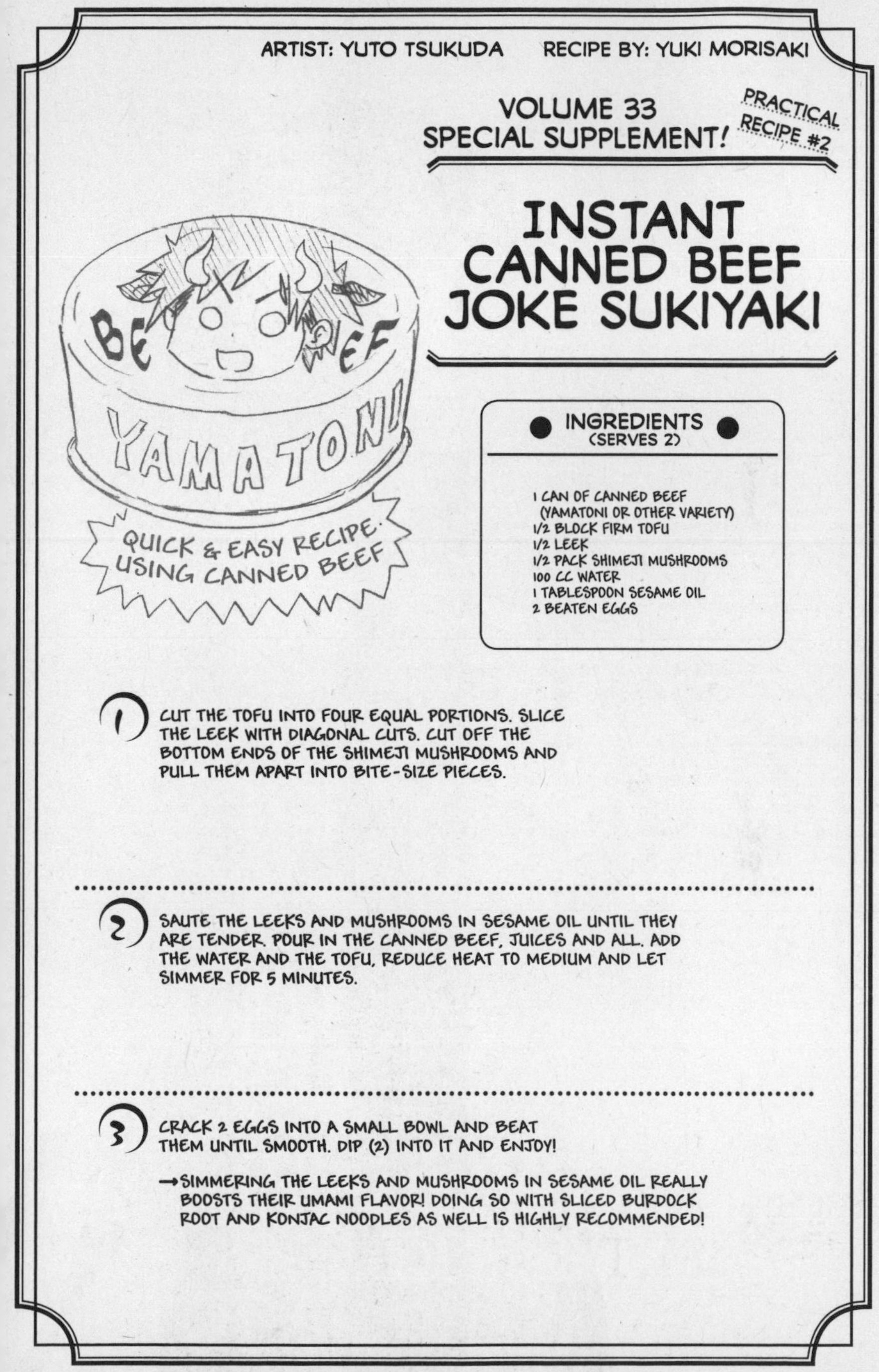
BEEF
YAMATONI
QUICK & EASY RECIPE USING CANNED BEEF

INGREDIENTS
(SERVES 2)

1 CAN OF CANNED BEEF (YAMATONI OR OTHER VARIETY)
1/2 BLOCK FIRM TOFU
1/2 LEEK
1/2 PACK SHIMEJI MUSHROOMS
100 CC WATER
1 TABLESPOON SESAME OIL
2 BEATEN EGGS

1. CUT THE TOFU INTO FOUR EQUAL PORTIONS. SLICE THE LEEK WITH DIAGONAL CUTS. CUT OFF THE BOTTOM ENDS OF THE SHIMEJI MUSHROOMS AND PULL THEM APART INTO BITE-SIZE PIECES.

2. SAUTE THE LEEKS AND MUSHROOMS IN SESAME OIL UNTIL THEY ARE TENDER. POUR IN THE CANNED BEEF, JUICES AND ALL. ADD THE WATER AND THE TOFU, REDUCE HEAT TO MEDIUM AND LET SIMMER FOR 5 MINUTES.

3. CRACK 2 EGGS INTO A SMALL BOWL AND BEAT THEM UNTIL SMOOTH. DIP (2) INTO IT AND ENJOY!

→SIMMERING THE LEEKS AND MUSHROOMS IN SESAME OIL REALLY BOOSTS THEIR UMAMI FLAVOR! DOING SO WITH SLICED BURDOCK ROOT AND KONJAC NOODLES AS WELL IS HIGHLY RECOMMENDED!

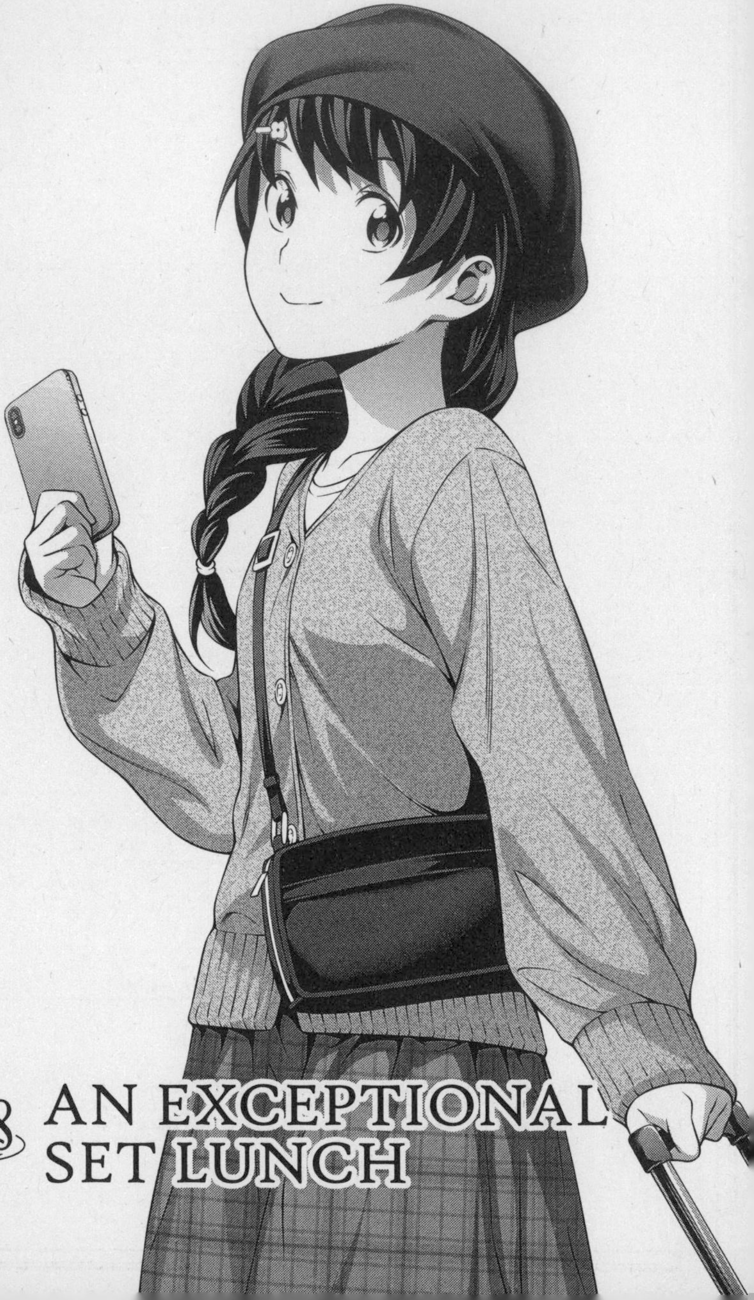

288 AN EXCEPTIONAL SET LUNCH

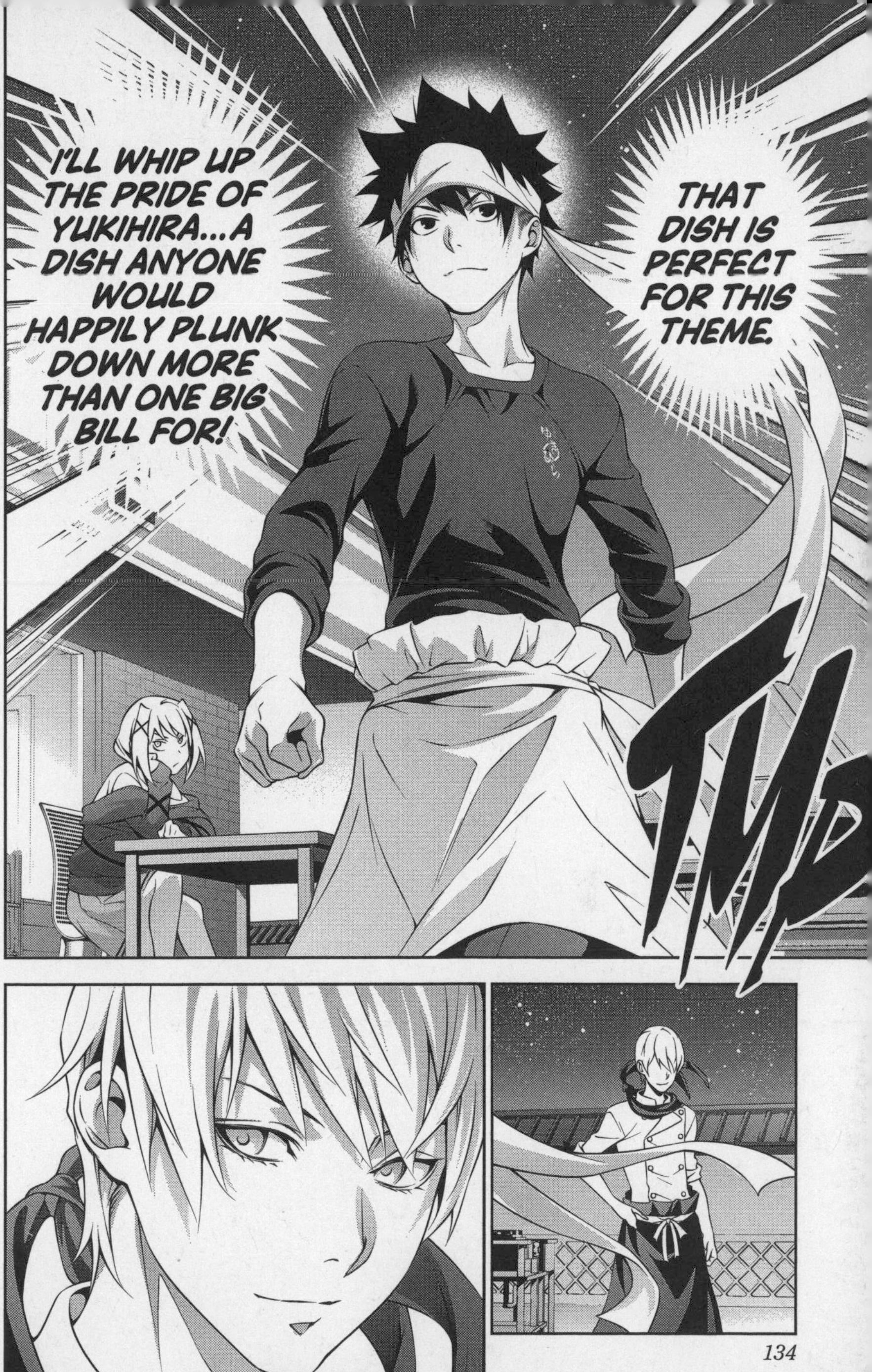
THAT DISH IS PERFECT FOR THIS THEME.
I'LL WHIP UP THE PRIDE OF YUKIHIRA...A DISH ANYONE WOULD HAPPILY PLUNK DOWN MORE THAN ONE BIG BILL FOR!

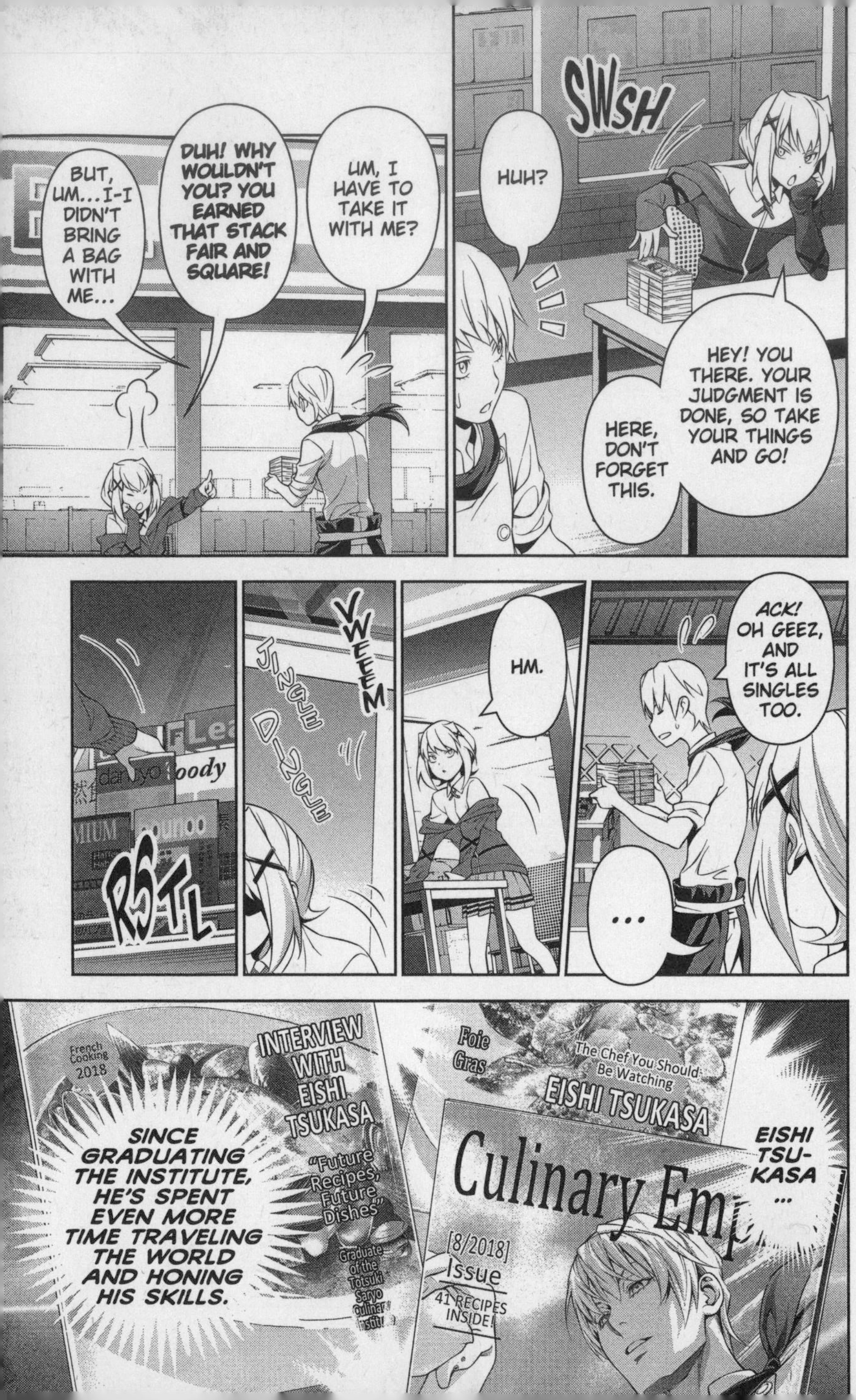

SWSH
HUH?
HEY! YOU THERE. YOUR JUDGMENT IS DONE, SO TAKE YOUR THINGS AND GO!
HERE, DON'T FORGET THIS.
UM, I HAVE TO TAKE IT WITH ME?
DUH! WHY WOULDN'T YOU? YOU EARNED THAT STACK FAIR AND SQUARE!
BUT, UM...I-I DIDN'T BRING A BAG WITH ME...
ACK! OH GEEZ, AND IT'S ALL SINGLES TOO.
...
HM.
VWEEEM
JINGLE DINGLE
RSTL
EISHI TSUKASA...
Foie Gras
The Chef You Should Be Watching
EISHI TSUKASA
Culinary Em
[8/2018] Issue
41 RECIPES INSIDE!
French Cooking 2018
INTERVIEW WITH EISHI TSUKASA
"Future Recipes, Future Dishes"
Graduate of the Totsuki Saryo Culinary
SINCE GRADUATING THE INSTITUTE, HE'S SPENT EVEN MORE TIME TRAVELING THE WORLD AND HONING HIS SKILLS.

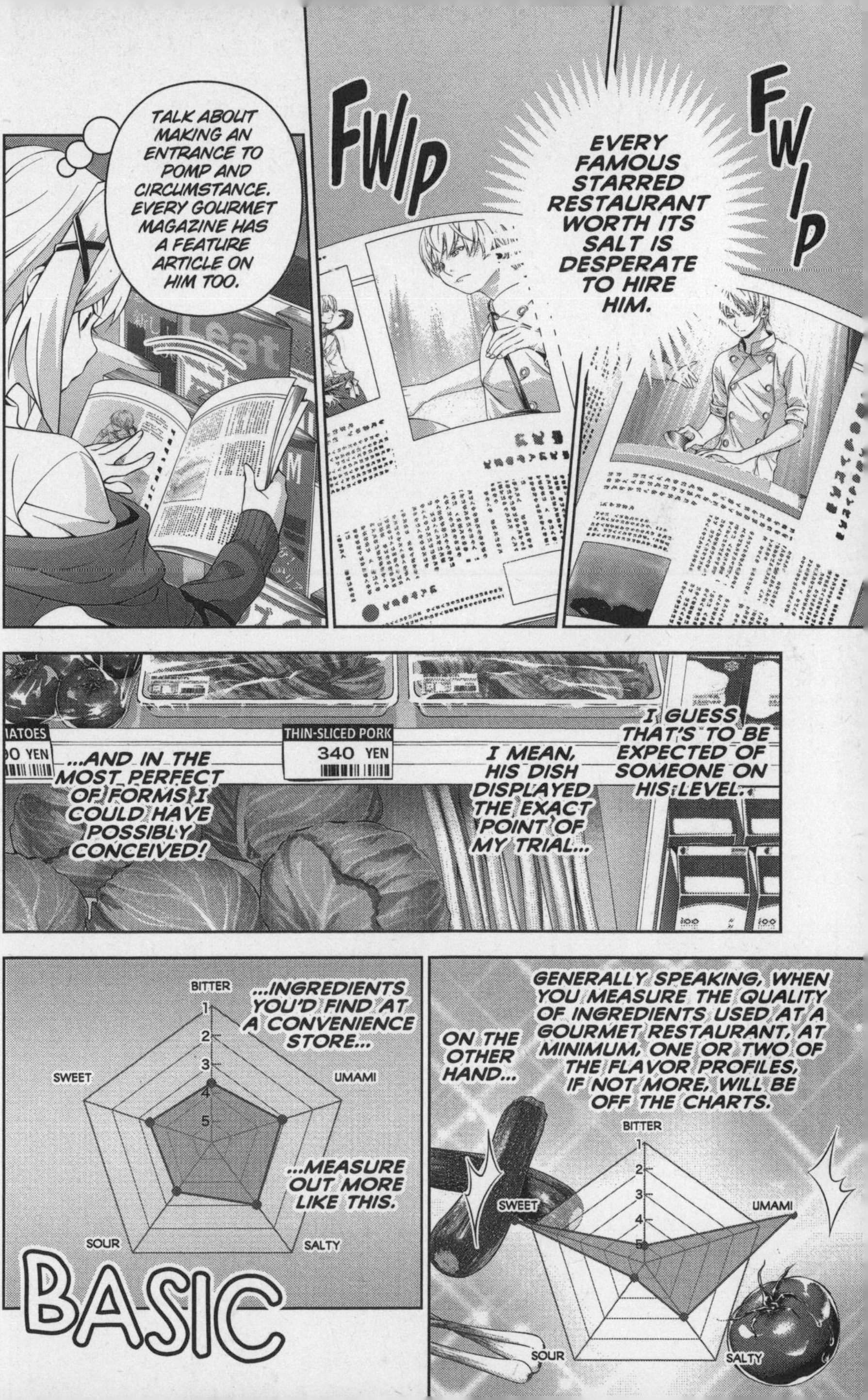
FWIP
FWIP
EVERY FAMOUS STARRED RESTAURANT WORTH ITS SALT IS DESPERATE TO HIRE HIM.
TALK ABOUT MAKING AN ENTRANCE TO POMP AND CIRCUMSTANCE. EVERY GOURMET MAGAZINE HAS A FEATURE ARTICLE ON HIM TOO.
I GUESS THAT'S TO BE EXPECTED OF SOMEONE ON HIS LEVEL.
I MEAN, HIS DISH DISPLAYED THE EXACT POINT OF MY TRIAL...
THIN-SLICED PORK
340 YEN
...AND IN THE MOST PERFECT OF FORMS I COULD HAVE POSSIBLY CONCEIVED!
GENERALLY SPEAKING, WHEN YOU MEASURE THE QUALITY OF INGREDIENTS USED AT A GOURMET RESTAURANT, AT MINIMUM, ONE OR TWO OF THE FLAVOR PROFILES, IF NOT MORE, WILL BE OFF THE CHARTS.
ON THE OTHER HAND...
BITTER
UMAMI
SALTY
SOUR
SWEET
1
2
3
4
5
...INGREDIENTS YOU'D FIND AT A CONVENIENCE STORE...
...MEASURE OUT MORE LIKE THIS.
BITTER
UMAMI
SALTY
SOUR
SWEET
1
2
3
4
5
BASIC

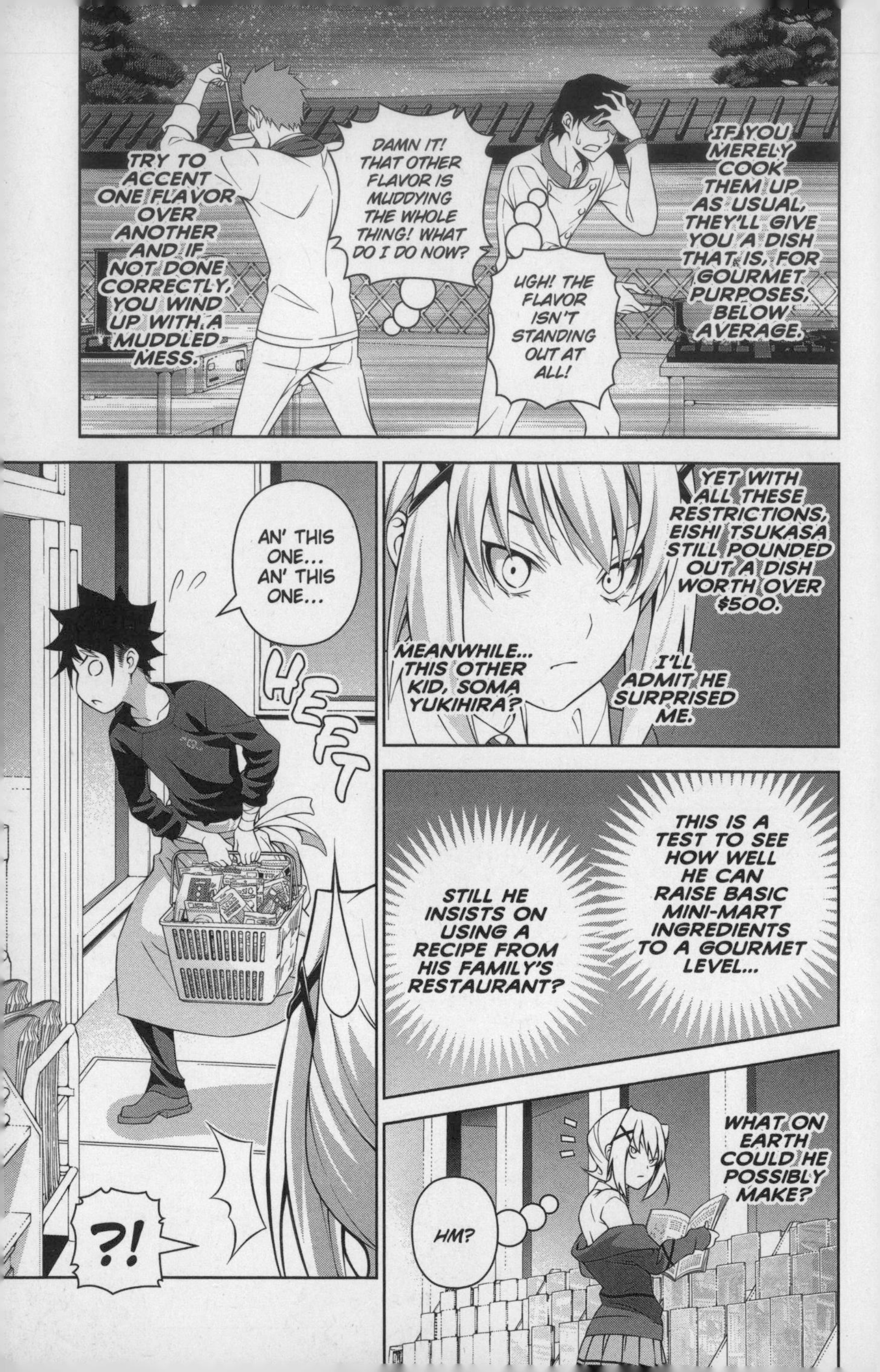
IF YOU MERELY COOK THEM UP AS USUAL, THEY'LL GIVE YOU A DISH THAT IS, FOR GOURMET PURPOSES, BELOW AVERAGE.
TRY TO ACCENT ONE FLAVOR OVER ANOTHER AND IF NOT DONE CORRECTLY, YOU WIND UP WITH A MUDDLED MESS.
DAMN IT! THAT OTHER FLAVOR IS MUDDYING THE WHOLE THING! WHAT DO I DO NOW?
UGH! THE FLAVOR ISN'T STANDING OUT AT ALL!
YET WITH ALL THESE RESTRICTIONS, EISHI TSUKASA STILL POUNDED OUT A DISH WORTH OVER $500.
I'LL ADMIT HE SURPRISED ME.
MEANWHILE... THIS OTHER KID, SOMA YUKIHIRA?
THIS IS A TEST TO SEE HOW WELL HE CAN RAISE BASIC MINI-MART INGREDIENTS TO A GOURMET LEVEL...
STILL HE INSISTS ON USING A RECIPE FROM HIS FAMILY'S RESTAURANT?
WHAT ON EARTH COULD HE POSSIBLY MAKE?
HM?
AN' THIS ONE... AN' THIS ONE...
HEFT
?!

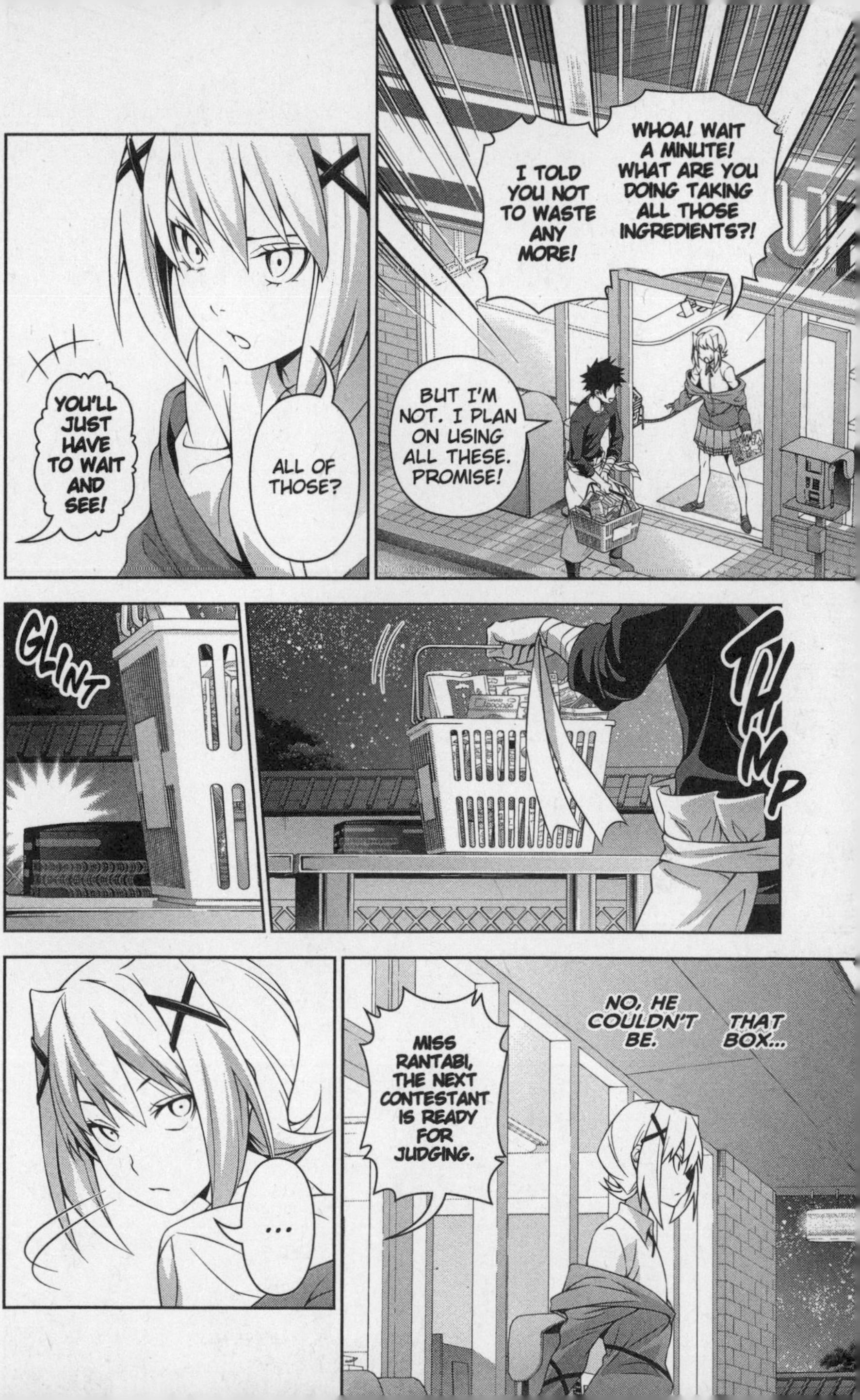
WHOA! WAIT A MINUTE! WHAT ARE YOU DOING TAKING ALL THOSE INGREDIENTS?!
I TOLD YOU NOT TO WASTE ANY MORE!
BUT I'M NOT. I PLAN ON USING ALL THESE. PROMISE!
ALL OF THOSE?
YOU'LL JUST HAVE TO WAIT AND SEE!
THUMP
GLINT
THAT BOX...
NO, HE COULDN'T BE.
MISS RANTABI, THE NEXT CONTESTANT IS READY FOR JUDGING.
...

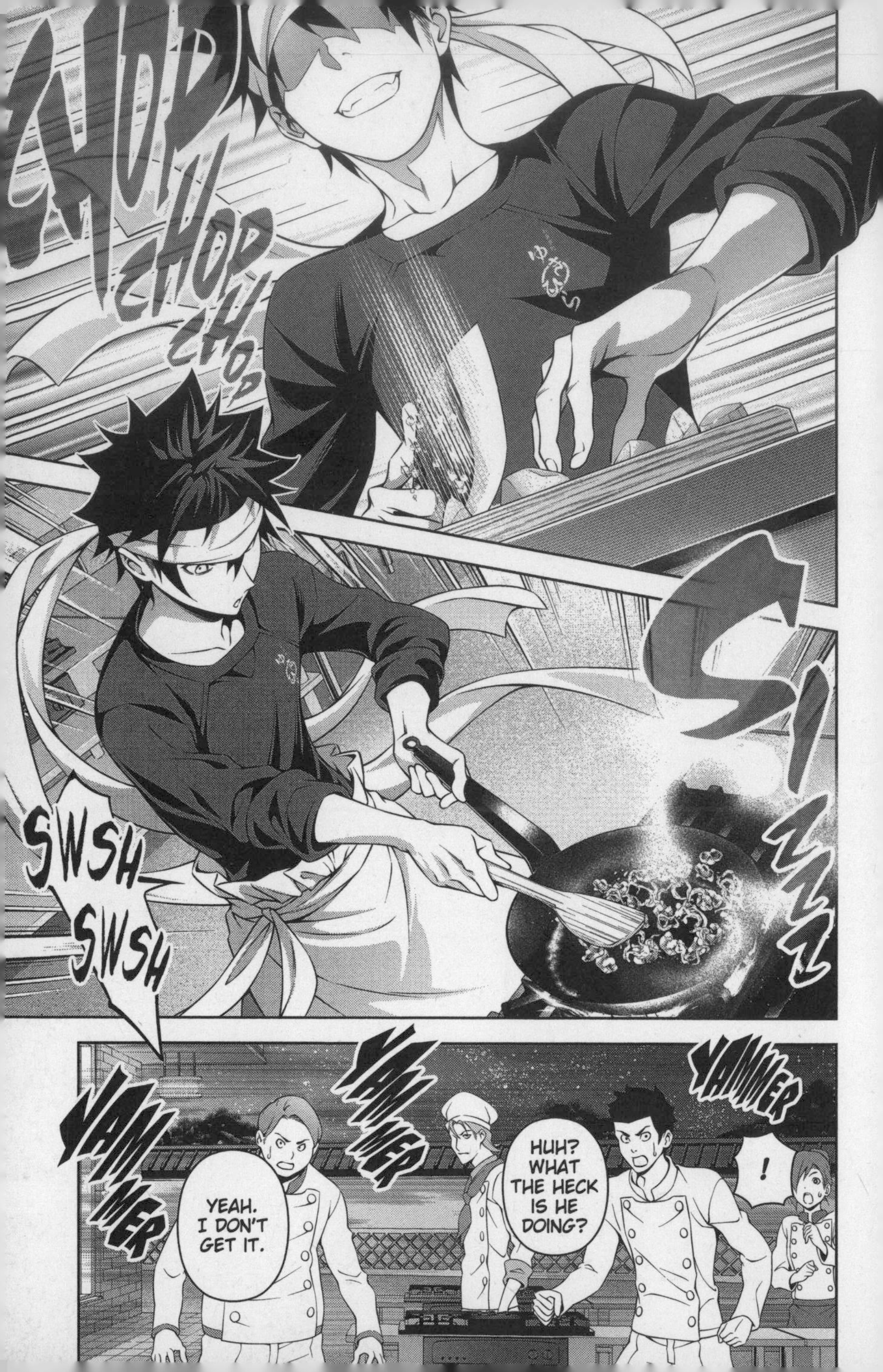
CHOP CHOP CHOP
SIZZZ
SWSH-SWSH
YAMMER
!
HUH? WHAT THE HECK IS HE DOING?
YAMMER
YEAH. I DON'T GET IT.
YAMMER

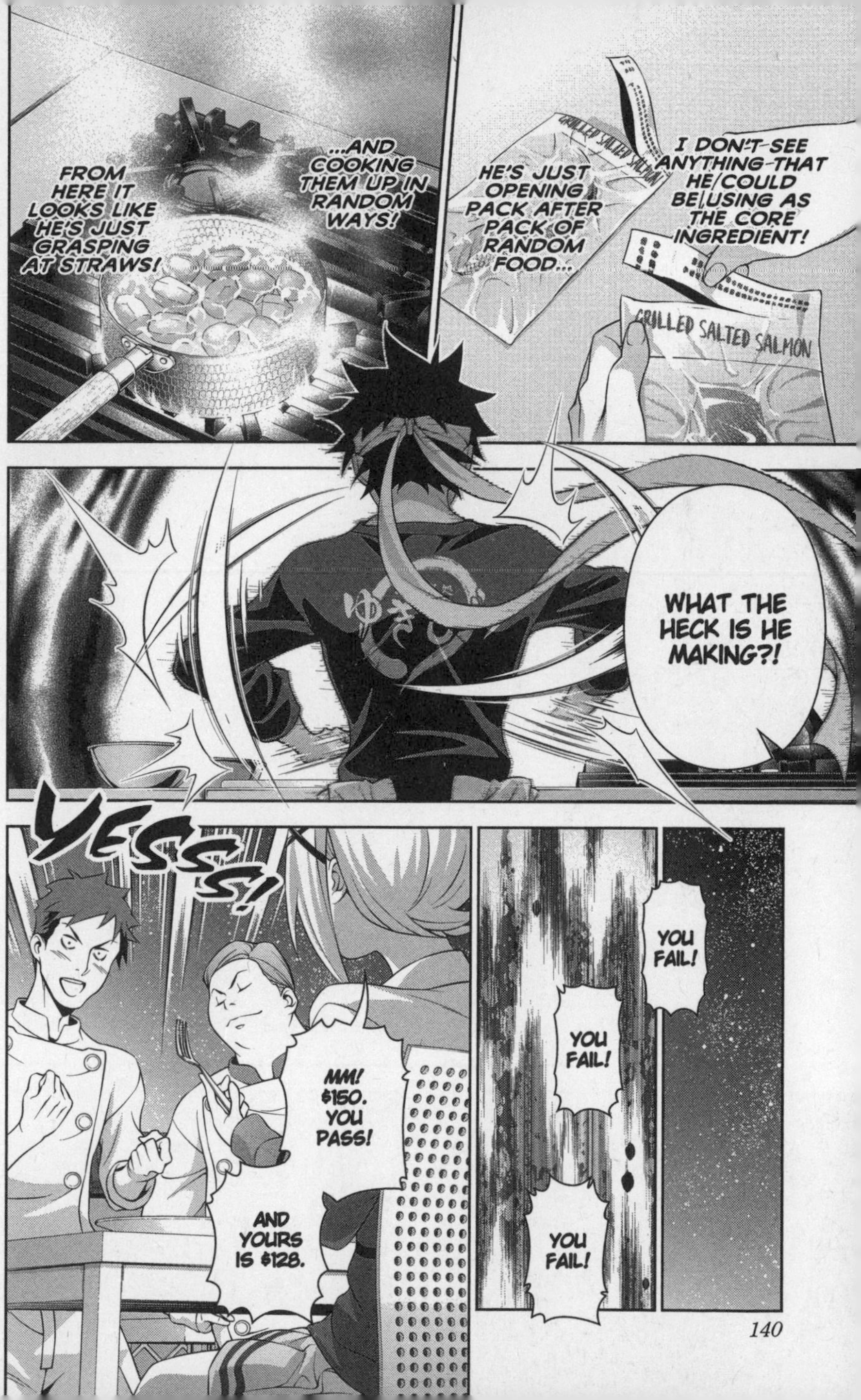
I DON'T SEE ANYTHING THAT HE COULD BE USING AS THE CORE INGREDIENT!
GRILLED SALTED SALMON
HE'S JUST OPENING PACK AFTER PACK OF RANDOM FOOD...
GRILLED SALTED SALMON
...AND COOKING THEM UP IN RANDOM WAYS!
FROM HERE IT LOOKS LIKE HE'S JUST GRASPING AT STRAWS!
WHAT THE HECK IS HE MAKING?!
YOU FAIL!
YOU FAIL!
YOU FAIL!
YESSS!
MM! $150. YOU PASS!
AND YOURS IS $128.

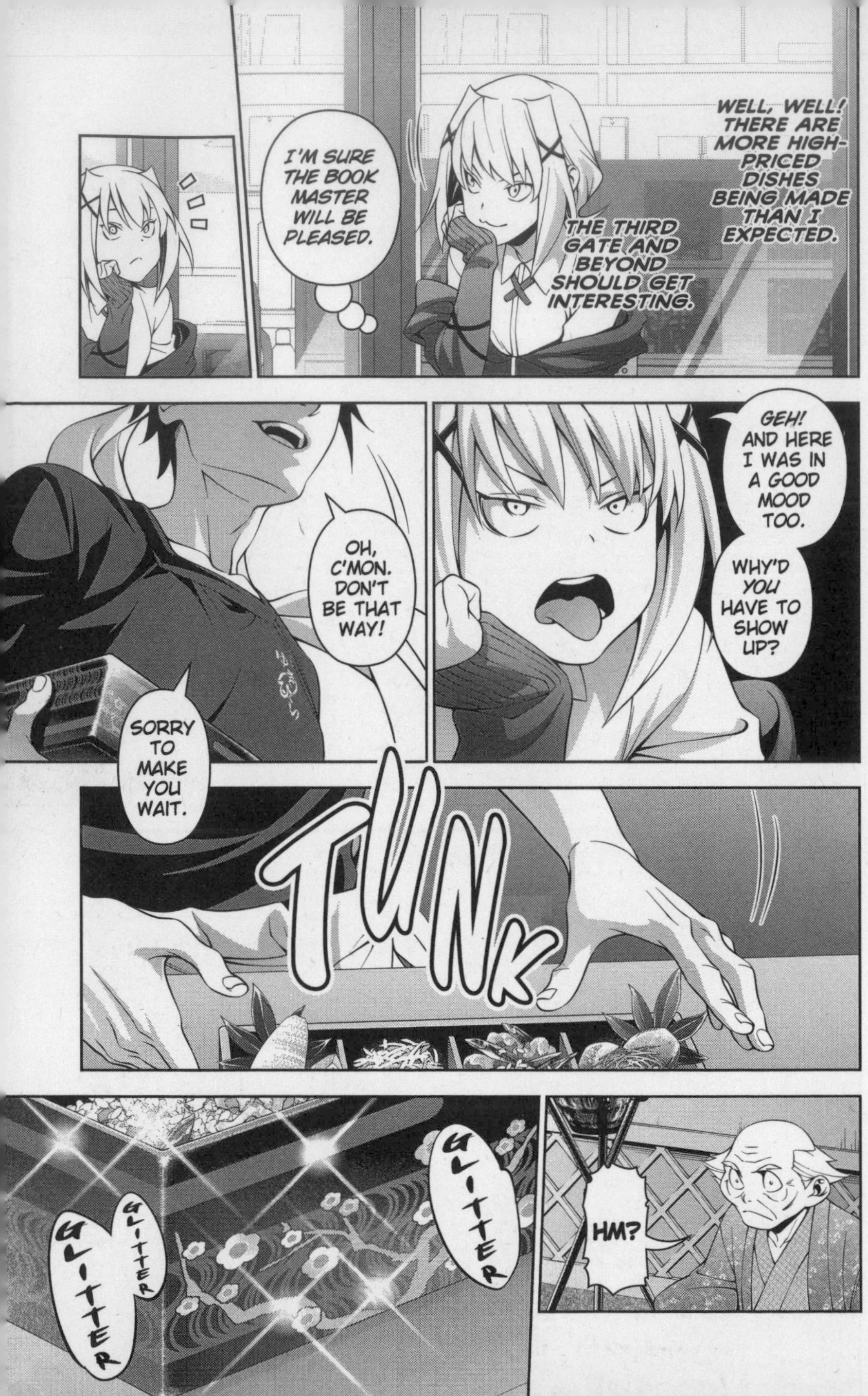
WELL, WELL! THERE ARE MORE HIGH-PRICED DISHES BEING MADE THAN I EXPECTED.
THE THIRD GATE AND BEYOND SHOULD GET INTERESTING.
I'M SURE THE BOOK MASTER WILL BE PLEASED.
GEH! AND HERE I WAS IN A GOOD MOOD TOO.
WHY'D YOU HAVE TO SHOW UP?
OH, C'MON. DON'T BE THAT WAY!
SORRY TO MAKE YOU WAIT.
TUNK
HM?
GLITTER
GLITTER
GLITTER

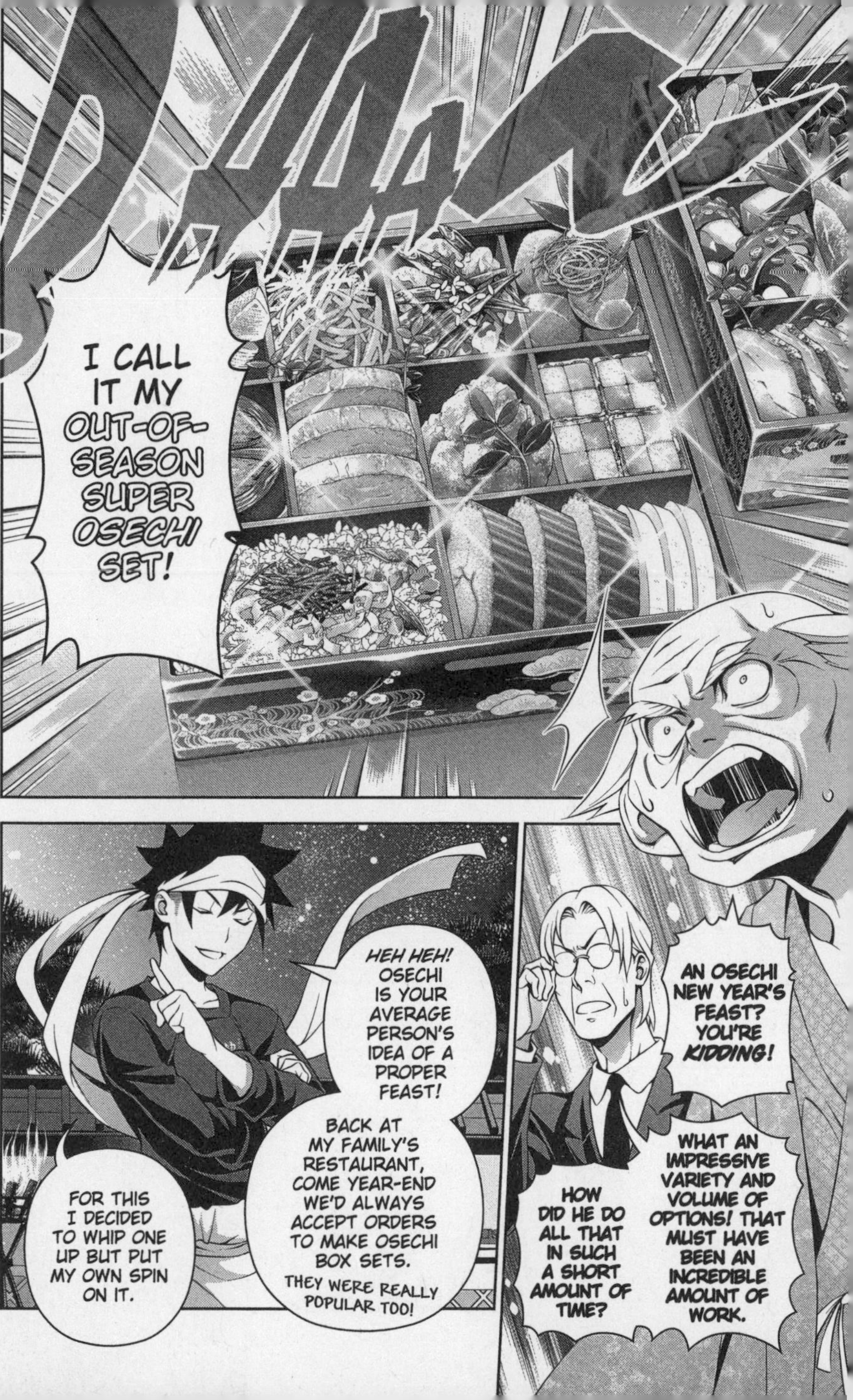
I CALL IT MY OUT-OF-SEASON SUPER OSECHI SET!
AN OSECHI NEW YEAR'S FEAST? YOU'RE KIDDING!
WHAT AN IMPRESSIVE VARIETY AND VOLUME OF OPTIONS! THAT MUST HAVE BEEN AN INCREDIBLE AMOUNT OF WORK.
HOW DID HE DO ALL THAT IN SUCH A SHORT AMOUNT OF TIME?
HEH HEH! OSECHI IS YOUR AVERAGE PERSON'S IDEA OF A PROPER FEAST!
BACK AT MY FAMILY'S RESTAURANT, COME YEAR-END WE'D ALWAYS ACCEPT ORDERS TO MAKE OSECHI BOX SETS.
THEY WERE REALLY POPULAR TOO!
FOR THIS I DECIDED TO WHIP ONE UP BUT PUT MY OWN SPIN ON IT.

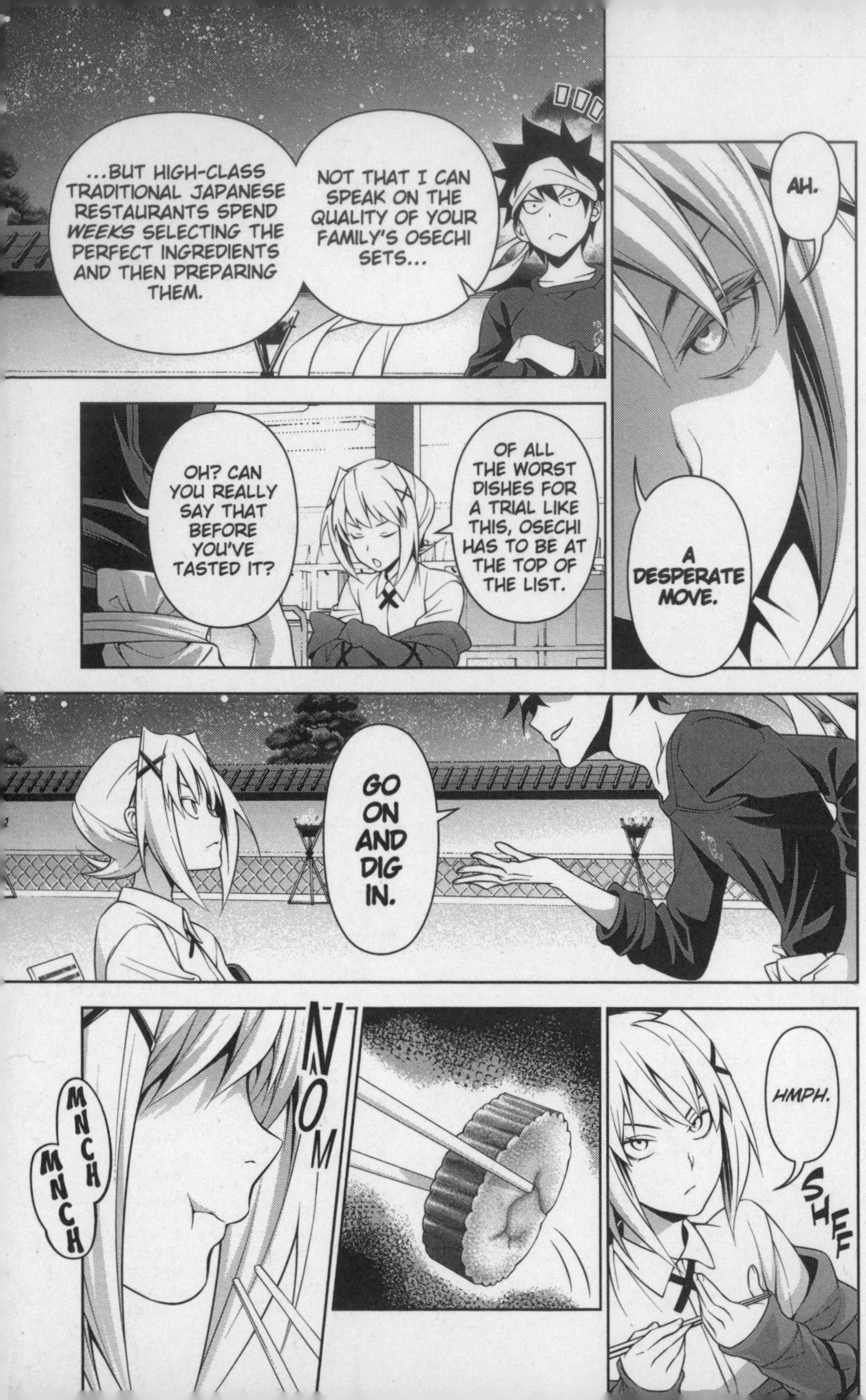
AH.
A DESPERATE MOVE.
NOT THAT I CAN SPEAK ON THE QUALITY OF YOUR FAMILY'S OSECHI SETS...
...BUT HIGH-CLASS TRADITIONAL JAPANESE RESTAURANTS SPEND *WEEKS* SELECTING THE PERFECT INGREDIENTS AND THEN PREPARING THEM.
OF ALL THE WORST DISHES FOR A TRIAL LIKE THIS, OSECHI HAS TO BE AT THE TOP OF THE LIST.
OH? CAN YOU REALLY SAY THAT BEFORE YOU'VE TASTED IT?
GO ON AND DIG IN.
HMPH.
SHFF
NOM
MNCH
MNCH
MNCH

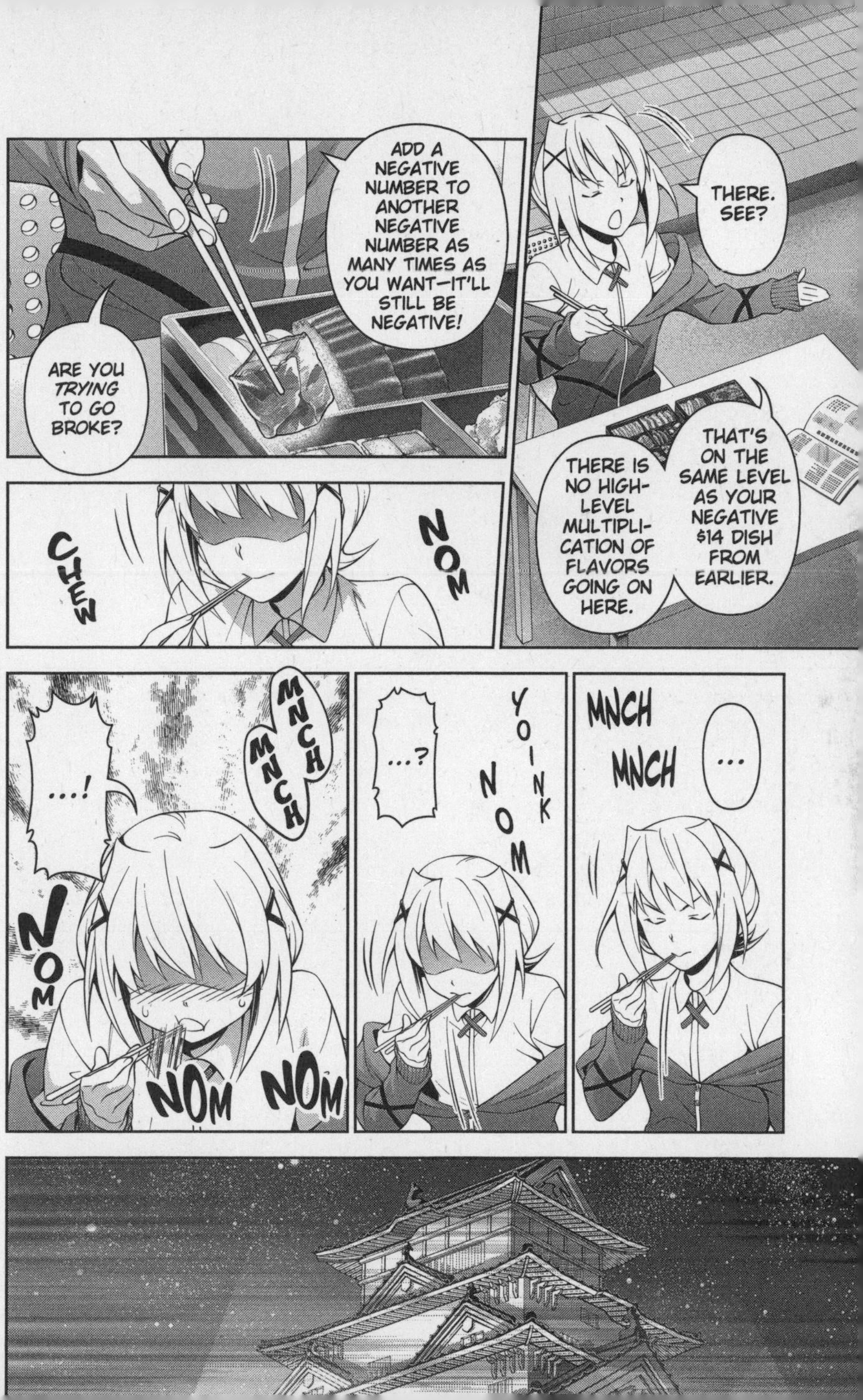
THERE. SEE?
THAT'S ON THE SAME LEVEL AS YOUR NEGATIVE $14 DISH FROM EARLIER.
THERE IS NO HIGH-LEVEL MULTIPLICATION OF FLAVORS GOING ON HERE.
ADD A NEGATIVE NUMBER TO ANOTHER NEGATIVE NUMBER AS MANY TIMES AS YOU WANT—IT'LL STILL BE NEGATIVE!
ARE YOU *TRYING* TO GO BROKE?
NOM
CHEW
MNCH
MNCH
...
YOINK
NOM
...?
MNCH MNCH
...!
NOM
NOM NOM

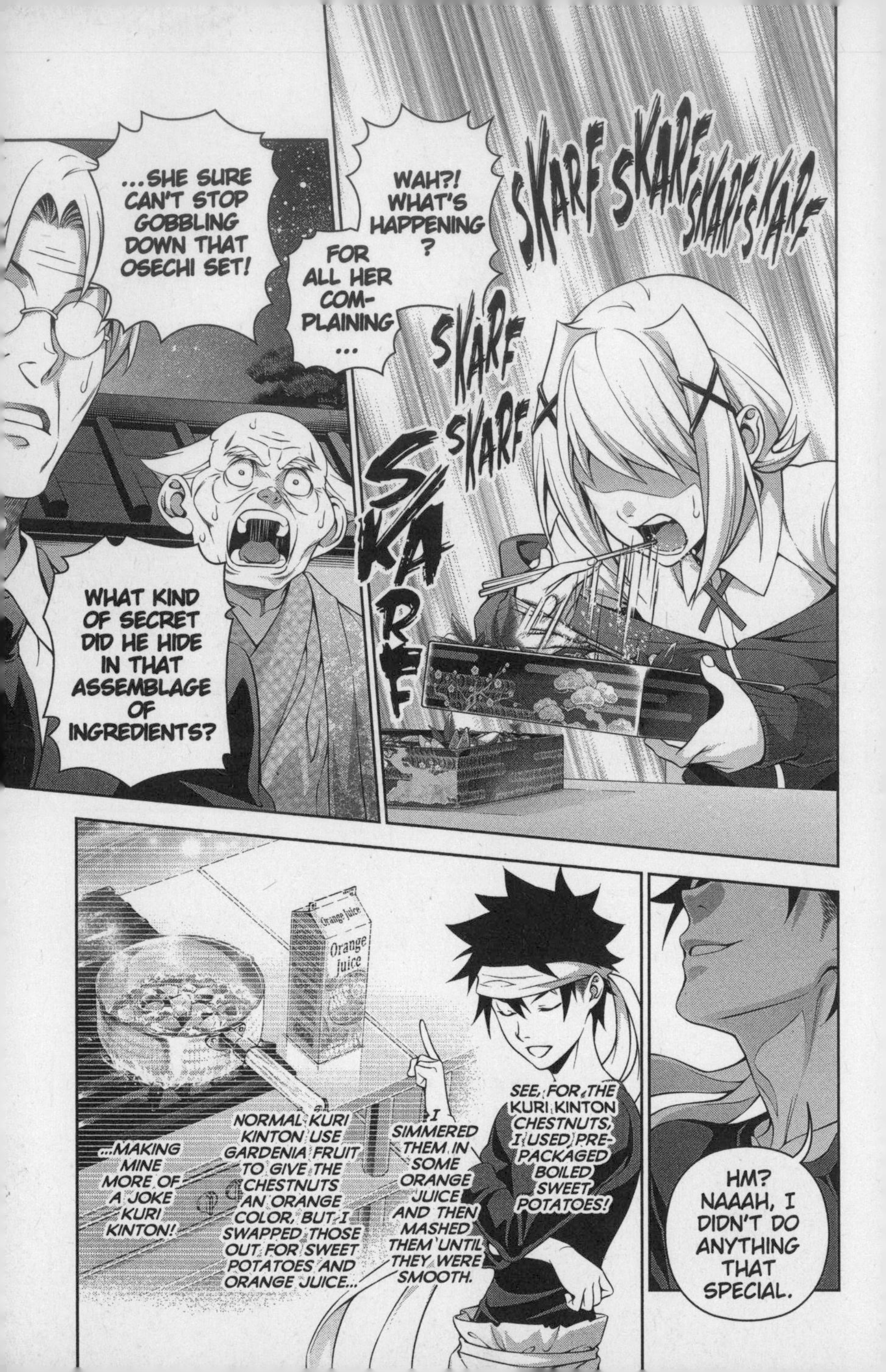
SKARF SKARF SKARF SKARF
WAH?! WHAT'S HAPPENING?
SKARF SKARF
FOR ALL HER COM-PLAINING...
SKARF
...SHE SURE CAN'T STOP GOBBLING DOWN THAT OSECHI SET!
WHAT KIND OF SECRET DID HE HIDE IN THAT ASSEMBLAGE OF INGREDIENTS?
HM? NAAAH, I DIDN'T DO ANYTHING THAT SPECIAL.
SEE, FOR THE KURI KINTON CHESTNUTS, I USED PRE-PACKAGED BOILED SWEET POTATOES!
I SIMMERED THEM IN SOME ORANGE JUICE AND THEN MASHED THEM UNTIL THEY WERE SMOOTH.
Orange Juice
Orange Juice
NORMAL KURI KINTON USE GARDENIA FRUIT TO GIVE THE CHESTNUTS AN ORANGE COLOR, BUT I SWAPPED THOSE OUT FOR SWEET POTATOES AND ORANGE JUICE...
...MAKING MINE MORE OF A JOKE KURI KINTON!

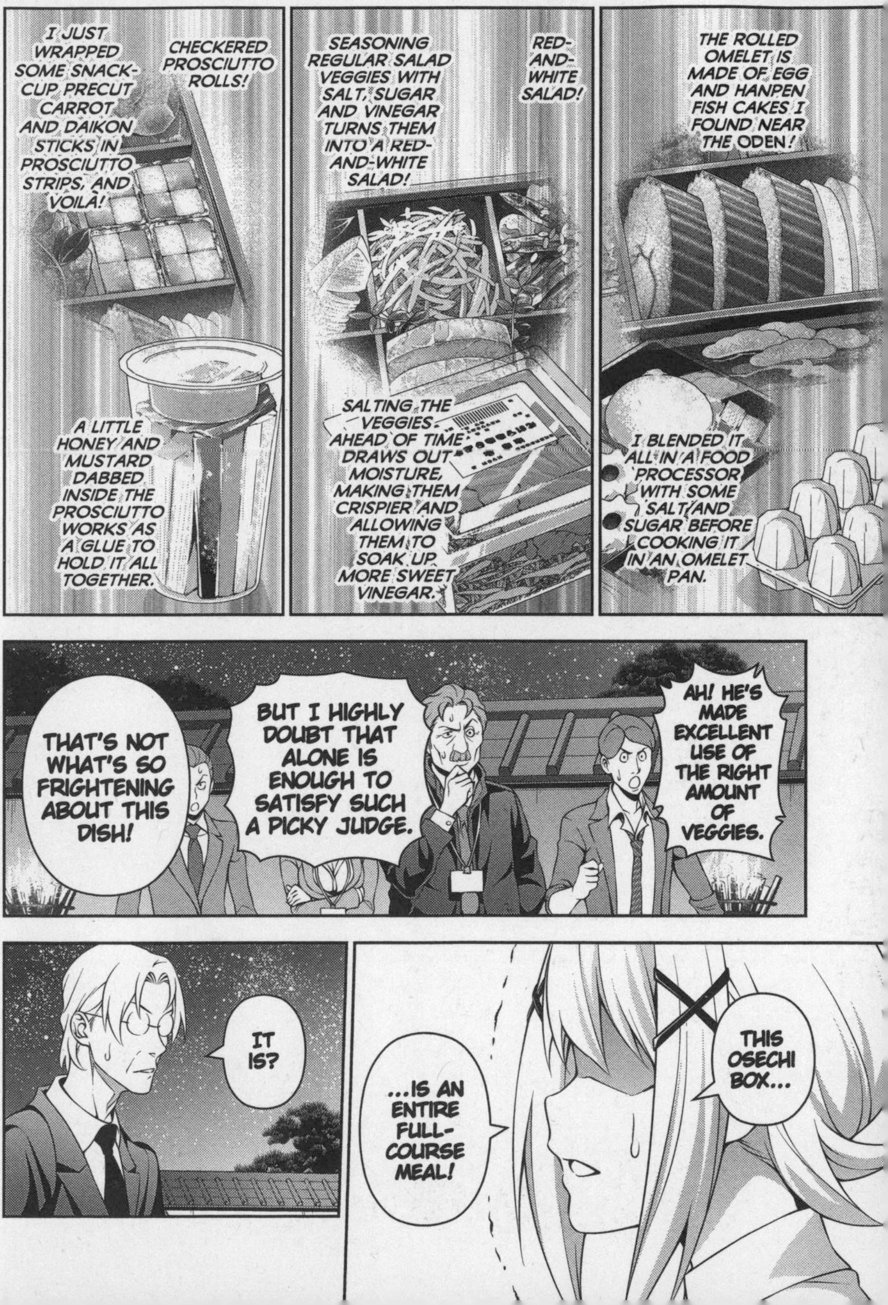
THE ROLLED OMELET IS MADE OF EGG AND HANPEN FISH CAKES I FOUND NEAR THE ODEN!
I BLENDED IT ALL IN A FOOD PROCESSOR WITH SOME SALT AND SUGAR BEFORE COOKING IT IN AN OMELET PAN.
RED-AND-WHITE SALAD!
SEASONING REGULAR SALAD VEGGIES WITH SALT, SUGAR AND VINEGAR TURNS THEM INTO A RED-AND-WHITE SALAD!
SALTING THE VEGGIES AHEAD OF TIME DRAWS OUT MOISTURE, MAKING THEM CRISPIER AND ALLOWING THEM TO SOAK UP MORE SWEET VINEGAR.
CHECKERED PROSCIUTTO ROLLS!
I JUST WRAPPED SOME SNACK-CUP PRECUT CARROT AND DAIKON STICKS IN PROSCIUTTO STRIPS, AND VOILÀ!
A LITTLE HONEY AND MUSTARD DABBED INSIDE THE PROSCIUTTO WORKS AS A GLUE TO HOLD IT ALL TOGETHER.
AH! HE'S MADE EXCELLENT USE OF THE RIGHT AMOUNT OF VEGGIES.
BUT I HIGHLY DOUBT THAT ALONE IS ENOUGH TO SATISFY SUCH A PICKY JUDGE.
THAT'S NOT WHAT'S SO FRIGHTENING ABOUT THIS DISH!
THIS OSECHI BOX...
...IS AN ENTIRE FULL-COURSE MEAL!
IT IS?

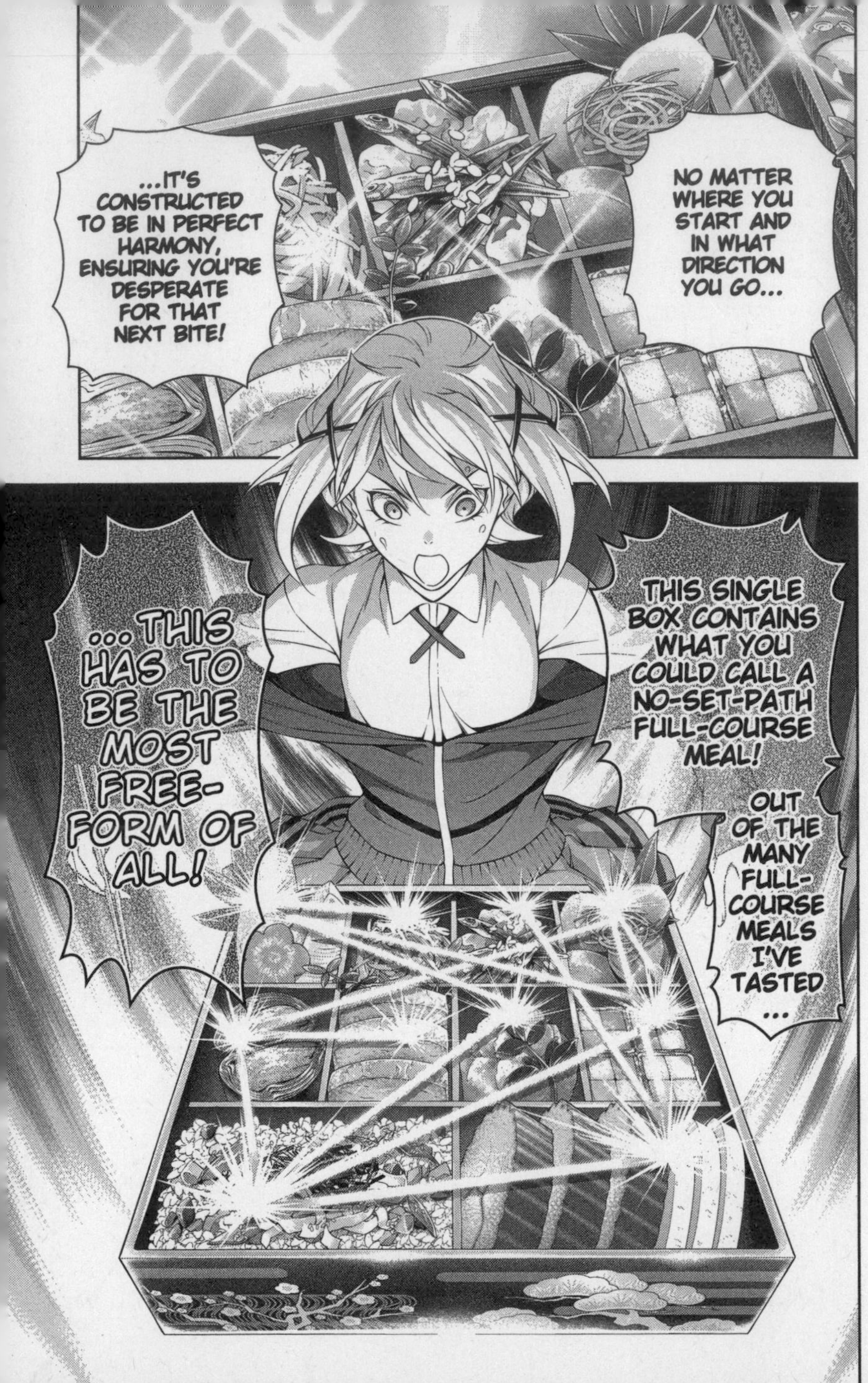
NO MATTER WHERE YOU START AND IN WHAT DIRECTION YOU GO...
...IT'S CONSTRUCTED TO BE IN PERFECT HARMONY, ENSURING YOU'RE DESPERATE FOR THAT NEXT BITE!
THIS SINGLE BOX CONTAINS WHAT YOU COULD CALL A NO-SET-PATH FULL-COURSE MEAL!
OUT OF THE MANY FULL-COURSE MEALS I'VE TASTED...
...THIS HAS TO BE THE MOST FREE-FORM OF ALL!

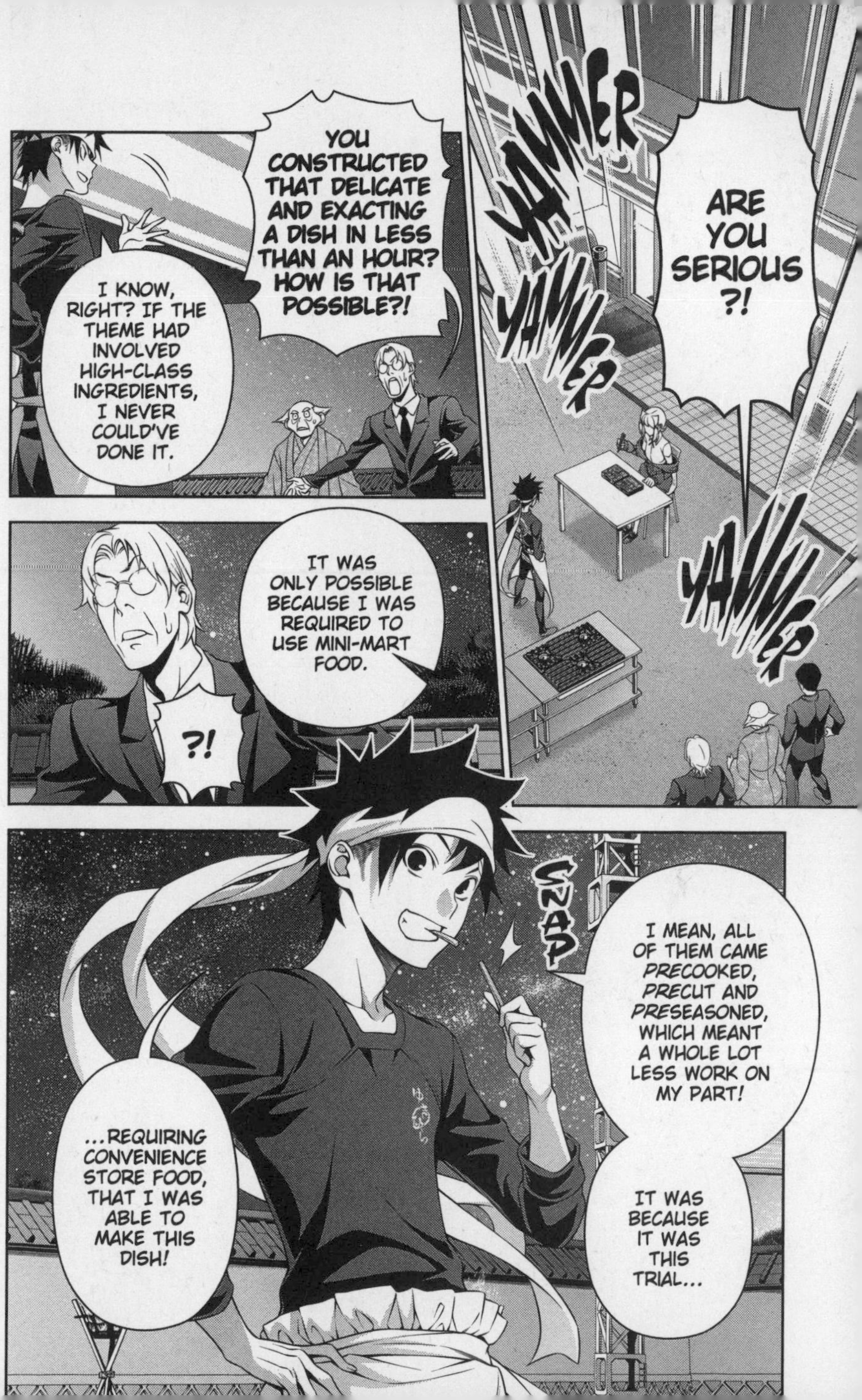
YAMMER
YAMMER
ARE YOU SERIOUS?!
YAMMER
YOU CONSTRUCTED THAT DELICATE AND EXACTING A DISH IN LESS THAN AN HOUR? HOW IS THAT POSSIBLE?!
I KNOW, RIGHT? IF THE THEME HAD INVOLVED HIGH-CLASS INGREDIENTS, I NEVER COULD'VE DONE IT.
IT WAS ONLY POSSIBLE BECAUSE I WAS REQUIRED TO USE MINI-MART FOOD.
?!
SNAP
I MEAN, ALL OF THEM CAME *PRECOOKED*, *PRECUT* AND *PRESEASONED*, WHICH MEANT A WHOLE LOT LESS WORK ON MY PART!
IT WAS BECAUSE IT WAS THIS TRIAL...
...REQUIRING CONVENIENCE STORE FOOD, THAT I WAS ABLE TO MAKE THIS DISH!

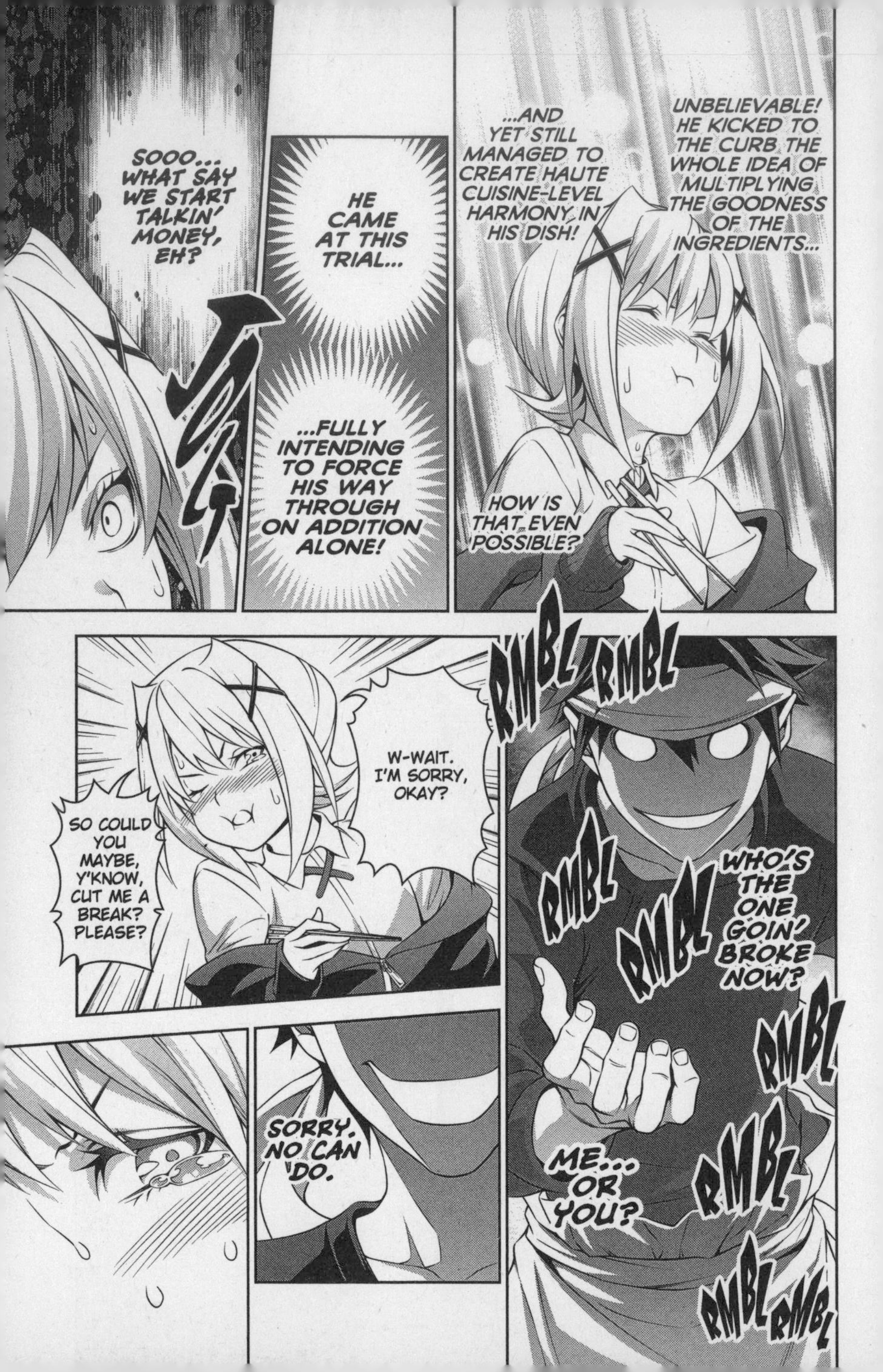
UNBELIEVABLE! HE KICKED TO THE CURB THE WHOLE IDEA OF MULTIPLYING THE GOODNESS OF THE INGREDIENTS...
...AND YET STILL MANAGED TO CREATE HAUTE CUISINE-LEVEL HARMONY IN HIS DISH!
HOW IS THAT EVEN POSSIBLE?
HE CAME AT THIS TRIAL...
...FULLY INTENDING TO FORCE HIS WAY THROUGH ON ADDITION ALONE!
SOOO... WHAT SAY WE START TALKIN' MONEY, EH?
RMBL RMBL
RMBL
RMBL
WHO'S THE ONE GOIN' BROKE NOW?
RMBL
RMBL
ME... OR YOU?
RMBL RMBL
W-WAIT. I'M SORRY, OKAY?
SO COULD YOU MAYBE, Y'KNOW, CUT ME A BREAK? PLEASE?
SORRY. NO CAN DO.

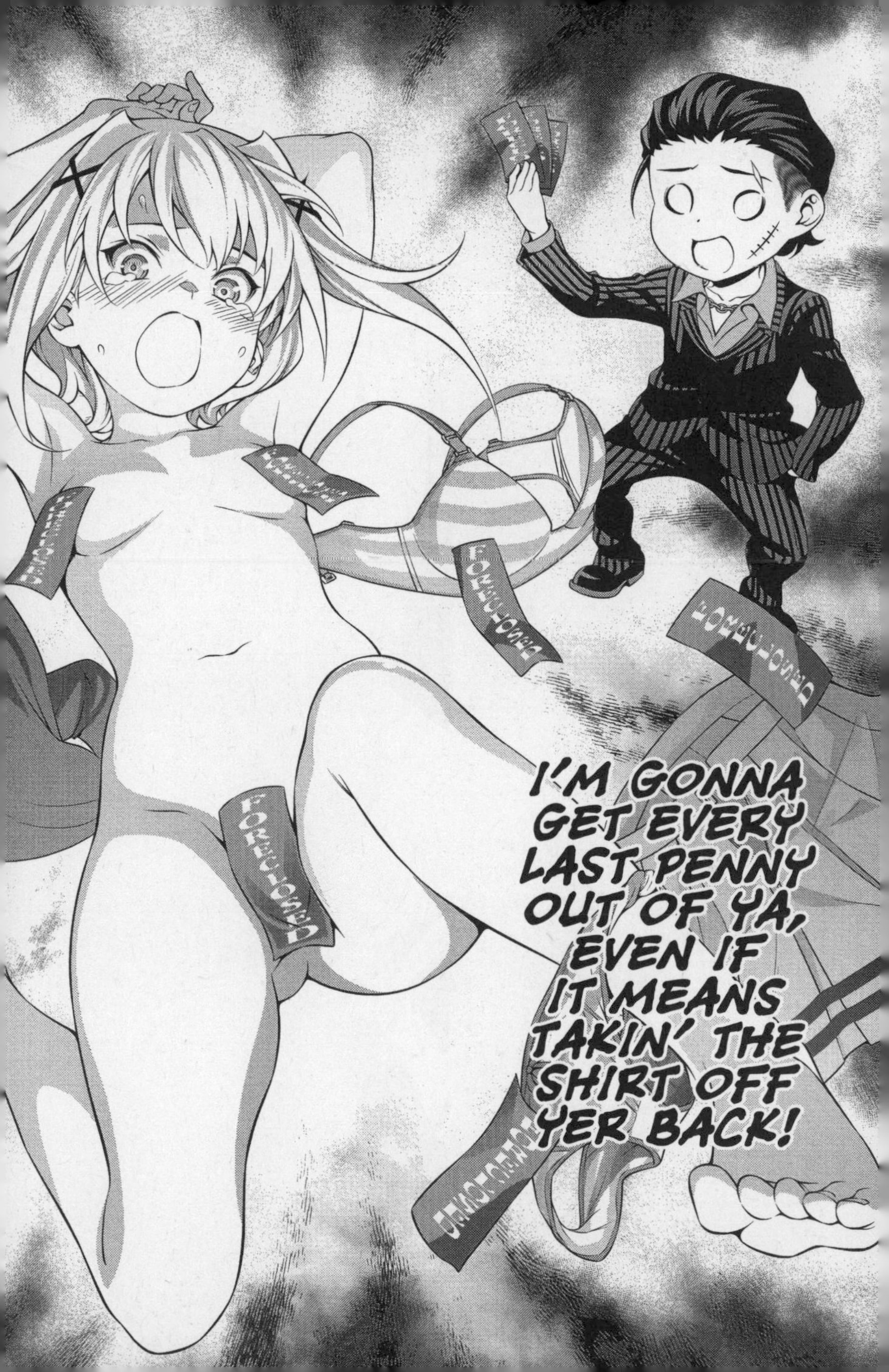
I'M GONNA GET EVERY LAST PENNY OUT OF YA, EVEN IF IT MEANS TAKIN' THE SHIRT OFF YER BACK!
FORECLOSED
FORECLOSED

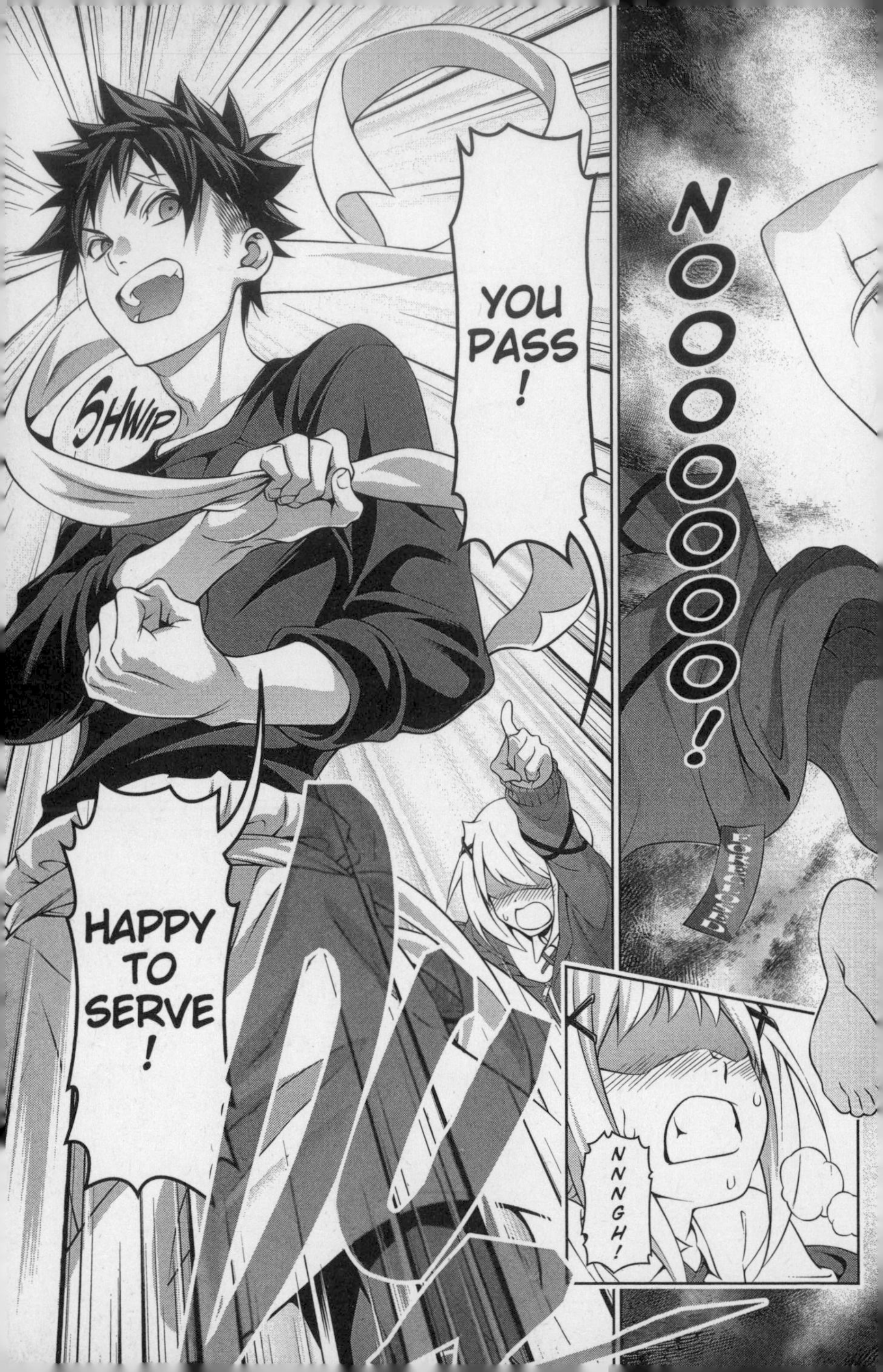
NOOOOOOOO!
NNNGH!
YOU PASS!
SHWIP
HAPPY TO SERVE!

ARTIST: YUTO TSUKUDA RECIPE BY: YUKI MORISAKI

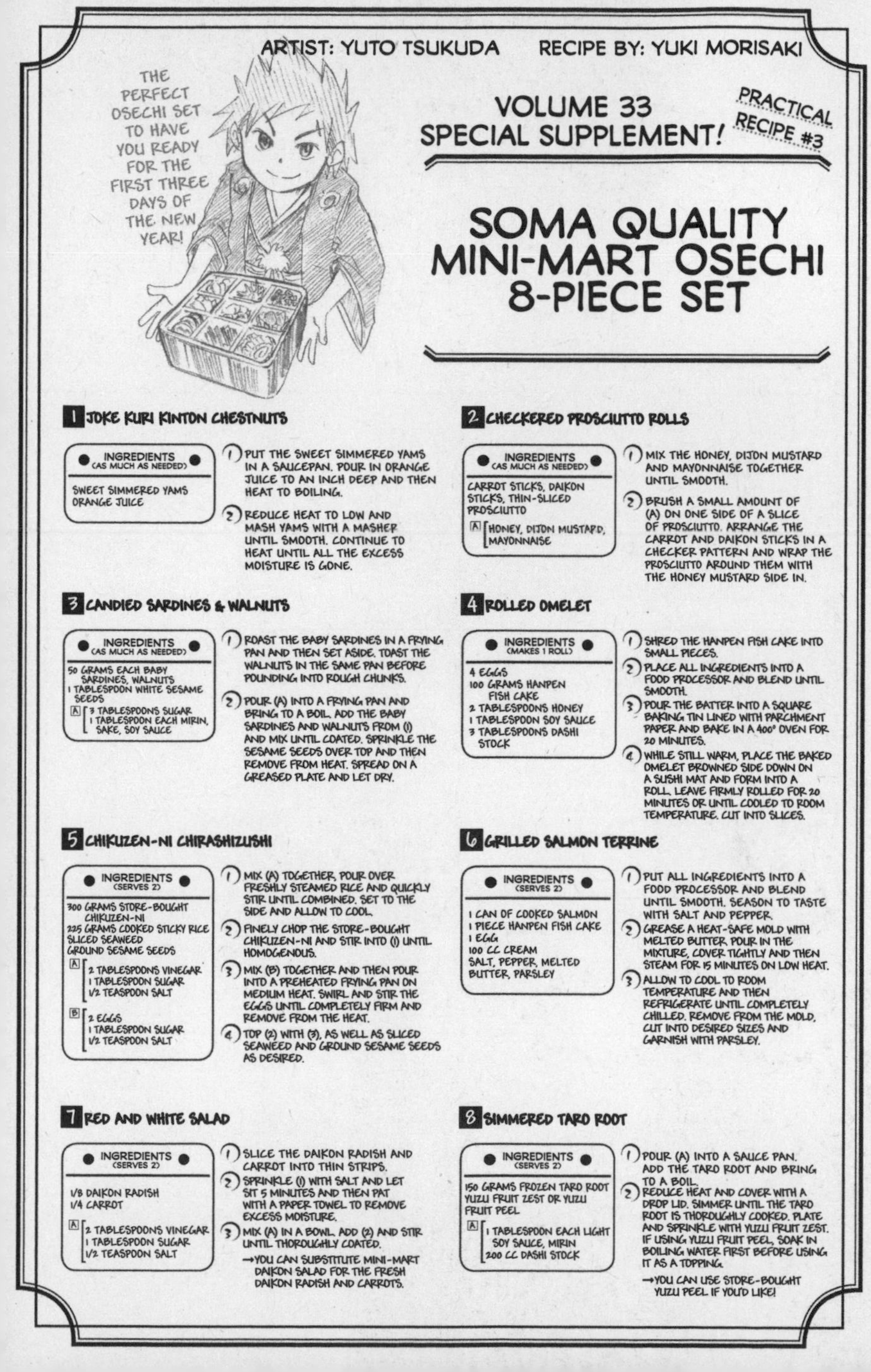
THE PERFECT OSECHI SET TO HAVE YOU READY FOR THE FIRST THREE DAYS OF THE NEW YEAR!

VOLUME 33 SPECIAL SUPPLEMENT!

PRACTICAL RECIPE #3

SOMA QUALITY MINI-MART OSECHI 8-PIECE SET

1 JOKE KURI KINTON CHESTNUTS

INGREDIENTS (AS MUCH AS NEEDED)

SWEET SIMMERED YAMS
ORANGE JUICE

1. PUT THE SWEET SIMMERED YAMS IN A SAUCEPAN. POUR IN ORANGE JUICE TO AN INCH DEEP AND THEN HEAT TO BOILING.
2. REDUCE HEAT TO LOW AND MASH YAMS WITH A MASHER UNTIL SMOOTH. CONTINUE TO HEAT UNTIL ALL THE EXCESS MOISTURE IS GONE.

2 CHECKERED PROSCIUTTO ROLLS

INGREDIENTS (AS MUCH AS NEEDED)

CARROT STICKS, DAIKON STICKS, THIN-SLICED PROSCIUTTO

A [HONEY, DIJON MUSTARD, MAYONNAISE

1. MIX THE HONEY, DIJON MUSTARD AND MAYONNAISE TOGETHER UNTIL SMOOTH.
2. BRUSH A SMALL AMOUNT OF (A) ON ONE SIDE OF A SLICE OF PROSCIUTTO. ARRANGE THE CARROT AND DAIKON STICKS IN A CHECKER PATTERN AND WRAP THE PROSCIUTTO AROUND THEM WITH THE HONEY MUSTARD SIDE IN.

3 CANDIED SARDINES & WALNUTS

INGREDIENTS (AS MUCH AS NEEDED)

50 GRAMS EACH BABY SARDINES, WALNUTS
1 TABLESPOON WHITE SESAME SEEDS

A [3 TABLESPOONS SUGAR
1 TABLESPOON EACH MIRIN, SAKE, SOY SAUCE

1. ROAST THE BABY SARDINES IN A FRYING PAN AND THEN SET ASIDE. TOAST THE WALNUTS IN THE SAME PAN BEFORE POUNDING INTO ROUGH CHUNKS.
2. POUR (A) INTO A FRYING PAN AND BRING TO A BOIL. ADD THE BABY SARDINES AND WALNUTS FROM (1) AND MIX UNTIL COATED. SPRINKLE THE SESAME SEEDS OVER TOP AND THEN REMOVE FROM HEAT. SPREAD ON A GREASED PLATE AND LET DRY.

4 ROLLED OMELET

INGREDIENTS (MAKES 1 ROLL)

4 EGGS
100 GRAMS HANPEN FISH CAKE
2 TABLESPOONS HONEY
1 TABLESPOON SOY SAUCE
3 TABLESPOONS DASHI STOCK

1. SHRED THE HANPEN FISH CAKE INTO SMALL PIECES.
2. PLACE ALL INGREDIENTS INTO A FOOD PROCESSOR AND BLEND UNTIL SMOOTH.
3. POUR THE BATTER INTO A SQUARE BAKING TIN LINED WITH PARCHMENT PAPER AND BAKE IN A 400° OVEN FOR 20 MINUTES.
4. WHILE STILL WARM, PLACE THE BAKED OMELET BROWNED SIDE DOWN ON A SUSHI MAT AND FORM INTO A ROLL. LEAVE FIRMLY ROLLED FOR 20 MINUTES OR UNTIL COOLED TO ROOM TEMPERATURE. CUT INTO SLICES.

5 CHIKUZEN-NI CHIRASHIZUSHI

INGREDIENTS (SERVES 2)

300 GRAMS STORE-BOUGHT CHIKUZEN-NI
225 GRAMS COOKED STICKY RICE
SLICED SEAWEED
GROUND SESAME SEEDS

A [2 TABLESPOONS VINEGAR
1 TABLESPOON SUGAR
1/2 TEASPOON SALT

B [2 EGGS
1 TABLESPOON SUGAR
1/2 TEASPOON SALT

1. MIX (A) TOGETHER, POUR OVER FRESHLY STEAMED RICE AND QUICKLY STIR UNTIL COMBINED. SET TO THE SIDE AND ALLOW TO COOL.
2. FINELY CHOP THE STORE-BOUGHT CHIKUZEN-NI AND STIR INTO (1) UNTIL HOMOGENOUS.
3. MIX (B) TOGETHER AND THEN POUR INTO A PREHEATED FRYING PAN ON MEDIUM HEAT. SWIRL AND STIR THE EGGS UNTIL COMPLETELY FIRM AND REMOVE FROM THE HEAT.
4. TOP (2) WITH (3), AS WELL AS SLICED SEAWEED AND GROUND SESAME SEEDS AS DESIRED.

6 GRILLED SALMON TERRINE

INGREDIENTS (SERVES 2)

1 CAN OF COOKED SALMON
1 PIECE HANPEN FISH CAKE
1 EGG
100 CC CREAM
SALT, PEPPER, MELTED BUTTER, PARSLEY

1. PUT ALL INGREDIENTS INTO A FOOD PROCESSOR AND BLEND UNTIL SMOOTH. SEASON TO TASTE WITH SALT AND PEPPER.
2. GREASE A HEAT-SAFE MOLD WITH MELTED BUTTER. POUR IN THE MIXTURE, COVER TIGHTLY AND THEN STEAM FOR 15 MINUTES ON LOW HEAT.
3. ALLOW TO COOL TO ROOM TEMPERATURE AND THEN REFRIGERATE UNTIL COMPLETELY CHILLED. REMOVE FROM THE MOLD, CUT INTO DESIRED SIZES AND GARNISH WITH PARSLEY.

7 RED AND WHITE SALAD

INGREDIENTS (SERVES 2)

1/8 DAIKON RADISH
1/4 CARROT

A [2 TABLESPOONS VINEGAR
1 TABLESPOON SUGAR
1/2 TEASPOON SALT

1. SLICE THE DAIKON RADISH AND CARROT INTO THIN STRIPS.
2. SPRINKLE (1) WITH SALT AND LET SIT 5 MINUTES AND THEN PAT WITH A PAPER TOWEL TO REMOVE EXCESS MOISTURE.
3. MIX (A) IN A BOWL. ADD (2) AND STIR UNTIL THOROUGHLY COATED.

→YOU CAN SUBSTITUTE MINI-MART DAIKON SALAD FOR THE FRESH DAIKON RADISH AND CARROTS.

8 SIMMERED TARO ROOT

INGREDIENTS (SERVES 2)

150 GRAMS FROZEN TARO ROOT
YUZU FRUIT ZEST OR YUZU FRUIT PEEL

A [1 TABLESPOON EACH LIGHT SOY SAUCE, MIRIN
200 CC DASHI STOCK

1. POUR (A) INTO A SAUCE PAN. ADD THE TARO ROOT AND BRING TO A BOIL.
2. REDUCE HEAT AND COVER WITH A DROP LID. SIMMER UNTIL THE TARO ROOT IS THOROUGHLY COOKED. PLATE AND SPRINKLE WITH YUZU FRUIT ZEST. IF USING YUZU FRUIT PEEL, SOAK IN BOILING WATER FIRST BEFORE USING IT AS A TOPPING.

→YOU CAN USE STORE-BOUGHT YUZU PEEL IF YOU'D LIKE!

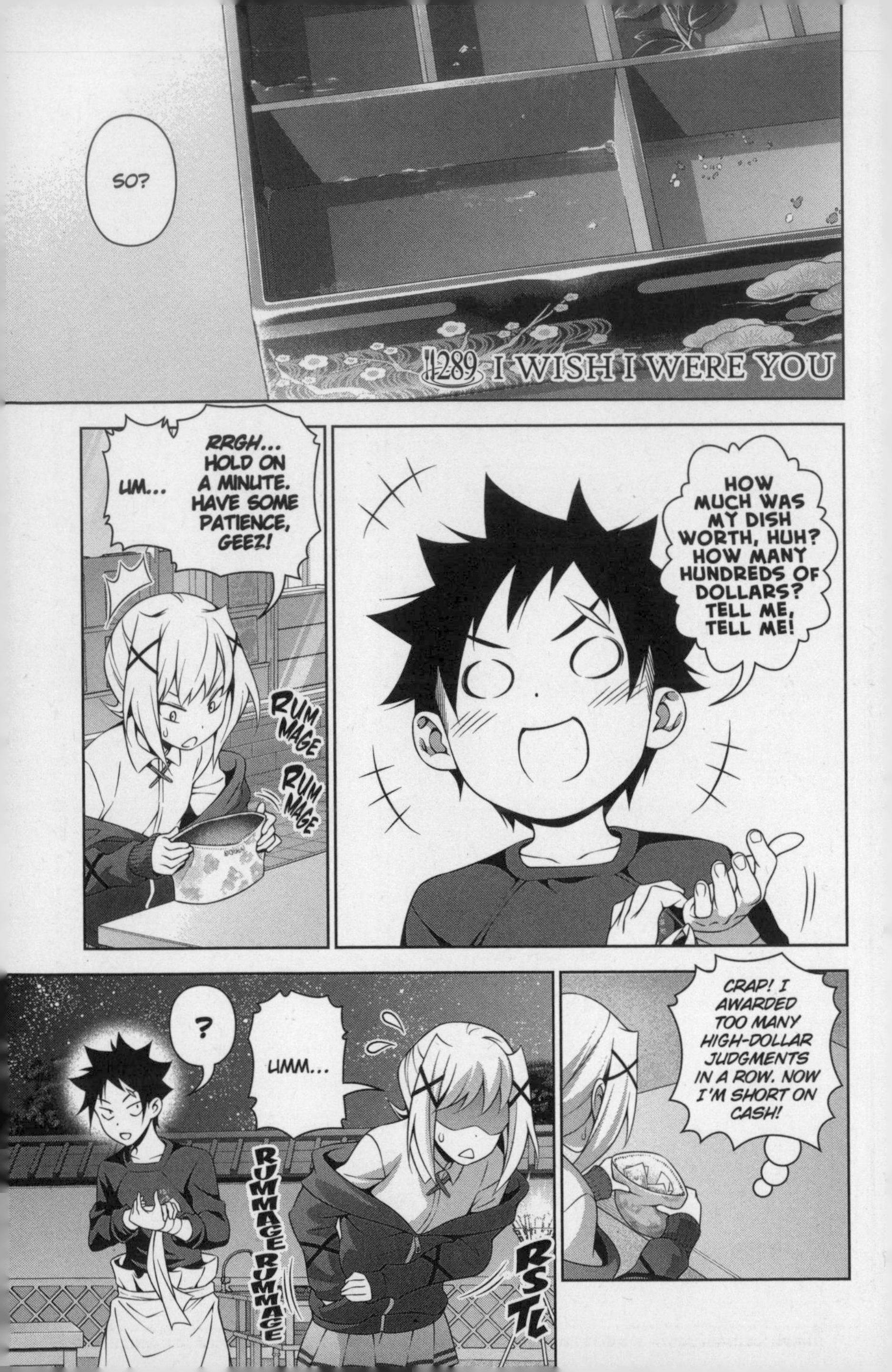
SO?
289 I WISH I WERE YOU
HOW MUCH WAS MY DISH WORTH, HUH? HOW MANY HUNDREDS OF DOLLARS? TELL ME, TELL ME!
RRGH... HOLD ON A MINUTE. HAVE SOME PATIENCE, GEEZ!
UM...
RUMMAGE RUMMAGE
CRAP! I AWARDED TOO MANY HIGH-DOLLAR JUDGMENTS IN A ROW. NOW I'M SHORT ON CASH!
UMM...
?
RUMMAGE RUMMAGE
RSTL

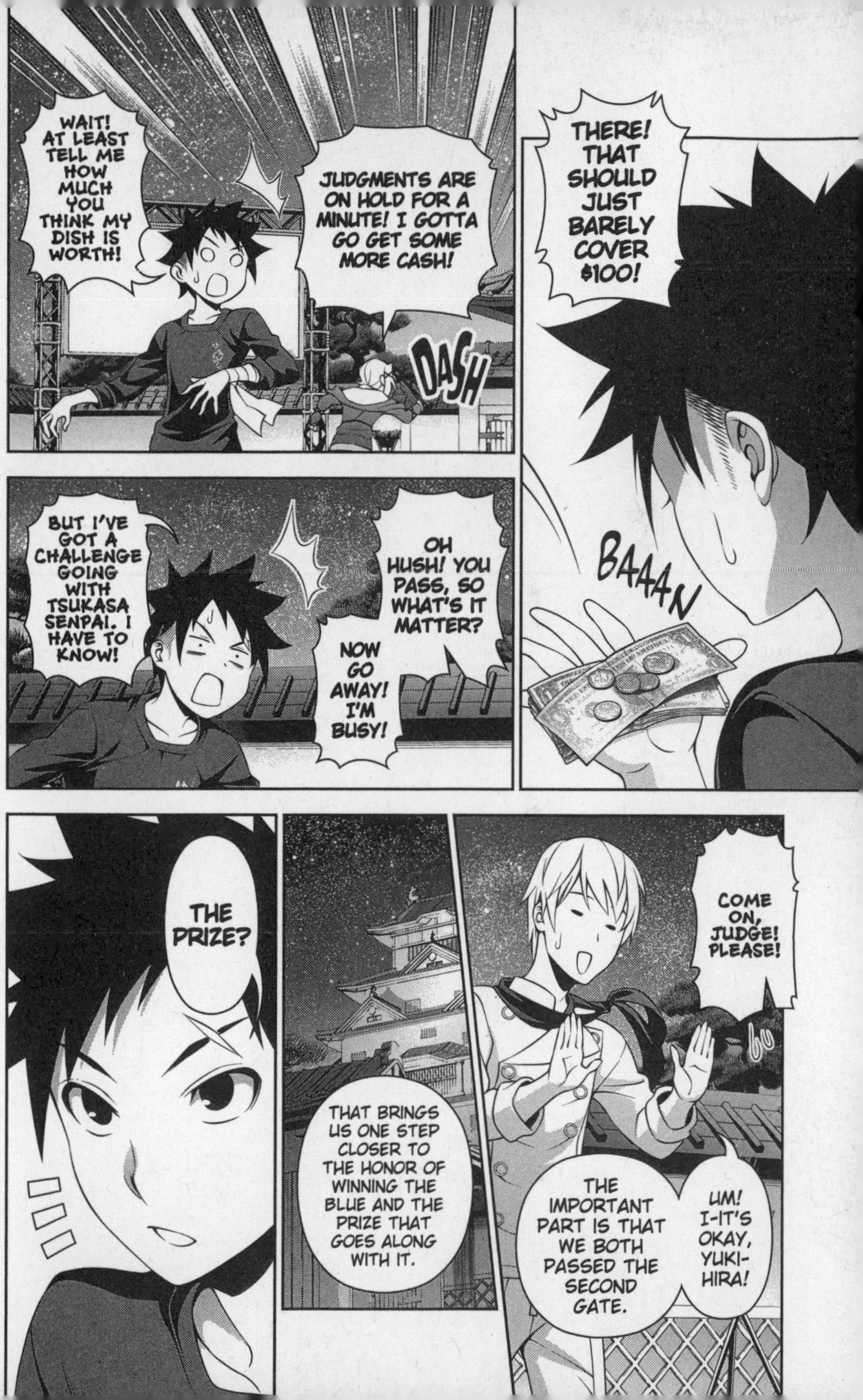
THERE! THAT SHOULD JUST BARELY COVER $100!
BAAAAN
JUDGMENTS ARE ON HOLD FOR A MINUTE! I GOTTA GO GET SOME MORE CASH!
DASH
WAIT! AT LEAST TELL ME HOW MUCH YOU THINK MY DISH IS WORTH!
OH HUSH! YOU PASS, SO WHAT'S IT MATTER?
NOW GO AWAY! I'M BUSY!
BUT I'VE GOT A CHALLENGE GOING WITH TSUKASA SENPAI. I HAVE TO KNOW!
COME ON, JUDGE! PLEASE!
UM! I-IT'S OKAY, YUKIHIRA!
THE IMPORTANT PART IS THAT WE BOTH PASSED THE SECOND GATE.
THAT BRINGS US ONE STEP CLOSER TO THE HONOR OF WINNING THE BLUE AND THE PRIZE THAT GOES ALONG WITH IT.
THE PRIZE?

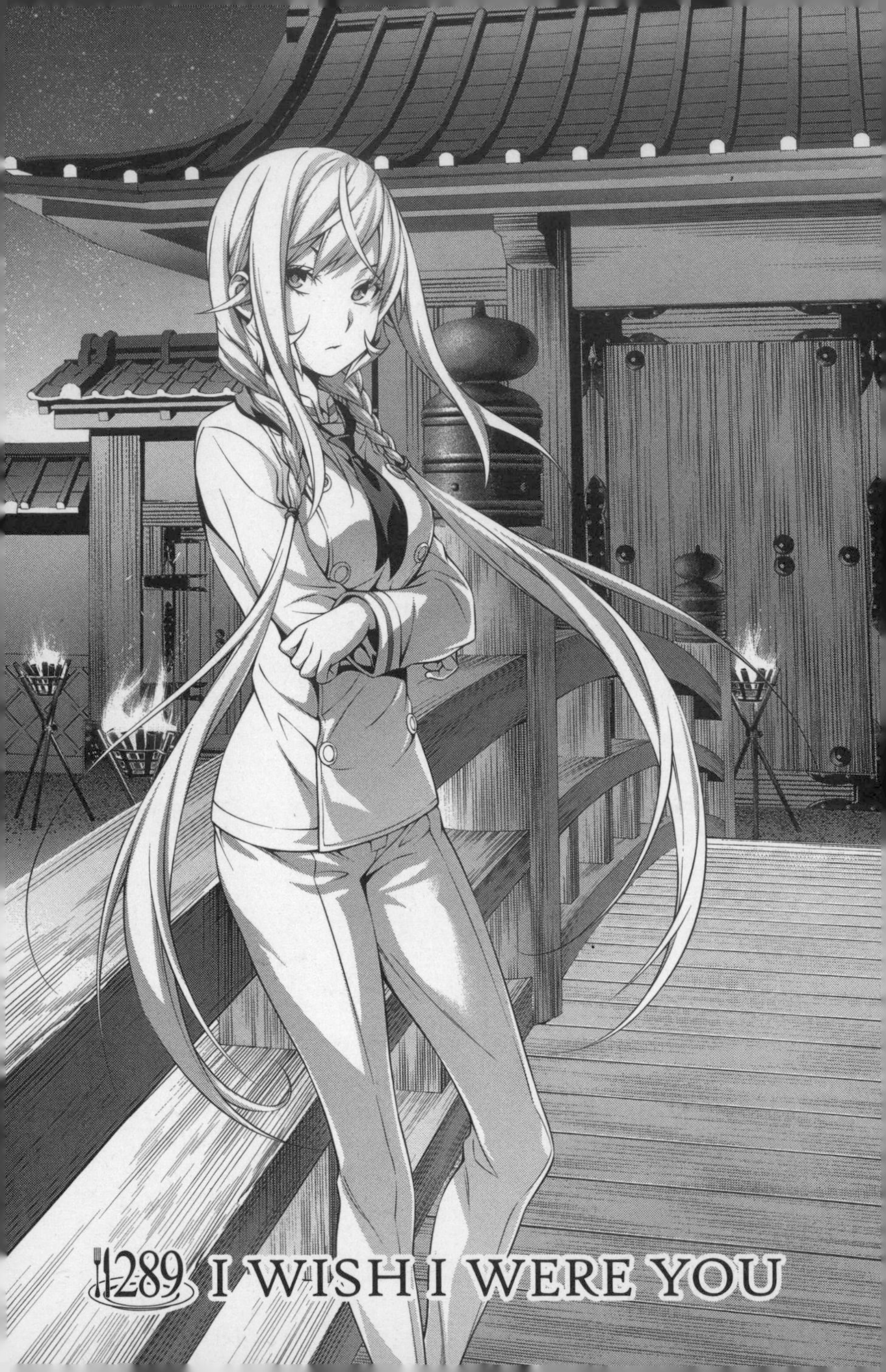
289
I WISH I WERE YOU

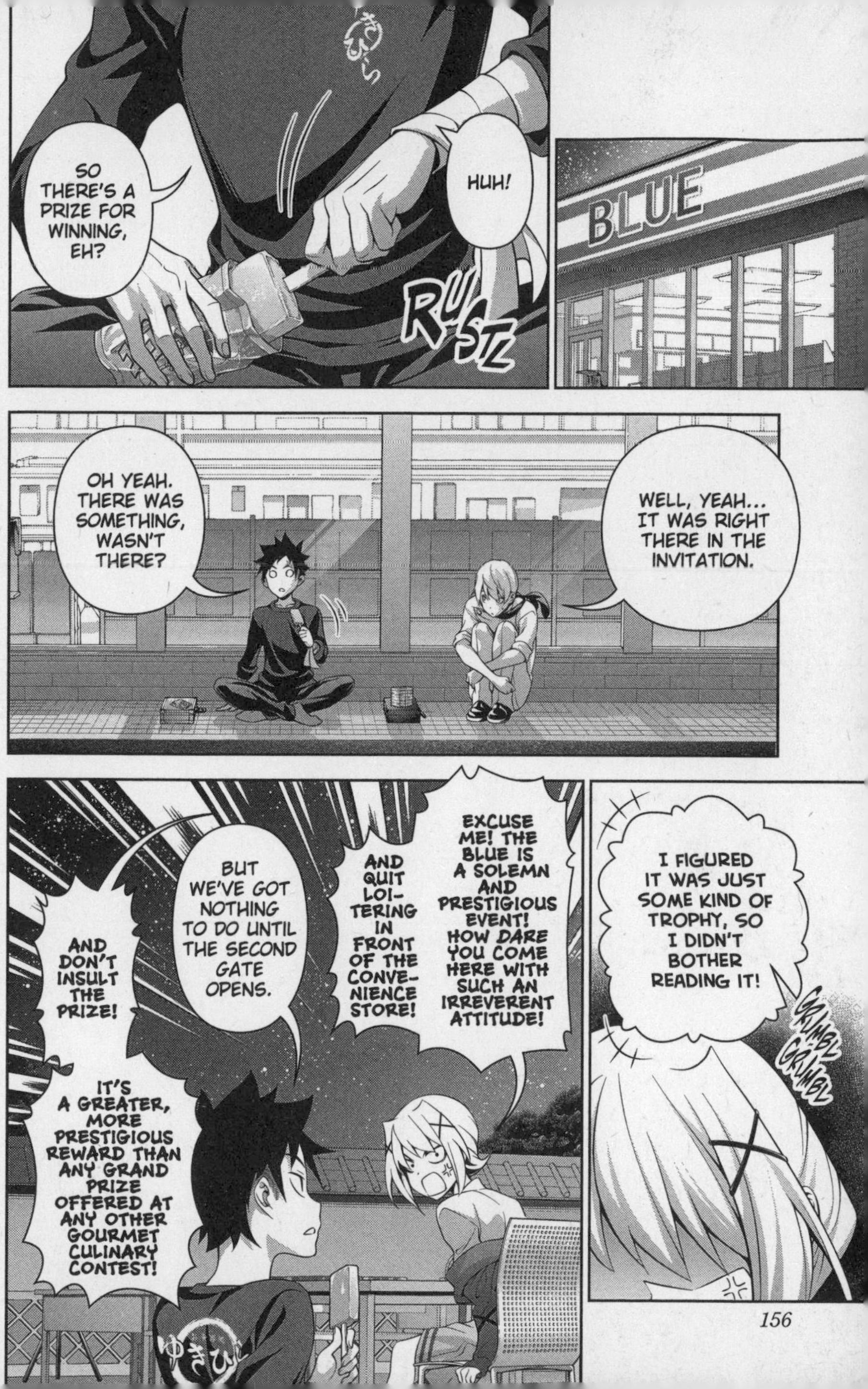
BLUE
HUH!
SO THERE'S A PRIZE FOR WINNING, EH?
RUSTL
WELL, YEAH... IT WAS RIGHT THERE IN THE INVITATION.
OH YEAH. THERE WAS SOMETHING, WASN'T THERE?
I FIGURED IT WAS JUST SOME KIND OF TROPHY, SO I DIDN'T BOTHER READING IT!
GRUMBL GRUMBL
EXCUSE ME! THE BLUE IS A SOLEMN AND PRESTIGIOUS EVENT! HOW DARE YOU COME HERE WITH SUCH AN IRREVERENT ATTITUDE!
AND QUIT LOITERING IN FRONT OF THE CONVENIENCE STORE!
BUT WE'VE GOT NOTHING TO DO UNTIL THE SECOND GATE OPENS.
AND DON'T INSULT THE PRIZE!
IT'S A GREATER, MORE PRESTIGIOUS REWARD THAN ANY GRAND PRIZE OFFERED AT ANY OTHER GOURMET CULINARY CONTEST!

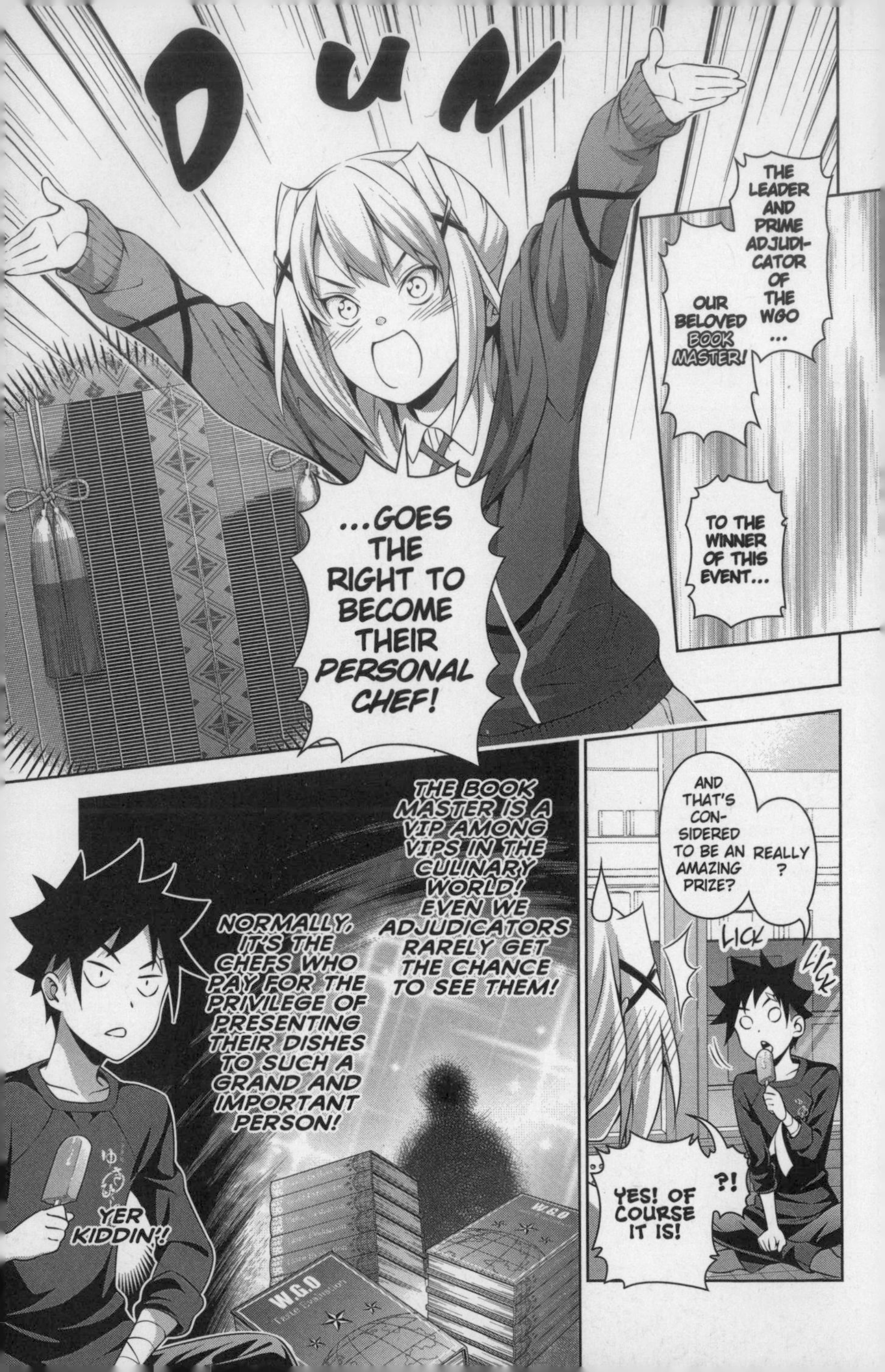

THE LEADER AND PRIME ADJUDICATOR OF THE WGO...
OUR BELOVED BOOK MASTER!
TO THE WINNER OF THIS EVENT...
DUN
...GOES THE RIGHT TO BECOME THEIR PERSONAL CHEF!
REALLY?
AND THAT'S CONSIDERED TO BE AN AMAZING PRIZE?
LICK
LICK
?!
YES! OF COURSE IT IS!
THE BOOK MASTER IS A VIP AMONG VIPS IN THE CULINARY WORLD! EVEN WE ADJUDICATORS RARELY GET THE CHANCE TO SEE THEM!
NORMALLY, IT'S THE CHEFS WHO PAY FOR THE PRIVILEGE OF PRESENTING THEIR DISHES TO SUCH A GRAND AND IMPORTANT PERSON!
YER KIDDIN'!
W.G.O
W.G.O

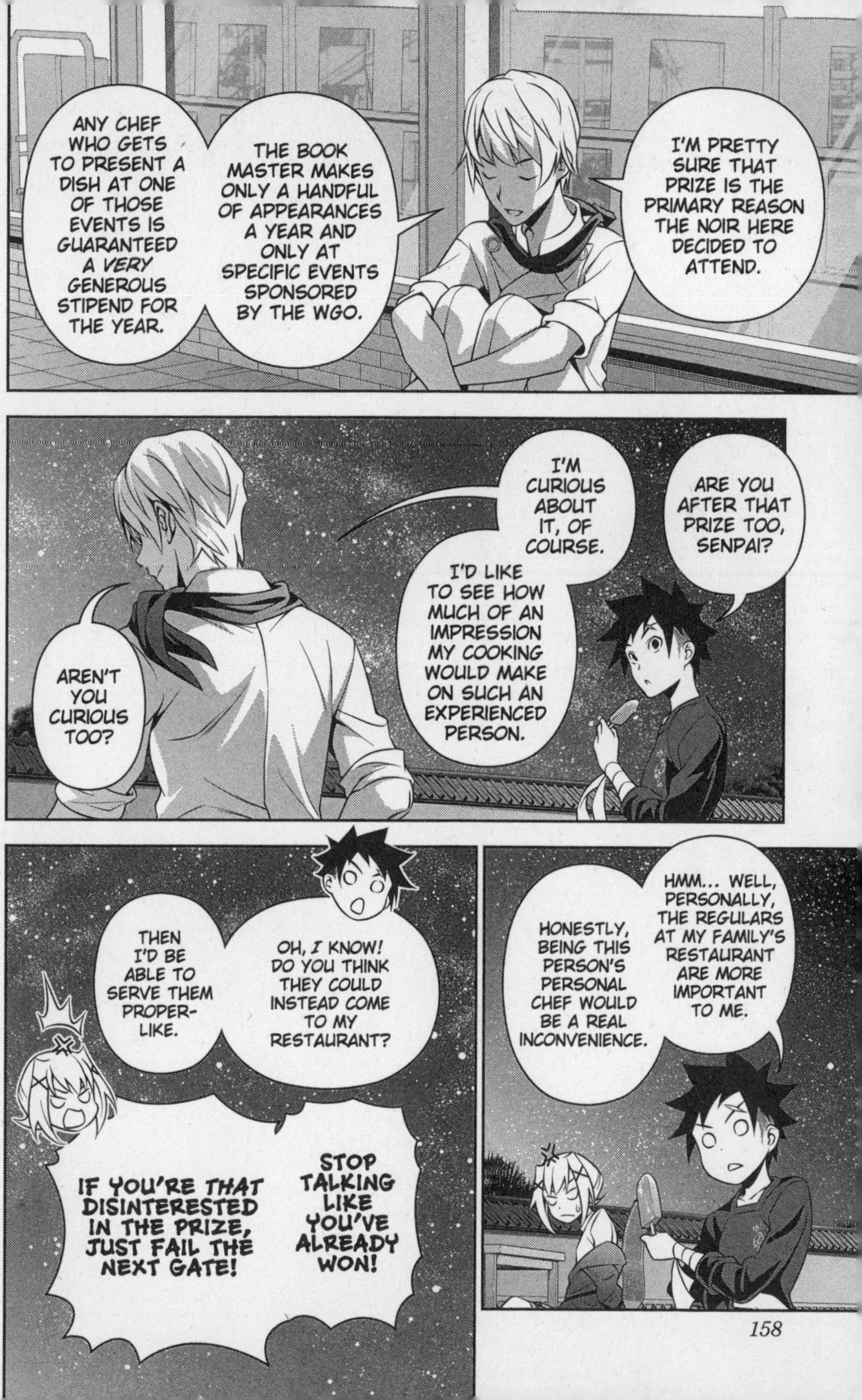
I'M PRETTY SURE THAT PRIZE IS THE PRIMARY REASON THE NOIR HERE DECIDED TO ATTEND.
THE BOOK MASTER MAKES ONLY A HANDFUL OF APPEARANCES A YEAR AND ONLY AT SPECIFIC EVENTS SPONSORED BY THE WGO.
ANY CHEF WHO GETS TO PRESENT A DISH AT ONE OF THOSE EVENTS IS GUARANTEED A *VERY* GENEROUS STIPEND FOR THE YEAR.
ARE YOU AFTER THAT PRIZE TOO, SENPAI?
I'M CURIOUS ABOUT IT, OF COURSE.
I'D LIKE TO SEE HOW MUCH OF AN IMPRESSION MY COOKING WOULD MAKE ON SUCH AN EXPERIENCED PERSON.
AREN'T YOU CURIOUS TOO?
HMM... WELL, PERSONALLY, THE REGULARS AT MY FAMILY'S RESTAURANT ARE MORE IMPORTANT TO ME.
HONESTLY, BEING THIS PERSON'S PERSONAL CHEF WOULD BE A REAL INCONVENIENCE.
OH, *I* KNOW! DO YOU THINK THEY COULD INSTEAD COME TO MY RESTAURANT?
THEN I'D BE ABLE TO SERVE THEM PROPER-LIKE.
STOP TALKING LIKE YOU'VE ALREADY WON!
IF YOU'RE *THAT* DISINTERESTED IN THE PRIZE, JUST FAIL THE NEXT GATE!

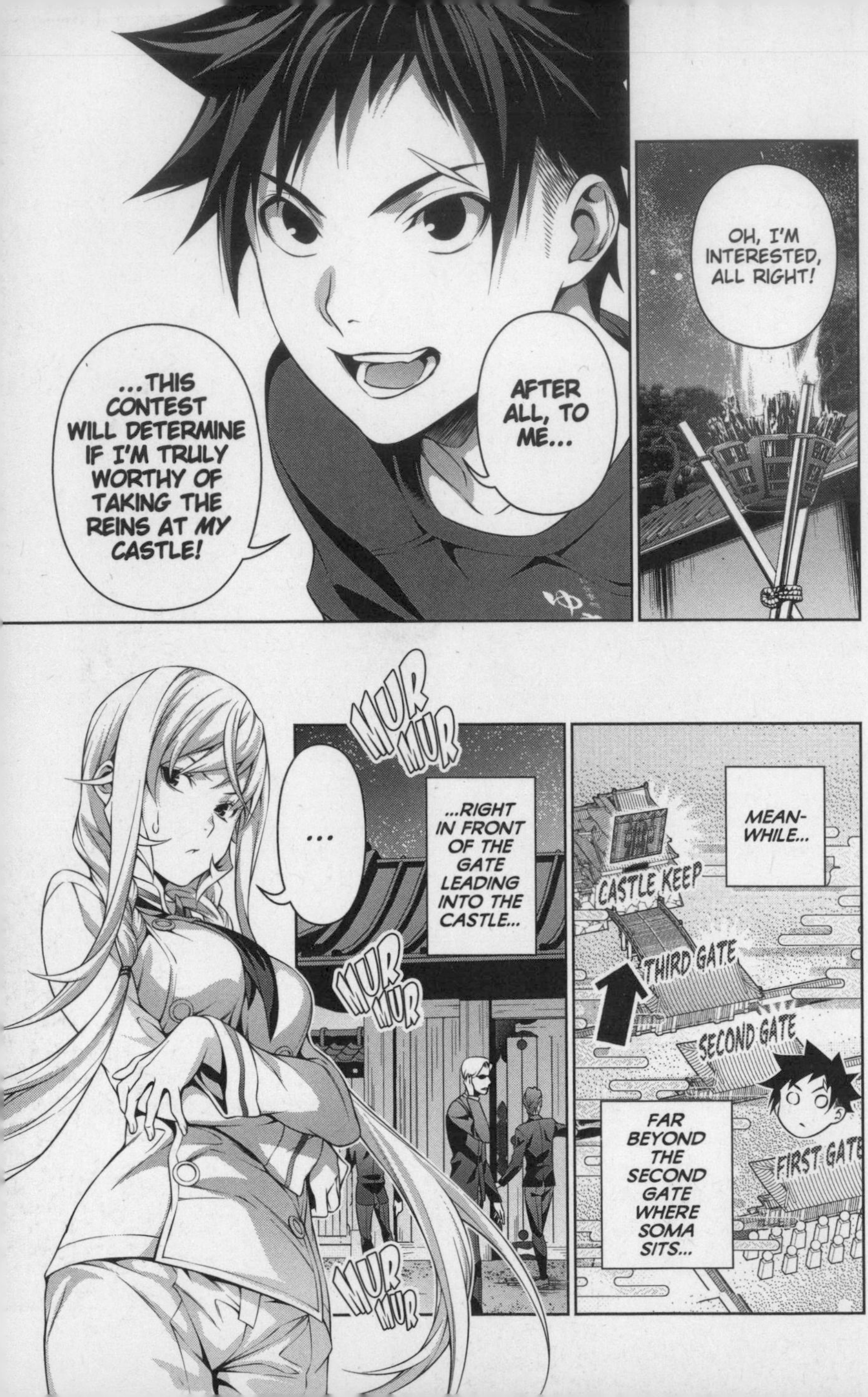
OH, I'M INTERESTED, ALL RIGHT!
AFTER ALL, TO ME...
...THIS CONTEST WILL DETERMINE IF I'M TRULY WORTHY OF TAKING THE REINS AT MY CASTLE!
MEAN-WHILE...
CASTLE KEEP
THIRD GATE
SECOND GATE
FIRST GATE
FAR BEYOND THE SECOND GATE WHERE SOMA SITS...
MUR MUR
...RIGHT IN FRONT OF THE GATE LEADING INTO THE CASTLE...
MUR MUR
MUR MUR
...

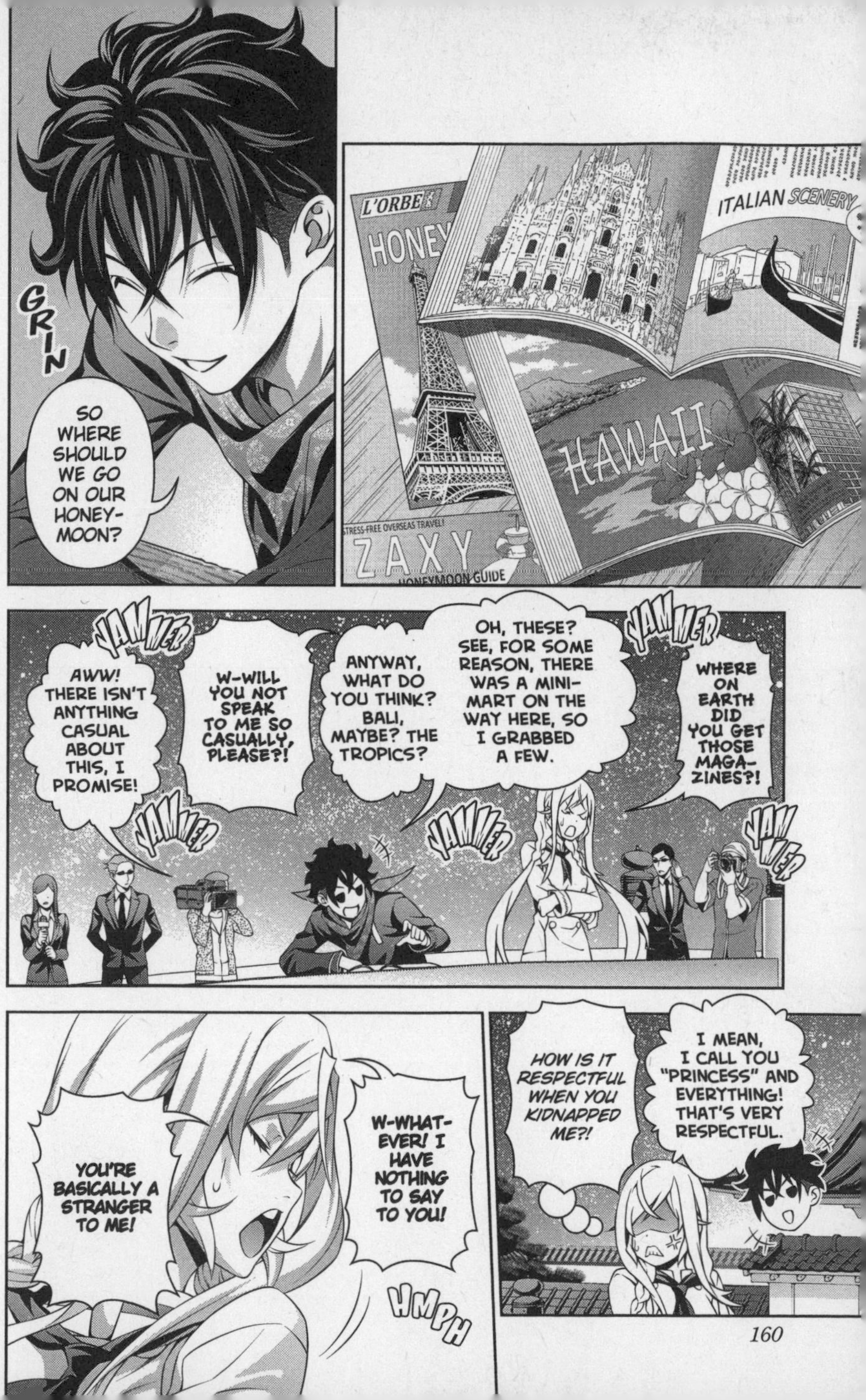
L'ORBE
HONEY
ITALIAN SCENERY
HAWAII
STRESS-FREE OVERSEAS TRAVEL!
ZAXY
HONEYMOON GUIDE
GRIN
SO WHERE SHOULD WE GO ON OUR HONEY-MOON?
YAMMER
WHERE ON EARTH DID YOU GET THOSE MAGA-ZINES?!
YAMMER
OH, THESE? SEE, FOR SOME REASON, THERE WAS A MINI-MART ON THE WAY HERE, SO I GRABBED A FEW.
ANYWAY, WHAT DO YOU THINK? BALI, MAYBE? THE TROPICS?
YAMMER
W-WILL YOU NOT SPEAK TO ME SO CASUALLY, PLEASE?!
AWW! THERE ISN'T ANYTHING CASUAL ABOUT THIS, I PROMISE!
YAMMER
YAMMER
I MEAN, I CALL YOU "PRINCESS" AND EVERYTHING! THAT'S VERY RESPECTFUL.
HOW IS IT RESPECTFUL WHEN YOU KIDNAPPED ME?!
W-WHAT-EVER! I HAVE NOTHING TO SAY TO YOU!
YOU'RE BASICALLY A STRANGER TO ME!
HMPH

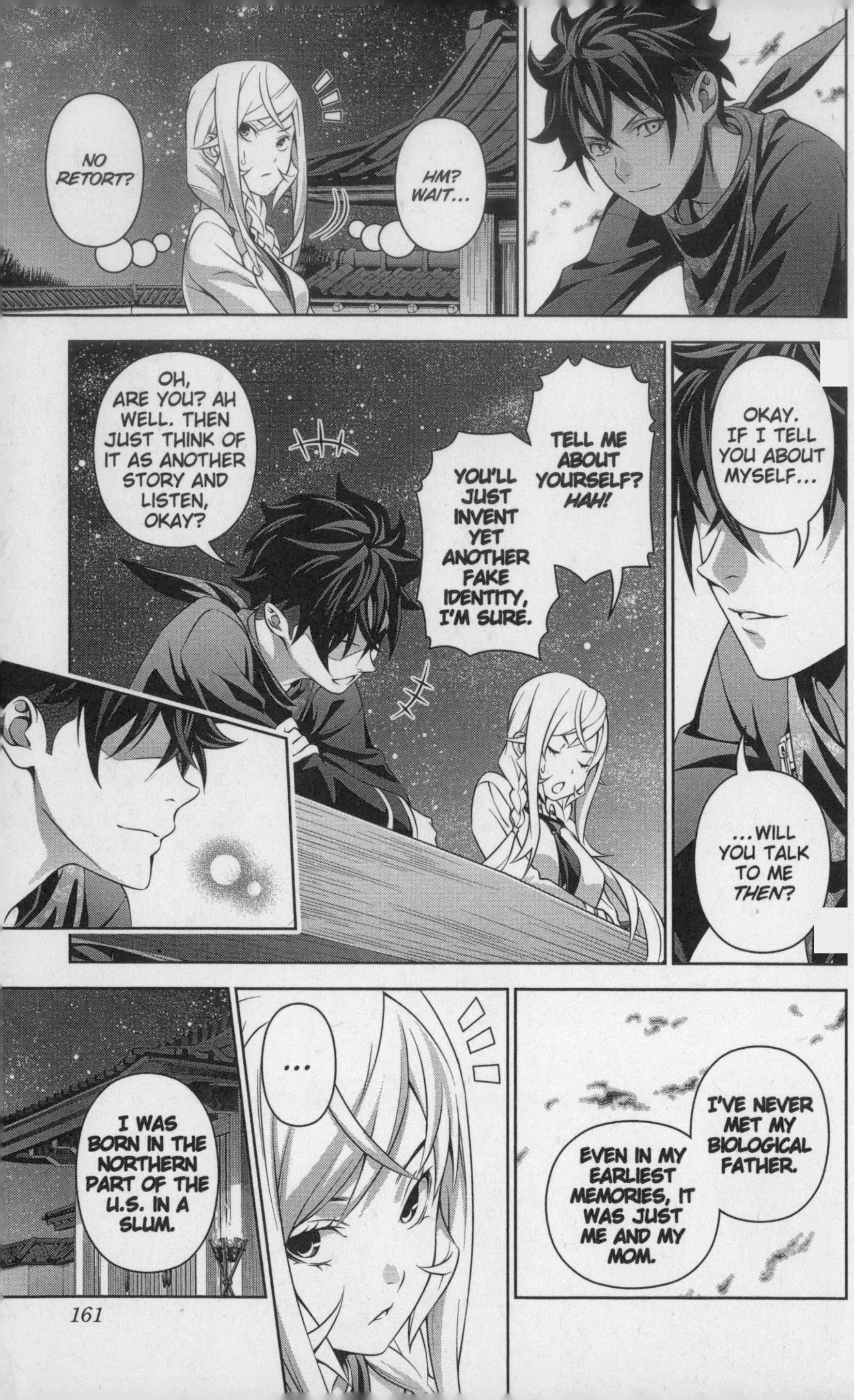
HM? WAIT...
NO RETORT?
OKAY. IF I TELL YOU ABOUT MYSELF...
...WILL YOU TALK TO ME *THEN*?
TELL ME ABOUT YOURSELF? *HAH!*
YOU'LL JUST INVENT YET ANOTHER FAKE IDENTITY, I'M SURE.
OH, ARE YOU? AH WELL. THEN JUST THINK OF IT AS ANOTHER STORY AND LISTEN, OKAY?
I'VE NEVER MET MY BIOLOGICAL FATHER.
EVEN IN MY EARLIEST MEMORIES, IT WAS JUST ME AND MY MOM.
...
I WAS BORN IN THE NORTHERN PART OF THE U.S. IN A SLUM.

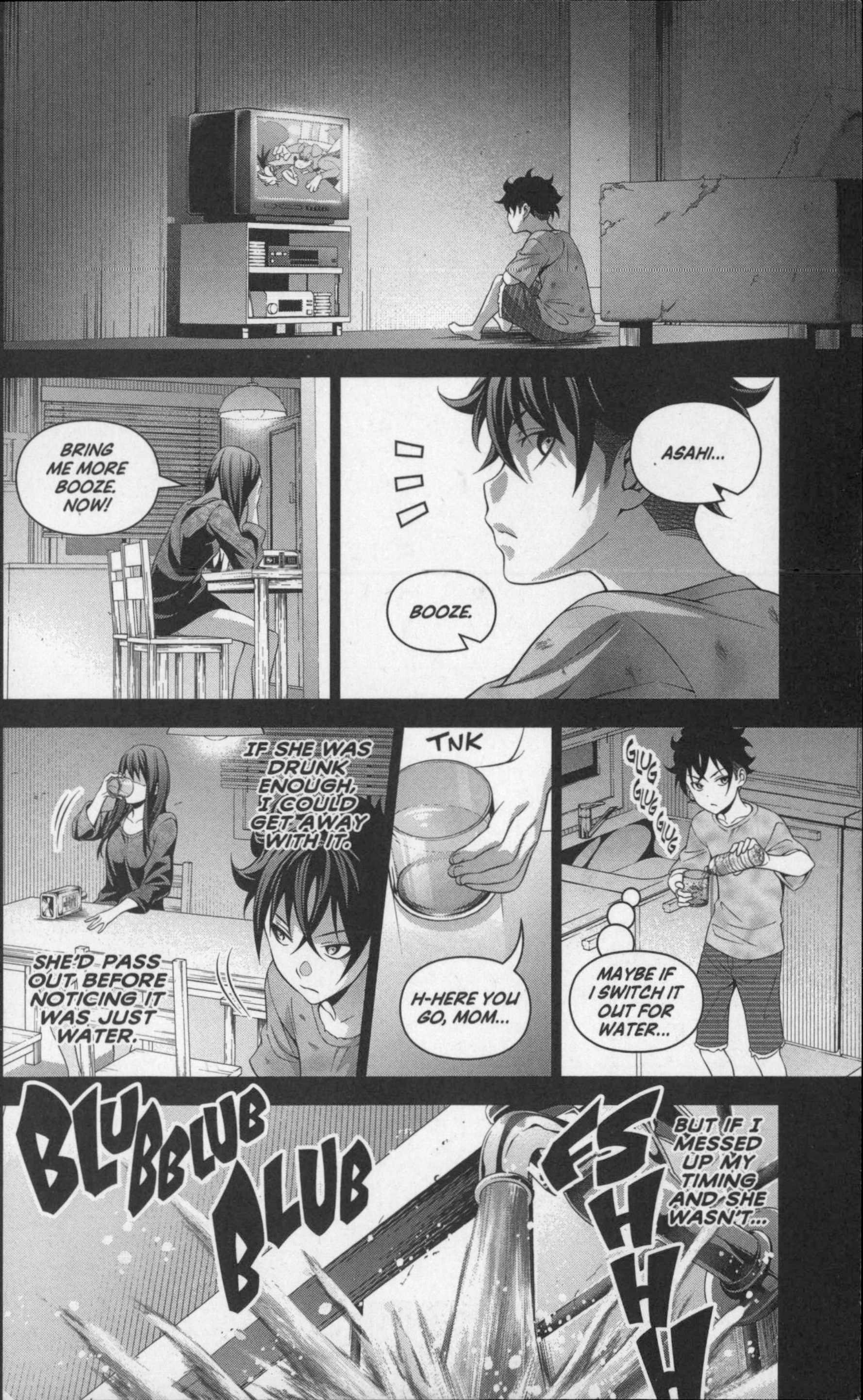
ASAHI...
BOOZE.
BRING ME MORE BOOZE. NOW!
GLUG GLUG GLUG
MAYBE IF I SWITCH IT OUT FOR WATER...
TNK
H-HERE YOU GO, MOM...
IF SHE WAS DRUNK ENOUGH, I COULD GET AWAY WITH IT.
SHE'D PASS OUT BEFORE NOTICING IT WAS JUST WATER.
BUT IF I MESSED UP MY TIMING AND SHE WASN'T...
FSHH!!
BLUBBLUB BLUB

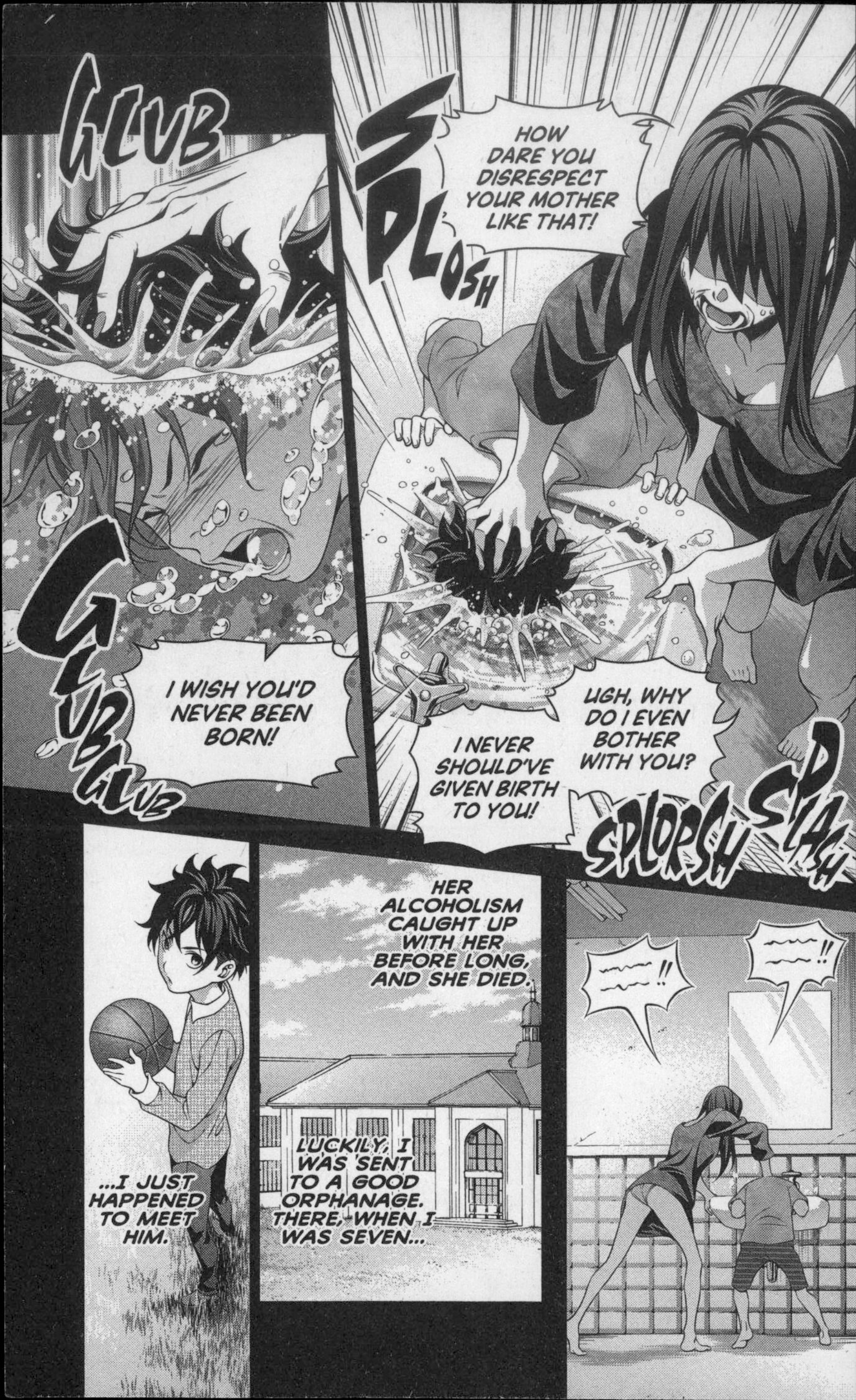
HOW DARE YOU DISRESPECT YOUR MOTHER LIKE THAT!
SPLOSH
UGH, WHY DO I EVEN BOTHER WITH YOU?
I NEVER SHOULD'VE GIVEN BIRTH TO YOU!
SPLASH
SPLORSH
GLUB
I WISH YOU'D NEVER BEEN BORN!
GLUBGLUB
HER ALCOHOLISM CAUGHT UP WITH HER BEFORE LONG, AND SHE DIED.
LUCKILY, I WAS SENT TO A GOOD ORPHANAGE. THERE, WHEN I WAS SEVEN...
...I JUST HAPPENED TO MEET HIM.

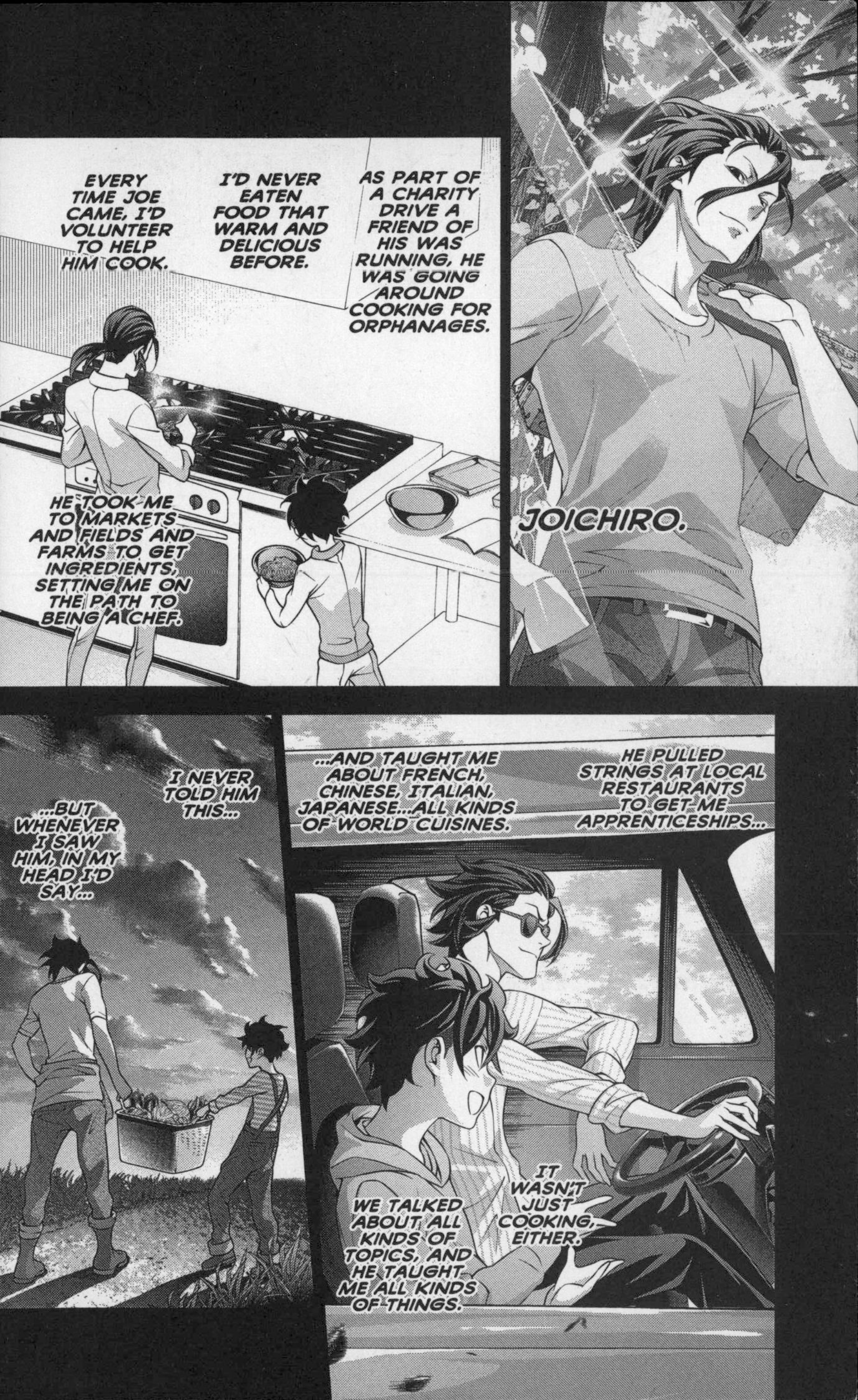
JOICHIRO.
AS PART OF A CHARITY DRIVE A FRIEND OF HIS WAS RUNNING, HE WAS GOING AROUND COOKING FOR ORPHANAGES.
I'D NEVER EATEN FOOD THAT WARM AND DELICIOUS BEFORE.
EVERY TIME JOE CAME, I'D VOLUNTEER TO HELP HIM COOK.
HE TOOK ME TO MARKETS AND FIELDS AND FARMS TO GET INGREDIENTS, SETTING ME ON THE PATH TO BEING A CHEF.
HE PULLED STRINGS AT LOCAL RESTAURANTS TO GET ME APPRENTICESHIPS...
...AND TAUGHT ME ABOUT FRENCH, CHINESE, ITALIAN, JAPANESE...ALL KINDS OF WORLD CUISINES.
IT WASN'T JUST COOKING, EITHER.
WE TALKED ABOUT ALL KINDS OF TOPICS, AND HE TAUGHT ME ALL KINDS OF THINGS.
I NEVER TOLD HIM THIS...
...BUT WHENEVER I SAW HIM, IN MY HEAD I'D SAY...

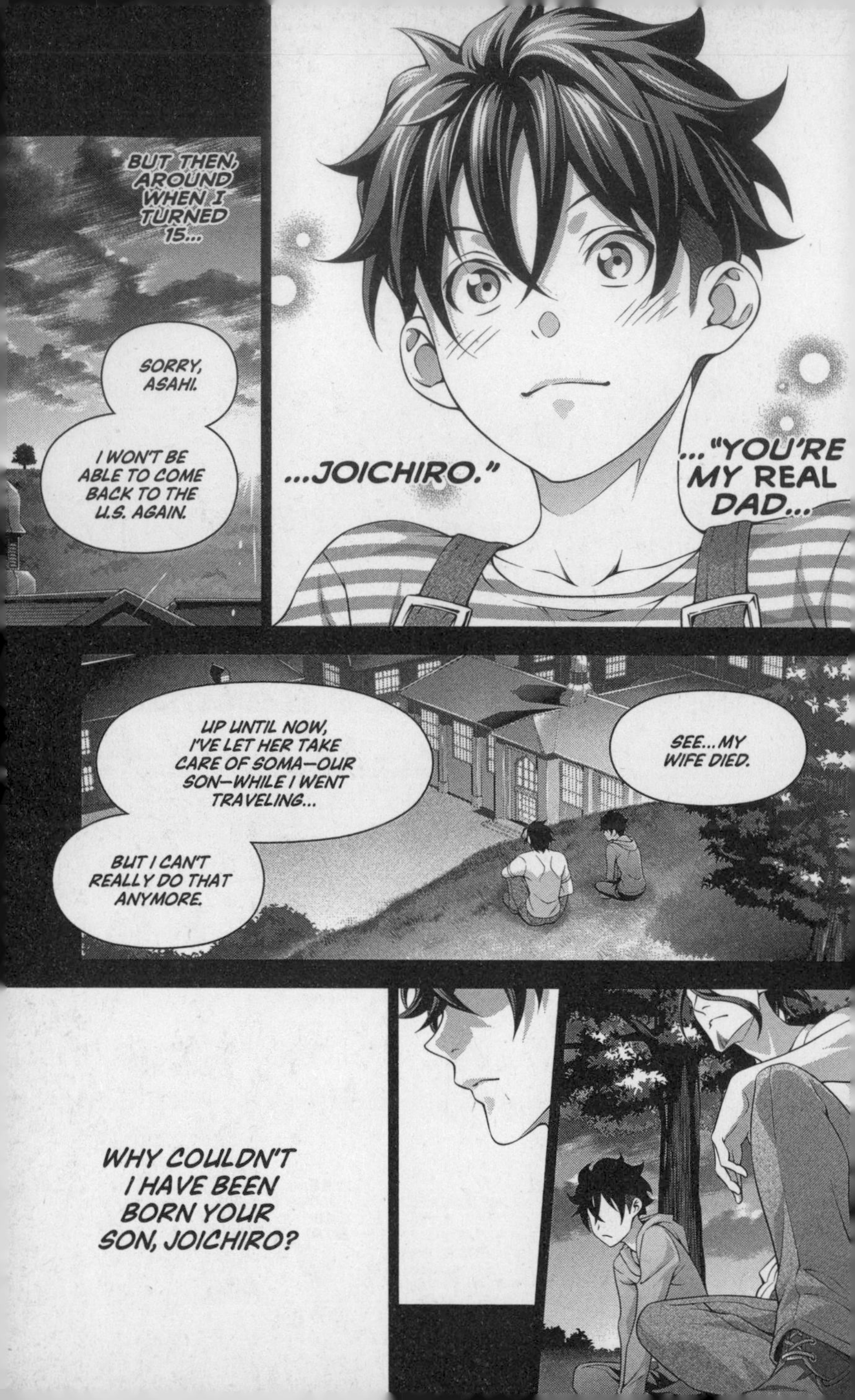
..."YOU'RE MY REAL DAD...
...JOICHIRO."
BUT THEN, AROUND WHEN I TURNED 15...
SORRY, ASAHI.
I WON'T BE ABLE TO COME BACK TO THE U.S. AGAIN.
SEE... MY WIFE DIED.
UP UNTIL NOW, I'VE LET HER TAKE CARE OF SOMA—OUR SON—WHILE I WENT TRAVELING...
BUT I CAN'T REALLY DO THAT ANYMORE.
WHY COULDN'T I HAVE BEEN BORN YOUR SON, JOICHIRO?

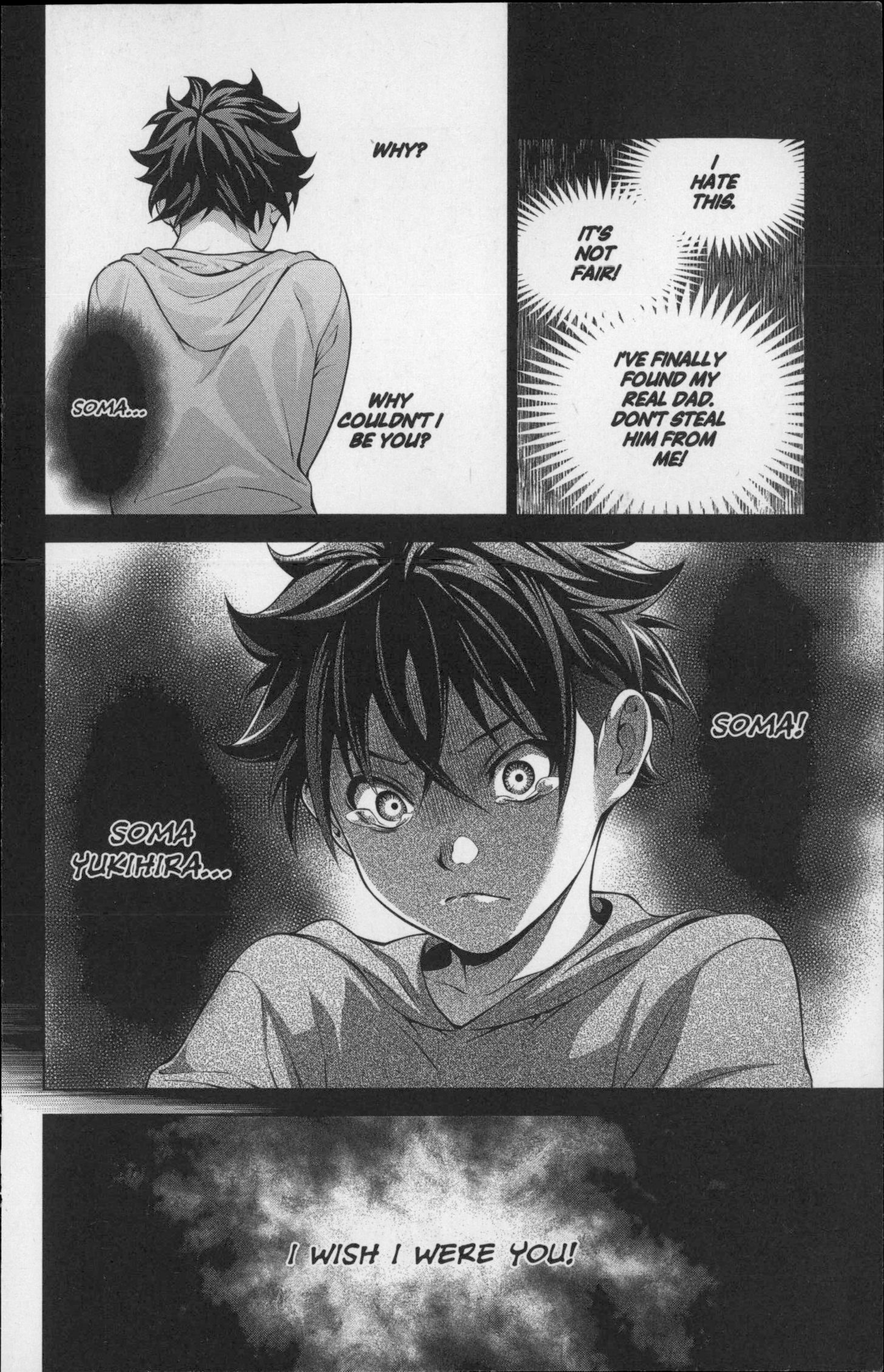
I HATE THIS.
IT'S NOT FAIR!
I'VE FINALLY FOUND MY REAL DAD. DON'T STEAL HIM FROM ME!
WHY?
WHY COULDN'T I BE YOU?
SOMA...
SOMA!
SOMA YUKIHIRA...
I WISH I WERE YOU!

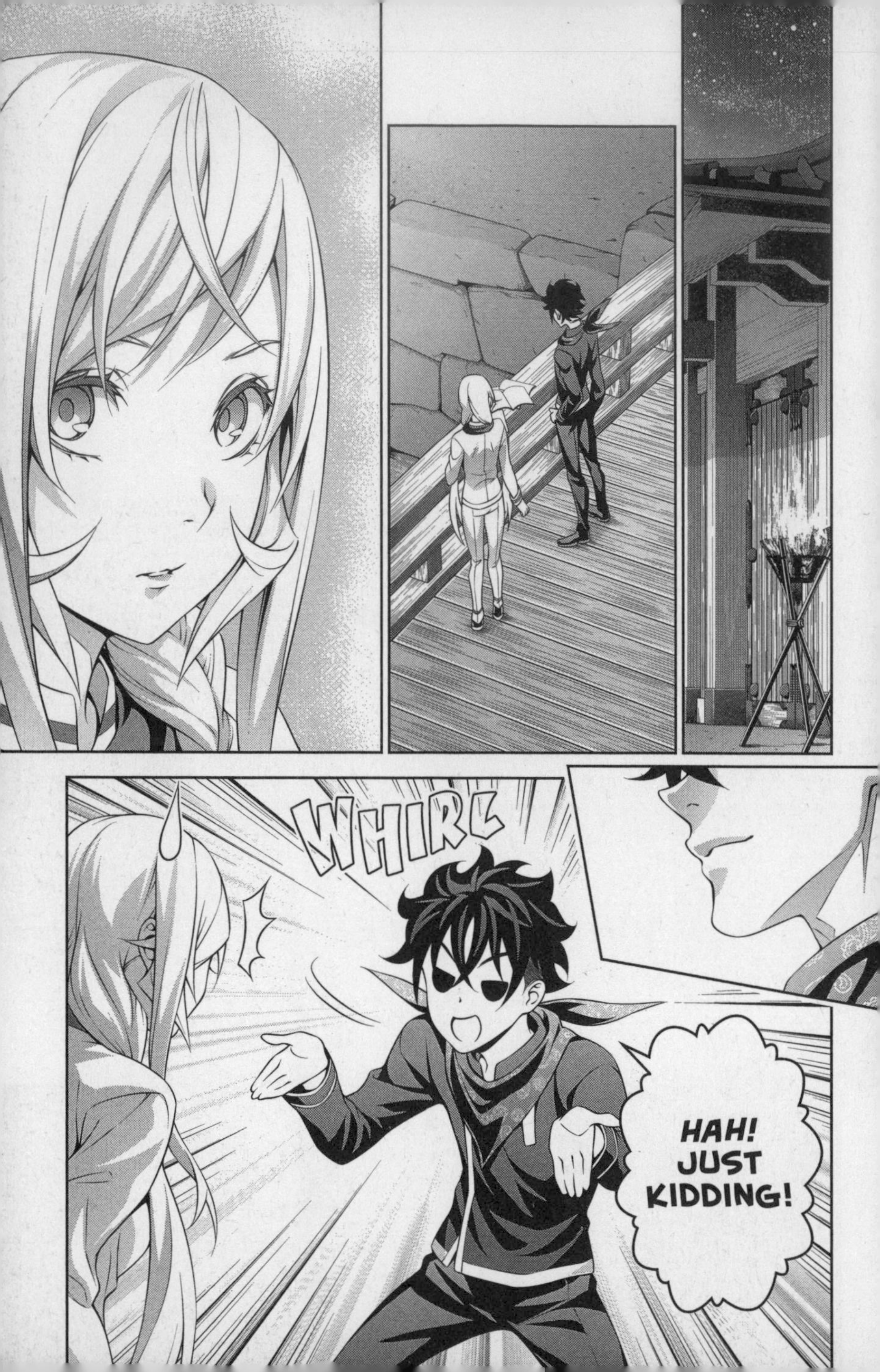
WHIRL
HAH! JUST KIDDING!

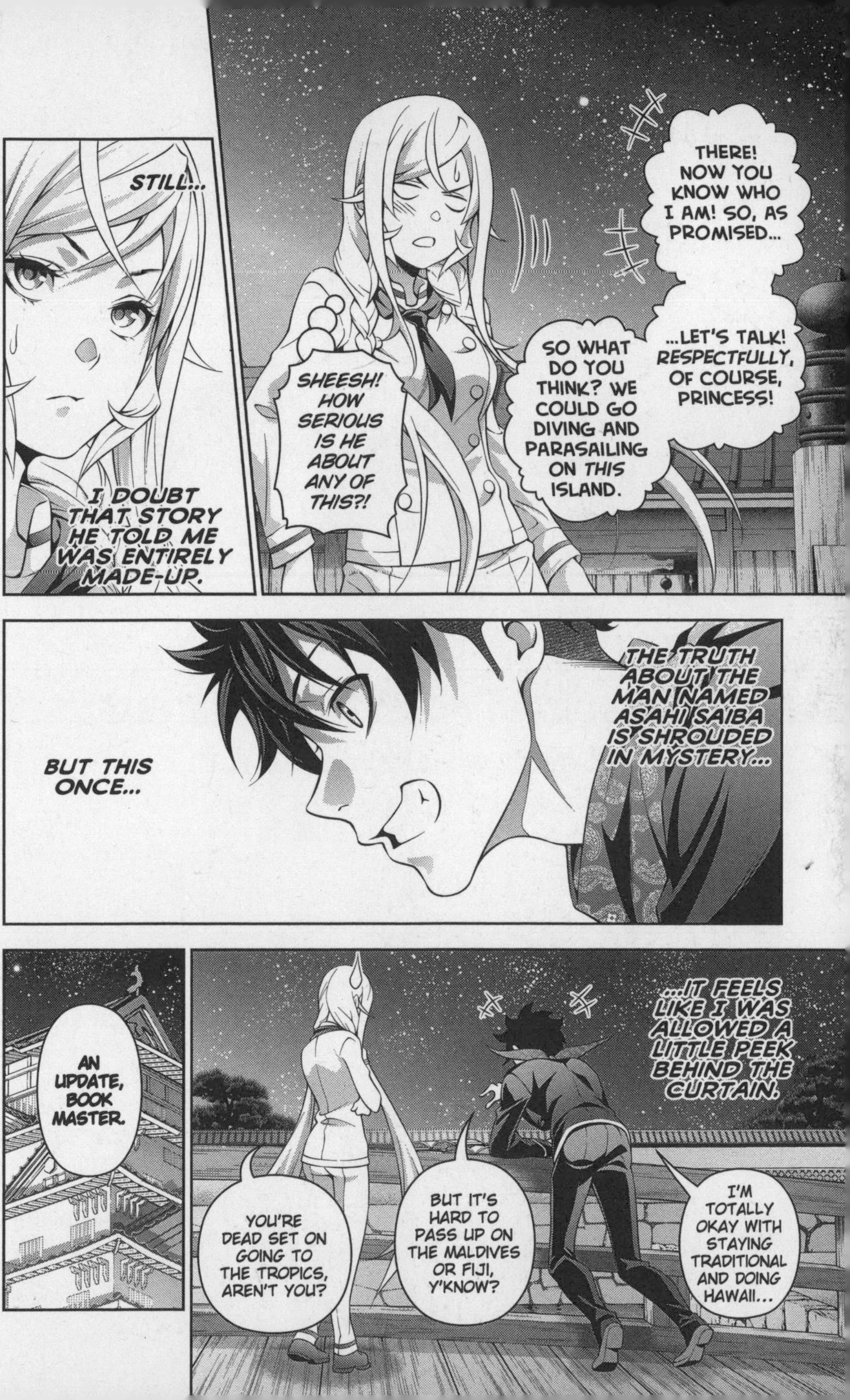
THERE! NOW YOU KNOW WHO I AM! SO, AS PROMISED...
...LET'S TALK! RESPECTFULLY, OF COURSE, PRINCESS!
SO WHAT DO YOU THINK? WE COULD GO DIVING AND PARASAILING ON THIS ISLAND.
SHEESH! HOW SERIOUS IS HE ABOUT ANY OF THIS?!
STILL...
I DOUBT THAT STORY HE TOLD ME WAS ENTIRELY MADE-UP.
THE TRUTH ABOUT THE MAN NAMED ASAHI SAIBA IS SHROUDED IN MYSTERY...
BUT THIS ONCE...
...IT FEELS LIKE I WAS ALLOWED A LITTLE PEEK BEHIND THE CURTAIN.
I'M TOTALLY OKAY WITH STAYING TRADITIONAL AND DOING HAWAII...
BUT IT'S HARD TO PASS UP ON THE MALDIVES OR FIJI, Y'KNOW?
YOU'RE DEAD SET ON GOING TO THE TROPICS, AREN'T YOU?
AN UPDATE, BOOK MASTER.

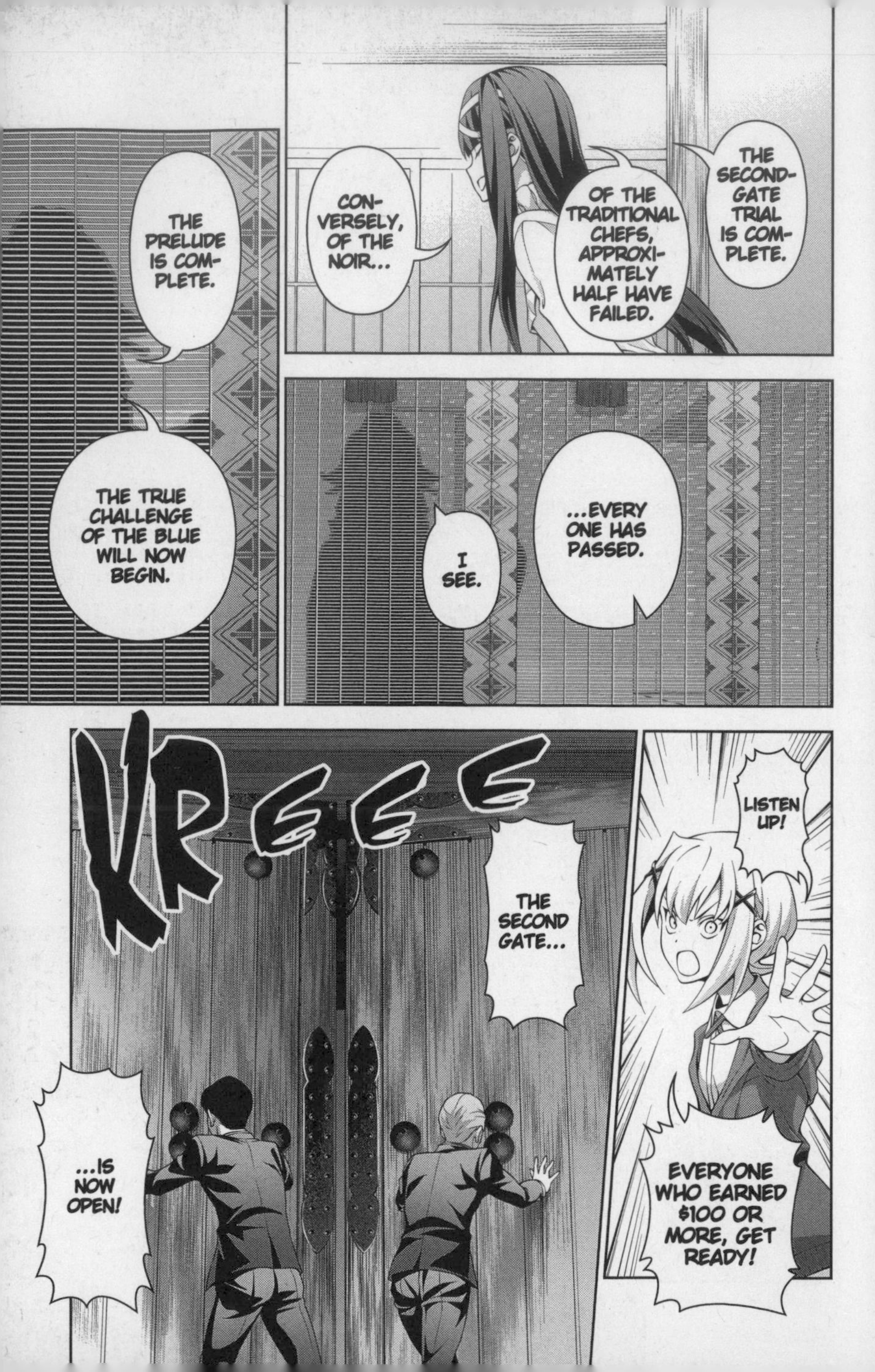
THE SECOND-GATE TRIAL IS COMPLETE.
OF THE TRADITIONAL CHEFS, APPROXIMATELY HALF HAVE FAILED.
CONVERSELY, OF THE NOIR...
...EVERY ONE HAS PASSED.
I SEE.
THE PRELUDE IS COMPLETE.
THE TRUE CHALLENGE OF THE BLUE WILL NOW BEGIN.
LISTEN UP!
EVERYONE WHO EARNED $100 OR MORE, GET READY!
KREEE
THE SECOND GATE...
...IS NOW OPEN!

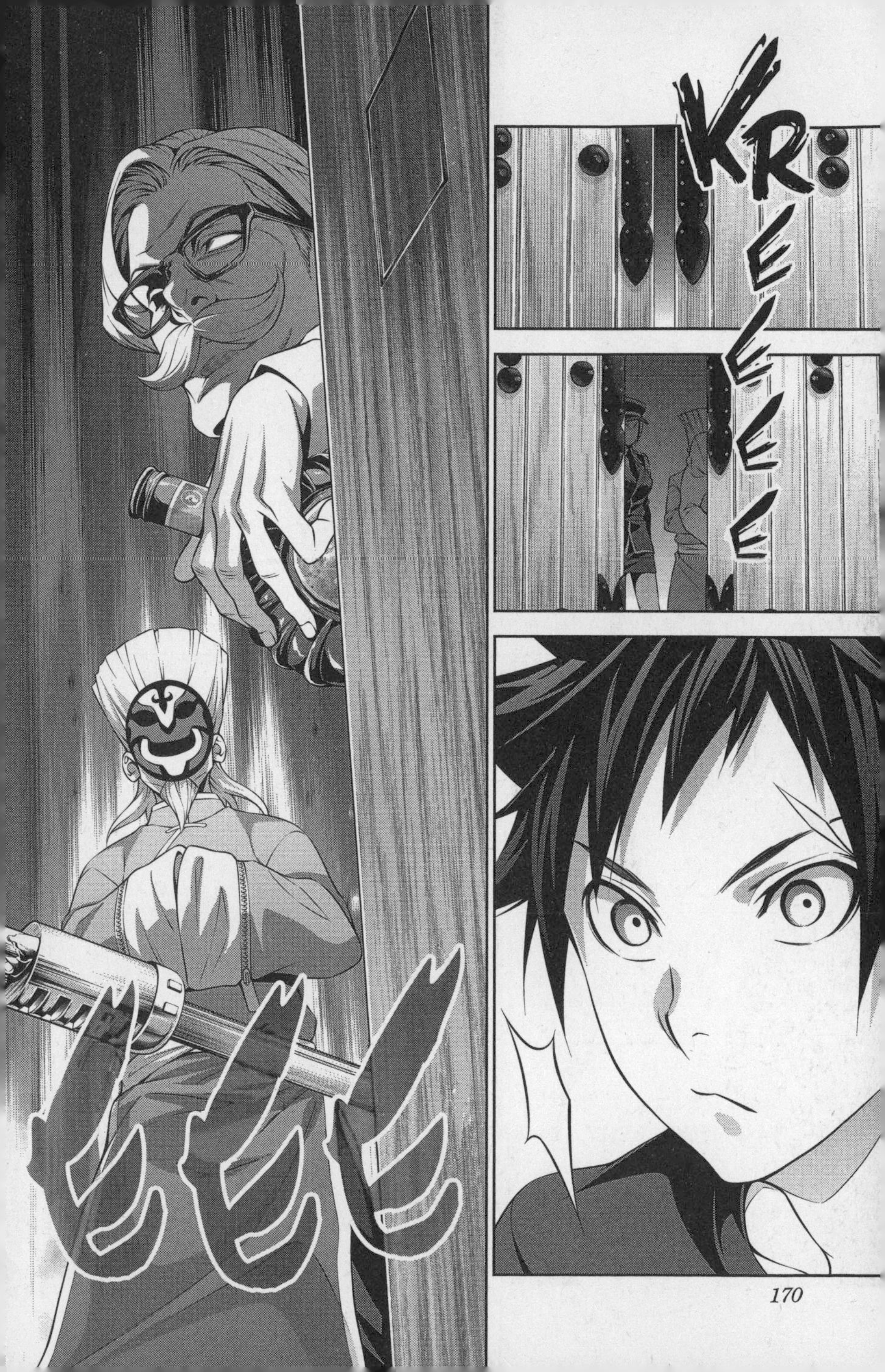
KREEEE

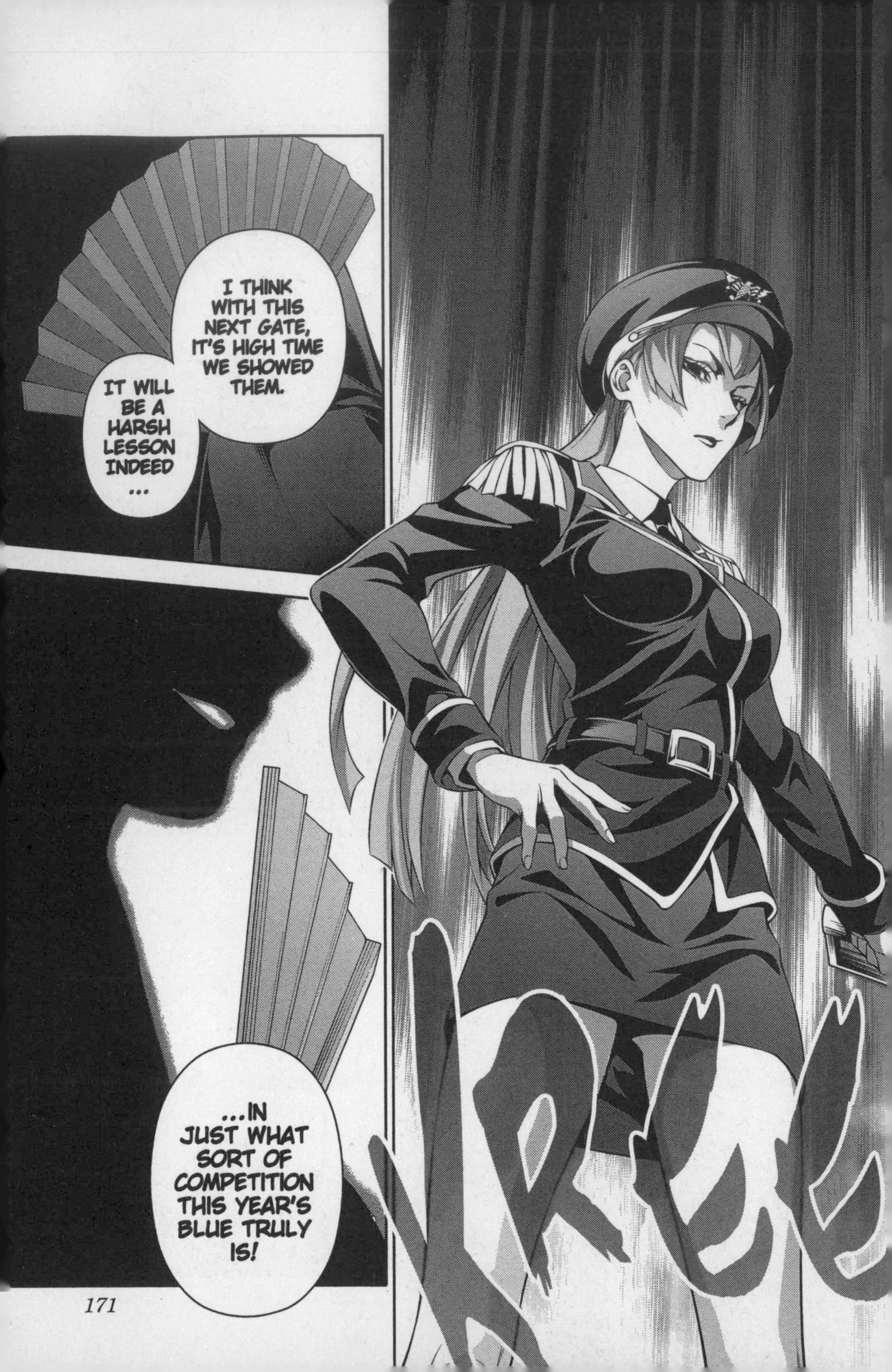
I THINK WITH THIS NEXT GATE, IT'S HIGH TIME WE SHOWED THEM.
IT WILL BE A HARSH LESSON INDEED...
...IN JUST WHAT SORT OF COMPETITION THIS YEAR'S BLUE TRULY IS!

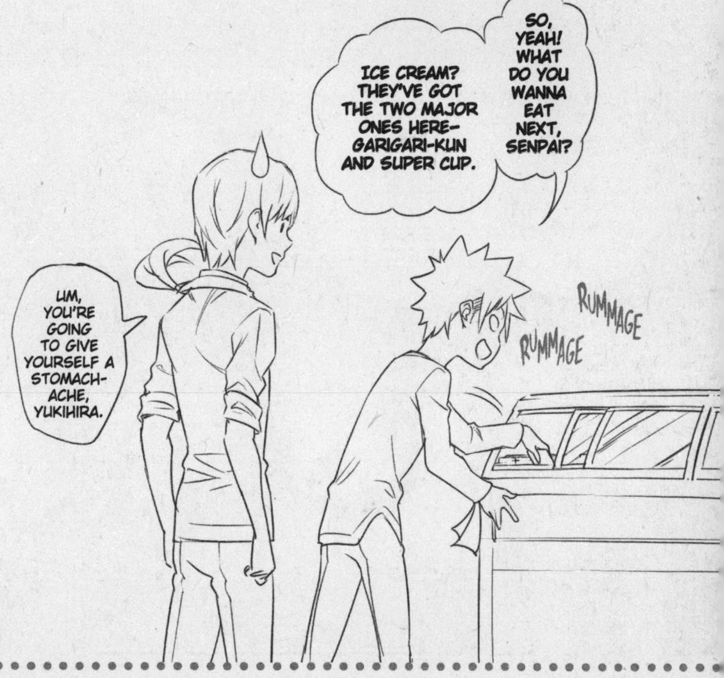
SO, YEAH! WHAT DO YOU WANNA EAT NEXT, SENPAI?
ICE CREAM? THEY'VE GOT THE TWO MAJOR ONES HERE- GARIGARI-KUN AND SUPER CUP.
RUMMAGE
RUMMAGE
UM, YOU'RE GOING TO GIVE YOURSELF A STOMACH-ACHE, YUKIHIRA.

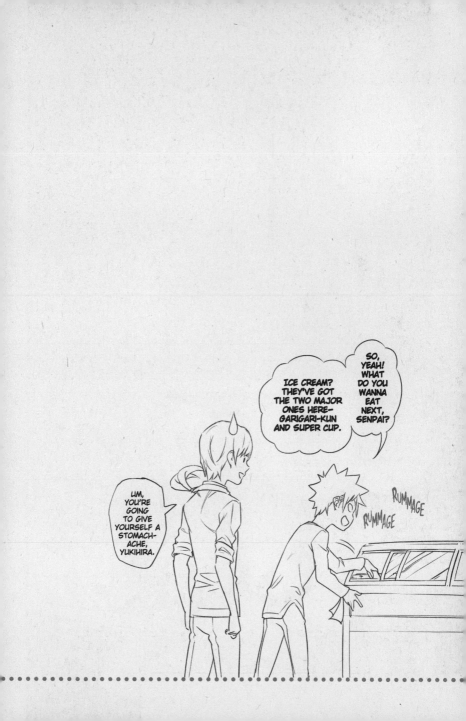

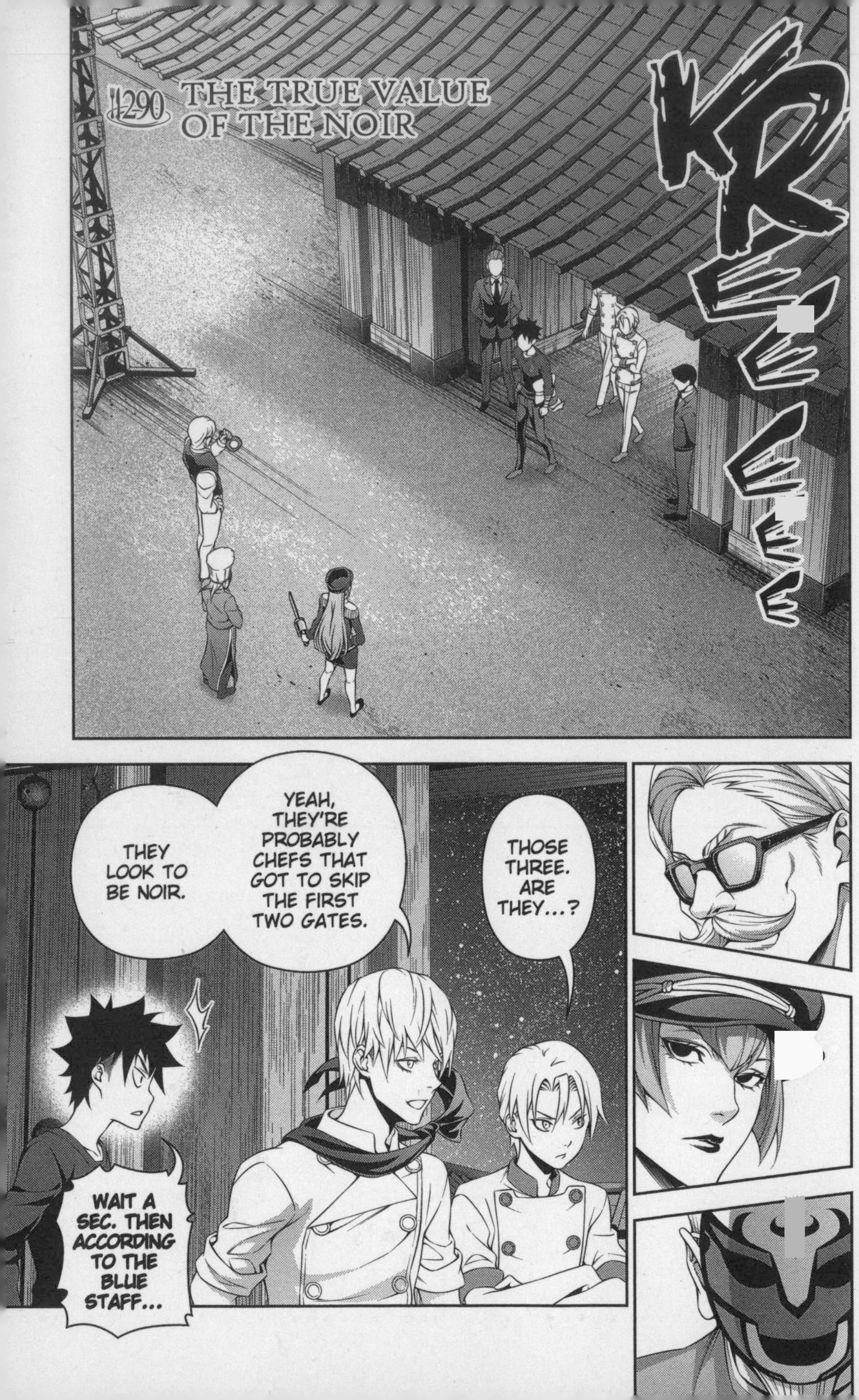
290
THE TRUE VALUE OF THE NOIR
THOSE THREE. ARE THEY...?
YEAH, THEY'RE PROBABLY CHEFS THAT GOT TO SKIP THE FIRST TWO GATES.
THEY LOOK TO BE NOIR.
WAIT A SEC. THEN ACCORDING TO THE BLUE STAFF...

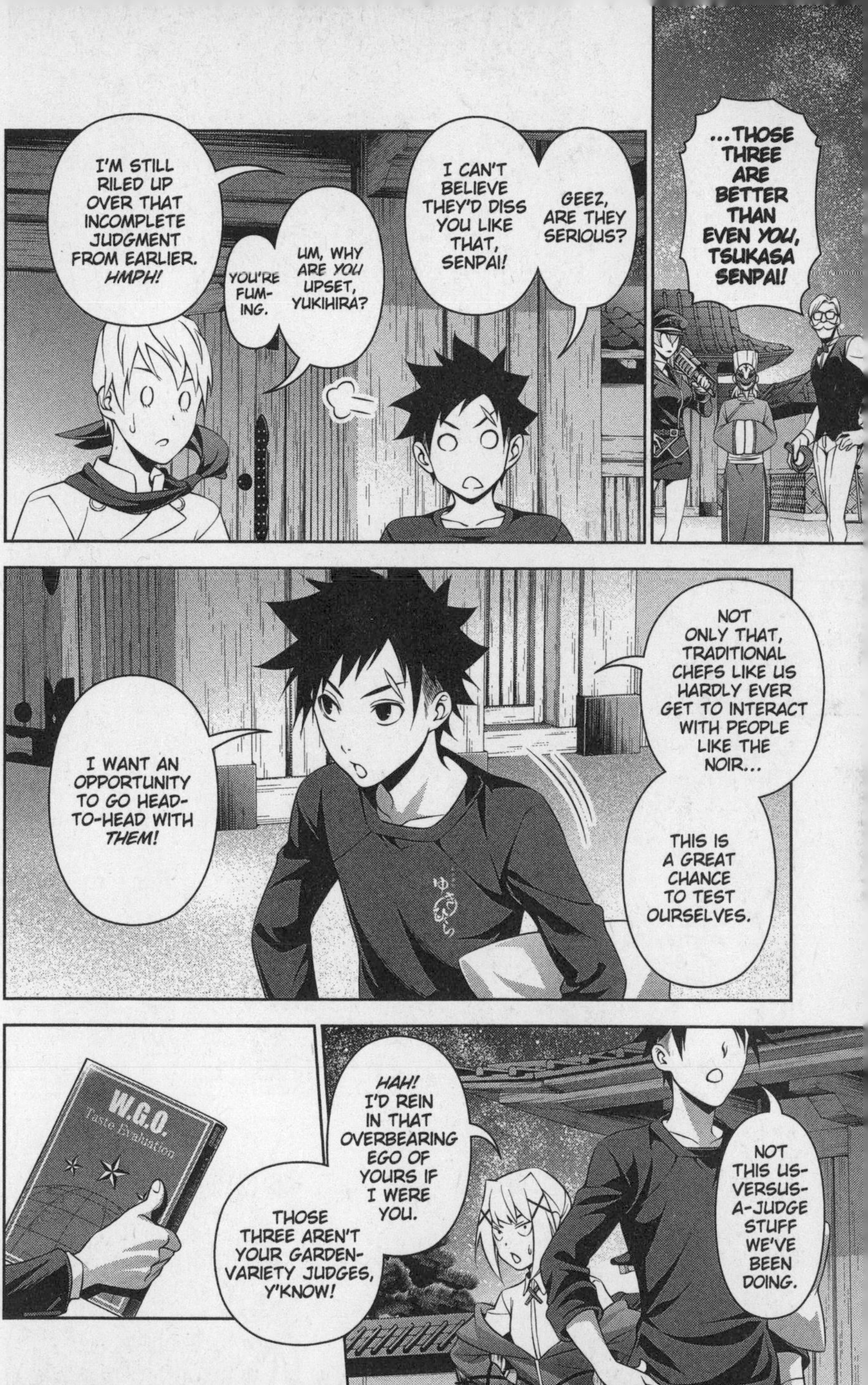
...THOSE THREE ARE BETTER THAN EVEN *YOU*, TSUKASA SENPAI!
GEEZ, ARE THEY SERIOUS?
I CAN'T BELIEVE THEY'D DISS YOU LIKE THAT, SENPAI!
UM, WHY ARE *YOU* UPSET, YUKIHIRA?
YOU'RE FUMING.
I'M STILL RILED UP OVER THAT INCOMPLETE JUDGMENT FROM EARLIER. *HMPH!*
NOT ONLY THAT, TRADITIONAL CHEFS LIKE US HARDLY EVER GET TO INTERACT WITH PEOPLE LIKE THE NOIR...
THIS IS A GREAT CHANCE TO TEST OURSELVES.
I WANT AN OPPORTUNITY TO GO HEAD-TO-HEAD WITH *THEM!*
NOT THIS US-VERSUS-A-JUDGE STUFF WE'VE BEEN DOING.
HAH! I'D REIN IN THAT OVERBEARING EGO OF YOURS IF I WERE YOU.
THOSE THREE AREN'T YOUR GARDEN-VARIETY JUDGES, Y'KNOW!
W.G.O.
Taste Evaluation

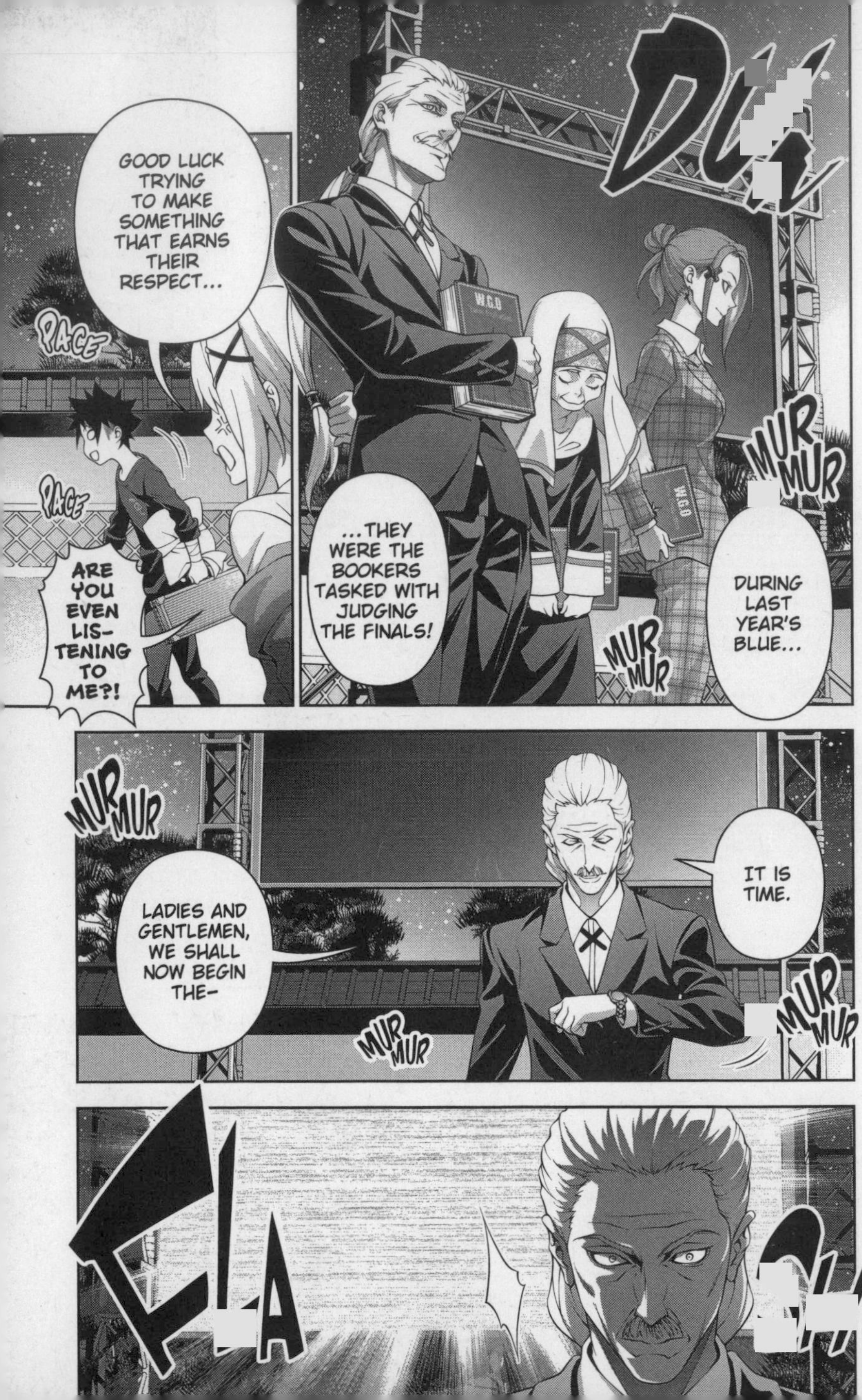

MUR MUR
DURING LAST YEAR'S BLUE...
...THEY WERE THE BOOKERS TASKED WITH JUDGING THE FINALS!
MUR MUR
GOOD LUCK TRYING TO MAKE SOMETHING THAT EARNS THEIR RESPECT...
PACE
PACE
ARE YOU EVEN LIS- TENING TO ME?!
IT IS TIME.
MUR MUR
LADIES AND GENTLEMEN, WE SHALL NOW BEGIN THE-
MUR MUR
MUR MUR

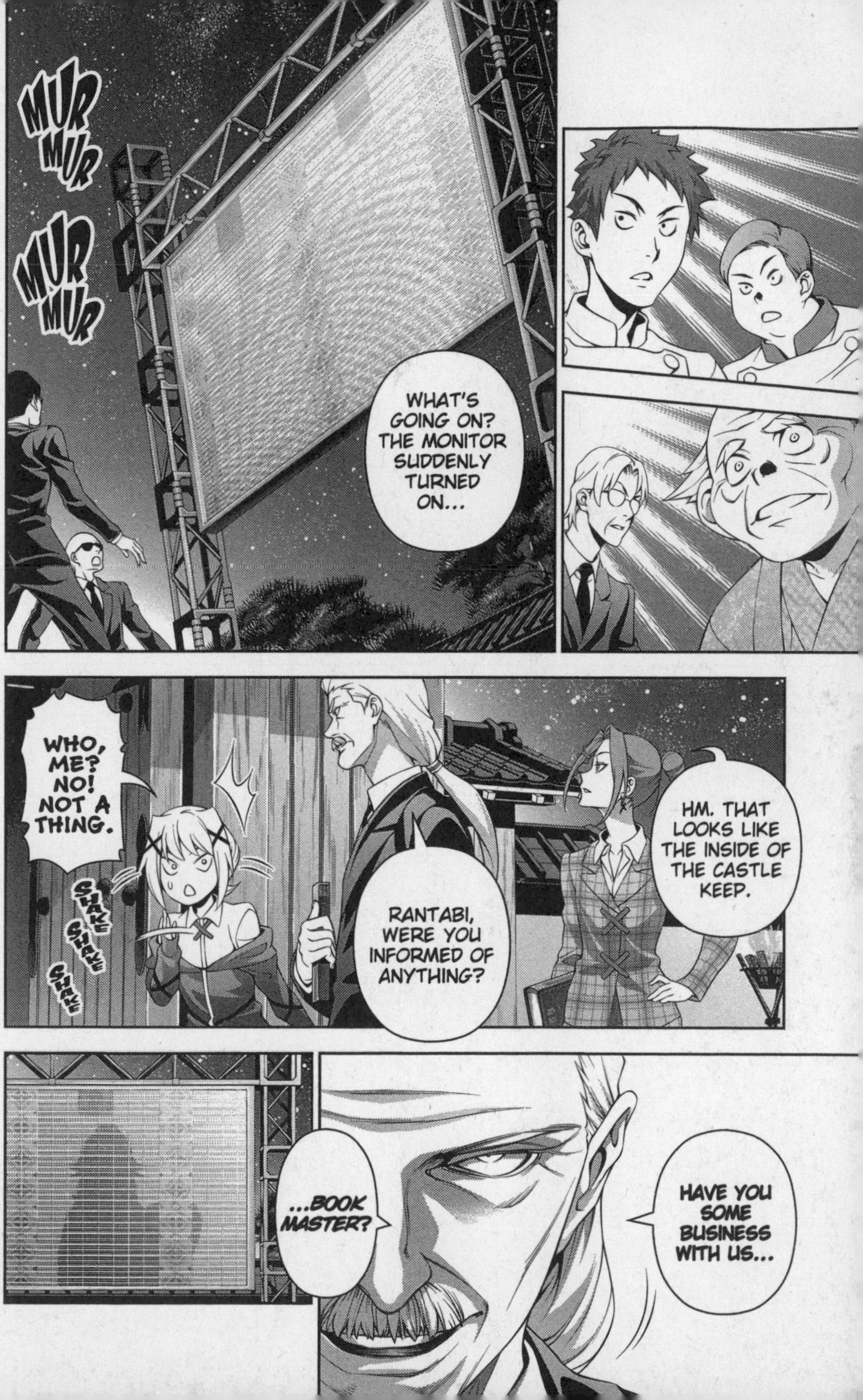
MUR MUR
MUR MUR
WHAT'S GOING ON? THE MONITOR SUDDENLY TURNED ON...
HM. THAT LOOKS LIKE THE INSIDE OF THE CASTLE KEEP.
RANTABI, WERE YOU INFORMED OF ANYTHING?
WHO, ME? NO! NOT A THING.
SHAKE SHAKE SHAKE
HAVE YOU SOME BUSINESS WITH US...
...BOOK MASTER?

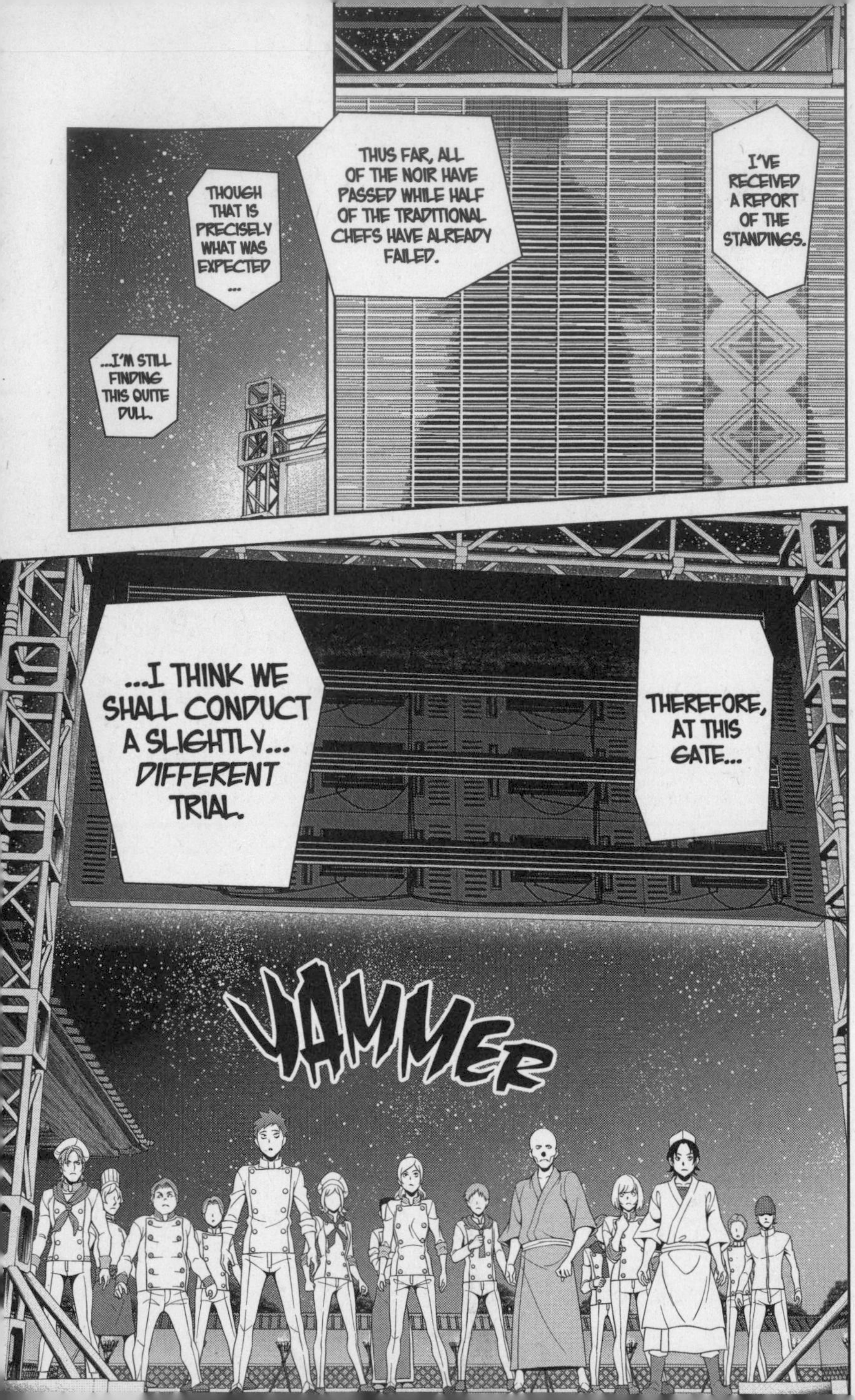
I'VE RECEIVED A REPORT OF THE STANDINGS.
THUS FAR, ALL OF THE NOIR HAVE PASSED WHILE HALF OF THE TRADITIONAL CHEFS HAVE ALREADY FAILED.
THOUGH THAT IS PRECISELY WHAT WAS EXPECTED ...
...I'M STILL FINDING THIS QUITE DULL.
THEREFORE, AT THIS GATE...
...I THINK WE SHALL CONDUCT A SLIGHTLY... DIFFERENT TRIAL.
VAMMER

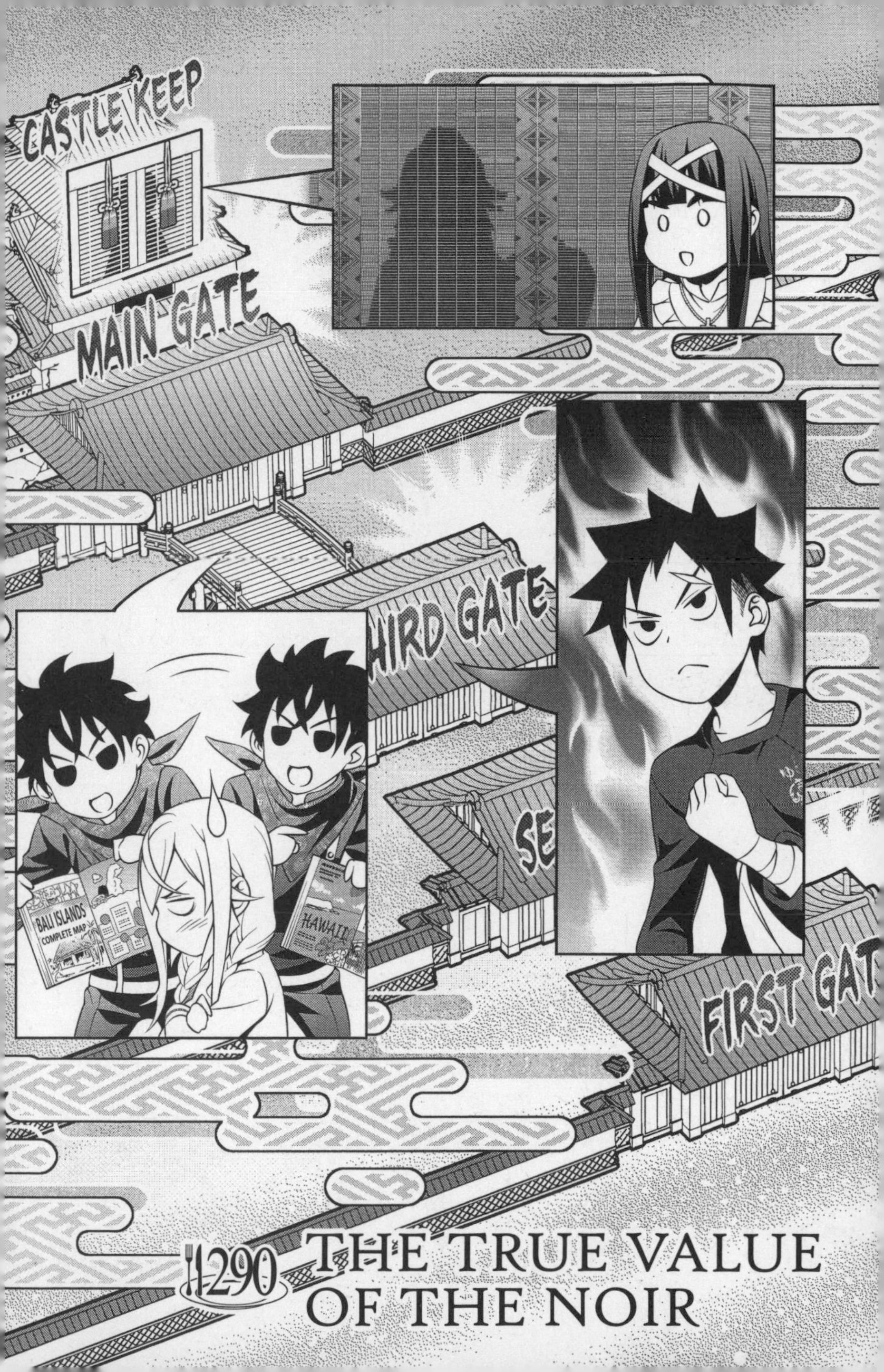
CASTLE KEEP
MAIN GATE
HIRD GATE
SE
FIRST GAT
BALI ISLANDS
COMPLETE MAP
HAWAII

290 THE TRUE VALUE OF THE NOIR

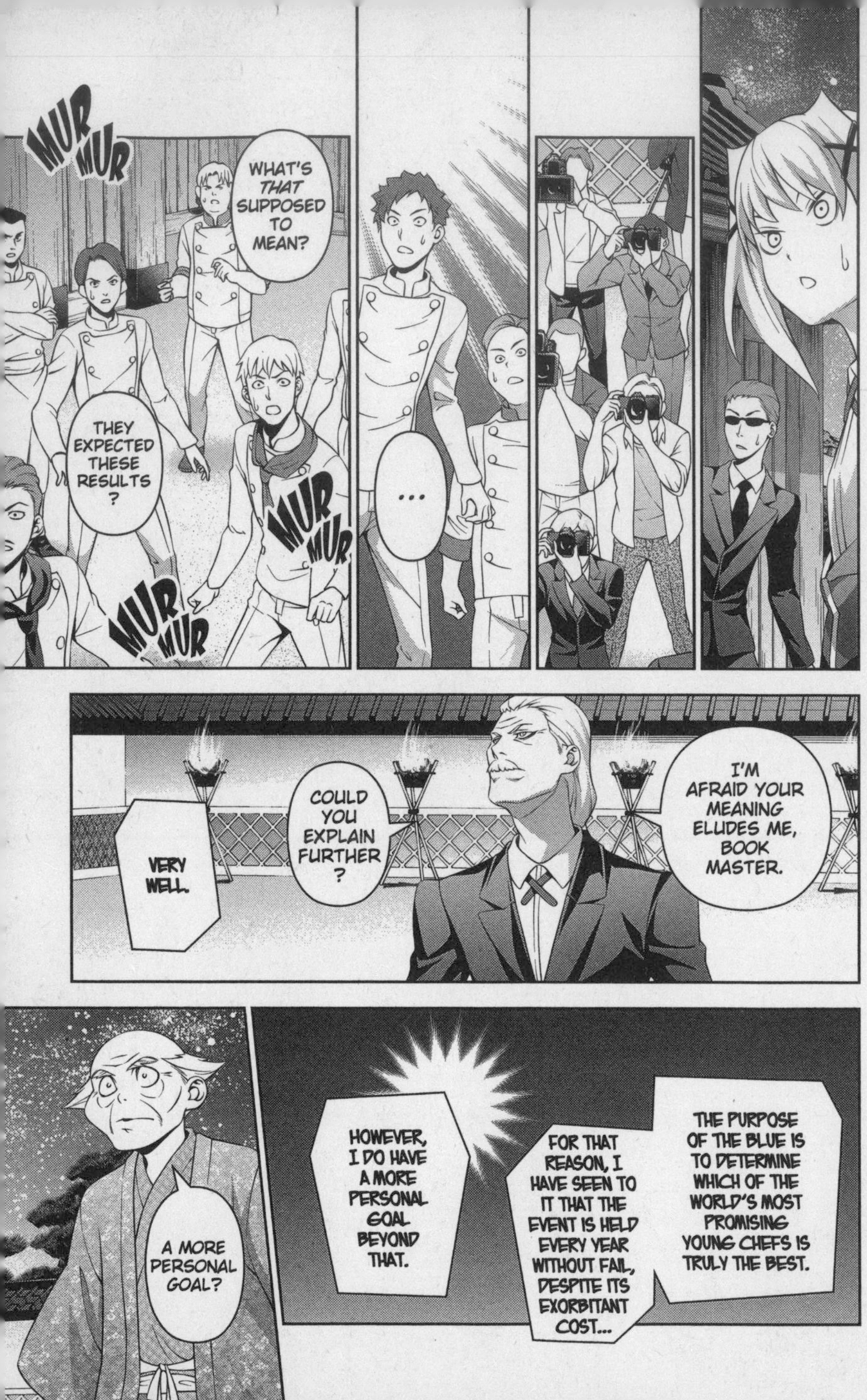
...
WHAT'S THAT SUPPOSED TO MEAN?
MUR MUR
THEY EXPECTED THESE RESULTS?
MUR MUR
MUR MUR
I'M AFRAID YOUR MEANING ELUDES ME, BOOK MASTER.
COULD YOU EXPLAIN FURTHER?
VERY WELL.
THE PURPOSE OF THE BLUE IS TO DETERMINE WHICH OF THE WORLD'S MOST PROMISING YOUNG CHEFS IS TRULY THE BEST.
FOR THAT REASON, I HAVE SEEN TO IT THAT THE EVENT IS HELD EVERY YEAR WITHOUT FAIL, DESPITE ITS EXORBITANT COST...
HOWEVER, I DO HAVE A MORE PERSONAL GOAL BEYOND THAT.
A MORE PERSONAL GOAL?

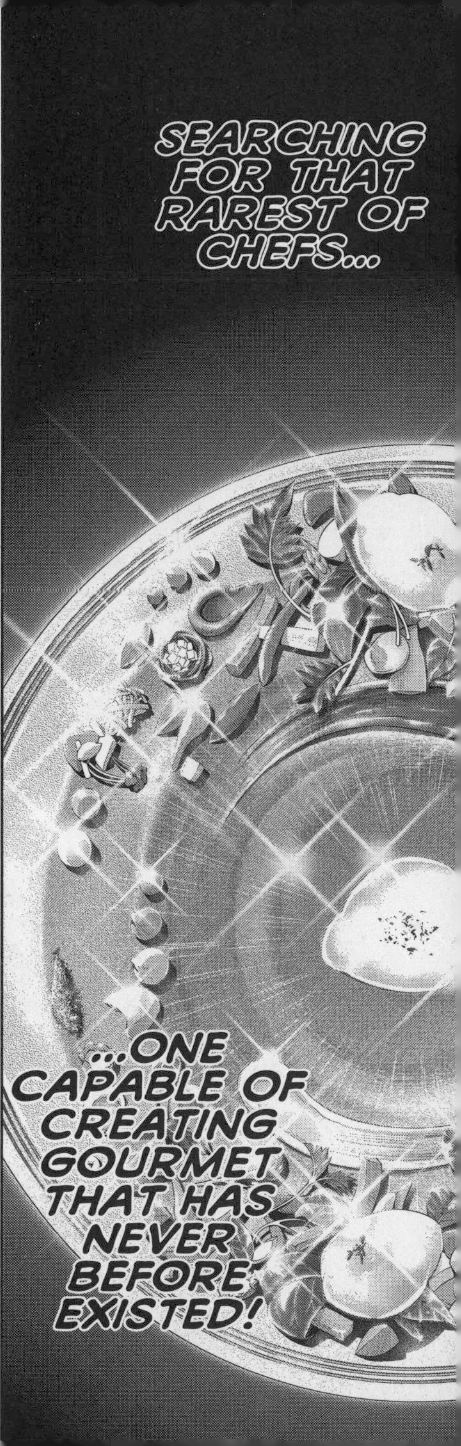
SEARCHING FOR THAT RAREST OF CHEFS...
...ONE CAPABLE OF CREATING GOURMET THAT HAS NEVER BEFORE EXISTED!

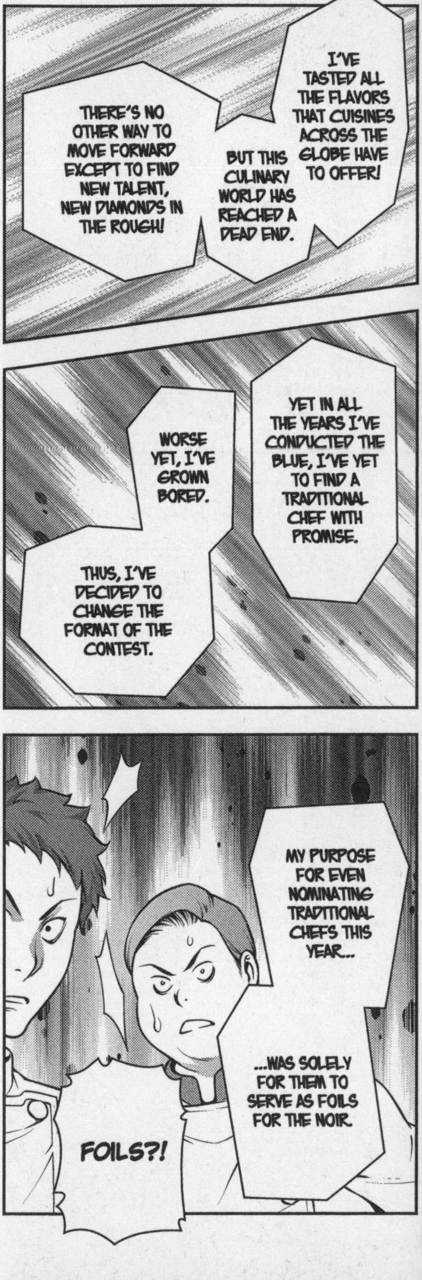
I'VE TASTED ALL THE FLAVORS THAT CUISINES ACROSS THE GLOBE HAVE TO OFFER!
BUT THIS CULINARY WORLD HAS REACHED A DEAD END.
THERE'S NO OTHER WAY TO MOVE FORWARD EXCEPT TO FIND NEW TALENT, NEW DIAMONDS IN THE ROUGH!
YET IN ALL THE YEARS I'VE CONDUCTED THE BLUE, I'VE YET TO FIND A TRADITIONAL CHEF WITH PROMISE.
WORSE YET, I'VE GROWN BORED.
THUS, I'VE DECIDED TO CHANGE THE FORMAT OF THE CONTEST.
MY PURPOSE FOR EVEN NOMINATING TRADITIONAL CHEFS THIS YEAR...
...WAS SOLELY FOR THEM TO SERVE AS FOILS FOR THE NOIR.
FOILS?!

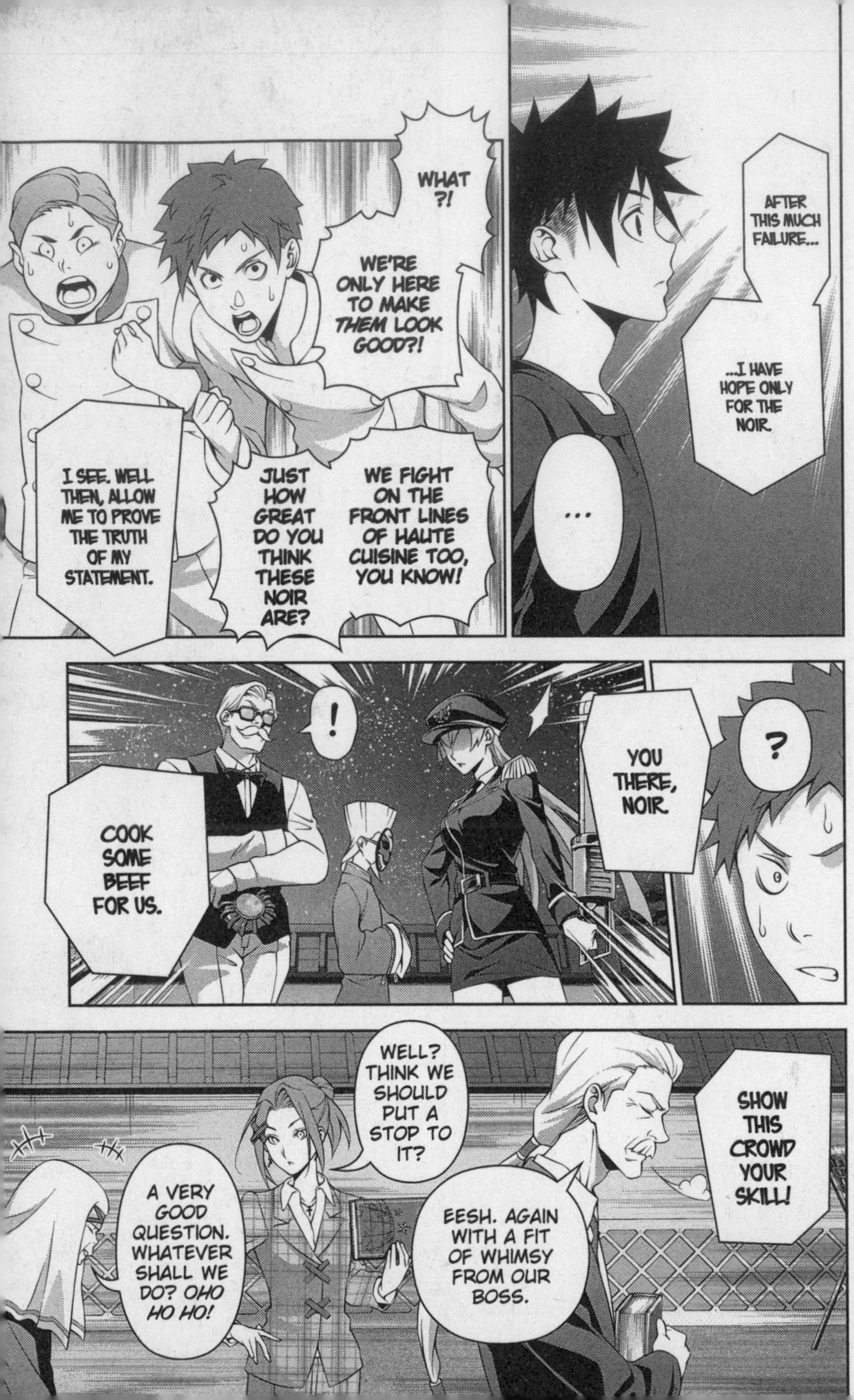
AFTER THIS MUCH FAILURE...
...I HAVE HOPE ONLY FOR THE NOIR.
...
WHAT ?!
WE'RE ONLY HERE TO MAKE *THEM* LOOK GOOD?!
WE FIGHT ON THE FRONT LINES OF HAUTE CUISINE TOO, YOU KNOW!
JUST HOW GREAT DO YOU THINK THESE NOIR ARE?
I SEE. WELL THEN, ALLOW ME TO PROVE THE TRUTH OF MY STATEMENT.
?
YOU THERE, NOIR.
!
COOK SOME BEEF FOR US.
SHOW THIS CROWD YOUR SKILL!
WELL? THINK WE SHOULD PUT A STOP TO IT?
EESH. AGAIN WITH A FIT OF WHIMSY FROM OUR BOSS.
A VERY GOOD QUESTION. WHATEVER SHALL WE DO? OHO HO HO!

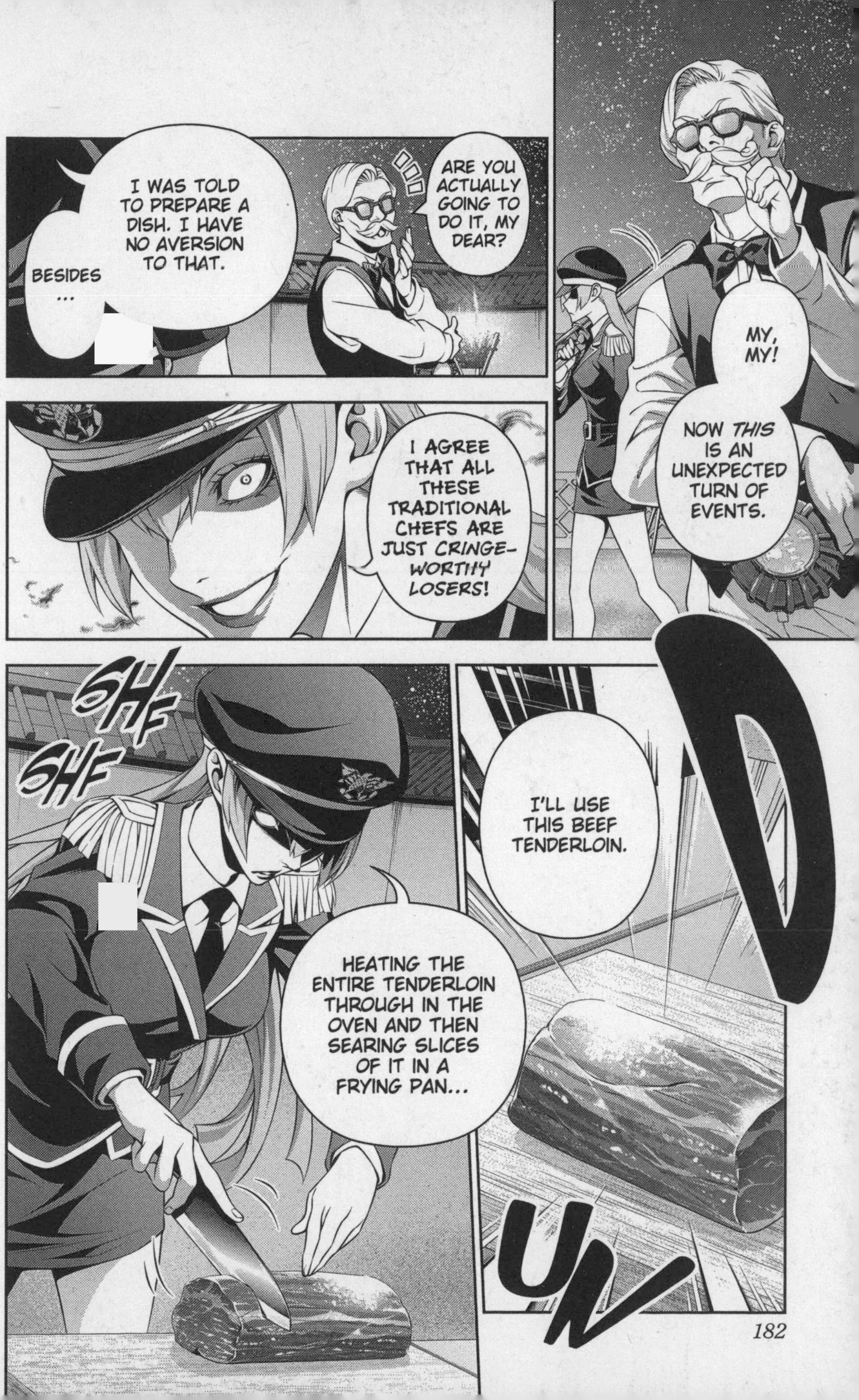
MY, MY!
NOW THIS IS AN UNEXPECTED TURN OF EVENTS.
ARE YOU ACTUALLY GOING TO DO IT, MY DEAR?
I WAS TOLD TO PREPARE A DISH. I HAVE NO AVERSION TO THAT.
BESIDES...
I AGREE THAT ALL THESE TRADITIONAL CHEFS ARE JUST CRINGE-WORTHY LOSERS!
D
I'LL USE THIS BEEF TENDERLOIN.
UN
SHF
SHF
HEATING THE ENTIRE TENDERLOIN THROUGH IN THE OVEN AND THEN SEARING SLICES OF IT IN A FRYING PAN...

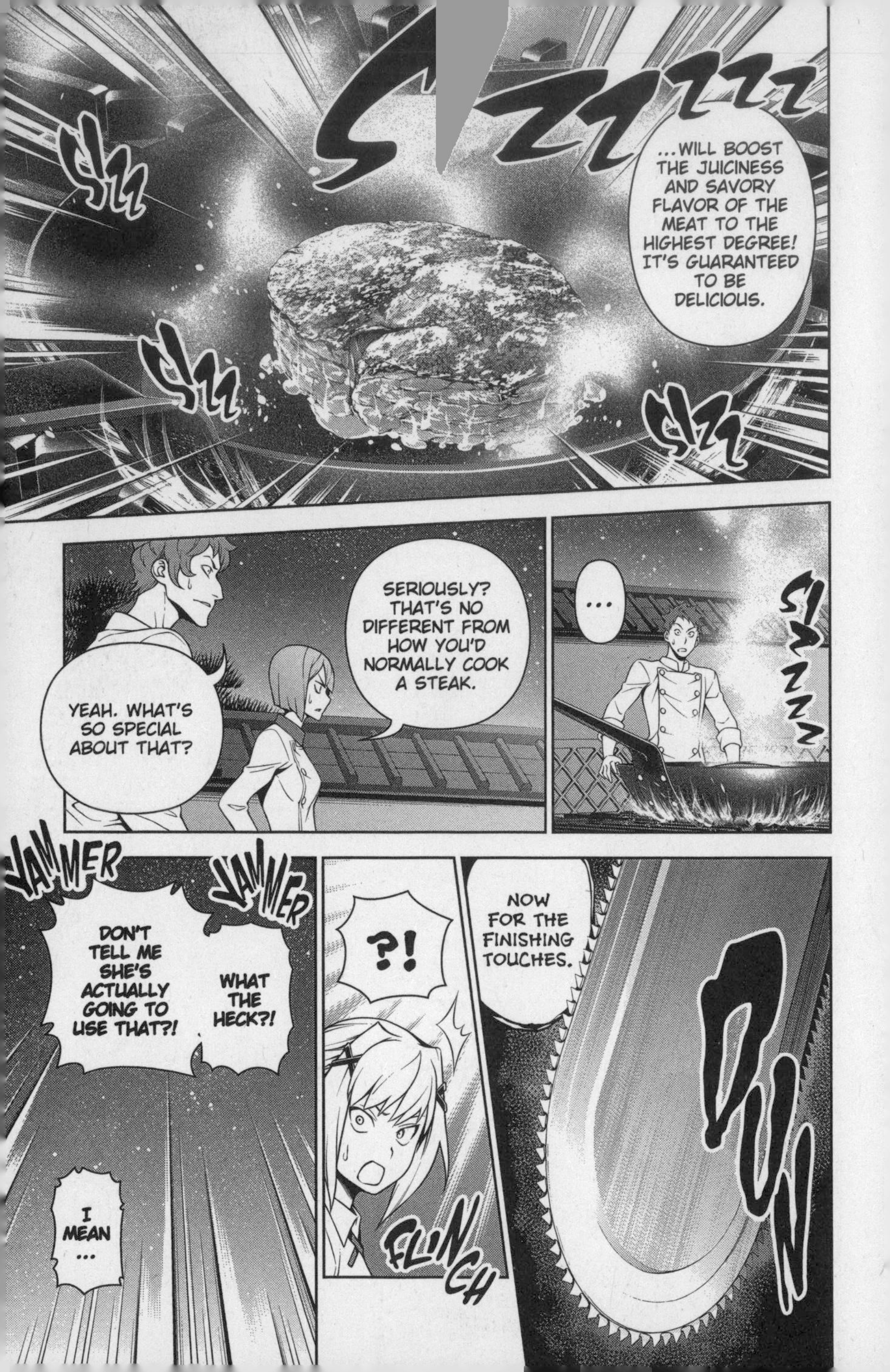
...WILL BOOST THE JUICINESS AND SAVORY FLAVOR OF THE MEAT TO THE HIGHEST DEGREE! IT'S GUARANTEED TO BE DELICIOUS.
...
SERIOUSLY? THAT'S NO DIFFERENT FROM HOW YOU'D NORMALLY COOK A STEAK.
YEAH. WHAT'S SO SPECIAL ABOUT THAT?
NOW FOR THE FINISHING TOUCHES.
?!
FLINCH
JAMMER
JAMMER
WHAT THE HECK?!
DON'T TELL ME SHE'S ACTUALLY GOING TO USE THAT?!
I MEAN ...

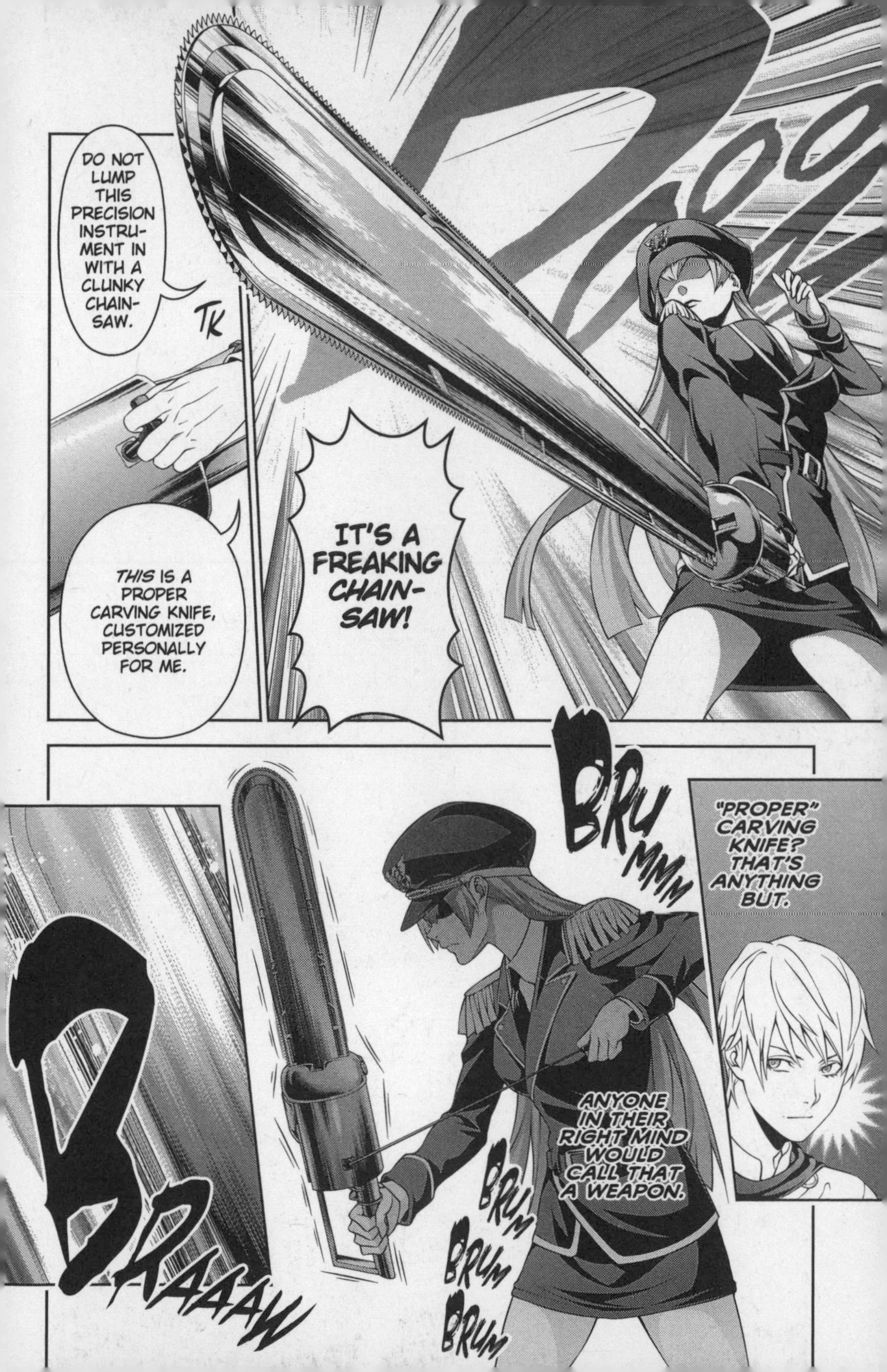
IT'S A FREAKING CHAIN-SAW!
DO NOT LUMP THIS PRECISION INSTRU-MENT IN WITH A CLUNKY CHAIN-SAW.
TK
THIS IS A PROPER CARVING KNIFE, CUSTOMIZED PERSONALLY FOR ME.
"PROPER" CARVING KNIFE? THAT'S ANYTHING BUT.
ANYONE IN THEIR RIGHT MIND WOULD CALL THAT A WEAPON.
BRUMMM
BRUM
BRUM
BRUM
BRUM
BRAAAAW

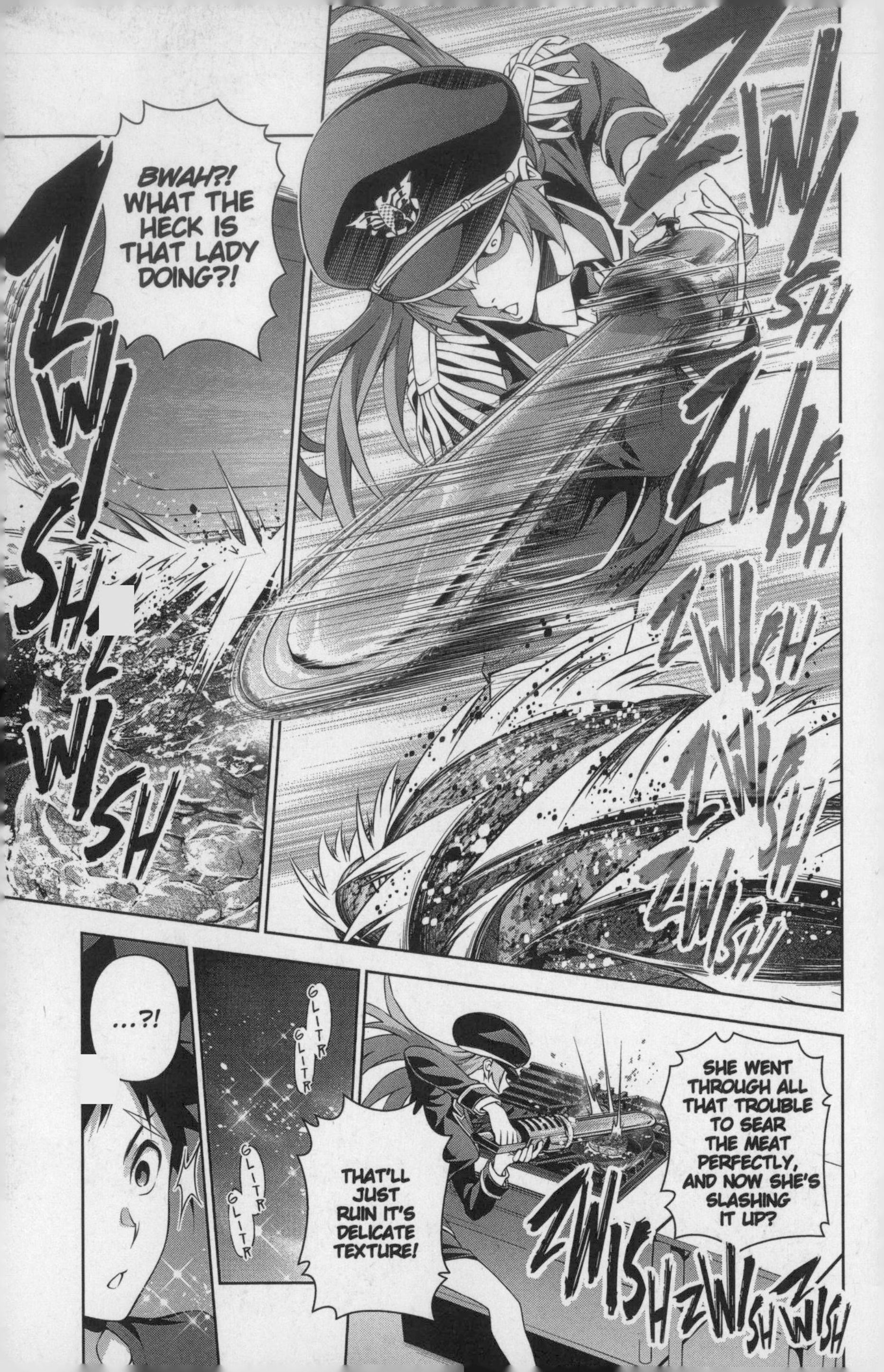
ZWISH
ZWISH
ZWISH
ZWISH
BWAH?! WHAT THE HECK IS THAT LADY DOING?!
ZWISH
SHE WENT THROUGH ALL THAT TROUBLE TO SEAR THE MEAT PERFECTLY, AND NOW SHE'S SLASHING IT UP?
ZWISH ZWISH ZWISH
THAT'LL JUST RUIN IT'S DELICATE TEXTURE!
GLITR GLITR
GLITR GLITR
...?!

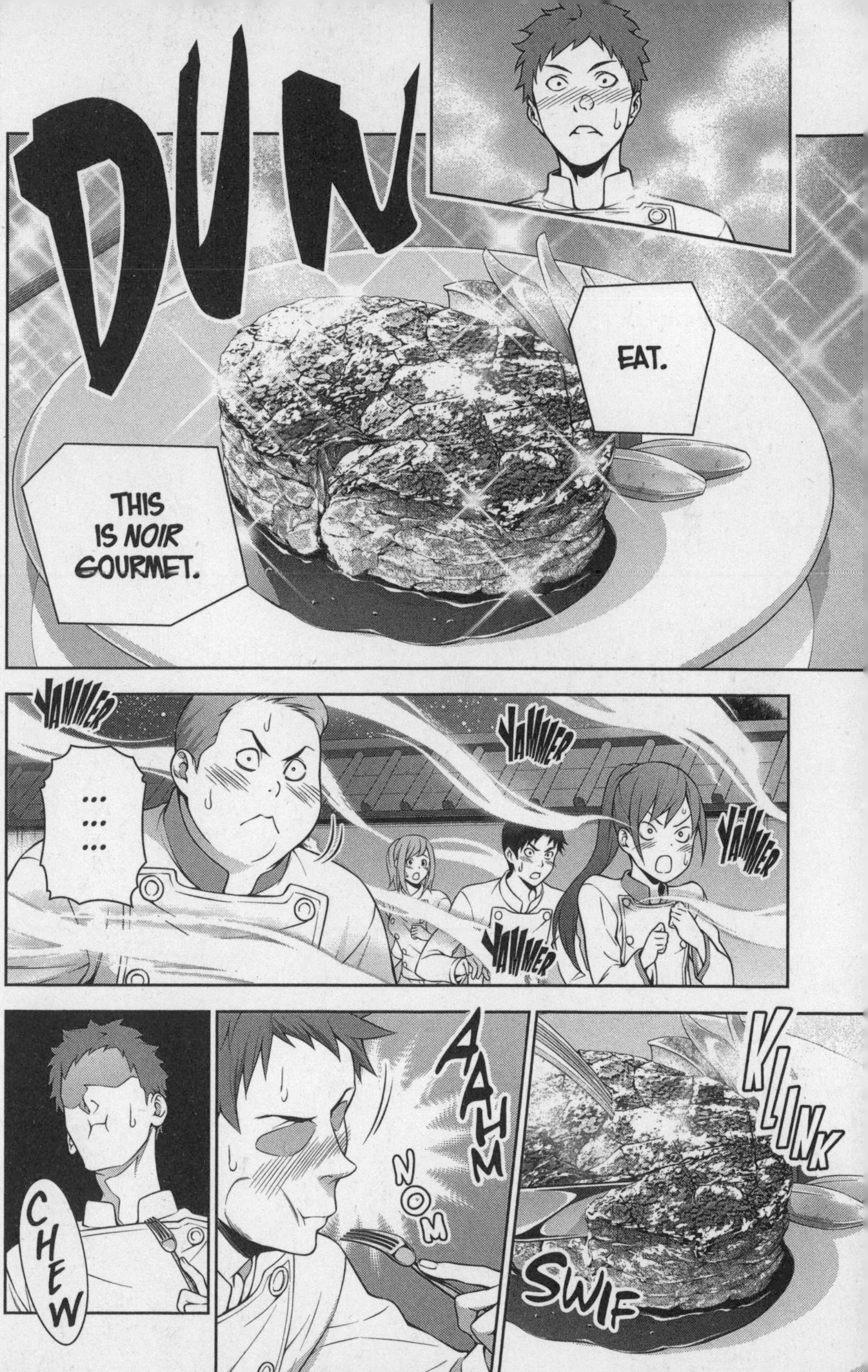
DUN
EAT.
THIS IS NOIR GOURMET.
YAMMER
YAMMER
YAMMER
...
...
...
YAMMER
KLINK
SWIF
AAHM
NOM
CHEW

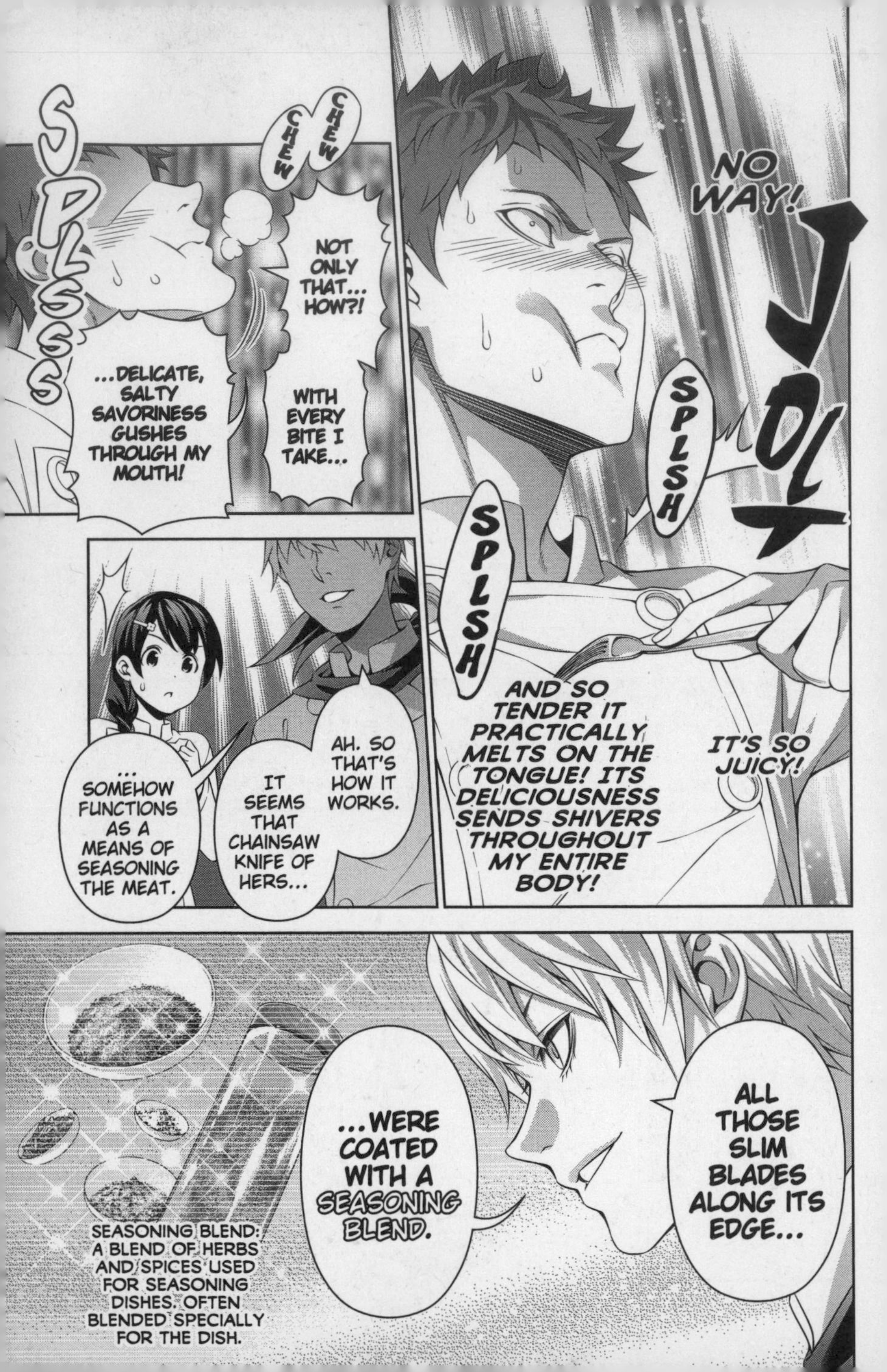
NO WAY!
JOLT
SPLSH
SPLSH
IT'S SO JUICY!
AND SO TENDER IT PRACTICALLY MELTS ON THE TONGUE! ITS DELICIOUSNESS SENDS SHIVERS THROUGHOUT MY ENTIRE BODY!
CHEW CHEW
NOT ONLY THAT... HOW?!
WITH EVERY BITE I TAKE...
SPLSS
...DELICATE, SALTY SAVORINESS GUSHES THROUGH MY MOUTH!
AH. SO THAT'S HOW IT WORKS.
IT SEEMS THAT CHAINSAW KNIFE OF HERS...
...SOMEHOW FUNCTIONS AS A MEANS OF SEASONING THE MEAT.
ALL THOSE SLIM BLADES ALONG ITS EDGE...
...WERE COATED WITH A SEASONING BLEND.
SEASONING BLEND: A BLEND OF HERBS AND SPICES USED FOR SEASONING DISHES. OFTEN BLENDED SPECIALLY FOR THE DISH.

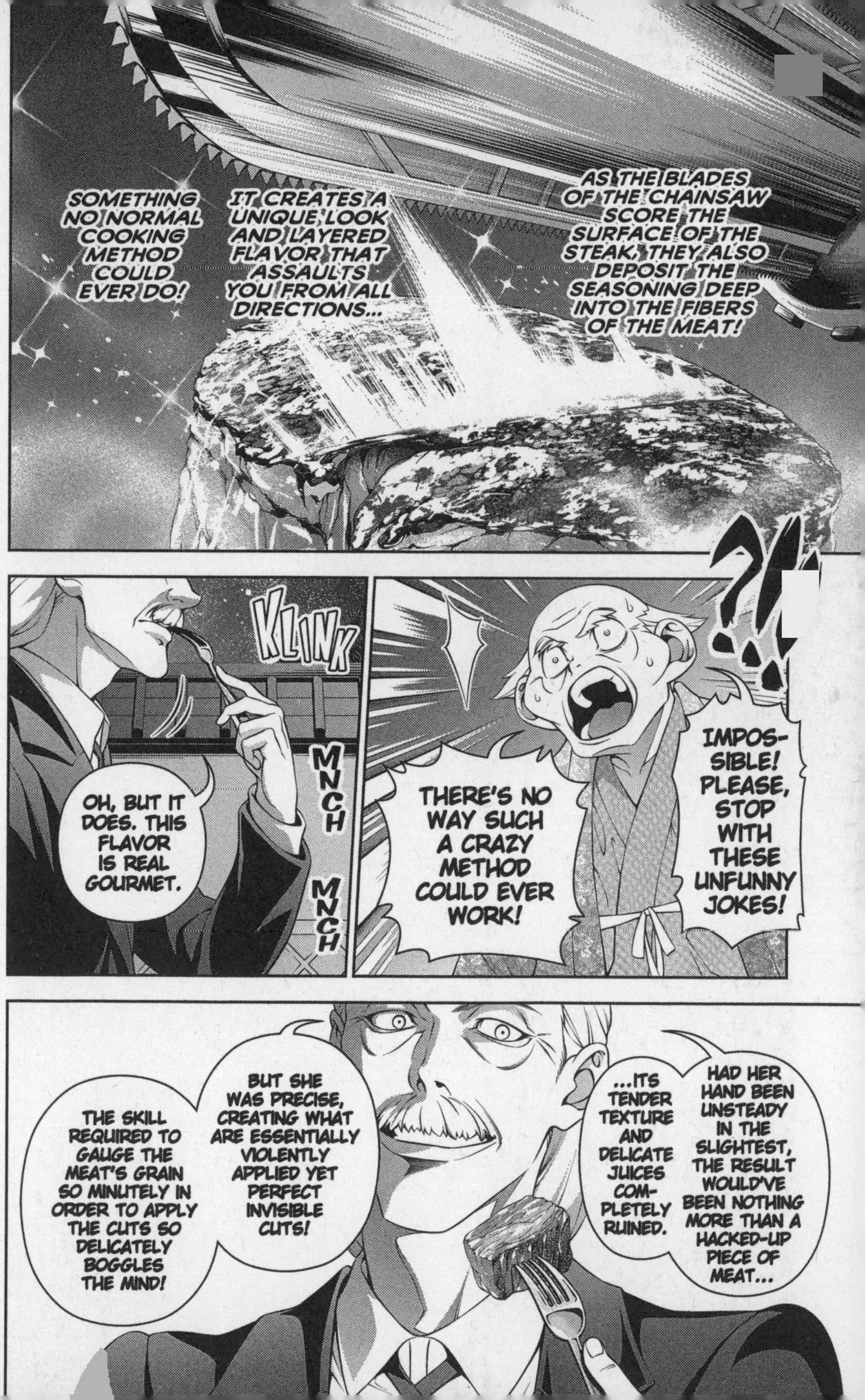
AS THE BLADES OF THE CHAINSAW SCORE THE SURFACE OF THE STEAK, THEY ALSO DEPOSIT THE SEASONING DEEP INTO THE FIBERS OF THE MEAT!
IT CREATES A UNIQUE LOOK AND LAYERED FLAVOR THAT ASSAULTS YOU FROM ALL DIRECTIONS...
SOMETHING NO NORMAL COOKING METHOD COULD EVER DO!
?!!
IMPOSSIBLE! PLEASE, STOP WITH THESE UNFUNNY JOKES!
THERE'S NO WAY SUCH A CRAZY METHOD COULD EVER WORK!
KLINK
MNCH
MNCH
OH, BUT IT DOES. THIS FLAVOR IS REAL GOURMET.
HAD HER HAND BEEN UNSTEADY IN THE SLIGHTEST, THE RESULT WOULD'VE BEEN NOTHING MORE THAN A HACKED-UP PIECE OF MEAT...
...ITS TENDER TEXTURE AND DELICATE JUICES COMPLETELY RUINED.
BUT SHE WAS PRECISE, CREATING WHAT ARE ESSENTIALLY VIOLENTLY APPLIED YET PERFECT INVISIBLE CUTS!
THE SKILL REQUIRED TO GAUGE THE MEAT'S GRAIN SO MINUTELY IN ORDER TO APPLY THE CUTS SO DELICATELY BOGGLES THE MIND!

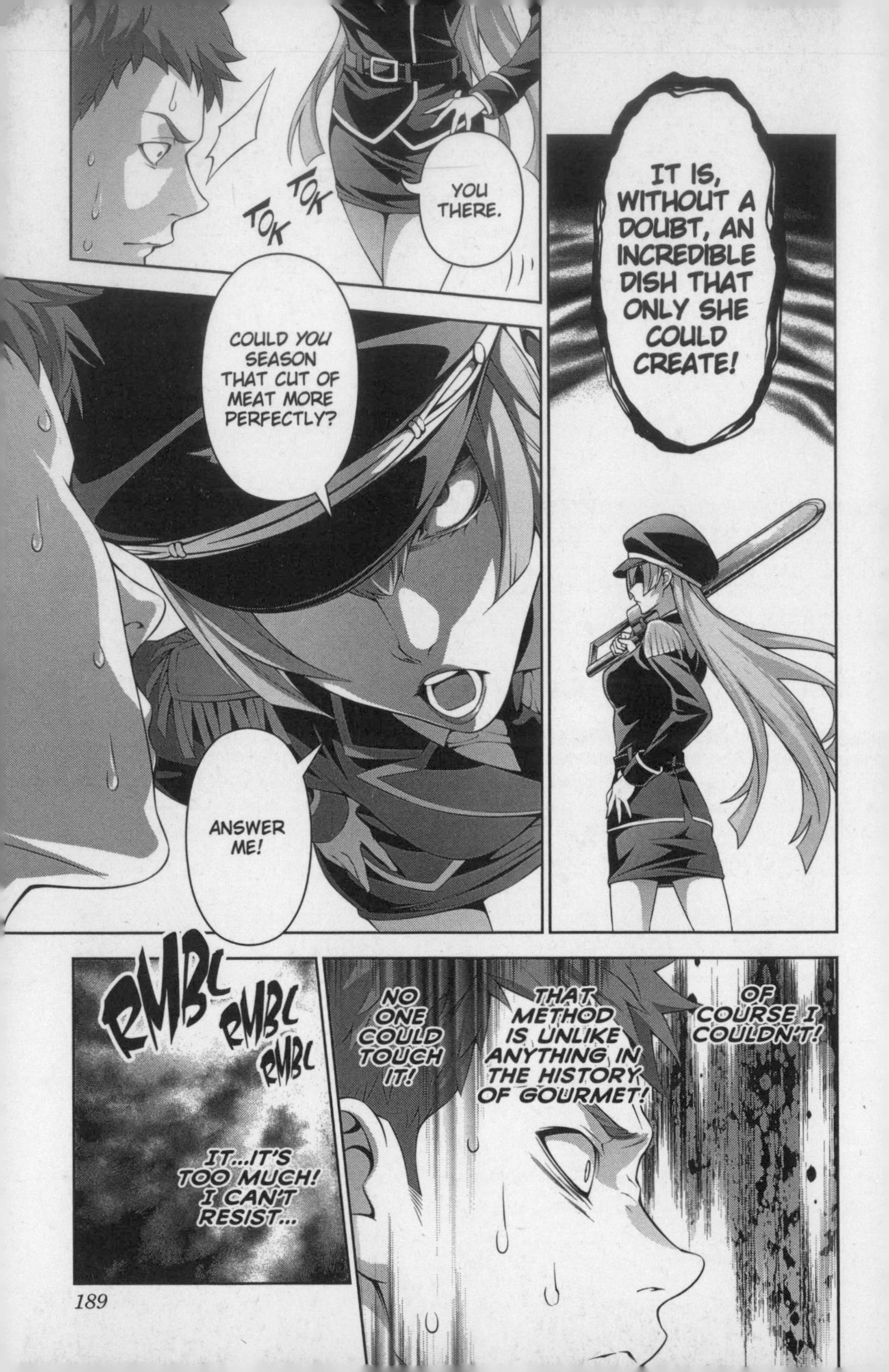
IT IS, WITHOUT A DOUBT, AN INCREDIBLE DISH THAT ONLY SHE COULD CREATE!
TOK TOK
YOU THERE.
COULD YOU SEASON THAT CUT OF MEAT MORE PERFECTLY?
ANSWER ME!
OF COURSE I COULDN'T!
THAT METHOD IS UNLIKE ANYTHING IN THE HISTORY OF GOURMET!
NO ONE COULD TOUCH IT!
RMBL RMBL RMBL
IT...IT'S TOO MUCH! I CAN'T RESIST...

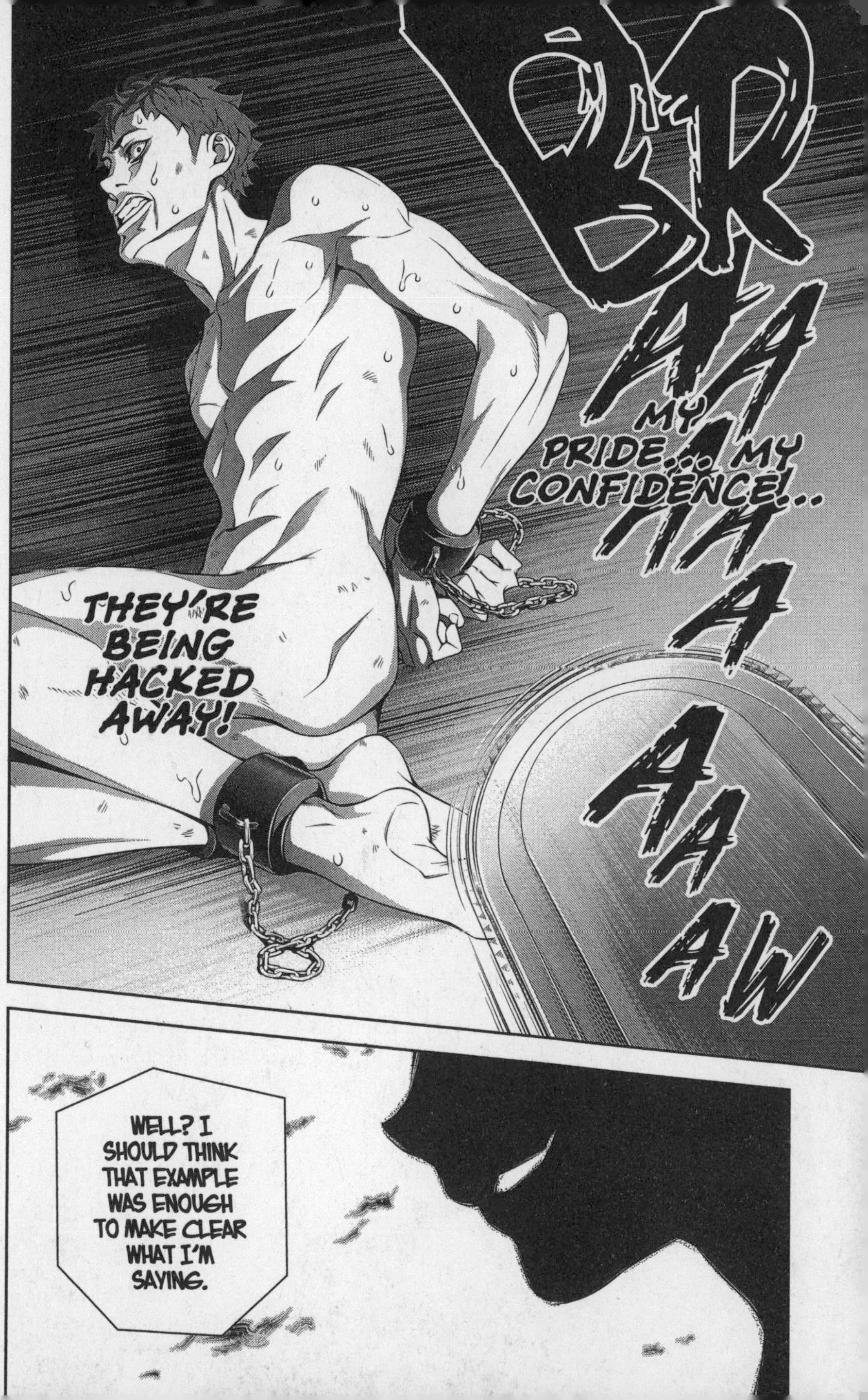
MY PRIDE... MY CONFIDENCE...
THEY'RE BEING HACKED AWAY!
WELL? I SHOULD THINK THAT EXAMPLE WAS ENOUGH TO MAKE CLEAR WHAT I'M SAYING.

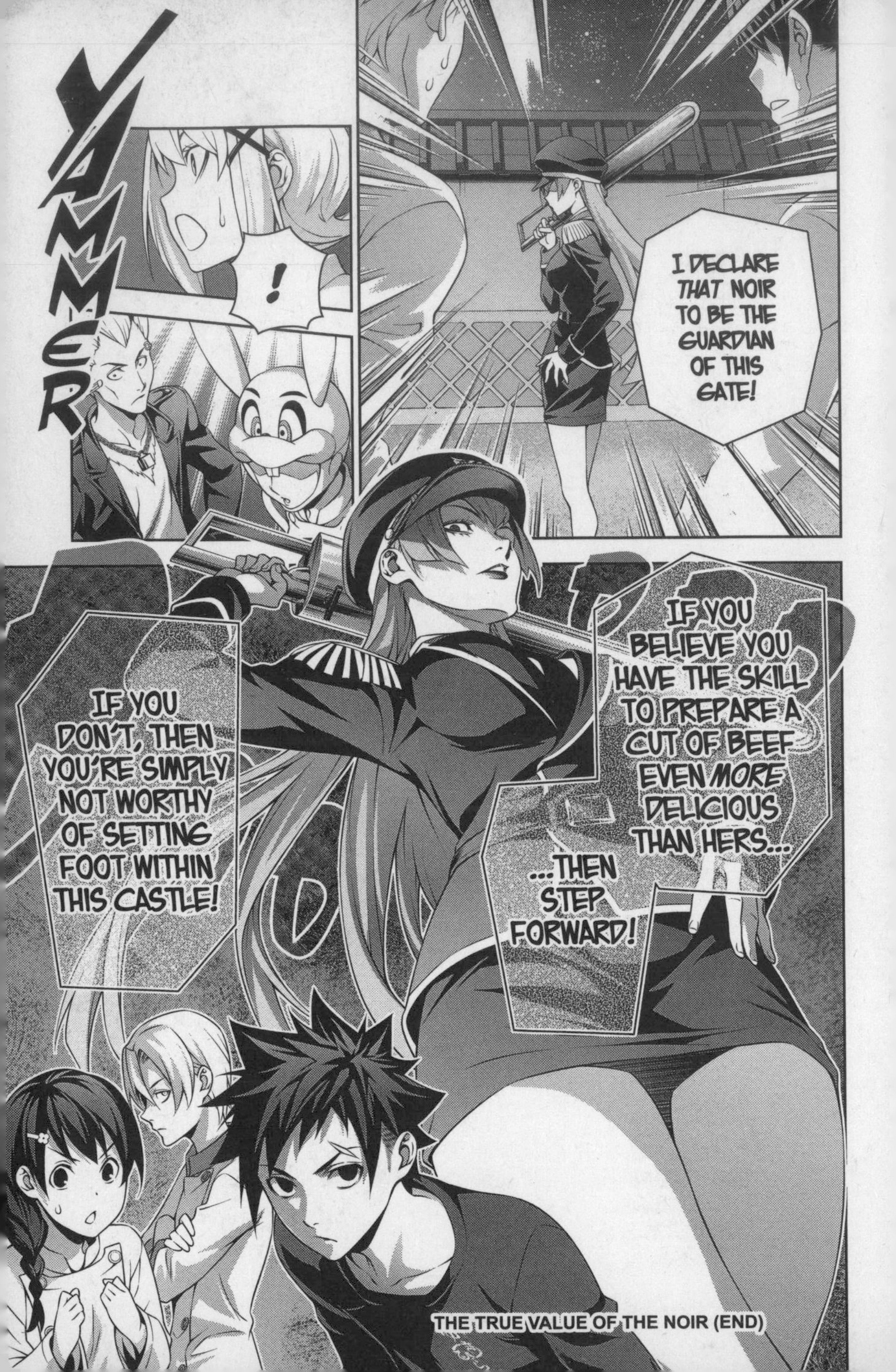
I DECLARE THAT NOIR TO BE THE GUARDIAN OF THIS GATE!
YAMMER
!
IF YOU BELIEVE YOU HAVE THE SKILL TO PREPARE A CUT OF BEEF EVEN MORE DELICIOUS THAN HERS...
...THEN STEP FORWARD!
IF YOU DON'T, THEN YOU'RE SIMPLY NOT WORTHY OF SETTING FOOT WITHIN THIS CASTLE!

THE TRUE VALUE OF THE NOIR (END)

You're Reading in the Wrong Direction!!

1
3
2
2
1
3
5
6
4

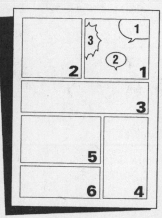

Whoops! Guess what? You're starting at the wrong end of the comic!

...It's true! In keeping with the original Japanese format, **Food Wars!** is meant to be read from right to left, starting in the upper-right corner.

Unlike English, which is read from left to right, Japanese is read from right to left, meaning that action, sound effects and word-balloon order are completely reversed... something which can make readers unfamiliar with Japanese feel pretty backwards themselves. For this reason, manga or Japanese comics published in the U.S. in English have sometimes been published "flopped"—that is, printed in exact reverse order, as though seen from the other side of a mirror.

By flopping pages, U.S. publishers can avoid confusing readers, but the compromise is not without its downside. For one thing, a character in a flopped manga series who once wore in the original Japanese version a T-shirt emblazoned with "M A Y" (as in "the merry month of") now wears one which reads "Y A M"! Additionally, many manga creators in Japan are themselves unhappy with the process, as some feel the mirror-imaging of their art skews their original intentions.

We are proud to bring you Yuto Tsukuda and Shun Saeki's **Food Wars!** in the original unflopped format.

For now, though, turn to the other side of the book and let the adventure begin...!

—Editor

PUSH A LITTLE HARDER
ER... I'M GOING ON AHEAD.

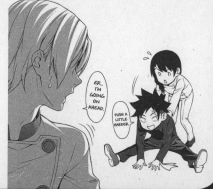